ADVANCED MICROSOFT® OFFICE POWERPOINT™ 2007

insights and advice from the experts

Wayne Kao
Jeff Huang

800 East 96th Street, Indianapolis, Indiana 46240 USA

Advanced Microsoft® Office PowerPoint™ 2007
Insights and Advice from the Experts

ISBN-13: 978-0-7897-3724-3
ISBN-10: 0-7897-3724-8

Library of Congress Cataloging-in-Publication Data

Kao, Wayne.

Advanced Microsoft Office PowerPoint 2007 : insights and advice from the experts / Wayne Kao, Jeff Huang.— 1st ed.

p. cm.

Includes index.

ISBN 0-7897-3724-8

1. Presentation graphics software. 2. Microsoft PowerPoint (Computer file) I. Huang, Jeff. II. Title.

T385.K35154 2007

005.5'8—dc22

2007044417

Printed in the United States on America

First Printing: December 2007

Trademarks

All terms mentioned in this book that are known to be trademarks or service marks have been appropriately capitalized. Que Publishing cannot attest to the accuracy of this information. Use of a term in this book should not be regarded as affecting the validity of any trademark or service mark.

Warning and Disclaimer

Every effort has been made to make this book as complete and as accurate as possible, but no warranty or fitness is implied. The information provided is on an "as is" basis. The authors and the publisher shall have neither liability nor responsibility to any person or entity with respect to any loss or damages arising from the information contained in this book.

Bulk Sales

Que Publishing offers excellent discounts on this book when ordered in quantity for bulk purchases or special sales. For more information, please contact

U.S. Corporate and Government Sales
1-800-382-3419
corpsales@pearsontechgroup.com

For sales outside the United States, please contact

International Sales
international@pearsoned.com

This Book Is Safari Enabled

The Safari® Enabled icon on the cover of your favorite technology book means the book is available through Safari Bookshelf. When you buy this book, you get free access to the online edition for 45 days.

Safari Bookshelf is an electronic reference library that lets you easily search thousands of technical books, find code samples, download chapters, and access technical information whenever and wherever you need it.

To gain 45-day Safari Enabled access to this book:

- Go to http://www.quepublishing.com/safarienabled
- Complete the brief registration form
- Enter the coupon code W4NT-PBNM-3U4S-PBLK-7EDA

If you have difficulty registering on Safari Bookshelf or accessing the online edition, please email customer-service@safaribooksonline.com.

Associate Publisher
Greg Wiegand

Acquisitions Editor
Loretta Yates

Development Editor
Laura Norman

Managing Editor
Gina Kanouse

Project Editor
Betsy Harris

Copy Editor
Rhonda Tinch-Mize

Indexer
Erika Millen

Proofreaders
Andy Beaster
Kathy Ruiz

Technical Editor
Kathy Jacobs

Publishing Coordinator
Cindy Teeters

Book Designer
Anne Jones

Compositor
Bronkella Publishing

CONTENTS AT A GLANCE

	Introduction	
PART I	**FINDING YOUR WAY AROUND**	**5**
1	Introducing the Office 2007 User Interface	7
PART II	**CREATING CONTENT**	**25**
2	Everything You Need to Know About Text	27
3	Text Support	41
4	Working with Pictures	63
5	Diagrams and SmartArt	85
6	Rediscover Charts	101
7	Working with Shapes	117
8	Tables Like You've Never Seen Before	137
9	Inserting Content into PowerPoint	151
PART III	**MANIPULATING CONTENT**	**171**
10	Formatting Your Presentation	173
11	Dissecting Themes	199
12	Formatting Shapes, Text, and More	217
13	Demystifying 3D	245
14	Positioning Slide Elements	265
PART IV	**WOWING YOUR AUDIENCE**	**281**
15	Going Beyond Slide-by-Slide	283
16	Running Slide Show Like a Pro	317
PART V	**POWERPOINT FILES UNLEASHED**	**335**
17	Migrating Files to PowerPoint 2007	337
18	Publishing Your Presentation to Any Format	351
PART VI	**FINDING HELP**	**379**
19	Using Help and Other Resources	381
	Index	385

TABLE OF CONTENTS

Introduction **1**

Who Should Buy This Book 1

Not for Newbies 1

Not a Comprehensive Dictionary 1

No Tips on Improving Your Presenting Skills 2

So What's in Here? 2

Applying to Business School? 2

How This Book Is Organized 2

Conventions Used in This Book 3

Icons 3

Text Conventions 4

Special Elements 4

I FINDING YOUR WAY AROUND

1 Introducing the Office 2007 User Interface **7**

The Ribbon Explained 7

Main Ribbon Tabs 8

Smart Ribbon Tabs 8

Ribbon Groups 9

Box Launcher 10

Minimizing the Ribbon 10

Galleries 11

Find Any Command 11

Introducing Live Preview 13

The Office Button 14

What Lives Here? 14

The File Menu in Disguise 15

Accelerate with the Alt Key 16

Finding New Shortcuts 16

Using Old Office Keyboard Shortcuts 16

Customizing the Office User Interface Using the Quick Access Toolbar 17

Customizing the QAT 18

Customization Limitations 19

Finding Hidden Commands 19
Customization Tips and Tricks 19
Contextual Text Formatting Using the Mini Toolbar 20
What's a Floatie? 20
Hate the Floatie? 21
Redesigned Status Bar 21
What's a Status Bar? 21
Anatomy of the Status Bar 22
Customizing the Status Bar 22
Other Useful Office 2007 Enhancements 22
What's That Noise? 23
Enhanced ScreenTips 23
Changing PowerPoint Skins 24

II CREATING CONTENT

2 Everything You Need to Know About Text 27
Selecting Multiple Ranges of Text 27
Text Selection Basics 27
New Multiple Selection Options 28
Easily Moving Text 28
Utilizing Copy/Paste 28
Drag 28
All Text Is WordArt 29
Modifying Text Direction/Orientation 30
Advanced Font Techniques 30
Live Preview 30
Theme Fonts 31
New Fonts for 2007 32
Replacing Fonts 33
Text Box Tricks 34
Advanced Text Box Options 34
Turn a Text Box into a Regular Shape 35
Advanced Character Formatting 36
Underline Style 36
Text Effects 38

Character Spacing 39
Kerning 40

3 Text Support 41

Bullets and Ordered Lists 41
Default Bullets 41
Ordered Lists 42
Your Face on a Bullet 42
AutoCorrect 44
Default Text Corrections 44
Creating Clickable Hyperlinks 45
Adding Your Own Phrases 46
Pranks 46
Understanding Tab Stops 46
Recognizing the Tab Symbols 47
Custom Tab Types 48
Shopping List Example 48
Tab Tips 50
Understanding Paragraph Formatting 50
Paragraph Markers 50
Justify and Distributed 52
Subtle Selection Handle Differences 53
Text Formatting for Placeholders and Shapes 54
Formatting Text Placeholders 54
Formatting Shapes 54
Formatting Placeholders on the Master 54
Transformed Text 55
Warping 55
Follow Path 56
Inline Editing 56
PowerPoint 2007's Proofing Tools 57
Translation 58
Spell Checking and Thesaurus 58
Proofing Example 58
What the Random? 60
Shortcut Keys for Newbies and Experts 61

4 **Working with Pictures** 63

Variations on Inserted Pictures 63

Regular Embedded Picture 63

Linked Picture 64

Linked Embedded Pictures 65

PowerPoint as an Advanced Picture Editor 66

Preset Picture Effects 66

Common Picture Adjustments 66

Cropping 71

Changing the Picture Shape 72

Text That Follows a Picture Around 73

Group Picture with Text 73

Shape with Picture Fill 73

Inserting Many Pictures at Once Using Photo Album 75

Using Photo Album 75

Edit Existing Photo Album 78

Picture Manager: The Hidden Application 78

Quick Edits in the Edit Pictures Workpane 79

Making Pictures Smaller 81

Why Not Just Use PowerPoint? 82

Changing a Picture's Format 82

Batch Editing 83

5 **Diagrams and SmartArt** 85

What's so Smart About It? 85

Inserting SmartArt 87

Using the Default 87

Convert Existing Content to SmartArt 88

Anatomy of a SmartArt Graphic 89

Content Pane 89

Text Pane 90

Nodes 90

Connectors 91

The Power of SmartArt Graphics 91

Working with SmartArt Layouts 92

Using Styles and Themes 94

Create Graphic Commands ... 95
Add Shape ... 95
Add Bullet ... 96
Right to Left ... 96
Layout ... 96
Formatting Nodes ... 96
Creating Animations ... 96
Placeholder Trick ... 97
Photos and SmartArt—Frame Your Pictures ... 98

6 Rediscover Charts ... 101

Inserting Excel Charts into PowerPoint ... 102
Copying and Pasting ... 102
Inserting an Excel Chart from Within PowerPoint ... 103
Getting Inside a Chart ... 105
Formatting ... 105
Formatting a Specific Piece of a Chart ... 106
Inserting Objects into a Chart ... 107
Understanding Chart Layouts ... 107
Understanding Chart Styles ... 108
Creating and Using Chart Templates ... 110
Creating a Template ... 110
Using an Existing Template ... 110
Managing Templates ... 111
Manipulating Data ... 111
Dragging the Pie ... 113
Working with Legacy Graphs and OLE Objects ... 114
Converting to Office 2007 Format ... 114
OLE Facts ... 115

7 Working with Shapes ... 117

Insertion Tricks ... 117
Who Knew There Were So Many Ways to Insert a Shape? ... 118
Lock Drawing Mode ... 119

Drawing Tools Format Tab ... 120
Using Shape Styles ... 120
Applying a Shape Fill ... 121
New Shapes ... 122
Creating Custom Shapes ... 122
Choosing a Shape Tool ... 122
Editing Shapes ... 124
Using Connectors to Save Time ... 126
How to Connect ... 128
Rerouting Lines ... 129
Customizing Lines ... 129
What Do Those Yellow Diamonds Do? ... 130
The Brand New Selection Pane ... 131
Embedding Objects from Other Applications ... 133
Grouping Shapes and Objects ... 135
Ungrouping and Regroup ... 135
Group Trivia ... 136

8 Tables Like You've Never Seen Before ... 137

Different Ways to Insert a Table ... 137
The Grid ... 137
Insert Table Dialog ... 138
Draw Table ... 139
Excel Spreadsheet ... 139
Copying and Pasting Excel Tables ... 141
Animating Table Cells ... 142
Adding Style to Tables ... 144
Applying Effects ... 146
Advanced Table Facts ... 146
Resize ... 147
Insert Rows and Columns ... 147
Cell Sizes ... 148
Cell Margins ... 149
Splitting and Merging Cells ... 149
Draw Table ... 149

9 Inserting Content into PowerPoint 151

Using Smart Tags to Customize Pasted Content 151

Paste Smart Tag 151

AutoCorrect Smart Tag 152

Overflowing Text Smart Tag 153

Smart Tags Are Contextual 154

Advanced Paste Techniques 154

Reusing Slides 156

Reusing a Slide from Another Presentation 156

Reusing Slides with Slide Library 157

Tell Me When This Slide Changes 162

Using Sounds and Videos Effectively 163

Linking Versus Embedding 164

Distributing a Presentation That Contains Movies or Large Sounds 165

Looping Sounds 166

Sounds Spanning Multiple Slides 166

Playlists 166

Tablet PC Features in PowerPoint (Ink) 168

How to Ink 168

Limitations of Ink 169

Inserting Mathematical Equations Using Word 169

III MANIPULATING CONTENT

10 Formatting Your Presentation 173

Uses of the PowerPoint Thumbnail Pane 173

Reordering Slides 174

Apply to Many Slides 175

Adding a Slide Background 175

Understanding Slide Masters 176

Additional Masters 177

Hide Background Graphics 178

Introducing Brand New Slide Layout Options 178

Layouts 101 179

New Slide 179

Change a Slide's Layout ... 179
Customize a Layout ... 181
Using the PowerPoint Outline Pane ... 182
Creating a Quick Presentation Outline ... 182
Creating Slides from the Outline ... 183
Placeholders Explained ... 185
Standard Placeholders ... 185
Custom Placeholders ... 187
Customized Headers and Footers ... 190
Presenter Notes ... 190
Using the Notes Pane ... 190
Using the Notes Page ... 191
When to Use Notes ... 192
Printed Handouts ... 192
Handout Master ... 193
Color Modes ... 195
Viewing the Presentation Color Mode ... 195
Choosing a Per-Object Color Mode ... 195
Programming PowerPoint with Macros ... 196
For Experts Only ... 196
Creating a Macro ... 196
Learn More ... 198

11 Dissecting Themes ... 199

Making Unique and Beautiful Presentations ... 199
Your Presentation Shouldn't Look Like You Stole It ... 199
It's Easy to Change Your Presentation's Look ... 200
Themes Across Office ... 200
Example of Using a Theme ... 200
Apply an Entire Theme ... 200
Apply Different Parts of Themes ... 202
Different Types of Theme Files ... 203
Theme Versus Effect Scheme Versus Font Scheme Versus Color Scheme ... 203
Theme Versus Presentation Versus Template ... 204

Core Parts of an Office Theme 205
Font Scheme 205
Color Scheme 208
Effect Scheme 210
Object Defaults and Extra Color Schema List 212
Thumbnails 212
Slide Layouts and Masters 213
Creating a Theme 214

12 Formatting Shapes, Text, and More 217

What Can I Format? 218
Three Ways to Apply Formatting 218
Gallery Styles 218
Formatting from the Ribbon 219
Format Shape Dialog 219
Impressive Fills 220
Solid Fills 220
Gradient Fills 220
Creating Gradient Overlays 223
Picture Fills 226
Textures and Picture Fills 227
Background Fill 229
Advanced Line Styles 231
Line Color 232
Line Style 232
Brand New Effects 235
Shadow 235
Reflection 237
Glow 237
Soft Edges 237
Bevel, 3D Rotation 238
Transparent Overlay 238
Customize the Default Shape 239

The Mysterious Paintbrush Icon (Format Painter) 239
Format Painter Example Using Shapes 240
Format Painter Works on Other Things Too! 240
Format Painter Tips 240
Using Repeat Can Save You Time 241
Mastering Multiple Undo 242
Change Shape 242

13 Demystifying 3D 245

3D Example 245
What Can Be 3D? 249
3D Rotation Explained 250
Preset Rotations 250
Custom Rotations 251
Text and 3D Objects 254
Object Position 255
Reset 255
Using 3D Formatting Effectively 255
Bevel 256
Depth 257
Contour 258
Surface 259
Reset 262
Be Careful! 262
Why? It Looks So Pretty! 262
Be Consistent 263

14 Positioning Slide Elements 265

Exact Positioning Using the Size and Position Dialog 265
Using the Dialog 266
Sizing Pictures 266
The Hidden Ruler 268
Aligning Objects 268
Adjusting the Unit of Measure 269
Snapping to Grids and Guides 269
Enabling Grids and Guides 270

Precise Positioning 271
Using the Mouse 271
Using Zoom 271
Using the Keyboard 272
Combining Positioning Tricks 273
Resize Tricks 273
Rotate Shortcuts 276
Move Shortcuts 277
Align and Distribute Tips 278

IV WOWING YOUR AUDIENCE

15 Going Beyond Slide-By-Slide 283
Using Animations 284
Preset Animations 284
Custom Animations 285
Custom Animation Types 288
Using Entrance, Emphasis, Exit 288
Motion Paths 292
Animating with Text 294
Triggers 296
Adding Transitions 297
Transition Sounds 298
Transition Speed 298
Advancing to the Next Slide 299
Creating Custom Shows 299
Hyperlinks 300
Set Off Actions During Your Presentation 301
Inserting Action Buttons 302
Mouse Over 303
Different Types of Actions 303
Nothing Special About These Buttons 305
Cool Things You Can Do with Actions 306
Presenting Tools 310
Rehearse Timings 310
Creating Self-Playing Presentations 311

Pre-Record Your Presentation (Record Narration) 313
Hide Slide 316

16 Running Slide Show Like a Pro 317

Four Ways to Start Slide Show 317
Working with the View Mode Buttons 318
Inking 320
Why Ink? 321
How to Ink 321
Saving Your Ink 322
Editing During a Presentation 323
Set Up Slide Show 324
Show Type 324
Present a Range of Slides 326
Presenting in Different Resolutions 326
View Notes on Your Laptop While the Audience Sees Normal Slides (Presenter View) 327
Presenter View Features 327
Setting Up Multiple Monitors for Use with Presenter View 328
Slide Show Keyboard Shortcuts 329
Widescreen (Custom Slide Sizes) 331
Fixing Flickering Problems 332
Getting New Graphics Drivers 332
Disabling Hardware Acceleration 333
Making Graphics Faster 333

V POWERPOINT FILES UNLEASHED

17 Migrating Files to PowerPoint 2007 337

Open Options 337
Converting Objects 338
Opening PowerPoint 2007 Files Using PowerPoint 97–2003 (Compatibility Pack) 340
How Presentations Are Windowed 341
PowerPoint Command-Line Parameters 342

What's a Command-Line Parameter? 342
Command-Line Parameters in PowerPoint 342
PowerPoint Parameter Example 342
Starting in PowerPoint Safe Mode 343
Inside the New PPTX File Format 344
Why a New File Format? 344
Peering Inside a PPTX File 345

18 Publishing Your Presentation to Any Format 351

PowerPoint File Format Types 351
Understanding PowerPoint File Formats 351
Macros 352
Embedding Fonts in a Presentation 352
Stick to the Office Fonts 353
Embedded Fonts 353
Making a Presentation That Just Plays (.ppsx) 354
Advanced Publishing Tricks 355
Mark as Final 355
Save as PDF/XPS 356
Collaboration Using Comments 357
Adding Comments 357
Using Comments 357
Encrypting Presentations with a Password 358
Password to Open 358
Setting a Password for Editing Privileges 360
Exporting a Presentation as a Picture Slide Show 361
Save Presentation as Pictures 361
Slides on an iPod 361
Save Anything as a Picture 362
Save a Picture as a Picture 362
Saving to a Network Share 363
Save as Web Page 364
Easily Extract Pictures, Movies, and Sounds from Your Presentation by Saving the Presentation as a Web Page 364
Ugly Office HTML 365

Removing Sensitive Information from Presentations (Document Inspector) 367
Using PowerPoint Shapes in Other Office Applications 368
Copying Shapes to Microsoft Excel 368
Copying Shapes to Microsoft Word 369
Saving to the 97–2003 File Format 369
Change Your Default File Format 370
Using the Compatibility Checker 371
Compatibility Mode 371
Compressing Pictures to Create Smaller Files 373
Publishing Your Presentation to a CD 373
Why Care About a Viewer If I Own PowerPoint? 374
Package for CD Customizations 375
Bypassing Package for CD 376
Other Notes About the Viewer 377

VI FINDING HELP

19 Using Help and Other Resources 381

Integrated Help 381
microsoft.public.powerpoint Newsgroup 382
Knowledge Base 383
Microsoft Employee Blogs 383
Community Sites 383

Index 385

About the Authors

Wayne Kao joined Microsoft in January 2003, working as a developer on the PowerPoint team. He developed PowerPoint 2007 features such as the pretty, new Effects and the new XML file formats; improved the undo, setup, placeholder, and Photo Album features; and worked to integrate SmartArt, chart, table, and picture improvements into PowerPoint 2007. Wayne also contributed to PowerPoint and Office Picture Manager 2003.

Jeff Huang is currently working as a developer for Microsoft on his second release of PowerPoint. He has learned the ins and outs of the product by implementing features and exposing himself to the inner workings of PowerPoint. Each day that he spends working with the talented people who make PowerPoint, he picks up an obscure new trick or shortcut.

Jeff hopes to empower you to create better presentations not only by making PowerPoint a better product, but also by helping you become an expert PowerPoint user. He wants you to be the person who does something new, cool, and unusual in PowerPoint, the person who makes others exclaim, "Wow! I didn't know you could do that!"

When not writing books about PowerPoint, Jeff can be found skiing, playing golf, or playing with his dog, Pouncer.

Acknowledgments

We are grateful to our project manager Loretta Yates, who believed in the book early on and championed it at Que Publishing. We are also truly indebted to Bill "Mr. Excel" Jelen who kindly put us in touch with Que. Thanks to the team at Que, without whom this book would not have been possible.

We are particularly thankful to our amazing reviewers Laura Norman, Kathy Jacobs, Stephanie Leung, and Melody Wu. Their honest feedback turned our mess of words into a coherent work.

Many thanks to Trang Pham for all her hard work. We'd also like to warmly thank Crystal Chen and Richard Bretschneider for their contributions.

We Want to Hear from You!

As the reader of this book, *you* are our most important critic and commentator. We value your opinion and want to know what we're doing right, what we could do better, what areas you'd like to see us publish in, and any other words of wisdom you're willing to pass our way.

As an associate publisher for Que Publishing, I welcome your comments. You can email or write me directly to let me know what you did or didn't like about this book—as well as what we can do to make our books better.

Please note that I cannot help you with technical problems related to the topic of this book. We do have a User Services group, however, where I will forward specific technical questions related to the book.

When you write, please be sure to include this book's title and author as well as your name, email address, and phone number. I will carefully review your comments and share them with the author and editors who worked on the book.

Email: feedback@quepublishing.com

Mail: Greg Wiegand
Associate Publisher
Que Publishing
800 East 96th Street
Indianapolis, IN 46240 USA

Reader Services

Visit our website and register this book at www.informit.com/title/9780789737243 for convenient access to any updates, downloads, or errata that might be available for this book.

Introduction

IN THIS INTRODUCTION

- Who Should Buy This Book
- How This Book Is Organized
- Conventions Used in This Book

Sure, you could go and spend your money on a book that calls you a dummy, but where's the dignity in that? Instead, imagine that a book exists that provides a detailed, under-the-hood look at PowerPoint 2007. Suppose that the two people who wrote this book actually work for Microsoft on the PowerPoint team, implemented PowerPoint 2007 features, and can write intelligently about them. Well, stop dreaming because you're holding it.

Who Should Buy This Book

So, you're wondering if this book is right for you and how it could possibly be different from the 20 other PowerPoint books on the shelf.

Not for Newbies

If you have *never used PowerPoint* before and you are looking for a book to teach you the bare basics, this is not it. We're not going to walk through how to turn on your computer. Unlike every other PowerPoint book currently on the market, we're not even going to walk through creating a basic presentation. Chances are you already know how to do that. We assume that you are reasonably comfortable using a computer, at ease with the bare PowerPoint basics, and have survived creating a presentation or two. That lets us focus our time on what you probably don't know.

Not a Comprehensive Dictionary

If you're looking for an *exhaustive guided tour* through every single PowerPoint feature, this is not it. Many basic PowerPoint tasks won't even be mentioned. Unlike those other books, we do our best not to baby you through every single feature, just to claim that it's in the book.

The exception to this rule is if we present to you a feature that is new to PowerPoint 2007, and not in previous versions. We might go into more detail, which might seem basic, to introduce you to how it works.

No Tips on Improving Your Presenting Skills

If you want to learn how to present in front of large audiences without your voice cracking, you will get better tips from joining Toastmasters than reading this book. We cannot help you deliver your presentations any better than you already do. What we can do is turn you into a PowerPoint power user, making your presentations better.

PowerPoint is a tool. Consider us the rugged hardware store employee ready to help you understand exactly what potential you can unleash with the tool. With these tools, you will be able to create richer, more interesting presentations in less time, which gives you more time to focus on the content and delivery.

So What's in Here?

Consider this a tour through the back roads of PowerPoint—an advanced insider look at what PowerPoint can do from two guys who have worked on the product itself. Our goal with this book is to provide a sampler of what's out there. We hope to show you things you didn't know were in PowerPoint and demonstrate the value in features you've long cursed or glossed over as uninteresting.

If you have recently upgraded to Office 2007, want to know what cool new features are included in PowerPoint 2007, and are curious how to use them, you will enjoy our introduction to those as well. If you are already a seasoned PowerPoint veteran and feel as if you have mastered it all, give us a shot, and we'll show you something that you didn't know existed.

Applying to Business School?

Recently, the University of Chicago School of Business decided to require applicants to submit a PowerPoint presentation as part of the application. This book will definitely help if you plan on applying to business school or are already in business school and want to become a PowerPoint expert.

How This Book Is Organized

If you read this book front to back, you might think that two separate books have somehow been interleaved. This is because every section in this book belongs to one of two categories:

- An advanced feature that is not well-known and contains many tips and tricks for saving you time and energy
- A feature that is new to PowerPoint 2007 and did not exist in previous versions of PowerPoint

You might ask why we did not organize the book by splitting it in half and covering each category in one half, and the answer is because some features rely on others.

There is a natural progression to the book that you will notice after you can create pieces of your presentation, position and manipulate them, and then finally put them all together and blow away your audience.

This book is organized into six major parts according to this progression:

- **Part I: "Finding Your Way Around"**—PowerPoint has undergone a makeover, and this part aims at helping you adjust to the new user interface. This section is helpful regardless of whether you know where features are in older versions of PowerPoint or you are brand new to them.
- **Part II: "Creating Content"**—This part might appear more basic than it really is. First things first: you must know how to add the primitive PowerPoint pieces to your slides, such as text, shapes, images, and more. Don't assume that you know everything there is to know about these simple objects; we show you a trick or two here that can save you some time.
- **Part III: "Manipulating Content"**—After you have content on your slides, we show you how to give it a common design, make everything match, position it exactly where it needs to be, and really give it the fit and finish that your presentation needs to be heads above the rest.
- **Part IV: "Wowing Your Audience"**—Creating presentations is not all that PowerPoint can do. This part shows you how to fully use PowerPoint while presenting and also how to perfect animations and transitions to avoid looking cheesy, yet still impress an audience.
- **Part V: "PowerPoint Files Unleashed"**—PowerPoint 2007 introduces a new file format (`.pptx`), which can be confusing if you have questions about upgrading and are worried about compatibility. We ease your concerns and, in addition, discuss the numerous formats that presentations can be exported to, as well as why that is important.
- **Part VI: "Finding Help"**—If you still have unanswered questions after going through this book, we provide some resources to help you get answers.

Conventions Used in This Book

Here are the conventions used to help you get the most from this book and from PowerPoint 2007.

Icons

As we mentioned before, this book contains two types of sections.

When you see this, it means that the content is primarily about a new feature in PowerPoint 2007, and the level of detail might be higher and more broadly discussed.

This icon indicates that the tip or trick is not well known or not for beginners; and even if you are familiar with the feature, you can still learn a thing or two here.

Text Conventions

Key combinations are represented with a plus sign. For example, if the text calls for you to enter Ctrl+S, you would press the Ctrl key and the S key at the same time.

Code continuation arrows (➥) are used to indicate when lines of code are too long to fit on one line on the printed page, and we have broken them manually. Lines broken with the code continuation arrow should be entered on one line when programming.

Special Elements

Throughout this book, you can find Tips, Notes, Cautions, and Sidebars. These elements provide a variety of information, ranging from warnings, extra tips, and side information that sometimes only serves the purpose of entertaining. We end up sprinkling anecdotal facts about PowerPoint features that we picked up along the way.

TIP

Tips show you how to do something easier, save you some time, or find something that might not be obvious.

NOTE

Notes are helpful for learning more about certain features and sometimes contain history about how something came to be the way it is.

CAUTION

Cautions are primarily here to prevent you from doing something that might end up causing you some grief.

SIDEBARS

Sidebars contain smaller topics that didn't quite fit into a section on their own but contain a lot of useful information.

The first thing you will notice about PowerPoint 2007 is that it looks and feels very different from previous versions. The chapter in this part takes you on a little tour through the ins and outs of the new look and feel of the product and explains a few of the new features that will make your life a little easier.

I

Finding Your Way Around

1 Introducing the Office 2007 User Interface 7

1

Introducing the Office 2007 User Interface

IN THIS CHAPTER

- The Ribbon Explained
- Introducing Live Preview
- The Office Button
- Accelerate with the Alt Key
- Customizing the Office User Interface Using the Quick Access Toolbar
- Contextual Text Formatting Using the Mini Toolbar
- Redesigned Status Bar
- Other Useful Office 2007 Enhancements

Just about every new release of Office has changed the user interface, but nothing compares to the drastic changes and innovation offered in Office 2007 compared to previous versions of Microsoft Office. This chapter introduces you to the concept of the Ribbon, the Office button, new accelerator shortcut keys including the new purpose of the Alt button, the new mini floating toolbar, and changes to the status bar.

The Ribbon Explained

New The most obvious difference in the user interface is the absence of the traditional Office menus and toolbar. This is initially a huge shock because, for decades, menus have been the cornerstone of the user interface in previous Microsoft Office applications.

If you have spent any time using Office 2007, you have seen the Ribbon, which is essentially one fat toolbar that replaces the menus and toolbars from previous versions of Office. The old drop-down menus are missing because Microsoft performed studies and found that the Ribbon is more effective and intuitive at displaying the large number of features found in Office (see Figure 1.1).

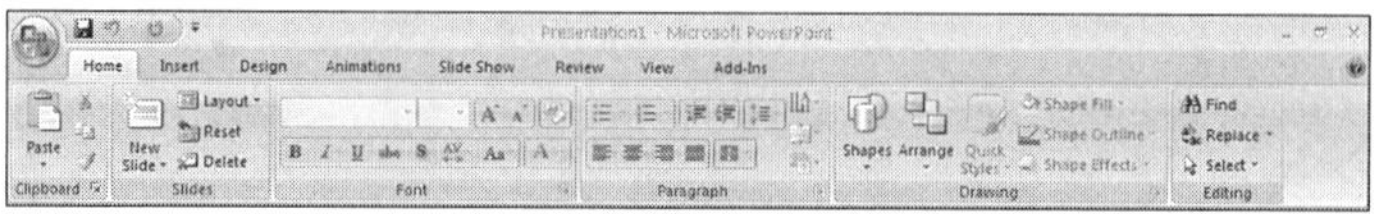

Figure 1.1

Enter the Ribbon.

NOTE

If you are interested in knowing more about the birth of the Ribbon, Microsoft has a funny comic strip describing the development of the new Office interface, including the Ribbon, at http://www.enhancedoffice.com.

Some advanced commands still spawn task panes, such as the Advanced Animation command found on the Animations ribbon tab in the Animations area when you select Custom Animation. But, these are all still launched from the Ribbon, and the goal is that you will be able to accomplish the vast majority of your tasks by just using the Ribbon itself.

Main Ribbon Tabs

The Ribbon is composed of top-level tasks such as inserting content (the Insert tab), setting the theme of the presentation (the Design tab), or giving a presentation (the Slide Show tab).

The standard PowerPoint Ribbon tabs are Home, Insert, Design, Animations, Slide Show, Review, and View.

Smart Ribbon Tabs

Various other tabs appear, depending on the content selected. This is the power of contextual user interfaces: The commands available change depending on what is relevant and helpful to you.

The standard Ribbon tabs mentioned in the previous section are always shown in PowerPoint. Additional Ribbon tabs exist that are contextual, meaning that they appear and disappear depending on what you are doing in PowerPoint at any given time. The appearance of smart tabs keeps the Ribbon uncluttered when you aren't doing something for which you need specific commands or tools.

For instance, when you are inserting text, the Text Formatting ribbon shows up, offering you various text formatting options. Similarly, you could select a shape, chart, or SmartArt, and the corresponding Ribbon tab for that object appears automatically, providing options specific to that task (see Figure 1.2). These tabs appear to the right of the standard Ribbon tabs described in the previous section.

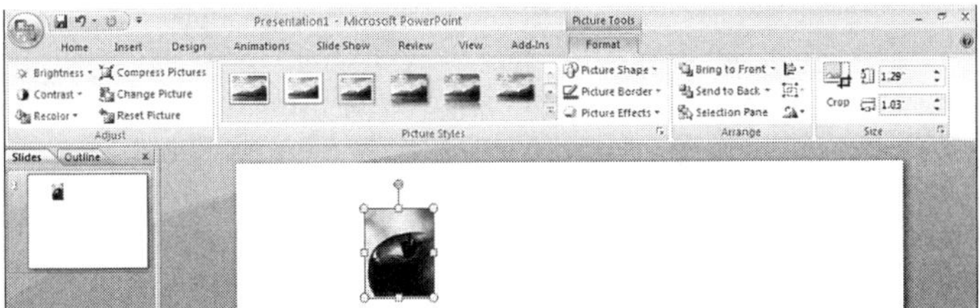

Figure 1.2

This Picture Tools Format tab appears to the right of the standard tabs when a picture is selected.

Compare this efficient design with the myriad of menu items from previous versions of PowerPoint—menus that would appear and disappear after activating an obscure option and might require assistance from your friendly neighborhood geek to understand. You have the same level of power in PowerPoint 2007. But, there are fewer options to sort through because relevant options appear right in front of you and irrelevant options remain hidden, making it all easier to use.

Ribbon Groups

Inside each Ribbon tab, items are divided into areas called *groups*. For example, on the main Home tab, groups exist for Clipboard, Slides, Font, Paragraph, Drawing, and Editing (see Figure 1.3). Now you can say "the Slides group," and other Office nerds will know what you're talking about.

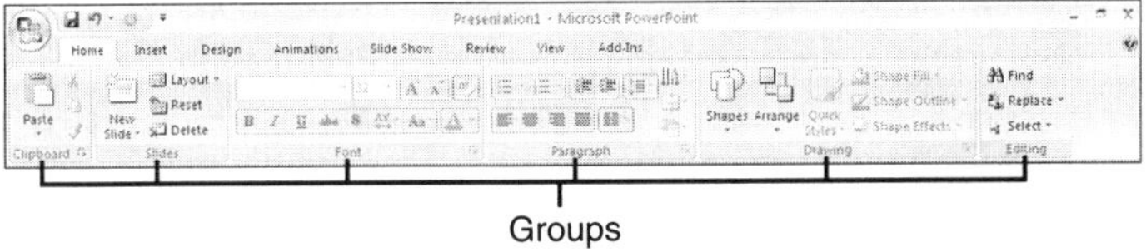

Figure 1.3

The six groups on the Home tab.

Depending on how wide your window is, PowerPoint fully expands some groups, showing all the items inside, and it shows other groups as just menus that you need to click before the additional commands are revealed. If your window is extremely wide and you have a widescreen monitor, all groups appear fully expanded. Give it a try. Make your PowerPoint window narrow and watch as the Ribbon groups change.

NOTE

Dynamically changing the user interface based on window size was first tried by Microsoft in OneNote 2003 and is now used by all the Ribbon-aware Office 2007 applications.

Box Launcher

Despite the fatness of the Ribbon, Microsoft could still cram only the most popular features onto the main Ribbon. If you're a power user, you probably want to see more than that. To access features that didn't make the cut for the default Ribbon real estate, look for a dialog box launcher at the bottom right of the Ribbon groups that offers more advanced options (see Figure 1.4).

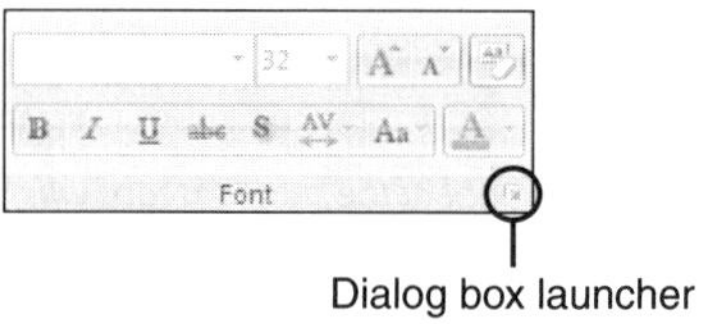

Figure 1.4

All the options are revealed after clicking the dialog box launcher in the Font check. The launcher brings up the Font dialog.

DESIGNING THE RIBBON

To decide which features to put on the main Ribbon and which advanced features to hide behind the box launcher, Office periodically tells Microsoft which features you're using the most. Microsoft can then sum up the totals using an internal tool called SQM (Service Quality Monitoring).

To build Office 2007, the Microsoft Office team looked closely at data gathered about Office 2003 usage. The really popular features ended up on the Home tab, the next most popular now live on groups in the Ribbon, and features that are only occasionally used ended up hidden behind the box launcher or in advanced dialogs.

The data is sent anonymously to respect your privacy, but you can opt-in or opt-out of the "program" by clicking the main Office button. Under PowerPoint Options, choose Trust Center in the left pane, Trust Center Settings, and, finally, Privacy Options. Check the Sign Up for the Customer Experience Improvement Program check box. Read more about SQM here at Jenson Harris' Office User Interface blog: http://blogs.msdn.com/jensenh/archive/2006/04/05/568947.aspx.

Minimizing the Ribbon

If you want to temporarily minimize the Ribbon to give yourself more screen real estate, just double-click any of the tabs or press Ctrl+F1 as a shortcut. This hides the bulk of the ribbon, including the groups, as shown in Figure 1.5, and you can also maximize the Ribbon by pressing Ctrl+F1 again to make it appear again.

NOTE

We often use this while reading a presentation when we don't anticipate making any changes—for example, reviewing a presentation for a friend.

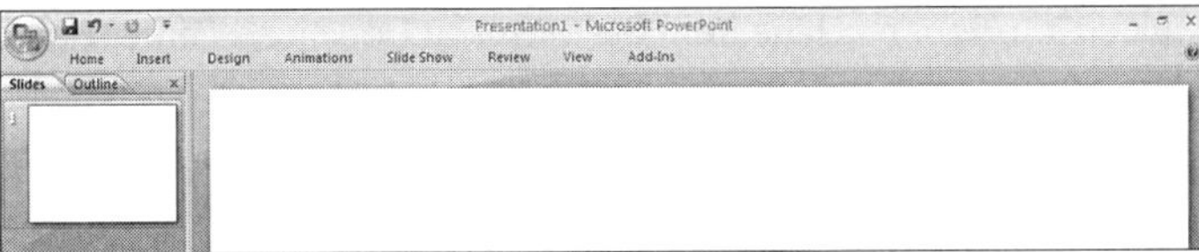

Figure 1.5

The Ribbon minimized.

Galleries

One common concept within the Ribbon is called a *gallery*. A gallery is a bunch of visual previews showing some results you can instantly apply to your presentation or to an object. For example, in the Design tab's Themes group, the Theme gallery shows visual previews of themes you can quickly apply to the entire presentation (see Figure 1.6). Clicking on a preview in the gallery instantly applies the look to your presentation, including the backgrounds, placeholder layouts, colors, and more.

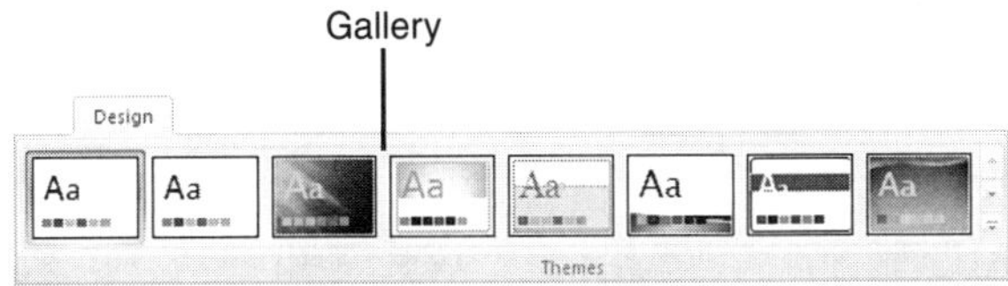

Figure 1.6

These theme choices appear in a gallery, a new user interface concept in Office 2007.

As you can see, there are always three buttons to the right of a gallery. The top two buttons are scroll buttons that let you scroll up and down to see more items in the gallery. The bottom button expands the gallery to a larger form so that you can see more items at one time.

To get slightly more information about any item in a gallery, park the mouse cursor above the item, and a ScreenTip appears, giving you more information. For example, hovering over a theme in the themes gallery tells you the name of the theme.

Find Any Command

Can't find your favorite PowerPoint command in the new user interface? Microsoft has a tool that shows you a mock version of the Office 2003 user interface with the old menus and toolbars. You can click on anything, and it tells you where the corresponding command is in the Office 2007 Ribbon-based user interface.

To get help:

1. Go to http://office.microsoft.com/en-us/powerpoint.
2. Then click PowerPoint 2007 Help in the left pane. Scroll down to Getting Help and then click it.
3. From the list, choose Interactive PowerPoint 2003 to PowerPoint 2007 Command Reference Guide.

You can also download it to your machine from the Microsoft Download Center. Here's how:

1. Go to http://www.microsoft.com/downloads.
2. Enter `Interactive PowerPoint 2003` in the search box and click Search.
3. This brings up the Results page. Click PowerPoint 2007 Guide: PowerPoint 2003 to PowerPoint 2007 Interactive Command Reference Guide.

WHY ANOTHER USER INTERFACE?

Many people have become increasingly bitter at Microsoft each year for making the user interface more complicated with each successive release of Office. Office 2000 introduced personalized menus that tried to hide some of the lesser used functionality, and Office XP introduced task panes, but neither was completely successful in distilling the sheer magnitude of Office down to an understandable user interface. When Office 2003 was released, it became especially difficult. Finding any particular command required hunting because there were so many places a command could be hidden in Office 2003 (see Figure 1.7). You'd have to hunt through:

- **Menus**—There were nine top-level menus, a few containing a dozen or more commands, some of each spawned yet another sub-sub-menu containing more choices.
- **Toolbars**—There were 20 of these.
- **Task panes**—There were 16 task panes in Office 2003.

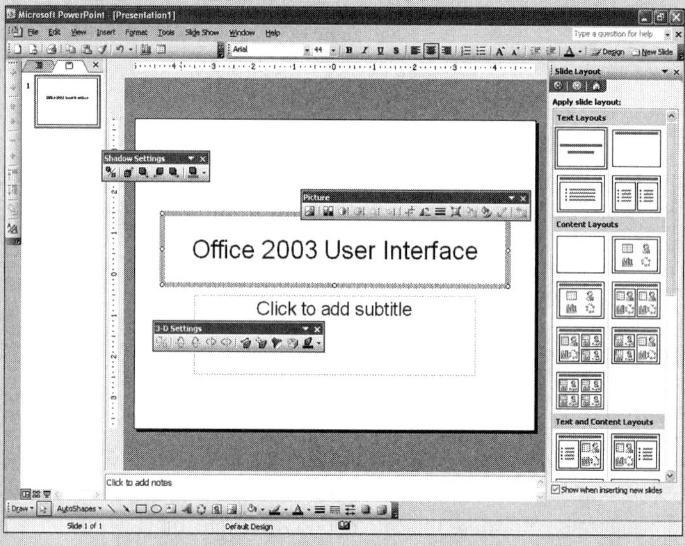

Figure 1.7

"We had some options in there that literally did nothing." —Paul Coleman, Microsoft product manager.

The name "Ribbon" comes from the fact that in original Office 2007 designs, there weren't any tabs. Instead, all the Office commands were just placed side-by-side in one super long strip that you could quickly scroll through, which was like one long Ribbon. Read more from one of the Office user interface designers: http://blogs.msdn.com/jensenh/archive/2005/10/07/478214.aspx.

Introducing Live Preview

One feature that goes hand in hand with galleries is Live Preview. Those of you who are as indecisive as we are will rejoice when you see this new feature in action. Live Preview allows you to see how formatting changes could look without actually having to apply them.

To give this feature a try, do the following:

1. Insert some text and select it.
2. Click the Format Tab.
3. Hover your mouse over one of the WordArt styles. The WordArt styles are in a gallery, similar to the Theme gallery shown in the previous section.
4. Even though you didn't click yet, notice that you now see a preview of what that change would do (see Figure 1.8).

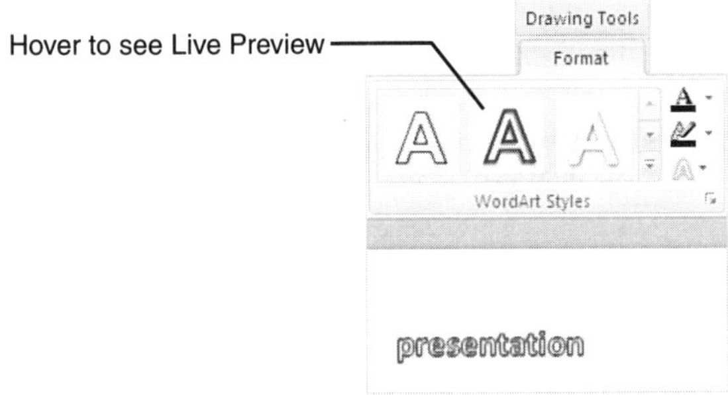

Figure 1.8

Live Preview shows a change without committing to it, so you can see what it would look like first.

This is useful not only for text, but also when applying styles to entire documents, single pictures, shapes, diagrams, charts, and tables, as well as just about anything else you can think of.

Live Preview allows you to preview style changes without actually making any changes.

NOTE

With the excellent undo features available in Office 2007, even if you apply a style that you don't like, you can always go back to a previous state. Learn more about styles in Chapter 11, "Dissecting Themes."

UNDER THE COVERS

Technically, this is what happens when you hover over something and Live Preview kicks in:

1. Live Preview makes an invisible clone of your presentation.
2. It applies the command you're previewing to the invisible copy. So, say that you're hovering over the WordArt style, as in the previous example. The style would be applied to the text in the clone document.
3. PowerPoint takes a screenshot picture of the clone document and displays it for you.
4. When you move your mouse off the object to kill Live Preview, the screenshot picture disappears and the clone document is destroyed.

Because the operation is only happening to this clone document, nothing happens to your actual document during a Live Preview.

TIP

If this feature slows down your computer, go to PowerPoint Options from the Office button, and, under the Popular tab, uncheck the Enable Live Preview check box.

The Office Button

Having redone all the toolbars from the User Interface, some leftover buttons/options from previous versions needed a place to live. Thus, the Office button (see Figure 1.9) was born.

Figure 1.9
The Office button.

What Lives Here?

If you ever find yourself looking for something pretty generic that used to be under the Tools drop-down menu in previous versions, try looking under the Office button first. Most importantly, the famous Options item under the Tools menu from previous versions of PowerPoint now lives under the PowerPoint Options item at the bottom of the main Office button menu.

In addition, the Office button menu contains many of the actions you perform at a document level—for example, Save, Save As, and so on, which were in the File menu of earlier versions, are found here.

The Save options reside here in addition to things such as Prepare, Send, and Publish. Options such as these produce flyouts that contain additional features such as those that allow you to send your presentation to Word as handouts, assign digital-rights management, or send the presentation as an email message or attachment. You'll be able to create a Document Workspace, publish slides to a Slide Library (via Publish Slides), or use Package for CD to publish to a CD. You'll also find the Printing options, which haven't changed much other than the cool new Quick Print option.

CAUTION

Be careful! If you double-click the Office button, it closes PowerPoint! Even though the Windows Start menu doesn't have this behavior, this is similar to what happens in other Windows applications when you double-click the icon in the top left, a holdover from the early days of Windows when there wasn't an "X" button at the top right of every window.

The File Menu in Disguise

Technically, the Office button is just the File menu with an extreme makeover. Hold down Alt+F, and the button opens, just like the File menu did in previous versions of Office. Beta test versions of Office 2007 called the Office button the "File menu" when you hovered over it, and even earlier betas had the word "File" in the upper left instead of the Office logo.

Despite its similarity to the File menu, we'll refer to this as the Office button throughout the rest of the book.

WHY THE FUNNY BUTTON IN THE CORNER? (FITTS LAW)

From a marketing perspective, Microsoft wanted Office 2007 to look visually similar to Windows Vista. Windows Vista has a round Start button, so we guess they figured Office 2007 needed a round button of menu options.

There's also a sound technical reason for putting the button in the corner. Most Office users maximize their windows so that it fills the entire computer screen. So, putting the Office button in the top-left of your window essentially puts it at the top-left corner of the entire monitor. It's a lot easier to click a target in one of the four corners of the screen than it is to click something, say, in the middle of the screen.

In research concerning the topic of computer mice, there exists a famous theory called Fitts Law, essentially stating that things on the computer screen are easier to click when the mouse is close to the target and when the target is large in size. When something, such as the Office button, is in the corner of the screen, it's essentially of infinite height and width because you can never overshoot it when you're trying to click it. So, it's really easy to click when the button is in the corner. This is the same reason that Windows puts the Start menu at the bottom left of the screen and Apple puts the Apple menu at the top left of the screen.

Read more about Fitts Law's impact on the Office 2007 user interface on the Jenson Harris: Office User Interface Blog website at http://blogs.msdn.com/jensenh/archive/2006/08/22/711808.aspx.

Accelerate with the Alt Key

Shortcuts are an important and interesting aspect to any application. The Alt key has always been used for finding shortcuts to certain menu commands (known as hotkeys). We'll show you what has changed and what hasn't with respect to these handy little time-savers.

Finding New Shortcuts

After you get used to them, using the keyboard shortcuts is normally a little faster than using the mouse. These shortcuts let you quickly access pieces of the Ribbon without ever touching the mouse.

In previous versions of PowerPoint, one letter in the name of each drop-down menus is underlined, which indicates that when that key is pressed in combination with the Alt key, the menu is expanded.

In PowerPoint 2007, try pressing the Alt key once by itself and notice that another set of small characters are immediately brought up underneath each tab (see Figure 1.10).

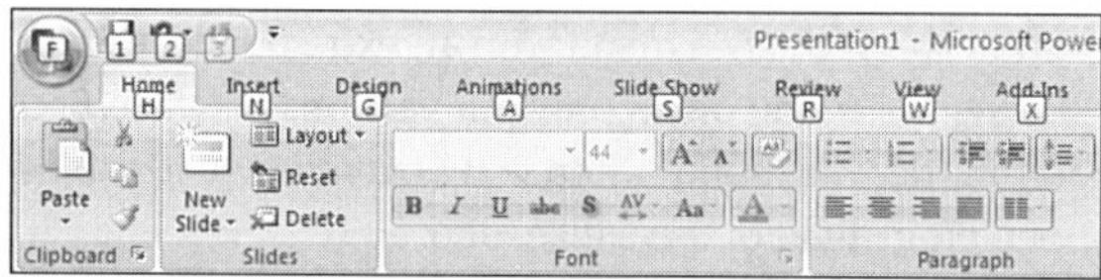

Figure 1.10

The new Alt key accelerators let you access parts of the user interface without ever leaving the comfort of your keyboard.

Now press one of the letters associated with the Alt key. If the group itself is a drop-down menu or exposes a gallery, pressing its letter reveals its contents and also another set of letters to access the subcommands (see Figure 1.11). This gives you a much faster way of accessing pieces of the user interface (UI) without using the mouse.

Figure 1.11

More little letters appear to help you select items within one of the Ribbon groups.

Using Old Office Keyboard Shortcuts

If you have used previous versions of Office 2003, you might have become accustomed to a few keyboard shortcuts that help you through the day and prevent carpal tunnel syndrome. After reading the previous section, you might be thinking that all this training will have been for naught, but don't worry because Office 2007 has taken this factor into consideration.

SELECT FROM A MENU

Most keyboard shortcuts from previous versions of Office still work. For example, to select something from a menu, simply press and hold the Alt key and begin the shortcut combination, just as you did in PowerPoint 2003.

For example, to insert a Picture from a File, you would do this in PowerPoint 2007: While pressing Alt, press the I key, the P key, and then the F key. This corresponds to pressing the Alt key in 2003, and then pressing I for Insert, P for Picture, and F for From file. This all still works in PowerPoint 2007, even though the menu items associated with the shortcut keys are no longer there.

SIMPLER KEYBOARD SHORTCUTS

Other simpler shortcuts, such as Ctrl+C for copy or Ctrl+B for bold, also work just as they did in PowerPoint 2003. All your favorite PowerPoint 2003 keyboard shortcuts should still work in PowerPoint 2007!

CYCLING THROUGH PANES USING F6

Have you ever tried to press F5 to enter Slide Show mode? Okay, that's an easy one; have you ever missed the F5 key and accidentally pressed F6? If you use F6 on purpose and can explain what it does, you are way ahead of the game.

F6 is a navigation shortcut that cycles through various parts of the Window to save you some time and relieves you of the stress of moving your mouse around so much.

The various parts of the Window that it cycles through include

- The Ribbon—With Accelerator keys highlighted
- The Thumbnail pane
- The Outline pane
- The Main slide
- The Notes pane

Customizing the Office User Interface Using the Quick Access Toolbar

New

Do you remember customizing all the toolbars in previous versions of Office? Do you remember how long it took you each time to customize each of the thirtysomething toolbars, adding buttons you wanted and removing the useless ones taking up valuable toolbar real estate?

Well, you will be pleasantly surprised with Office 2007 because the new Quick Access Toolbar, or QAT (pronounced "KWAT"), saves you the trouble of customizing multiple toolbars, letting you automatically create your own toolbar (see Figure 1.12).

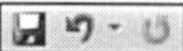

Figure 1.12

Quick Access Toolbar.

Customizing the QAT

To begin customizing your toolbar, click the Office button and choose PowerPoint Options. Click the Customize section on the left, and you are greeted by a dialog box of two panes next to one another vertically (see Figure 1.13).

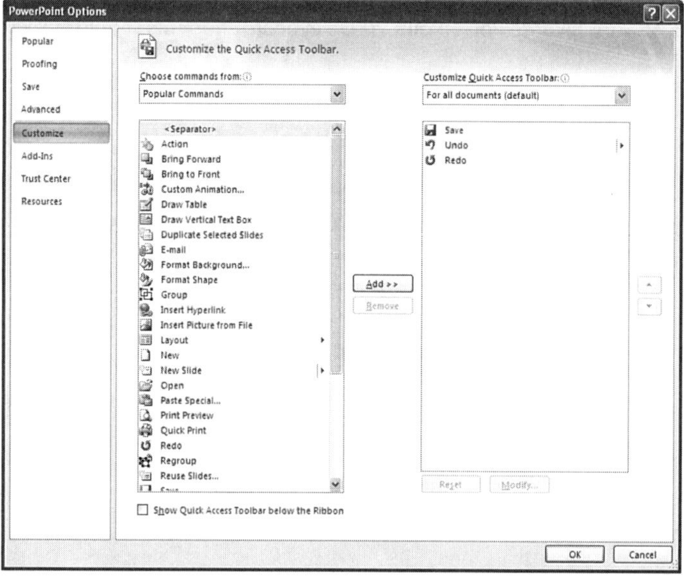

Figure 1.13

The pane on the left side allows you choose which command you want on the Quick Access Toolbar in the pane on the right side.

TIP

All the sections beginning with Customize and below, underneath the horizontal line, are the same in Word, Excel, and PowerPoint 2007. Learn about these once, and you should be able to use your skills across Office.

Click toolbar buttons from the left side of the dialog, and then click the Add button to add it to the QAT. If you accidentally choose one you don't want, you can remove it by selecting it on the right and clicking Remove.

Another easy way to modify the Quick Access Toolbar is to simply right-click on parts of the Ribbon and click Add to Quick Access Toolbar.

Customization Limitations

Two notable deficiencies of the Ribbon exist when you compare it to the Office 2003 toolbars:

1. The 2007 interface can't be heavily customized.
2. The Ribbon tabs can't be torn away and made floating.

NOTE

The Ribbon cannot be customized through the PowerPoint user interface, but if you're a developer willing to write some code, Office does offer Ribbon customization capabilities. It's easiest using XML and a .NET language such as C# or VB.NET. Read more on MSDN: http://msdn2.microsoft.com/en-us/library/aa338202.aspx. Third-party tools also might be of some help, so definitely check those out. One is called Ribbon Customizer.

Finding Hidden Commands

The QAT is useful not only for accessing certain features more quickly, but also for accessing some features that are not available from the standard user interface. If you find yourself unable to find a feature that existed in previous versions of the product, first check the QAT commands to see if you can add it there before you go searching to see if the feature was left out of the product for this release.

Customization Tips and Tricks

Here are some tips and tricks you might find useful as you manipulate the user interface to the way you work:

- If you find yourself using a piece of the Ribbon frequently and want to add it to your QAT, simply right-click it on the Ribbon and select Add to Quick Access Toolbar.
- One thing we like to do is to put the QAT below the Ribbon. This is how you do it: Right-click on the QAT and select Show Quick Access Toolbar Below the Ribbon, which moves it down below to make it resemble the screen shown in Figure 1.14. Try it out; you'll find that you have less screen real estate, but the QAT will be faster to reach and might not be in the way as much. (You won't need to move the mouse past the Ribbon each time you want to access it.)
- Using the Alt keys in combination with the QAT can produce some useful results. Pressing the Alt key assigns a number in ascending order to the items from left to right in your QAT. So, if you have an action that takes four or five Alt key combinations, just add it as an item to your QAT. You will automatically get the next higher number for that action. For instance, if the number assigned is 4, you can access this QAT item with a single Alt+4 combination key.

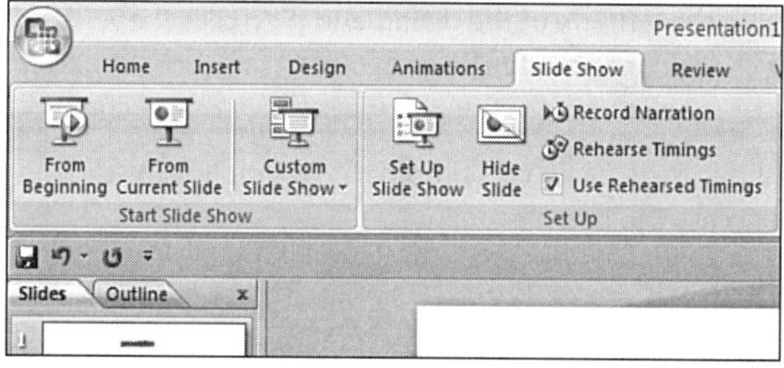

Figure 1.14

Example of the QAT below the Ribbon.

NOTE

Fun and Useless Fact: If you installed Beta 2 of Office 2007, the game Solitaire was available under All Commands, and you could add it to the QAT in Excel.

Contextual Text Formatting Using the Mini Toolbar

Another new addition to the user interface is that of the mini toolbar, which is often referred to as the floatie.

What's a Floatie?

The *floatie*, also known as the *mini toolbar*, is a little toolbar that appears when you're editing text. Shown in Figure 1.15, it contains the most popular and useful text editing buttons, which makes it easy to format your text without actually having to go to the Ribbon.

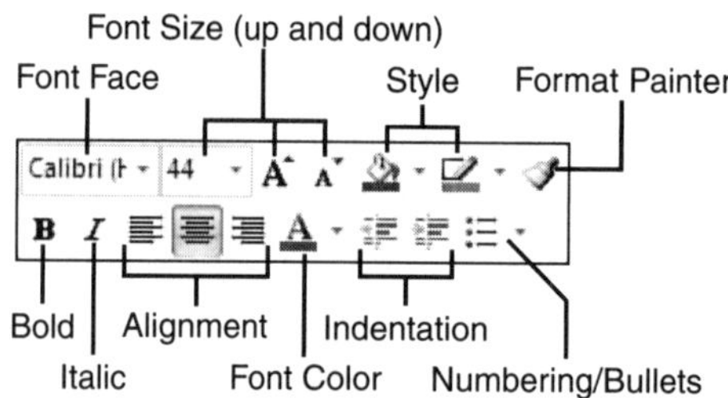

Figure 1.15

The anatomy of the floatie.

The floatie is contextual, meaning that it shows up when PowerPoint senses that you need it, such as in the following instances:

- It appears after you paste, alongside the Smart Tag (more on that in the beginning of Chapter 9, "Inserting Content into PowerPoint").

- Simply hover over some selected text, and you'll see it.
- Simply double-click on a word or another object or right-click on just about anything.

Notice that as you move the mouse away from the floatie, it becomes more and more transparent until it disappears entirely. As you move closer to the floatie, it becomes more opaque (see Figure 1.16).

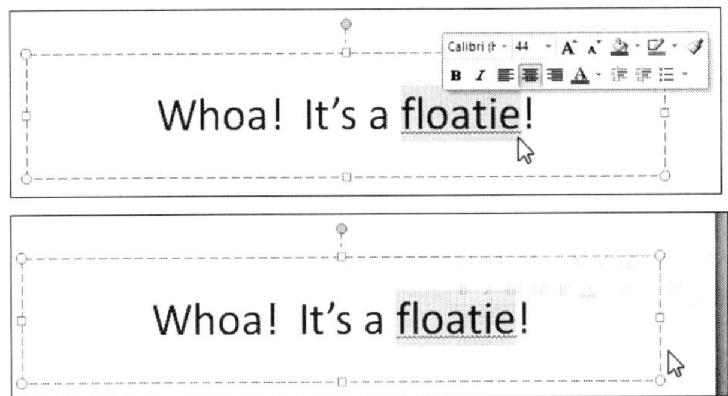

Figure 1.16

Here is the floatie in different opaque states.

Hate the Floatie?

The floatie can't be customized, but if you happen to find this feature cumbersome, you can turn it off completely by clicking the Office button, PowerPoint Options Popular (section in the left pane) and unchecking the Show MiniToolbar on Selection check box, which is the very first check box.

Redesigned Status Bar

The area at the bottom of your PowerPoint windows might look new to you. This area is known as the status bar.

What's a Status Bar?

The strip of real estate at the bottom of your PowerPoint window contains a ton of information about your presentation and has more features than the status bar from previous versions.

In earlier versions of PowerPoint, the status bar would show you what slide you're on, whether you've saved the presentation, and what Slide Design was applied to the document. The 2007 release adds new information to the status bar.

Anatomy of the Status Bar

Figure 1.17 shows the new PowerPoint 2007 status bar. Table 1.1 describes what each piece of the status bar does.

Figure 1.17

The PowerPoint status bar.

Table 1.1 The Status Bar

Status Bar	Component Description
Slide Number and Total Number of Slides	The status bar still reports which slide you're on and how many slides are in your current presentation in the lower left.
Theme	Right next to it, you'll see what theme has been applied to your presentation. You can change this by selecting the Design tab and choosing a new theme for your document.
Spell Check	The current state of the spell checker and whether you have errors.
Language	The status bar reports which locale is currently active. This isn't useful to most U.S. users because it does not show up if English is the default language to use, but is handy for people who create presentations that contain multiple languages.
Signatures	If your document is right protected or digitally signed, you will see an icon here.
The Square Triplets	On the lower-right side of your status bar, you'll see three buttons—each of which controls which view you're in. You can go to Normal Presentation, Slide Sorter, or Slider Show mode by clicking the appropriate box.
Zoom	Next to that is a really cool feature, which is the Zoom slider. With this, you can select in the level of zoom on your presentation without having to enter a number from the drop-down as in previous versions of Office. You can also click the square button to the right of the slider, which automatically chooses the appropriate zoom level for the current slide contents.

Customizing the Status Bar

Don't like the default items on the status bar or want to add more? Right-click the status bar to bring up the status bar customization menu. Check items you want to keep, and uncheck the ones you don't like.

Other Useful Office 2007 Enhancements

The following are a few interesting features that can make your presentation-authoring experience more enjoyable.

What's That Noise?

Maybe you didn't notice because it's usually so quiet, but Office can do sounds. To activate them, go to the Office button and select PowerPoint Options; then choose Advanced in the left pane, scroll to the bottom of the right pane, and check the Provide Feedback with Sound check box. Press OK. You'll probably get prompted to install the Microsoft Office Sounds add-in. Go ahead and do so.

NOTE

Okay, so this isn't really new. The Office sounds add-in has been available since PowerPoint 2002, but you probably haven't tried it out yet.

After the add-in is installed, crank up your computer speakers, try a few operations, and listen to the sounds. For example, you'll get a sound for each of these operations:

- Creating a new presentation (Ctrl+N)
- Inserting a slide (Ctrl+M)
- Undoing (Ctrl+Z)
- Redoing (Ctrl+Y)
- Clicking a button on a toolbar
- Closing the presentation without saving (Ctrl+F4)

If you find the sounds annoying, go back to PowerPoint Options and uncheck the Provide Feedback with Sound box to disable them.

Enhanced ScreenTips

ScreenTips are great. You love and use them, especially when a button itself is more generic than a shirt from the Gap. When you hover over a button with your mouse pointer, ScreenTips help you figure out what a button does. New to Office 2007 are Super ScreenTips, which have the same functionality as the regular ScreenTips, but are much larger and provide more information and sometimes pictures that are helpful (see Figure 1.18).

If you find that these giant ScreenTips annoy you, click the Office button and choose PowerPoint Options. Choose Popular in the left pane and look for the ScreenTip Style drop-down. Choose Don't Show Feature Descriptions in ScreenTips to make them smaller or Don't Show ScreenTips to make them go away altogether.

NOTE

In development, the giant ScreenTips were called "Super ScreenTips." Eventually, the "Super" moniker was dropped, and in the final product, Office just calls these extra large ScreenTips "Screen Tips."

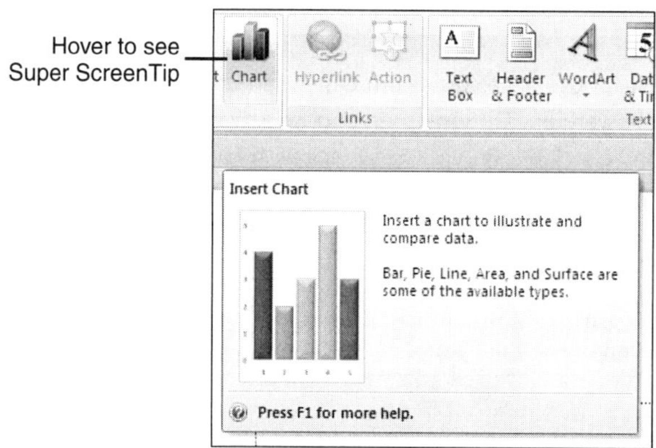

Figure 1.18

A big, fat enhanced ScreenTip.

Changing PowerPoint Skins

One of the first things we did after installing Office is change the skin, which Office calls a color scheme. The three main color options that you can use for Office applications—which recolor the background, the toolbars, and the look and feel—are Blue, Silver, and Black.

> **NOTE**
>
> More information about Office 2007 color schemes can be found on the Web from Microsoft Office's user interface guru: http://blogs.msdn.com/jensenh/archive/2006/08/14/699304.aspx.

The default Office color scheme is blue. To change the scheme, click the Office button and choose PowerPoint Options, and then click Popular in the left pane. Find the Color Scheme drop-down and pick your favorite color.

> **NOTE**
>
> It's incredibly confusing that Office calls these "color schemes," but these have nothing to do with PowerPoint colors, schemes, or themes used to style your documents. You'll learn more about those concepts in Chapter 11.

The content of a presentation is as important as how it is presented. Imagine a cake that looks beautiful but tastes horrible.

This part of the book helps you create PowerPoint content that will augment the ideas you are trying to convey. You will learn to make a beautiful presentation with ease, giving you more time to concentrate on the material you are presenting.

Creating Content

2 Everything You Need to Know About Text ... 27

3 Text Support ... 41

4 Working with Pictures ... 63

5 Diagrams and SmartArt ... 85

6 Rediscover Charts ... 101

7 Working with Shapes ... 117

8 Tables Like You've Never Seen Before ... 137

9 Inserting Content into PowerPoint ... 151

2

Everything You Need to Know About Text

IN THIS CHAPTER

- Selecting Multiple Ranges of Text
- Easily Moving Text
- All Text Is WordArt
- Modifying Text Direction/Orientation
- Advanced Font Techniques
- Replacing Fonts
- Text Box Tricks
- Advanced Character Formatting

When people think of Microsoft Office and text, they usually think of Word. Word's text handling is undoubtedly more powerful in most areas, but PowerPoint is no slouch. In this chapter, we'll take a close look at PowerPoint's text functionality and show you some powerful features that you might not have known about.

Selecting Multiple Ranges of Text

This section talks about selecting text, from the basic to some more advanced tips.

Text Selection Basics

The methods for selecting paragraphs or portions of text have been around seemingly since the beginning of time, or at least since the beginning of Microsoft Word. You can click and drag across the text you want to select, click into the selection, and then press Shift and an arrow key until you get to the end point of the selection, or simply triple-click in the paragraph to select it in its entirety. That's about all there is to it.

If you want to extend a selection you already made, you can either Shift+click again at the new end point, or press Shift and the arrow key in the direction of the remainder of the desired selection.

Voilà! Your new selection is complete.

New Multiple Selection Options

New to PowerPoint 2007, you can select text discontinuously, meaning that all your text selections don't have to touch one another as one giant selection. Here's how:

1. Type in some text.
2. Select some of it.
3. Hold down the Ctrl key and select another range of text. You just selected two parts of text that aren't at all connected (see Figure 2.1).

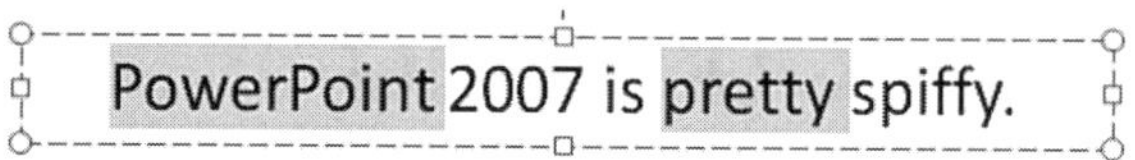

Figure 2.1

Select two discontinuous parts of the text.

4. Now you can do something to both of these ranges at the same time. For example, press Ctrl+B to make them bold.

Easily Moving Text

Advanced Now, let's talk about two ways to move the text you selected somewhere else.

Utilizing Copy/Paste

The most straightforward way most people move text is a simple copy/paste. Select the text, press Ctrl+C or choose Clipboard on the Home ribbon tab and then click the Copy icon to copy the text. Then, put the text cursor where you want to move the text and press Ctrl+V or click the large Paste Icon on the Home ribbon tab to paste it.

Drag

Another way to move text is to simply drag it. After selecting the text, click and hold your mouse on top of the selected text, and then drag it to where you want to move it.

Here are some interesting drag tips:

- You can drag text within the same text box, but as with copy/paste, you can also move it to one or more text boxes on the same slide or to the notes pane at the bottom of the PowerPoint window.
- If you drag text to a place on the slide where there's no target text box and release the mouse button, PowerPoint creates a new text box and drops the text into it.

- You can drag text to other PowerPoint windows. Go to the View ribbon tab, Windows group and select Arrange All to get multiple PowerPoint windows on the screen at the same time.
- You can even drag to other applications, such as Microsoft Word. Make the target window smaller, so you can see that window and your PowerPoint window at the same time. Then, just drag the text from one window to another.
- Windows lets you drag text to other Windows application windows (for example, a PowerPoint slide window, a Word document window) that you don't currently see:
    1. Select the text, move your cursor above it, and hold down the mouse button to begin a drag.
    2. Drag the text to the very bottom of the monitor to the Windows taskbar and move your mouse to another application on the taskbar. Windows will bring that window to the front.
    3. With your mouse button still pressed, move your cursor up into to the new application window onto some text.
    4. Release the mouse button to drop the text in its new location.
- Holding down Ctrl while you're dragging text copies the text instead of moving it.

All Text Is WordArt

New One of the best features in PowerPoint 2007 is the unified editing experience for both text and shapes. In PowerPoint 97–2003, there was WordArt, which could be richly styled with all the same formatting as a shape, but regular text was relegated to simple formatting such as solid color fills, bold, italics, and underline.

In PowerPoint 2007, there is no longer the distinction. Type in a text placeholder, select a few of the characters, and then you can apply a gradient fill, add a glow, or even apply 3D effects (see Figure 2.2). You'll learn more about formatting text in Chapters 11 through 13, where we discuss themes and formatting.

Figure 2.2

Richly styled text.

WORDART OR TEXT?

Despite the WordArt/text unification, PowerPoint is somewhat inconsistent in its terminology—sometimes calling it WordArt and sometimes calling it Text. On the Insert tab, in the Text group, you find an entire WordArt section. If you right-click some selected text though, the contextual menu contains a Format Text Effects option.

Some of this is a holdover from previous versions of Office, where there was a difference between the two; but rest assured that there's no difference any more in Office 2007 between WordArt and regular text, and the two terms can be used interchangeably.

Modifying Text Direction/Orientation

Advanced Here's an example of changing text direction. This lets you set different rotation values on text and the shape in which it's contained. For example, you could rotate text 90 degrees and rotate the shape it's inside 25 degrees. Here's how you set text rotation:

1. Type a few words into the title placeholder.
2. Give the placeholder shape a gradient fill by selecting the placeholder shape, and then going to the Shape Styles group of the Format tab and choosing Shape Fill item, Gradient, and selecting your favorite gradient.
3. On the Home tab in the Paragraph group, choose Text Direction, and then choose a text direction like Rotate All Text 270 degrees. Notice how the gradient is unchanged, but the text all rotates.

TIP

New to PowerPoint 2007 is the ability to set text columns inside a shape. Just select a shape; then go to the Home tab, and in the Paragraph group, click the Columns icon and choose how many columns of text that you want. It's useful if you have a long block of text you want to break up.

Advanced Font Techniques

Select some text, and then you can change fonts on the Home tab in the Font group using the Font drop-down.

Live Preview

One of our favorite Office 2007 features is Live Preview, which we first mentioned in Chapter 1, "Introducing the Office 2007 User Interface." Try it:

1. Type some text and select it.
2. Click on the Font drop-down to show the list of fonts, but don't click on any of the font names.
3. Hover over one of the font names. Watch as your text changes instantly, giving you a preview of how it will look before you actually pick a new font (see Figure 2.3).

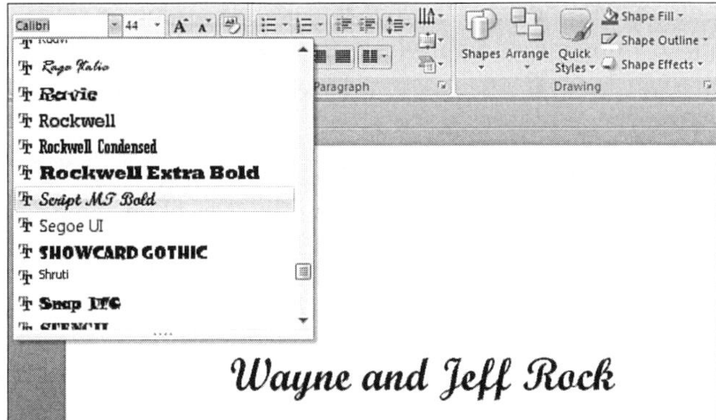

Figure 2.3

Preview how a font will look by hovering over it in the font picker.

Theme Fonts

The first two font choices in the Font drop-down are Theme Fonts—one marked for Headings and the other marked for Body. These two fonts are derived from the current Theme Fonts set in the Design tab on the Themes group under Fonts.

Here are some reasons why you would pick a Theme Font when formatting text:

- By default, these two fonts are picked by the theme designer, who probably makes a living designing stuff you wouldn't dream of designing. It will probably look better and be better coordinated with the rest of the presentation's visuals.
- If you later change your mind about, say, how all the Body fonts in your presentation look, you can easily change that font (again, on the Design tab in the Themes group under Fonts), and all text in your presentation that you formatted as Body font will automatically update. This won't happen if you select a non-theme font.
- If you copy/paste text formatted with a themed font to another presentation, or to a Word or Excel file, the pasted text automatically updates to whatever the font is in the target file's theme. For example, if the Body font in your presentation is Helvetica, and the Body font in the file you pasted your text into is Garamond, the pasted text automatically becomes formatted with the Garamond font without you having to do anything else to it.

Anything you ever wanted to know about font schemes and themes is described in Chapter 11, "Dissecting Themes."

New Fonts for 2007

Windows Vista and Office 2007 come with a few new fonts. This means that PowerPoint 2007 now has them as well.

The new fonts were designed to look best with ClearType enabled, which is a sub-pixel antialiasing technology first introduced in Windows XP in 2001. It makes everything on your computer screen look smoother. Windows Vista turns on ClearType by default. You can enable it in Windows XP by using Microsoft's ClearType tuner at http://www.microsoft.com/typography/cleartype/tuner/Step1.aspx.

Microsoft's promotion literature writes paragraphs about each new font. There's a lot to say about each one, but we'll keep it short here and just include a brief description about each of the main new PowerPoint 2007 fonts (see Table 2.1).

Table 2.1 New Fonts in PowerPoint 2007

Font Name	Description	Serif/Sans-serif
Consolas	For computer programmers. Each letter has the same width (monospaced) as in old-school typewriters.	Sans-serif
Calibri	Has a warm and fuzzy feel.	Sans-serif
Cambria	For formal or business documents. Good for onscreen reading and at small sizes.	Serif
Constantia	For printing and electronic media. Has wedge-serifs, so letters look more square but are easier to read at smaller sizes.	Serif
Corbel	Designed to look very simple and clean.	Sans-serif
Candara	Is less smooth and straight compared to the others, making it look more calligraphic.	Sans-serif
Segoe UI	Is used for all the text in the ribbon and in the user interface.	Sans-serif

Sans-serif means that a font doesn't have the little "serif" features at the end of each stroke but soft rounded corners instead. Serif means that it does have these little feet (see Figure 2.4).

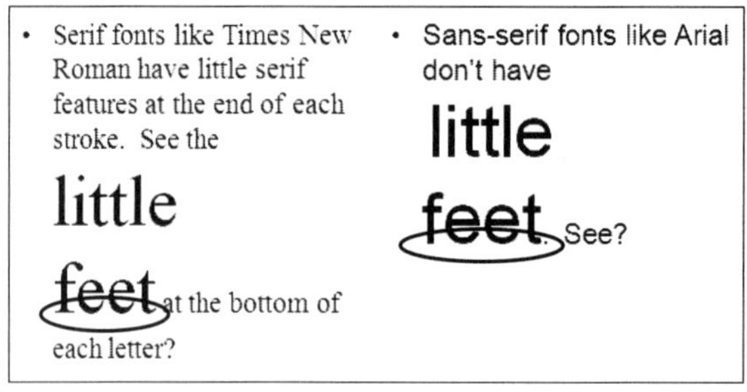

Figure 2.4

Serifs and sans-serif.

Replacing Fonts

Advanced Replacing fonts is a helpful way to save time if you need to quickly change the look of all the text in your document. All you have to do is make sure that you use the same font when you start typing. When you decide you want to change all words of that same font to something different, do the following:

Click the Home tab, and in the Editing group, click the little arrow to the right of Replace and choose Replace Fonts (see Figure 2.5).

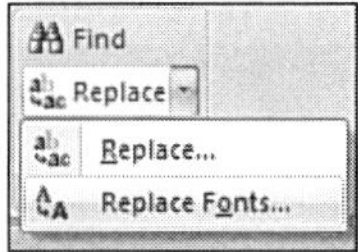

Figure 2.5

Find the Replace Fonts option in the Editing group of the Home tab.

NOTE

Question marks in front of the font name in the Replace box indicate that the font is not available on the current system.

You'll notice that the simple dialog has two options, Replace and With. These options enable you to select two fonts, and then after clicking the Replace button, all text is changed from one font to another (see Figure 2.6).

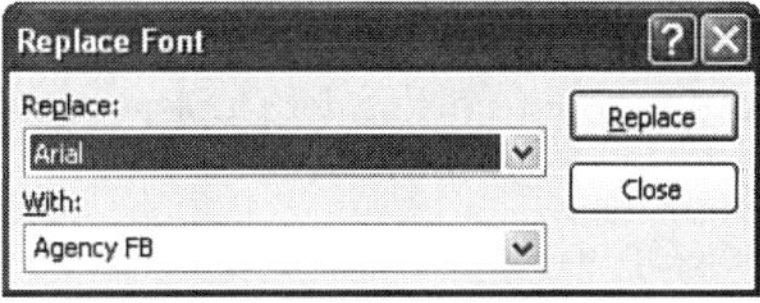

Figure 2.6

Choose the font to replace and what to replace it with.

You can distinguish text by choosing different temporary font types while you type, and then make a second pass later to revise the fonts to their final types.

One example of when you might use this is when you're editing a presentation you got from a colleague and it uses a font that isn't installed on your computer. Without having the font used to create the text, it shows up as Times New Roman by default. Fear not! All you have to do is go to the Replace Fonts dialog and replace Times New Roman with a font that looks similar to what you desire.

CAUTION

This feature does not replace text within Pictures, even Metafiles (Windows Metafile Format, Enhanced Metafile Format).

Text Box Tricks

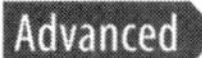

PowerPoint allows for text boxes to make it especially easy to add text anywhere on the slide (Insert tab on the Text group under the Text Box button). Let's explore text boxes for a little bit.

HORIZONTAL AND VERTICAL TEXT BOXES

PowerPoint users who use Asian languages can create both horizontal and vertical text boxes. To make the Vertical Text Box option appear, click the Office Button and choose PowerPoint Options. In the Popular section on the left, click the Language Settings button and add an Asian language such as Chinese. Restart PowerPoint.

After you've done this, if you click the arrow on the Text Box button on the Insert tab in the Text group, you'll see two types of text boxes that can be inserted—Horizontal Text Box and Vertical Text Box.

CAUTION

Language Setting choices change your settings in all Office applications, not just PowerPoint.

Advanced Text Box Options

While we're in the advanced Text Box options dialog, let's look at some of these other choices (see Figure 2.7 and Table 2.2).

Table 2.2 Advanced Text Box Options

Text Option	Description
Vertical alignment	Choose where you want the text to float in your text box when the text inside your text box doesn't quite take up all the vertical space: Should the text float up, to the middle, or to the bottom of the box? Should it be centered?
Autofit	What happens when you type more text into a text box? Either nothing happens (Do Not Autofit is selected), the text gets smaller so that it still fits inside the text box (Shrink Text on Overflow is selected), or the text box gets bigger so the extra text still fits inside (Resize Shape to Fit Text is selected).
Internal margin	Leave a little slack around the inside edges of the text box so that the text doesn't touch the edges of the text box.
Wrap text in shape	If this is unchecked, the text won't automatically break into multiple lines—all the text will be in one long line.

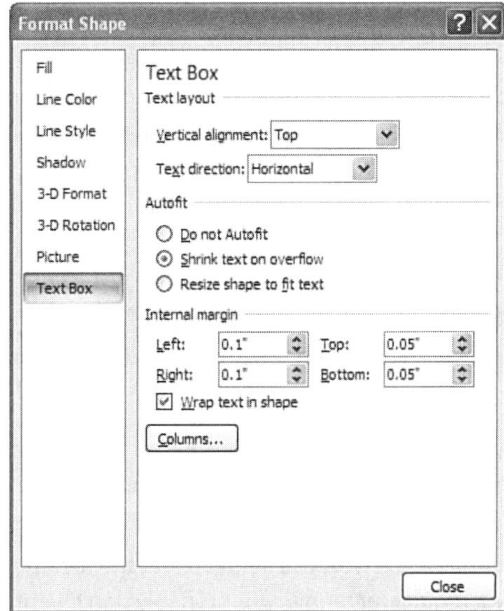

Figure 2.7

Advanced Text Box tweaks.

Turn a Text Box into a Regular Shape

It is not well known that text can be placed inside nearly all PowerPoint shapes. In this section, we explain the relationship between PowerPoint text and PowerPoint shapes.

AUTOMATIC TEXT POSITIONING INSIDE SHAPES

The cool thing about text in shapes is that the text knows where to live inside the shape. So, even if you insert text into a right triangle, as in the example shown in Figure 2.8, the text won't be placed in the exact center of the shape's bounds (sticking half inside the shape and half outside), but rather where the shape thinks text should go.

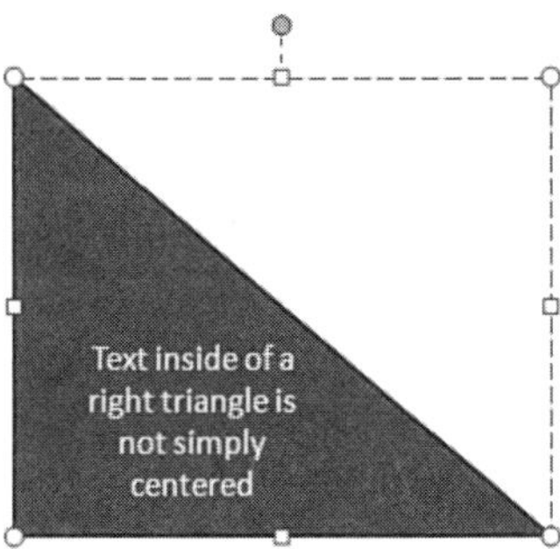

Figure 2.8

This is a great example of how text will be smart and follow where the shape tells it to go. Notice that the text does not simply land in the middle of the shape.

TEXT OPERATIONS WITH A SHAPE SELECTION

When you have a shape selected, you can perform any text operation on it, and the text inside of it will be affected. You can apply text operations, such as bold and italics (for example, at the Home tab in the Font group, click the Bold icon that has a "B" on it, or Ctrl+B), and all the text inside the shape will be formatted.

TURNING A TEXT BOX INTO A SHAPE

There is nothing inherently special about a text box. In fact, it's just a customized rectangle shape with special settings. The following steps show you how to turn a text box into a rectangle:

1. Insert a text box by clicking on the Insert tab and choosing Text Box.
2. Type some text in it.
3. Next, let's give it a line and a fill by using the controls on the Format tab. In the Shape Styles group, choose Shape Fill and Shape Outline. After the line and fill is applied, we already have something that looks just like a rectangle!
4. If you type a lot of text into a text box, you'll notice that the rectangle grows to fit the text. If you want it to be truly a regular rectangle, you probably don't want this behavior. You can turn off that setting by doing the following: Right-click the shape and select Format Shape. Choose the Text Box section on the left and then choose Do Not Autofit. You now have a shape that's completely a rectangle in every way.

TIP

One change of the *Format Shape* dialog from previous versions of Office is that it's modeless. This means that your dialog can stay up and its values immediately change depending on what you click. Try it: Launch the dialog and then click on different shapes in your presentation. Also, if you make any changes in the dialog, the changes are made immediately, without requiring you to hit an OK button at the end.

Advanced Character Formatting

Advanced The Font dialog has been beefed up in PowerPoint 2007. Select some text and access a dialog by choosing the Home tab and clicking the box launcher on the Font group, which is the little rectangle at the bottom right (see Figure 2.9).

Underline Style

Set an underline style by selecting one of the many choices from the drop-down (see Figure 2.10). These affect how dashed the underline is. You can select a color for the underline right next to it.

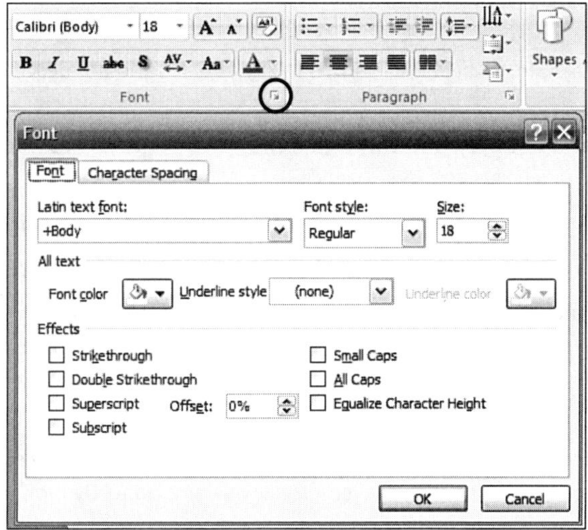

Figure 2.9

The PowerPoint 2007 Font dialog.

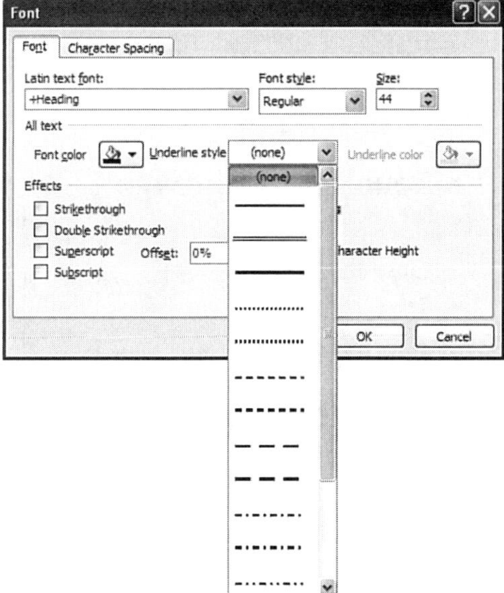

Figure 2.10

Choose an underline style from the drop-down.

Text Effects

Several text effect features are available, as shown in Figure 2.11, and are described in the following list:

- **Strikethrough and double-strikethrough**—Draws one or two lines through the middle of the text.
- **Superscript**—Raises the text higher than it usually is. You can specify an exact percentage.
- **Subscript**—The opposite of superscript. Makes the text lower than it usually is.
- **Small caps and all caps**—Changes the case of the text to "SMALL CAPS" or "ALL CAPS." Unlike the others, selecting this is a one-time deal. In other words, if you set some text to small caps and then type some capitalized words in the middle of that text, the newly inserted text will stay capitalized.
- **Equalize character heights**—Makes all the letters the same height by stretching the shorter letters to be the same height as the taller letters. This one honestly looks pretty ugly for most text.

TIP

Select some text and use Shift+F3 to toggle between the three different case settings: small case, UPPERCASE, and Camel Case.

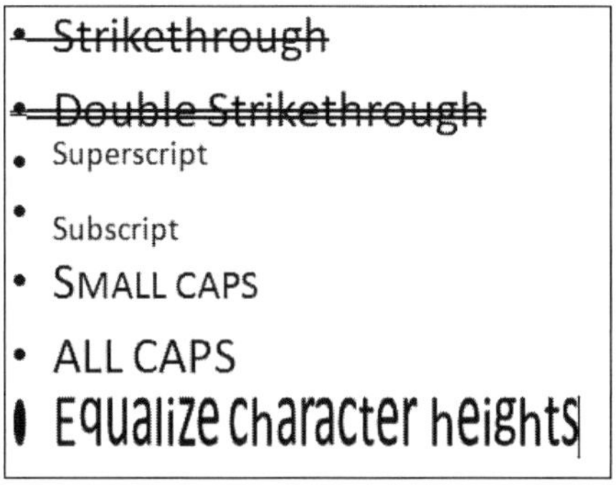

- ~~Strikethrough~~
- ~~Double Strikethrough~~
- Superscript
- Subscript
- SMALL CAPS
- ALL CAPS
- Equalize character heights

Figure 2.11

PowerPoint text effects.

Single strikethrough is available as an icon that shows a line across the letters on Home tab in the Font group (see Figure 2.12). Interestingly enough, you can click the down arrow next to the Change Case icon in the Font group to drop down a list of choices—some of which don't appear in the Font dialog: Sentence Case, Lowercase, Uppercase, Capitalize Each Word, and Toggle Case.

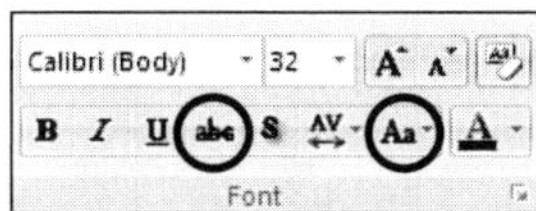

Figure 2.12

Several text effects are available on the ribbon, as shown here.

You can choose Double Strikethrough, Small Caps, All Caps, and Equalize Character Height in the Effects section of the Font dialog.

NOTE

Strikethrough, double-strikethrough, the casing options, and Equalize Character Heights are new in PowerPoint 2007.

Character Spacing

The Character Spacing tab on the Font dialog lets you be very specific about how much spacing you want between letters (see Figure 2.13). The default Spacing option is Normal, but you can choose Expanded to increase the space between letters or Condensed to decrease the space between letters.

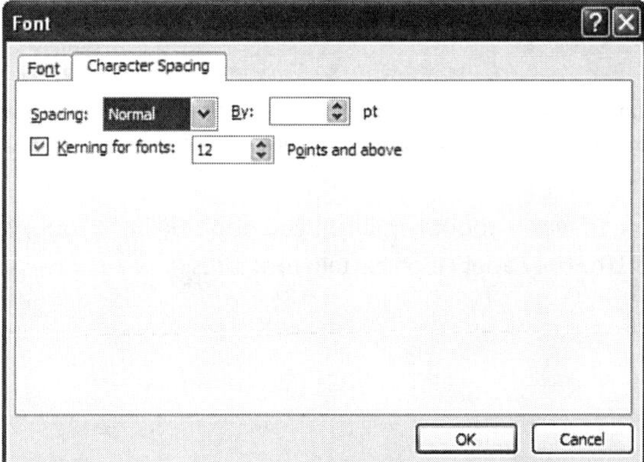

Figure 2.13

Character Spacing tab on the Font dialog.

Additionally, you can choose a point size for the spacing, although we don't often find a need to be this precise. You can generally pick from the spacing choices on the ribbon's Home tab in the Font group, and then click the character spacing button labeled with "AV" and a double-arrow (see Figure 2.14).

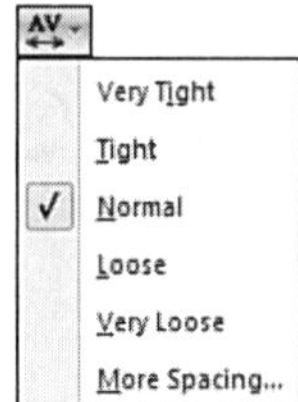

Figure 2.14

A drop-down list of character spacing options.

Kerning

You probably also noticed the kerning choices on the Character Spacing tab. *Kerning* is a typographical concept in which letters are spaced closer together, depending on which particular two letters are close to each other. For example, PowerPoint 2003 didn't support kerning, and so there was the same distance between the A and the V as the S and the T. With kerning turned on, the first two are packed closer together (see Figure 2.15).

AVAVAVSTSTST AVAVAVSTSTST

With kerning applied Without kerning applied

Figure 2.15

With kerning and tight spacing set, the V and A are noticeably spaced closer together in PowerPoint 2007 compared to PowerPoint 2003. Only certain letters will affect how close they fit together.

In general, you don't have to worry about kerning. If you don't like it, though, you can turn it off on the Character Spacing tab or only apply it on certain font sizes.

3

Text Support

IN THIS CHAPTER

- Bullets and Ordered Lists
- AutoCorrect
- Understanding Tab Stops
- Understanding Paragraph Formatting
- Subtle Selection Handle Differences
- Text Formatting for Placeholders and Shapes
- Transformed Text
- PowerPoint 2007's Proofing Tools
- What the Random?
- Shortcut Keys for Newbies and Experts

Now that you are familiar with actual text and how it works, let's walk through some helpful text-related features that can enhance and aid your journey through creating a presentation with great text.

Bullets and Ordered Lists

Advanced Many people suffer from boring "bullet-itus." If you're one of those who find themselves using boring, plain, soporific bullets, pay attention because we're about to show you how to put some life back into your presentation.

Default Bullets

There is a time and place for plain bullets, and if you find yourself stuck using them, it's easy to create nice-looking default bullets.

If you want to just do the default circle bullet, select some text and click the Home tab, Paragraph group, and then the Bullets button, and PowerPoint inserts a bullet in front of the text (see Figure 3.1). Most placeholders already contain these regular bullets by default.

Let's say that you want something slightly fancier. Instead of clicking the Bullets button on the Home tab, click the arrow to the right of it to open the gallery of bullet types (see Figure 3.2).

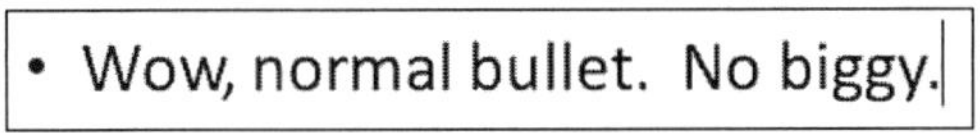

• Wow, normal bullet. No biggy.

Figure 3.1

Default circle bullet.

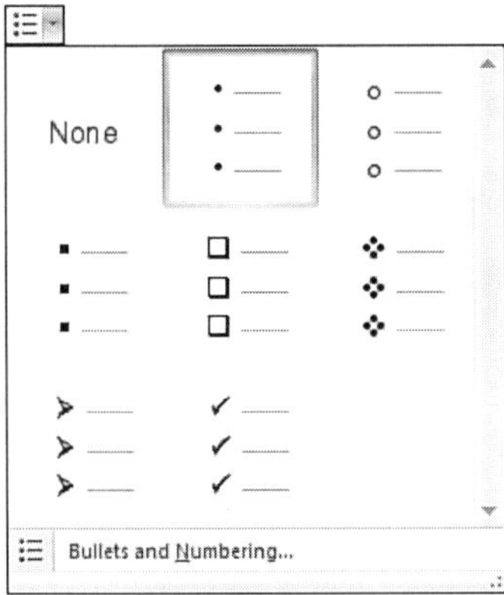

Figure 3.2

Other default bullets choices.

Ordered Lists

Creating an ordered list uses the same techniques. The button for creating an ordered list is right next to the bullets button. Click the arrow next to the Ordered List button to select from some canned ordered lists such as 1., 2., 3.; i., ii., iii; and a), b), c).

Your Face on a Bullet

No, we're not making a threat. But consider this: your face on a bullet. Yes, even better than on a billboard, all you need is a picture of your face and some bullet points in your presentation (see Figure 3.3).

Figure 3.3

Jeff's dog was gracious enough to let us use her beautiful face as an example.

Here's how it is done:

1. Select the text being bulleted.
2. Click the Home tab, the Paragraph group, and then the arrow to the right of the bullet icon. This time, click the Bullets and Numbering button at the bottom of the gallery (see Figure 3.4), which brings up the Bullets and Numbering dialog.

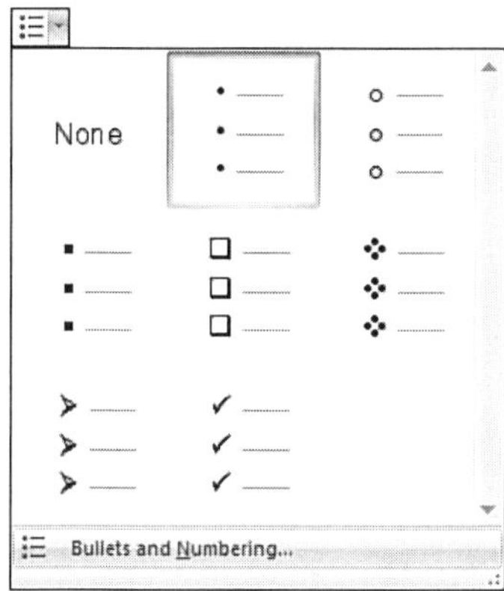

Figure 3.4

Use this button to access the Bullets and Numbering dialog from the ribbon.

3. Assuming that the defaults didn't meet with your satisfaction, you can change the size or color of the bullets in the dialog. Or, if you want to use another symbol for the bullet, click the Customize button to open the Symbol dialog (see Figure 3.5).

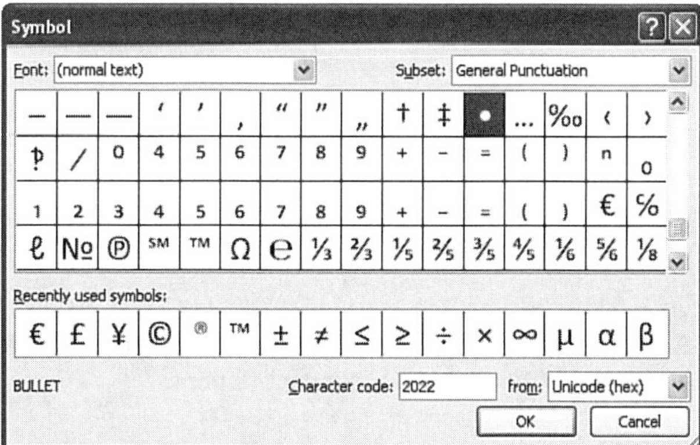

Figure 3.5

You can select some preset bullets types.

4. Let's suppose that even a crazy symbol isn't custom enough for us. Exit the Symbol and the Customize dialogs, and then click the Picture button.

5. You can click one of the old-school images that ships with Office, but it's more interesting to use your own image. Click the Import button (see Figure 3.6).

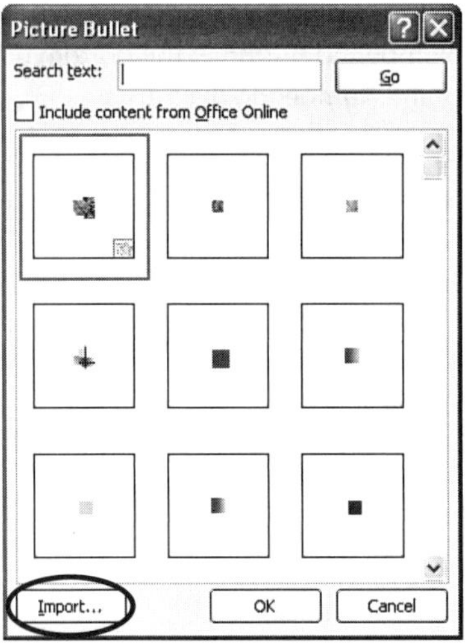

Figure 3.6

Click the Import button and select an image to use as a bullet.

6. Find your way to that picture of your face (or whatever image fits your purpose) and select it. You can use a picture of any format that PowerPoint supports.

What a great way to customize such a basic feature as bullet points and numbering.

AutoCorrect

Advanced AutoCorrect is another one of those Office features that everyone loves to hate. You're happily typing some text into PowerPoint, and PowerPoint changes it into something else, thinking that it's smarter than you are.

Fortunately, this feature is fairly customizable, and you can disable it completely if it annoys you. Bring up the AutoCorrect dialog by clicking the Office button and choosing PowerPoint Options (at the bottom). Click Proofing (on the left), and then AutoCorrect Options.

Default Text Corrections

You can change everything from whether "eyt" becomes "yet" to whether straight quotes become smart quotes. Many of the tabs in the AutoCorrect options are rare corner cases that will convert certain types of text you type into something else, so if you still want AutoCorrect on but find it wrong in certain cases, look for that specific case before you disable it altogether.

NOTE

These options are shared between all Microsoft Office applications, so if you change it in PowerPoint, it applies in Word as well.

We both love AutoCorrect, though, and happily use it daily. Table 3.1 shows some of the corrections we rely on.

Table 3.1 AutoCorrect Defaults

Type	Becomes
:)	☺
(tm)	™
(c)	©
-->	→
<--	←

Don't forget; AutoCorrect also handles all of the grammar, spelling, and autocapitalization that we take for granted.

TIP

If AutoCorrect fixes something for you that you didn't want to happen, simply Undo (Ctrl+Z), and it will go back to how you originally had it.

Creating Clickable Hyperlinks

Typing a URL (a web address) becomes a clickable URL, just as you find on websites:

http://www.waynekao.com

But, there's a problem if you have spaces in the URL. The AutoCorrect feature only converts the first part of the URL into an actual hyperlink that can be clicked. Just look at this:

http://waynekao.com/the first page.html

Luckily, there's a workaround; to get spaces in a URL, simply surround it with angle braces (the "less than" and "greater than" symbols):

<http://www.waynekao.com/the first page.html>

Then press Enter or the spacebar, and voilà:

http://www.waynekao.com/the first page.html

Note that these hyperlinks are only clickable in slideshow mode, so don't panic if you click on a link in default edit mode and nothing happens. Auto-hyperlink underlining can also be disabled by clicking the Office button and choosing PowerPoint Options. Click Proofing (in the left pane), and then AutoCorrect Options, AutoFormat As You Type. Uncheck the Internet and Network Paths with Hyperlinks box.

TIP

This hyperlink angle brace trick also works in Word and Outlook.

Adding Your Own Phrases

Beyond its traditional uses, AutoCorrect can also be used to automate typing of phrases that you type often. You can have "address" or "!address" or the word "addy" turn into your actual mailing address if you need to type it a lot or if your address is very long.

Pranks

Finally, AutoCorrect can be used to pull some great pranks. When your buddy leaves his computer unlocked, you can append words to his AutoCorrect list and really confuse him. Using opposite and intentional misspellings are the best (see Table 3.2).

Table 3.2 Fake AutoCorrect Entries Just For Fun

Type	Becomes
dumb	great
great	dumb
the	teh
me	Britney Spears
orange	ahrnge
water	wauder
forest	farst

Understanding Tab Stops

Advanced Tabs stops are one of those features everyone has seen but few fully understand. Tab stops have been around since the days of the typewriter, and at a high level, they let you specify precisely what happens to your text after you press the Tab key.

Let's first look at the ruler in PowerPoint, which is basically the holding tank for all the available Tab stops.

1. Start a new PowerPoint presentation.
2. Make sure that the Ruler is turned on by checking the View tab in the Show/Hide group to see that Ruler is selected.

3. Click into the content placeholder on your slide to make sure that you're in text-editing mode. Notice how the sides of the ruler just darkened to draw attention to the editable text area.
4. Click on the ruler between inches 1 and 2. You should see something like the symbol shown in Figure 3.7. If you don't see that symbol, continue clicking a few times until you do.

Figure 3.7

Notice the "L" shaped Tab stop inserted between inches 1 and 2.

Recognizing the Tab Symbols

Let's now take a closer look at each of these tab symbols. There are five of them shown in Figure 3.8, which we'll decrypt for you right here.

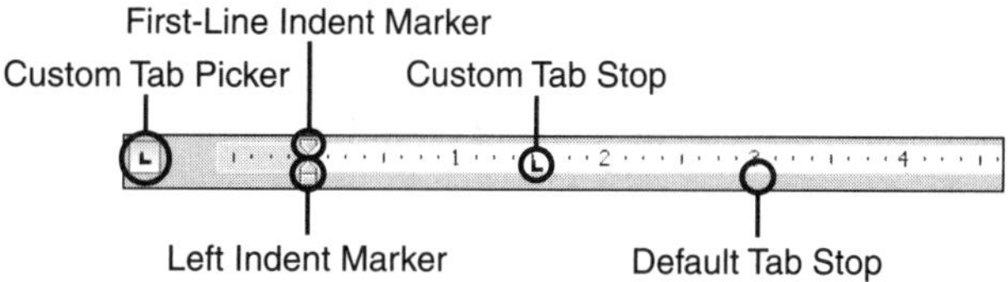

Figure 3.8

Let's look at what each of these tab symbols means.

- **Custom Tab Picker**—Clicking this button cycles through all the available Tab stops, which are detailed in "Custom Tab Types" later in this chapter . After you have cycled to a Tab stop type that you want to insert, just click on the ruler and the currently selected Tab type will be inserted at that position. If you change your mind, you can drag the inserted Tab stop somewhere else on the ruler or drag the Tab stop off the ruler and release the mouse to delete the stop.
- **First-Line Indent Marker**—This specifies where you want the first line in a paragraph to be lined up. For a bulleted or numbered list, this specifies where the bullet or number appears.
- **Left Indent Marker**—This specifies where you want the second line in a paragraph to be lined up. For a bulleted or numbered list, this specifies where the text appears.
- **Custom Tab Stop**—This is a custom tab that you inserted using the Custom Tab Picker.
- **Default Tab Stop**—These faint gray lines are default Tab stops that PowerPoint creates for you. You can drag them around if you don't like where they are.

TIP

All these skills are transferable to Microsoft Word, which has a nearly identical user interface for creating and using tabs.

Custom Tab Types

There are four custom tab types in PowerPoint:

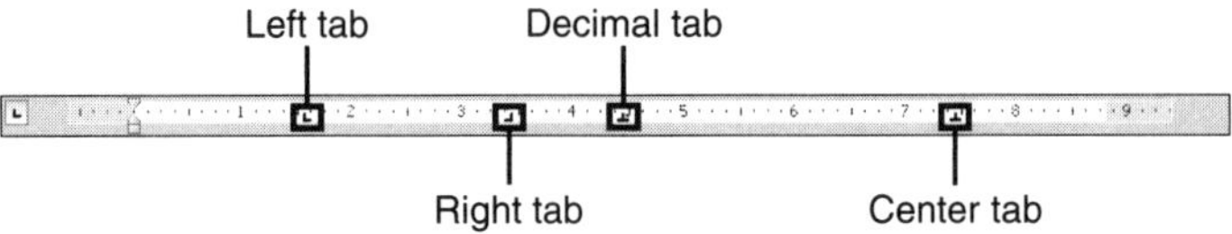

Figure 3.9

Here are four custom tab types.

- **Left tab**—Text at this tab stop is left-aligned with the tab stop.
- **Center tab**—Ditto, but the text is center-aligned at the top.
- **Right tab**—Ditto again, but text is right-aligned such that the right edge of the text is flush with the Tab stop.
- **Decimal tab**—The decimal point of the text lines up with the Tab stop.

Shopping List Example

Okay, now let's see some of this mumbo jumbo in action. Say that we want to list some purchase transactions in a text box, and we don't want to use a table:

PowerPoint	$229.00
PowerPoint Book	$100.00
6-pack of TAB Soft Drink	$2.99

Notice how the decimal points of all the dollar amounts line up nicely. Here's how you can join in on the fun:

1. Insert a new slide (Ctrl+M) in an open presentation and go to the second slide (see Figure 3.10).

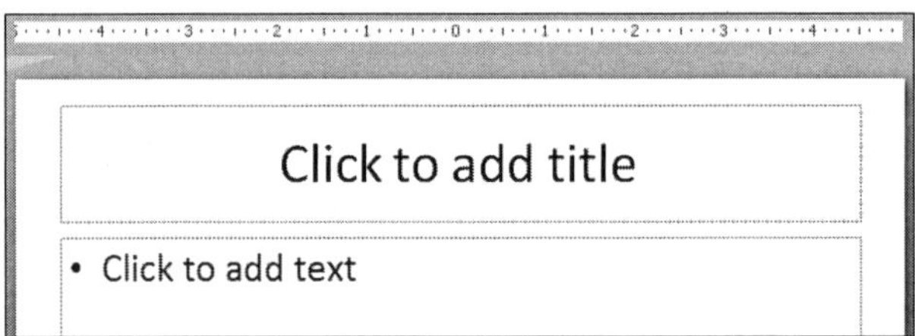

Figure 3.10

Look at the tabs on the Ruler at the top of the slide.

2. Click into the large placeholder. Notice again how the sides of the ruler darkened after you clicked into the placeholder (see Figure 3.11).

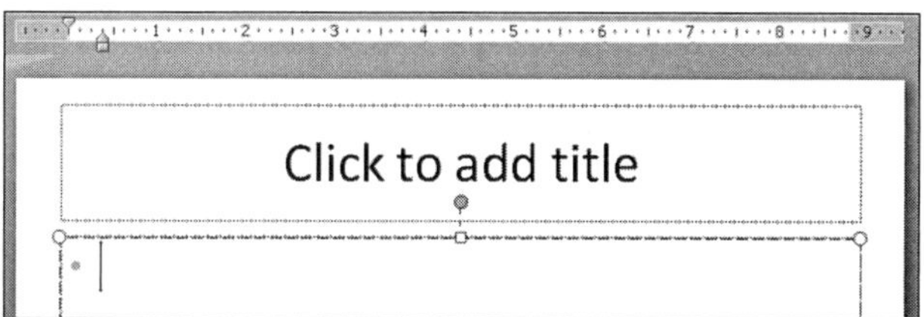

Figure 3.11

The ruler is darkened to let you know that you are in text editing mode.

3. Let's say that we want the decimal points to line up roughly where the 6 inch mark is on the ruler. Find the Custom Tab Picker (refer back to Figure 3.8) and click it until it shows the decimal Tab stop (shown previously in Figure 3.9). Notice how each click switches to a different Tab stop.
4. Now we want to insert the decimal Tab stop onto the ruler. Click the 6 inch mark on the ruler. Notice how the Tab stop symbol appears where you clicked.
5. Okay, now let's start typing. Type **`PowerPoint`**. Press the Tab key and type **`$229.00`**. The decimal point in the "$229.00" lines up with the 6 inch mark on the ruler, just as we predicted (see Figure 3.12).
6. Now, you just need to type in the rest of the list. Press Enter to go to the beginning of the next line. Type **`PowerPoint book`**, press Tab, type **`$100.00`**, and then press Enter. For the last line, type **`6-pack of TAB Soft Drink`**, press Tab, and then type **`$2.99`**.

Figure 3.13 shows the finished list.

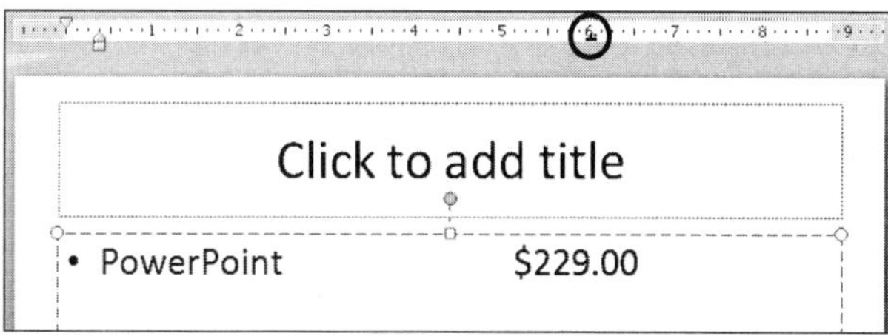

Figure 3.12

The numbers are centered around the decimal tab stop, which is where the decimal resides.

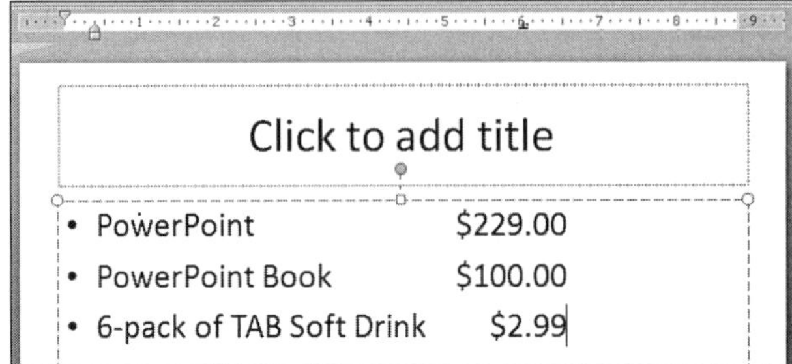

Figure 3.13

See how nicely the numbers line up?

Tab Tips

Following is a list of tips to be aware of when working with tabs:

- To move a default Tab stop (symbol #5 in Figure 3.8), just drag it to the new location.
- When you're adding or moving a Tab stop, hold the mouse button down, and you should see a temporary vertical dotted line from the Tab stop down. This line indicates where the tabbed text will be aligned when the Tab stop is placed.
- Inserting a new custom Tab stop, as we did in the shopping list example, removes all default Tab stops to its left.
- To remove a custom Tab stop, just drag it off the ruler, and it disappears.
- If you hold down the Ctrl key while dragging Tab stops around, the movement will be slower and you should be able to place the Tab stops more precisely.
- You can also set Tabs by selecting some text, right-clicking, and choosing Paragraph. Then, click the Tabs button.

Understanding Paragraph Formatting

Advanced Text is grouped into paragraphs, and it's convenient and logical to format all words and letters in a paragraph together. Let's take a look at how you can format paragraphs and save some time over formatting each word individually.

Paragraph Markers

Text formatting can throw you for a loop if you don't have a solid understanding of paragraph markers.

A WORD DETOUR

PowerPoint has no way to allow you to view paragraph markers, so let's make a quick detour into Word 2007:

1. Launch Word. Click Start, All Programs, Microsoft Office, and then Microsoft Office Word 2007.
2. Open a Word document you have sitting around, or type a few paragraphs of text.
3. Now, let's turn on paragraph markers. On the Home tab in the Paragraph group, click Show/Hide ¶. It's the big ¶ symbol in the top right of that Ribbon group.

Whoa, now there are ¶ symbols at the end of every paragraph. What's up with that? Well, those are paragraph markers.

NOTE

Early word processors, such as Microsoft Word, had paragraph markers turned on by default, which forced users to understand them. But, people kept complaining about weird symbols in their documents, so, a few releases back, Microsoft decided to hide them by default.

POWERPOINT PARAGRAPH MARKERS

Okay, back to PowerPoint. PowerPoint has paragraph markers too, but unlike Word, there's no way to make them visible. But, there's a space-like character at the end of each paragraph, which you can select (see Figure 3.14). This paragraph marker holds all the paragraph properties for that paragraph, essentially everything on the Home tab in the Paragraph group.

Here's some paragraph marker–related behavior. This is all identical to behavior in Word:

- Creating a new paragraph copies the paragraph formatting from the previous paragraph marker to the new paragraph.
- Deleting a paragraph marker deletes all of that paragraph's formatting and merges that text into the next paragraph, adopting the next paragraph's paragraph formatting.
- If you copy text without copying the paragraph marker, the paragraph properties won't be copy/pasted and your text adopts the target text's paragraph settings. So, copy that paragraph marker at the end if you want paragraph properties copied over.

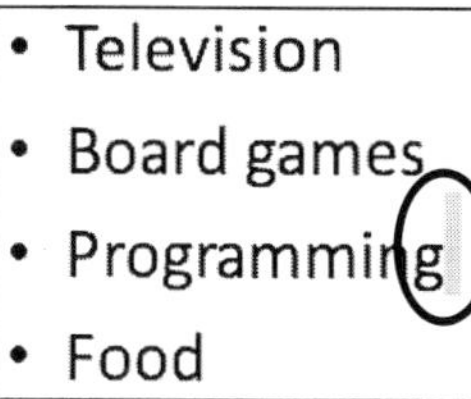

Figure 3.14

Select the space at the end of the paragraph to format the paragraph.

NOTE

Paragraph behavior in previous versions of PowerPoint was not as well-defined, and there was no way to select the paragraph marker.

PowerPoint goes out of its way to try to do the right thing, so nine times out of ten, you won't have to care about the paragraph marker and the right behavior will just happen. But remember your friend the paragraph marker the next time paragraph formatting is applied the way you expect.

NOTE

Just to make things more confusing, PowerPoint title placeholders are just one large paragraph. There's no way to have different paragraph formatting for different parts of the title placeholder, and there's only one paragraph marker per title placeholder to select.

Justify and Distributed

The Justify and Distributed alignment options give your text a clean look by aligning the text to both the left and right margins, as shown in Figure 3.15. You can find these options on the Home tab at the bottom left of the Paragraph group near the Columns drop down.

- Justify is the traditional setting that aligns text to both the left and right margins by adding spaces between words.
- Distributed is a newer setting that aligns text to both the left and right margins by adding spaces between letters. The Distributed option is not available to users who only use Latin languages such as English. To make the Distributed icon appear, click the Office button and choose PowerPoint Options. In the Popular section on the left, choose the Language Settings button and then add an Asian language such as Chinese. Restart PowerPoint.

- This text is justified. Look how spaces are added between words so that the paragraph touches the sides of the text box.
- This text is distributed. Look how spaces are added between letters so that the paragraph touches the side of the box.

Figure 3.15

Justified and distributed text.

Subtle Selection Handle Differences

Advanced Some commands do different things, depending on what editing mode you're in. For example, if you have some text selected in a title placeholder (see Figure 3.16) and you press Delete, the text gets deleted, but the placeholder remains.

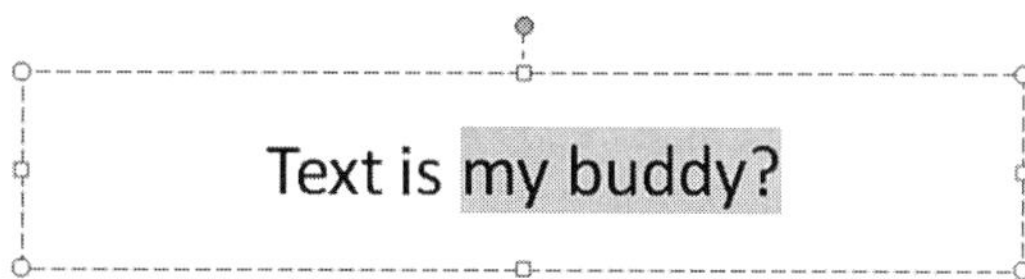

Figure 3.16

Here we have some text selected.

If you select the entire placeholder as shown in Figure 3.17, and then press Delete, the entire placeholder gets deleted.

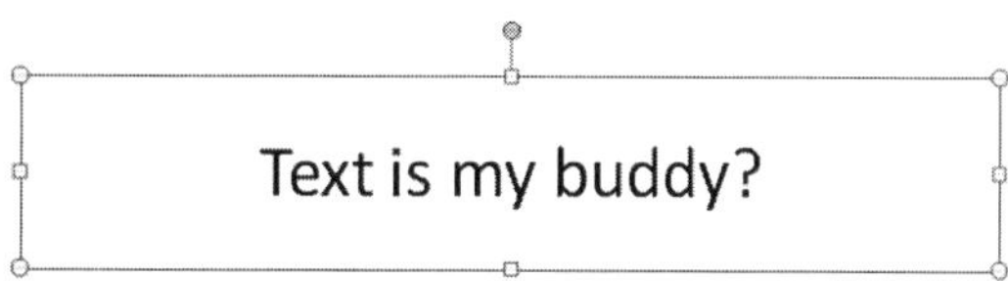

Figure 3.17

Here we have the entire placeholder selected.

Aside from the text cursor, do you notice the difference between those two screenshots? In Figure 3.16, the selection handle consists of dotted lines. This means that we're in text-editing mode. In Figure 3.17, the selection is solid, indicating that we're in shape-editing mode.

NOTE

In previous versions of PowerPoint, the border is much thicker, but there's still a difference: Text selections had diagonal lines and shape selections had a dotted line.

Look for these subtle changes in the handles whenever you're trying to figure out what's selected.

TIP

You can exit from text-editing mode into shape-editing mode by pressing the Esc key.

Text Formatting for Placeholders and Shapes

Advanced Although many believe that text operations such as bold and italic can only be applied to text, you can apply these operations to other PowerPoint objects as well. This section discusses performing text operations to placeholders and shapes.

Formatting Text Placeholders

Text formatting isn't just for text selections. It can be applied to placeholders as well, which affects any text typed into the placeholder after the formatting is applied. For example:

1. Create a new presentation (Ctrl+N).
2. Select the title placeholder. You want a shape selection, not a text selection, so make sure that the selection border is not dotted (see the section, "Subtle Selection Handle Differences," earlier in this chapter).
3. Click on the bold button from the Home tab (or press Ctrl+B). Notice how the prompt text becomes bold.
4. Click into the placeholder and type—the new text becomes bold.

Formatting Shapes

Placeholder text formatting works on shapes too:

1. Insert a circle from the Insert tab on the Shapes group by choosing a circle shape and then clicking somewhere on the slide.
2. Select the inserted circle.
3. Click on the bold button on the Home tab (or press Ctrl+B).
4. Type text into the circle and the text becomes bold.

Formatting Placeholders on the Master

So far, formatting placeholders is somewhat of a novelty, but this is actually useful for placeholders on the master.

1. Go to the slide master by choosing the View tab and clicking Slide Master on the Presentation Views group.
2. Select the title placeholder on the Master Slide.
3. Underline the text by clicking the Underline button on the Home tab or by pressing Ctrl+U.
4. Let's go crazy and apply a 3D bevel, too. On the Format tab in the WordArt Styles group, choose Text Effects, 3-D Rotation, and select your favorite effect.

5. Return to normal view by clicking the Close Master View button on the ribbon (the big red X). Notice that the placeholder now includes the underline and 3D formatting you applied.
6. Just to prove that this works, click into the placeholder and type. Notice how the text takes on the underline and the 3D formatting.
7. Create a new slide (Ctrl+M). Notice how the placeholder is formatted here, too.

This is neat because it means that you can go to the master, apply text formatting to the master placeholders, and have it apply to all the placeholders in the presentation.

CLEAR ALL FORMATTING

Ever want to just strip out all the crazy formatting on a piece of text to make it simple, plain text? Just select the text, and click the Home tab, Font group, Clear All Formatting button. It looks like an eraser, and it's at the top right of the ribbon group. Note that this does not clear any formatting applied via the Master or Layout that the text inherits from.

Transformed Text

If you've been to a cheap restaurant, a garage sale, or a flea market, you have probably seen Office WordArt, which are predefined transformed text effects. PowerPoint 2007 has even more WordArt-like effects, which you can use to make text really stand out. Figure 3.18 shows a gallery of text transform effects. As we mentioned before, in PowerPoint 2007, these effects can be applied to any text in PowerPoint because there is no distinction between WordArt and regular text.

Warping

Transformed text is another way of saying warped text or vector text because you can change the way the words are arranged and make them follow a certain pattern.

As with all things, use this in moderation. A great use of Text Transforms is using it to make your slide titles stand out or for a large sign. Please don't go around making your figure captions warped, or it will seem overplayed like a song on the radio. Serious content should be normal and non-transformed, but if you want to make a point or emphasize some words, transform away!

For example, if you want to make your text look like the *Star Wars* credits (without the animation), you can select the Fade Up Transform Effect:

1. Type some text, and then select it.
2. On the Format tab in the Text Effects group, choose Transform.
3. Scroll down to the bottom, and select the object that says Fade Up in the ScreenTip. The text now resembles what is shown in Figure 3.19.

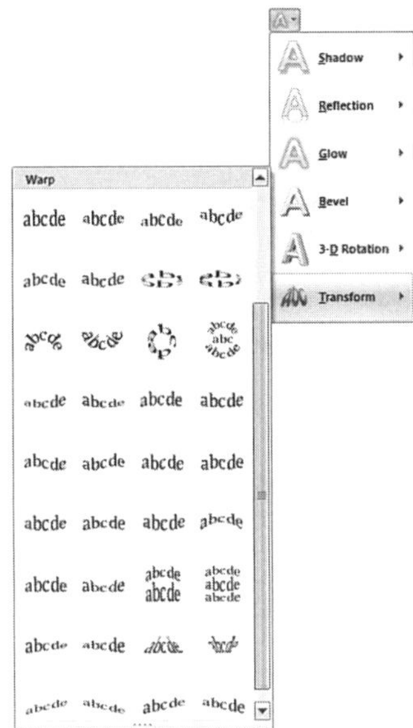

Figure 3.18

PowerPoint 2007 has a large collection of warped text effects from which you can choose.

Figure 3.19

You can make your text look exciting by using a Transform effect and making your text flow the way that you want it to.

Follow Path

The Follow Path Transforms, which are located above the Warp Effects, are good for making text look bannered. These are applied exactly the same as Warp Effects are.

Inline Editing

WordArt editing in previous versions of PowerPoint entailed typing unstyled text into a dialog box, clicking OK, and then seeing what you typed appear as WordArt. New to PowerPoint 2007, all this editing occurs inline, which means that you type directly into the transformed text instead of inside a separate box. You also get to see the results immediately without having to click a button.

If you edit a word that has a Text Transform applied to it, notice that the cursor will be modified in the way that your text is! Not only that, but if you have a misspelled word, the red line underneath the word becomes warped too (see Figure 3.20).

Figure 3.20

The spelling error indicator line also gets transformed!

PowerPoint 2007's Proofing Tools

Advanced When we were in high school, it was common to use a dictionary to check your spelling, a thesaurus to find word synonyms, and a foreign language dictionary to painfully translate words between languages. Those days are long behind us.

Table 3.3 shows some of the awesome proofing tools that are built into PowerPoint and other Office applications. You will find them on the Review tab in the Proofing group.

Table 3.3 Built-in Proofing Tools

Tool	Where	Shortcut Key	Description
Spelling checker	Spelling	F7	Starting from your current selection or cursor position, checks the spelling of everything in your presentation.
Thesaurus	Thesaurus	Shift+F7	Find words similar, and more intellectual sounding, than a word you can think of. Works after first selecting some text.
Translation	Translate		Instantly translates words between languages.
Dictionary	Research		Looks up definitions of words.

NOTE

In case you're wondering, PowerPoint doesn't do grammar checking, only Word and Outlook do. Few strive for perfect grammar when throwing together some presentation bullet points, so PowerPoint doesn't bother badgering you about your bad grammar.

Translation

We'll briefly touch on translation here because it's easily the coolest of the four proofing services.

Sometimes you receive presentations with words in a foreign language. Just select the foreign word, go to the Review tab in the Proofing group, and click Translate. Choose the language you're translating to and what language you're translating from. Follow the instructions to install the appropriate dictionary, if it's not already installed.

NOTE

This was more convenient in previous versions of Office. You could just hold down the Alt key and click the word you wanted to translate to open the Research pane. Because of a bug, this no longer works in PowerPoint 2007.

Spell Checking and Thesaurus

In the Proofing group of the Review tab, you'll also find the spell checker (under Spelling) and the thesaurus (under Thesaurus).

Even though it's as easy as pressing the F7 key to start the spell checker, all recent versions of Office make spell-checking and grammar-checking so easy that you don't even need to activate it at all. PowerPoint checks spelling as you type and underlines spelling mistakes in red.

NOTE

Word 2007 uses green underlines to show grammatical errors and blue underlines to show words that are spelled correctly but probably misspelled in the current context, such as "Jeff bought a pear of shoes" or "Wayne kept loosing his mind." Neither of these features is supported by PowerPoint 2007.

To use the thesaurus, highlight a word, right-click it, and PowerPoint shows a list of possible corrections to choose from. Choose a word from that list to use that correction.

Proofing Example

Let's walk through a quick example that shows many of PowerPoint's neat proofing capabilities:

1. In a new presentation, type "I am teh best" in the title placeholder. AutoCorrect automatically changes "teh" into "the," which is one way that PowerPoint prevents you from typing misspelled text. You can read more about AutoCorrect earlier in this chapter.
2. Okay, we're demonstrating something here, so manually change "the" back to "teh" and move the text cursor over to "best." Notice how PowerPoint underlines the word in red to show you that it's misspelled.

3. To correct it, right-click "teh." PowerPoint shows a list of recommended replacement words (as shown in Figure 3.21), and you can choose "the" to correct the spelling.

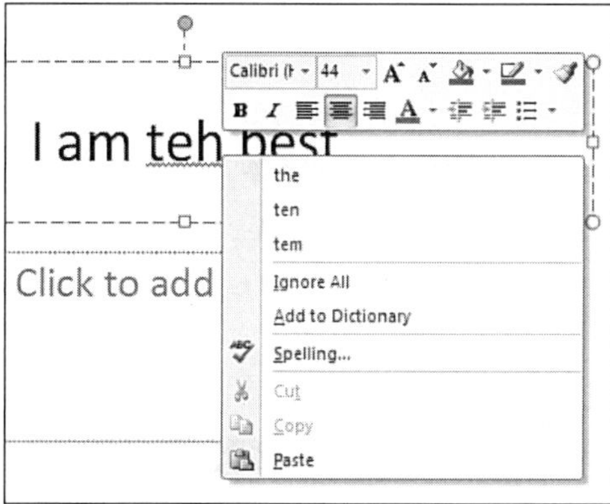

Figure 3.21

Right-clicking a misspelled word shows a list of correctly spelled similar words.

4. Now, let's say that we're putting this in an important presentation and we want a more refined word than "best." Right-click "best" and go to the Synonyms menu. This shows you a list of words that mean the same thing as "best" (see Figure 3.22). You can now choose a cooler word such as "preeminent."
5. Select "preeminent" and go to the Review tab in the Proofing group and click Translate. This brings up the Research pane that shows you the definition of the word, or you can choose to translate "preeminent" to another language (see Figure 3.23).

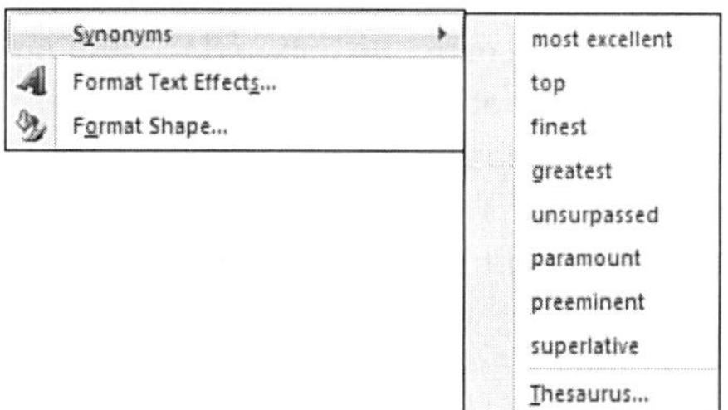

Figure 3.22

Right-clicking a word and going to Synonyms shows a list of similar words.

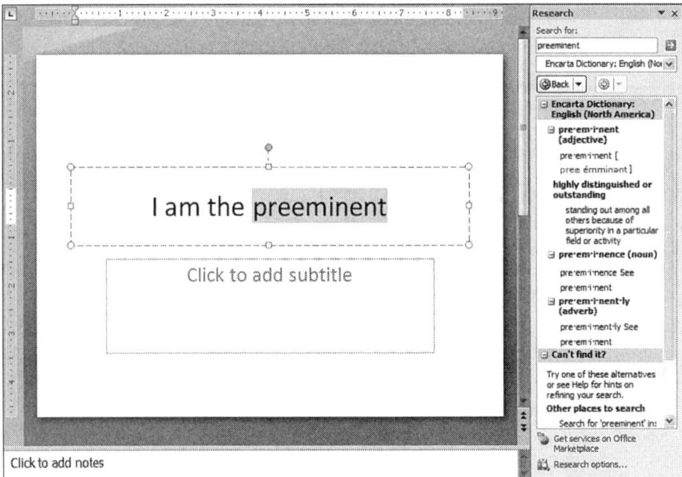

Figure 3.23

The Research pane can be used to look up word definitions, synonyms/antonyms, and for translation to and from other languages.

What the Random?

Advanced

Though we all like to believe that we focus on content first and worry about the look of the presentation afterward, sometimes we want to format the presentation without having any content.

To create some dummy text to insert, you might be tempted to bang on the keyboard. Fortunately, the development team at Microsoft cares about your poor keyboard and has an easier solution. Just type `=rand(3)` and press Enter. You can substitute another number for 3, which corresponds to the number of paragraphs you want to insert. The text that's inserted varies depending on which language version of PowerPoint you're using, but in U.S. English, I get this:

```
The quick brown fox jumps over the lazy dog. The quick brown fox jumps over the lazy
dog. The quick brown fox jumps over the lazy dog. The quick brown fox jumps over the
lazy dog. The quick brown fox jumps over the lazy dog.

The quick brown fox jumps over the lazy dog. The quick brown fox jumps over the lazy
dog. The quick brown fox jumps over the lazy dog. The quick brown fox jumps over the
lazy dog. The quick brown fox jumps over the lazy dog.

The quick brown fox jumps over the lazy dog. The quick brown fox jumps over the lazy
dog. The quick brown fox jumps over the lazy dog. The quick brown fox jumps over the
lazy dog. The quick brown fox jumps over the lazy dog.
```

NOTE

This trick also works in Word. Excel's `=rand()` function gives you a random real number between 0 and 1.

Shortcut Keys for Newbies and Experts

Advanced To really use PowerPoint with great speed, learning to use shortcuts is essential. Learning just a couple of keyboard shortcuts will save you time in the long run, especially if you're working with text a lot. Basic and advanced keyboard shortcuts are shown in Table 3.4 and Table 3.5. Start with the basic ones first if you're new to shortcut keys. Mouse shortcuts are shown in Table 3.6.

Table 3.4 Basic Keyboard Shortcuts

Key Combination	Effect
Ctrl+B	Bold
Ctrl+I	Italic
Ctrl+U	Underline
Ctrl+left arrow	Moves the cursor one word left
Ctrl+right arrow	Moves the cursor one word right
Ctrl+Home	Navigates to beginning of the text box
Ctrl+End	Navigates to end of the text box
Ctrl+down arrow	Moves the cursor one paragraph down
Ctrl+up arrow	Moves the cursor one paragraph up
Shift+right arrow	Selects one character to the right
Shift+left arrow	Selects one character to the right
Ctrl+Shift+right arrow	Selects one word to the right
Ctrl+Shift+left arrow	Selects one word to the left
Shift+up arrow	Selects everything from the current cursor up to the previous line
Shift+down arrow	Selects everything from the current cursor down to the next line
Ctrl+A	Selects all text in the current text box.

Table 3.5 Advanced Keyboard Shortcuts

Key Combination	Effect
Ctrl+Shift+F or Ctrl+Shift+P	Font dialog
Ctrl+Shift+→	Increases font size
Ctrl+Shift+←	Decreases font size
Alt+Ctrl+Shift+→	Superscript
Alt+Ctrl+Shift+←	Subscript
Ctrl+Shift+Z	Strips all formatting and reverts to plaintext
Shift+F3	Changes casing
Ctrl+backspace	Deletes word to the left
Ctrl+Delete	Deletes word to the right
Shift+Ctrl+Left/Right arrow	Selects text
Ctrl+click	Selects sentence
Ctrl+E	Center
Ctrl+J	Justified
Ctrl+L	Left-aligned
Ctrl+R	Right-aligned
Ctrl+K	Hyperlink

Table 3.6 Mouse shortcuts

Mouse Combination	Effect
Double-click text	Selects the word
Triple-click text	Selects the line
Select and drag text	Moves the selected text somewhere else
Ctrl+drag text	Duplicates the text and puts the duplicate somewhere else

4

Working with Pictures

IN THIS CHAPTER

- Variations on Inserted Pictures
- PowerPoint as an Advanced Picture Editor
- Text That Follows a Picture Around
- Inserting Many Pictures at Once Using Photo Album
- Picture Manager: The Hidden Application

Pictures are one of the most commonly inserted objects in PowerPoint. Few people know that PowerPoint can actually manipulate the pictures after they have been inserted into a presentation. Let's take a look at what you can do with pictures in PowerPoint.

Variations on Inserted Pictures

Advanced You're undoubtedly familiar with the basics of pictures. You go to the Insert tab in the Illustrations group and click Picture, select your favorite picture from your hard drive, press OK, and voilà: You have a picture in your presentation.

Now, if you save the presentation, where is that picture saved? There are a few possibilities.

Regular Embedded Picture

By default, pictures are saved inside the presentation. That's why you can typically copy a presentation to another computer, open it in PowerPoint on that machine, and all the pictures show up. Here are the advantages and disadvantages of this method:

Advantage

You can copy your presentation to another machine and pretty much be guaranteed that all your pictures will show up there, with very little headache.

Disadvantages

All your pictures are saved inside the presentation, so your presentation file can get pretty big.

Because PowerPoint is working on copies of the images, if you change any of the original pictures on your hard disk, you need to remember to update the image you're using in the presentation.

Linked Picture

Okay, let's say that you don't want to stuff the picture into your file. PowerPoint also lets you link to external pictures.

Let's go through the steps of inserting a picture again. On the Insert tab, go to the Illustrations group, click Picture, and then select a picture. Instead of just clicking OK, press the down arrow on the right side of the OK button. Don't see it? Look at Figure 4.1.

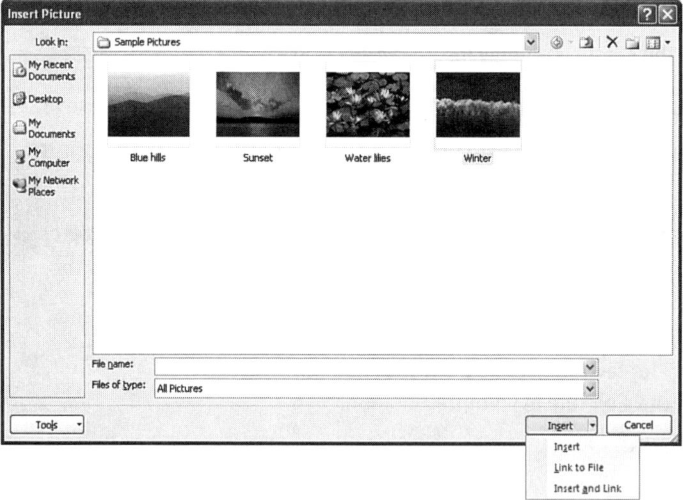

Figure 4.1

There is a hidden menu next to the OK button. Note that this looks different in Windows XP and Windows Vista.

Select Link to File. Now, instead of embedding the entire picture inside your file, it just references the picture that's already sitting on your hard disk. Here are the advantages and disadvantages of this method:

Advantages

Your file size will be smaller.

If you update the image, the image in your presentation is automatically updated.

Disadvantage

If you move this presentation to another machine, you must make sure that you copy those pictures over, too. Otherwise, when you open the presentation, your picture won't show up and you'll see the red X icon you're used to seeing on broken web pages (see Figure 4.2).

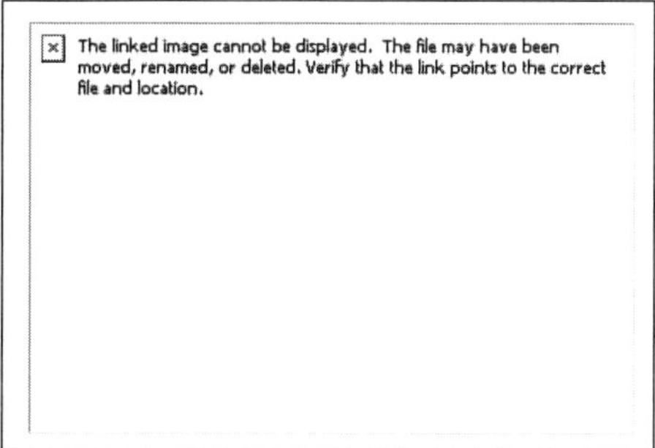

Figure 4.2

Broken picture produces a red X.

NOTE

In our example, we're linking to a picture on the same computer. If you instead link to a picture on another machine or hosted on a server, save your presentation, and the presentation is opened on another machine, PowerPoint warns you about the dangers of external content. This is another potential disadvantage of linking to pictures.

Linked Embedded Pictures

Office has a third insertion option that lets you do a hybrid of embedding and linking. This option embeds the picture into the PowerPoint file, but it also updates the picture if the original image is ever changed.

Again, go to the Insert tab in the Illustrations group, click Picture, and select a picture again. Click the down arrow on the right side of the OK button and select Insert and Link.

NOTE

In PowerPoint 2003, this option didn't work well because it required Photo Editor, which Microsoft replaced with Picture Manager in Office 2003. In even older versions of PowerPoint, linked and embedded pictures did work, but they required going to the Insert Object dialog and using the Create from File option. Linked embedded pictures are back and much easier to use in 2007.

Here are the advantages and disadvantages of this method:

Advantage

The picture updates whenever the original image on your hard drive updates. The PowerPoint file caches a temporary copy of the image so that if the presentation is moved to another computer, the last known picture still shows up. This is the best of both worlds.

Disadvantage

This method tends to bloat the file size quite a bit, even more than a regular embedded picture.

NOTE

As with linked pictures, be careful when adding linked embedded pictures that reside on a different machine. If you open the presentation on another machine, the picture shows up, but PowerPoint warns you about external content in the presentation.

PowerPoint as an Advanced Picture Editor

New

Select one of the photos that you inserted earlier in the chapter when we discussed adding pictures to your presentation. The Picture Tools Format tab should now appear, as shown in Figure 4.3. This is where the main picture editing tools reside. The sections that follow explore some of these tools and how to use them.

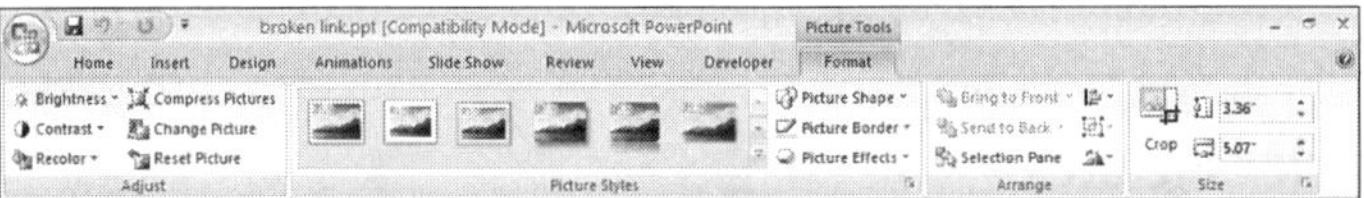

Figure 4.3

Picture Tools Format tab.

Preset Picture Effects

If you play around with the large Picture Styles gallery in the middle, you can experiment with some of the preset effects. Expand the gallery by clicking the More button at the bottom right of the gallery (see Figure 4.4). Just click a preset picture effect that you like, and that effect will instantly be applied to your photo.

Common Picture Adjustments

Typical PowerPoint users normally get by with just the canned picture effects, but you're more advanced than that, so let's dig in a little deeper. The Adjust group on the left side of the Picture Tools Format tab lets you fine-tune certain aspects of your pictures, such as

- Contrast
- Brightness
- Recolor
- Compress Pictures
- Change Picture
- Reset Picture

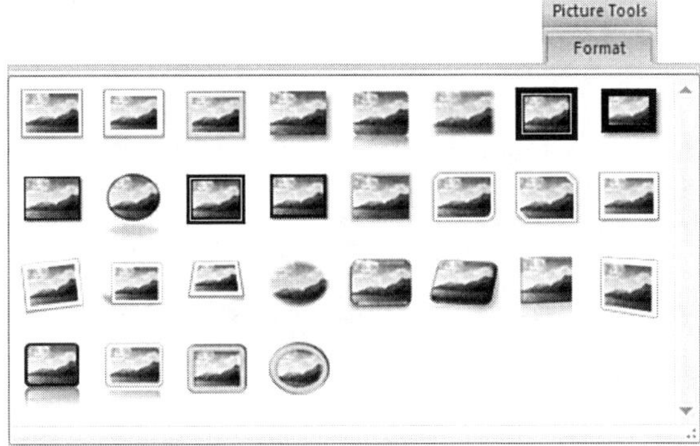

Figure 4.4
Canned picture effects gallery.

We look into a few of these in the following few sections, in addition to some other picture effects that we find particularly useful.

NOTE

Most effects that you will learn about in Chapters 12, "Formatting Shapes, Text, and More," and 13, "Demystifying 3D," can also be applied to pictures. Try applying different shadows, glows, and reflections to pictures, for instance.

BRIGHTNESS/CONTRAST

These are no-brainers. Select a picture and make it brighter or darker, or adjust its contrast by going to the Picture Tools Format tab, going to the Adjust group, and selecting Brightness or Contrast (refer back to Figure 4.3). If you want to select a value that isn't an increment of 10%, choose Picture Corrections Options at the bottom of either the Brightness or Contract drop-downs, and you can get really fine-grained, such as 27% brightness.

RECOLOR

The recoloring feature, also known as a duotone effect, is an effect that takes the darker colors in the picture and turns them into one color and takes the lighter colors in the picture and turns them into a second color. Algorithmically, that's the only thing happening. To make this easier, PowerPoint throws a nice, pretty list of these at you in a gallery under the Picture Tools Format tab, in the Adjust group under Recolor (see Figure 4.5).

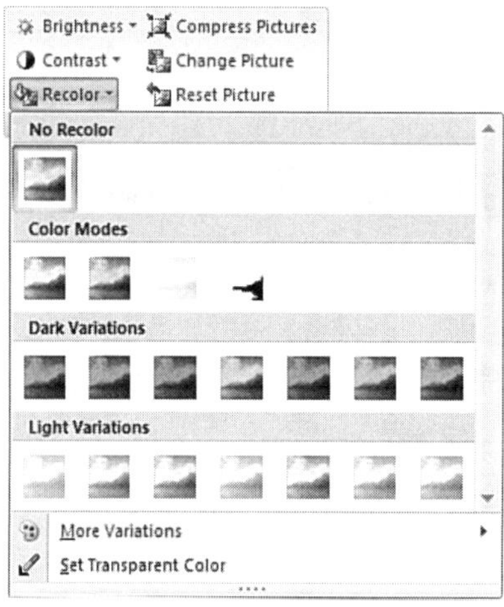

Figure 4.5

Recolor gallery.

The following sections go into more detail about each of the Recolor options.

DARK VARIATIONS

For these:

- The darker colors in your picture turn into shades of black.
- The lighter colors turn into shades of a given theme color.

For example, if you select the blue dark variation, the darker colors in your picture would become shades of black and the lighter colors in your picture would become shades of blue.

If the theme colors aren't enough, you can also select the More Dark Variations item near the bottom to choose any color you like. We'll talk more about themes in Chapter 11, "Dissecting Themes."

LIGHT VARIATIONS

These options do the opposite:

- The darker colors in your picture turn into shades of a given theme color.
- The lighter colors turn into shades of white.

For example, when blue is one of the theme colors for your presentation, there is a blue light variation in the drop-down list. If you select it, the darker colors in your picture become shades of blue and the lighter colors turn into shades of white.

COLOR MODES

Finally, there are four other recoloring effects in the Color Modes section of the gallery. These effects give pictures a retro look. From left to right in Figure 4.6, these color modes are

- **Grayscale**—The picture becomes shades of gray.
- **Sepia**—The picture changes to a brownish/gray color.
- **Washout**—Turns the picture really white, as if it has been overexposed.
- **True black and white**—This turns your photo into a truly two colors, black and white, which usually doesn't look great. Normally, instead of true black and white, you're better off using the grayscale effect.

Figure 4.6

Color mode effects.

Sepia is new, but the others are old PowerPoint 2003 effects that have been carried over.

NOTE

In previous PowerPoint versions, such as PowerPoint 2003, only metafiles (mostly used in clip art) had recoloring features. A dialog would list all the colors used in the metafile, and you could change each individual color to another color. In the early days of PowerPoint, bitmaps could be recolored like this as well, but that feature was removed long ago. These features were designed for the days when images were just a handful of colors, but this approach didn't scale to the modern era, where pictures typically contain millions of colors. So, color-by-color remapping was completely removed in PowerPoint 2007.

COMPRESS PICTURES

Compared to previous versions of PowerPoint, 2007 does such a good job compressing pictures in your presentation that there's really little need for you to do much else. By default, PowerPoint 2007:

- Compresses pictures every time you save
- Saves pictures to 220 pixels per inch, which is fine for printing and onscreen display
- Permanently deletes any regions of the picture you crop out

To change any of these three defaults or to compress pictures even more than the default (you can compress to 150 or 96 pixels per inch to save even more disk space), select a picture and then go to the Picture Tools Format tab. In the Adjust group, select Compress Picture, Options.

CAUTION

The three defaults mentioned previously are the default when you first install PowerPoint. If you've ever changed these settings, you might see different defaults when you open the Options dialog.

CHANGE PICTURE

Say that you've inserted a picture of your friend Willow and applied a lot of operations to it, but then you realize that you actually intended to apply those edits to a picture of your friend Melody instead. The Change Picture option (Picture Tools Format tab, Adjust group) lets you swap out the underlying picture file but keep all those effects and animations on the picture.

SET TRANSPARENT COLOR

Another neat tool is the Set Transparent Color wand. Go to the Picture Tools Format tab, to the Adjust group, click Recolor, and then select Set Transparent Color (an odd place to put it because technically you're applying transparency and not "recoloring").

After you click Set Transparent Color, your mouse pointer turns into a wand. You can then click on any color in the picture, and that color turns transparent. This isn't quite the same as simply "erasing" part of the picture, but it's similar. You're choosing one color and yanking it out of the picture.

Making parts of the picture transparent lets you create nonrectangular pictures, which can give your pictures a more interesting look. If you have anything behind the picture, such as a custom slide background, it shows through the hole. In Figure 4.7, we've clicked the bottom of the picture, which cuts out the bottom-left of the photo.

Figure 4.7

The bottom-left portion of the picture is now transparent.

RESET PICTURE

It's simple. This tool removes all the edits to the picture that you've done in PowerPoint. Say that you cropped something out or applied a recoloring effect, and now you realize that it was a horrible mistake. Just click the picture, go to the Picture Tools Format tab, and in the Adjust group, choose Reset Picture. The picture is restored to its original state.

This is possible because the .pptx files you save in PowerPoint contain your picture and some instructions (in XML) telling PowerPoint how to change the picture before it's shown onscreen. Reset Picture is just stripping out these instructions.

The downside to Reset Picture is that it truly restores everything. If you played with the size and the width, those changes are gone. Any picture brightness/contrast adjustments are gone. You're reverting the picture back to how it was on the hard drive before PowerPoint did anything to it.

Cropping

Cropping has been around in practically every picture tool throughout time. It lets you chop off parts of the picture you dislike or don't need to focus on a specific portion of the picture.

HOW TO CROP

Just select the picture you want to crop, click the Picture Tools Format tab, and in the Size group, select Crop. Doing this makes black crop handles appear around the picture (see Figure 4.8). Drag a handle to outline the parts of the picture you want to keep, which will remove the outer parts of the picture that you don't want. Then click the Crop button again to commit those changes.

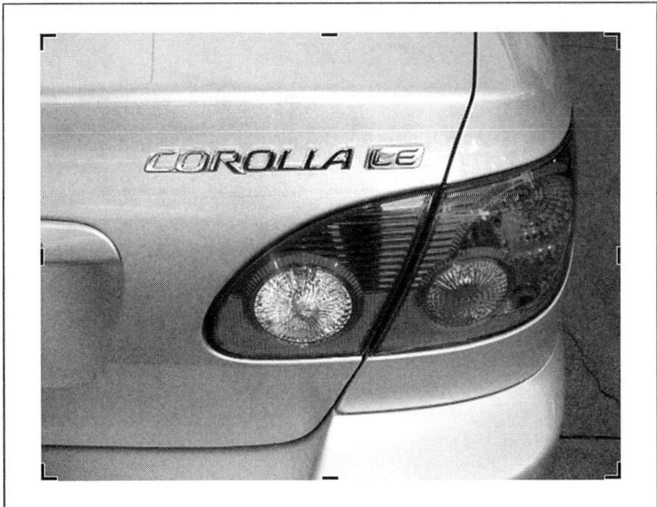

Figure 4.8

Crop handles are used to create the area to be cropped from your picture.

REVERTING CROPS

If you change your mind, as usual, use Undo (Ctrl+Z) to revert your last change. Or, to undo all your crops, go to Picture Tools Format tab, Size group, and click the box launcher in the bottom right. In the Size and Position dialog, click the Reset button at the bottom.

CAUTION

New to 2007, PowerPoint helpfully tries to reduce your file size when you save by automatically removing any cropped region. The downside to this is that using the Reset button in the Size and Position dialog or using the Reset Picture feature to restore a picture to its original state has no effect after the presentation has already been saved. It won't bring back cropped regions because they're truly gone. So, after you crop a picture, don't save the presentation unless you're sure that you never want to see those portions of the picture again, or be sure to save a copy of your original pictures.

Changing the Picture Shape

One fun effect is changing the shape of your picture. Select a picture and go to the Picture Tools Format tab in the Picture Styles group and select Picture Shape. Select your favorite shape from the list. You'll never use a rectangle again! See Figure 4.9 for an example.

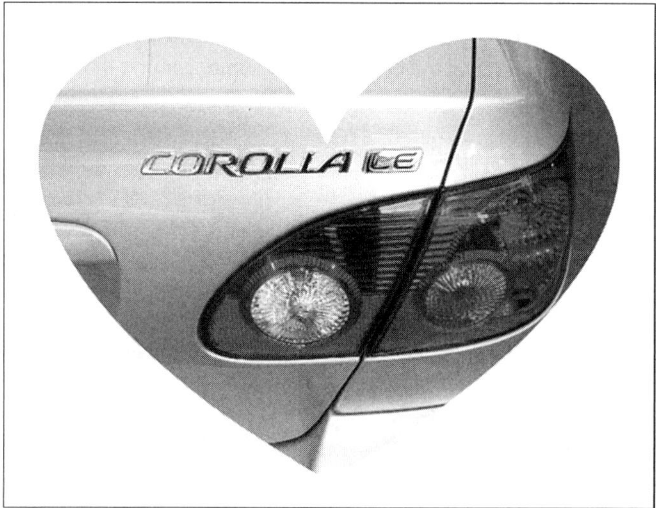

Figure 4.9

Heart-shaped picture.

TIP

Another powerful alternative for creating an interestingly shaped picture is to create a shape with a picture fill, described in the "Shape with Picture Fill" section later in this chapter. If you use that alternative, PowerPoint disables some of the Picture Tools Format abilities such as Reset Picture and the Picture Styles gallery. But, you then have the full power of PowerPoint shapes and can set a completely custom shape path (on the Drawing Tools Format tab, go to the Insert Shapes group and click Edit Shape), and you can type text inside your picture. It's definitely confusing that PowerPoint offers two ways to do something similar.

Text That Follows a Picture Around

Advanced One common challenge in PowerPoint is being able to associate text with a picture so that the text moves when you move the picture. The common tactic that people take is to create a picture and a text box and use Shift+click or Ctrl+click to multiselect the two and always move them together. But that's a pain to manage, and the ideal solution is for the text and the picture to just move together without you having to think about it every time you want to move them a little. The following sections give some techniques for getting over this PowerPoint hurdle.

Group Picture with Text

One way to get a text and picture to work together is to create a text box (Insert tab, Text group, choose Text Box) and a picture. Select them both and then group them together by going to the main Home tab, the Drawing group, the Arrange section, and then clicking Group. As shown in Figure 4.10, when the text or picture is clicked, bounding boxes appear around both items. Now, you can move the entire group around as one unit.

New New to PowerPoint 2007, you can select, edit, and move around individual items inside a group. In previous versions of PowerPoint, you had to first ungroup, make your edits, and regroup them, which was much more painful. The new PowerPoint 2007 functionality makes captioning much easier.

Shape with Picture Fill

Another way to associate text with a picture is to create a shape with a picture fill, and then type in the shape. To use this method, do the following:

1. Insert a shape onto a slide by selecting your favorite shape: Go to the Insert tab, the Illustrations group, the Shapes group, and then click somewhere on the slide.
2. Fill it with a picture by selecting the Drawing Tools Format tab. Under the Shape Styles group, click the Shape Fill drop-down and choose Picture. You might need to resize the shape to make the picture look decent.
3. Now to add text, just type, and the text appears in the body of the shape (see Figure 4.11).

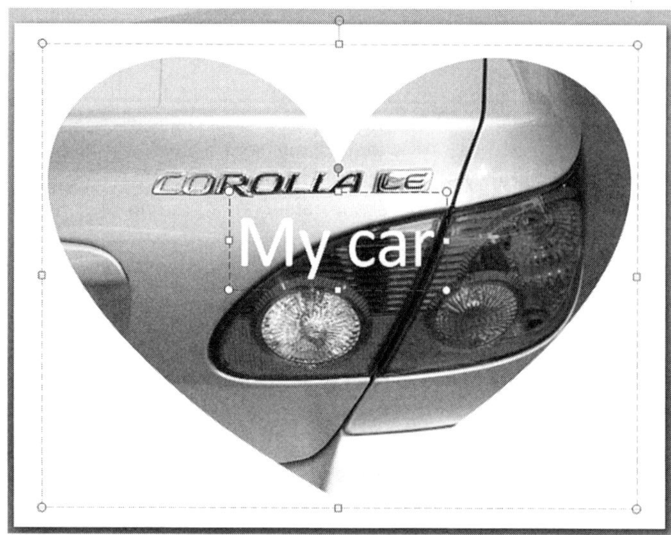

Figure 4.10

A picture grouped with text.

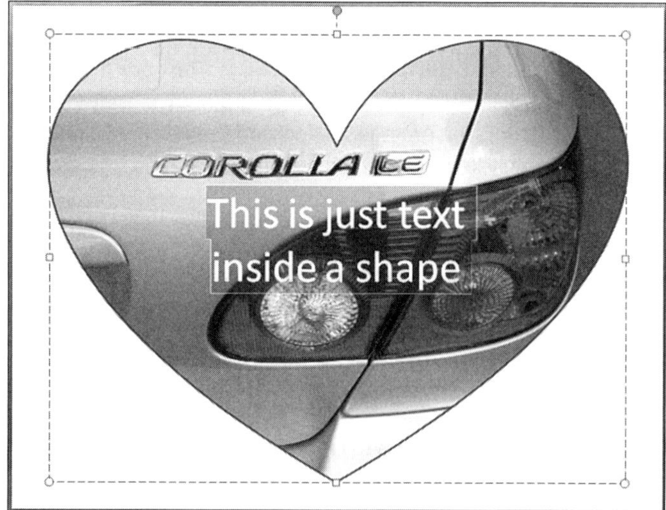

Figure 4.11

Type inside a shape that contains a picture fill.

By default, the text appears centered in the middle of the shape, which might not be what you want. You can change this by selecting the shape, going to the Format Tools Format tab, and clicking the box launcher at the bottom-right corner of the WordArt Styles group. In the Format Text Effects dialog, choose the Text Box category on the left. Here, you can adjust the text positioning using the

Internal Margin settings at the bottom of the dialog. For example, to get the text to float below the shape as a caption might, increase the value of the Top number until the text appears where you want it to appear.

Inserting Many Pictures at Once Using Photo Album

Advanced Need to insert a gazillion photos into PowerPoint? Maybe you want to show your crazy vacation photos to your friend, or you need to catalog product photos for a presentation to a vendor. Don't insert them one-by-one like we spent six hours doing one sad afternoon. Instead, use PowerPoint's Photo Album feature.

NOTE

Photo Album has been around since PowerPoint 2002 but was hard to find in the old menu system at Insert, Picture, New Photo Album. In PowerPoint 2007, it is much more discoverable because the Photo Album feature is right on the Insert tab.

Using Photo Album

PowerPoint's Photo Album feature is pretty easy to use, as you will see in the steps that follow.

1. To get started, go to the Insert tab's Illustrations group and click Photo Album. You'll see the Photo Album dialog shown in Figure 4.12.

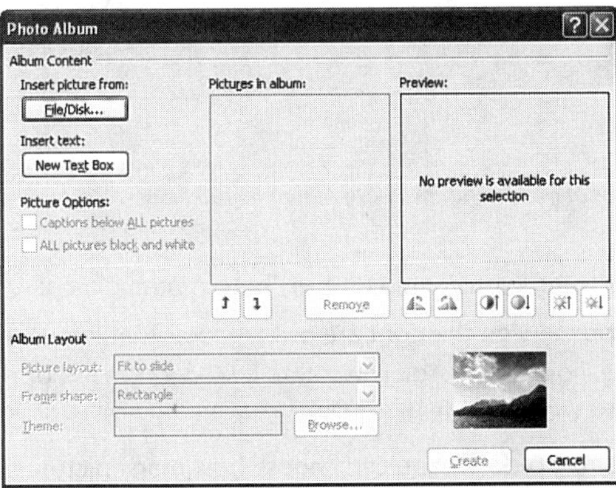

Figure 4.12

Photo Album dialog.

2. Using the buttons on the left, you can insert pictures from your hard disk. You can also insert text boxes to interleave some text between pictures. Everything you insert shows up in the middle list.

3. To reorder the items you've inserted, click the two buttons that have arrows on them to move things up and down the list. Click Remove if you made a mistake and want to remove something from the list.

NOTE

Previous versions of PowerPoint let you insert Photo Album pictures from a scanner or digital camera, but this was removed in PowerPoint 2007. The feature had remained static for several releases, and the PowerPoint team felt that most people would be more successful using the software that comes with their scanners or digital cameras.

---

4. Click the Create button, and now you've got a bunch of pictures inserted into PowerPoint (see Figure 4.13).

Figure 4.13

It's easy to insert several photos at once using the Photo Album feature.

Here are a few interesting things you can do on the Photo Album dialog:

- Under the picture preview on the right are picture tools that let you make minor adjustments to each picture (see Figure 4.14). You can rotate it 90 degrees left or right, adjust the contrast of the picture, or adjust the brightness.
- In the Picture layout drop-down, you can choose how many pictures you want to appear on each slide and whether you want a title to appear on each slide (see Figure 4.15). The Fit to Slide choice puts only the picture on the slide and disables other Photo Album options such as Frame shape, Design template, and Captions Below All Pictures, so choose another Picture layout option, such as 1 Picture, if you want to use any of those features.

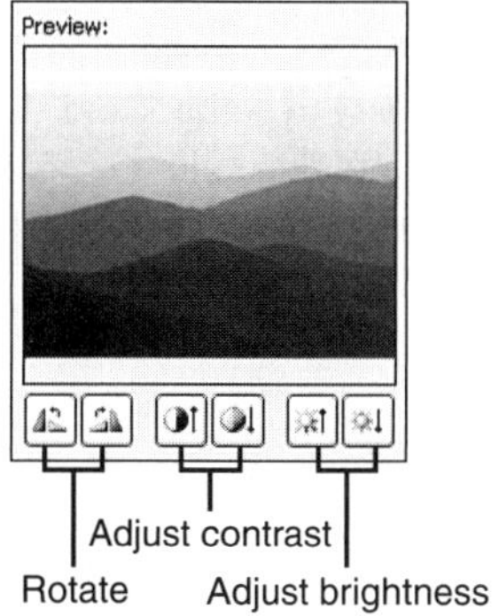

Figure 4.14

Photo Album picture tools let you make quick adjustments to your photographs.

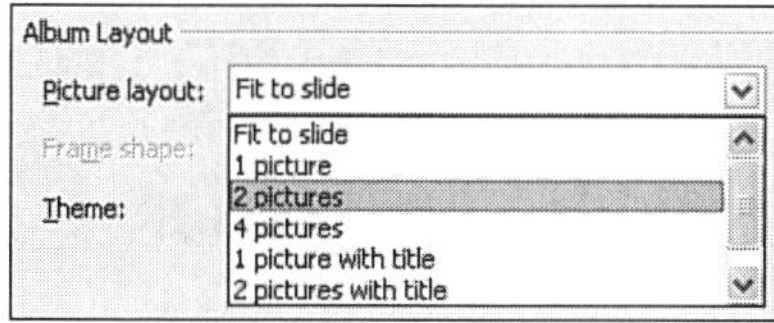

Figure 4.15

Photo Album layout features.

- The Frame shape drop-down lets you choose if you want a frame to appear around each picture. PowerPoint 2007 adds several new options here, including Center Shadow Rectangle. Here's a complete list of them:

  Rectangle

  Rounded Rectangle

  Simple Frame, White

  Simple Frame, Black

  Compound Frame, Black

  Center Shadow Rectangle

  Soft Edge Rectangle

- There are two Picture Options check boxes on the left. The first, Captions Below All Pictures, puts a little caption box under each inserted picture. This option will be grayed out if you choose Fit to Slide for the Picture layout.
- The other Picture Options check box, All Pictures Black and White, as the name suggests, makes all the pictures you insert black and white. This is cool for making your pictures look older than they really are.

Edit Existing Photo Album

After you've created a Photo Album, it's easy to go back and change your mind on some of these options. To do this, just go to the Insert tab's Illustrations group and choose Photo Album again; only this time, instead of clicking the main Photo Album button, click the arrow at the bottom part of the button. Then, choose Edit Photo Album (see Figure 4.16).

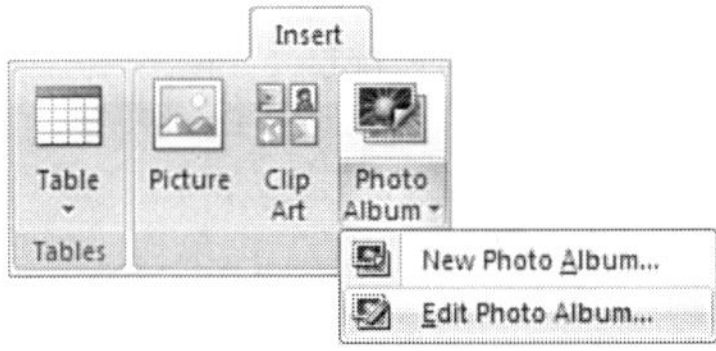

Figure 4.16

Click the bottom half of the Photo Album button to edit a Photo Album.

Picture Manager: The Hidden Application

Advanced Though not a part of PowerPoint, Picture Manager is a reliable Microsoft Office application that comes with PowerPoint. With Picture Manager, you can manage your picture collections and make quick photo edits. It's the fastest way to

- Crop a picture
- Change a picture's file format, say from .jpg to .png
- Resize a picture or compress a picture to reduce its file size
- Autocorrect a picture's brightness, contrast, and color

Picture Manager also lets you set the brightness and color manually, rotate and flip a picture, and remove red eye.

Let's walk through some of these features.

NOTE

Picture Manager was first introduced with Office 2003. It officially replaced Microsoft Photo Editor, which was present in Office 2000 and Office XP. Although Picture Manager has a more polished user interface, it's missing many of the Photo Editor effects such as chalk, charcoal, and watercolor. Photo Editor, on the other hand, doesn't allow importing images from cameras or scanners, it has fewer color correction options, and it couldn't print pictures on Windows 2000. Many users complained about the replacement when Office 2003 was first released, but Picture Manager is probably here to stay.

Quick Edits in the Edit Pictures Workpane

To edit a picture in Picture Manager, use Windows Explorer to locate a file, and then right-click it, choose Open With, and select Microsoft Office Picture Manager (see Figure 4.17).

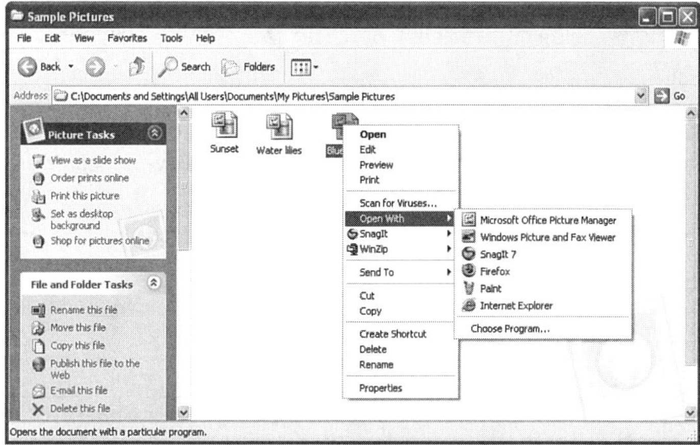

Figure 4.17

Launch Picture Manager by right-clicking a picture in Windows Explorer.

Click the Edit Pictures button on the toolbar (see Figure 4.18). This brings up the Edit Pictures workpane.

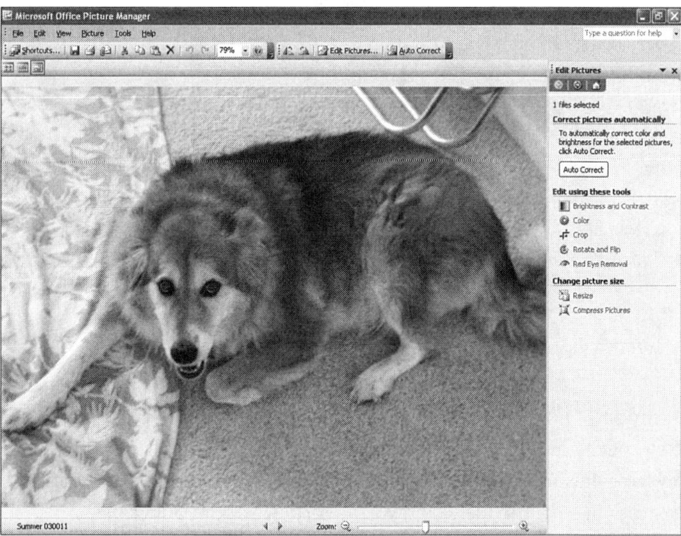

Figure 4.18

Bring up the Edit Pictures workpane by clicking on the Edit Pictures button on the toolbar.

AUTO CORRECT THE PICTURE

Next, choose what you want to do with the picture. Let's quickly fix the brightness and colors. Just click the Auto Correct button at the top to kick that off.

Look better? If not, undo the change by pressing Ctrl+Z or choosing Edit, Undo Auto Correct. Then choose File, Save (Ctrl+S) when you're sure that you're ready to save the changes.

CROPPING THE PICTURE

Now let's crop part of the picture to chop off the part of the picture that we don't like. Click the Crop link on the Edit Pictures workpane. Notice how eight black handles have appeared around your picture (see Figure 4.19).

NOTE

You can crop within PowerPoint as well. See the section titled "Cropping," earlier in this chapter.

Figure 4.19

Crop handles appear around the picture.

Drag the handles around to cut off parts of the picture. Or, to be more precise, enter numbers in pixels in the workpane to specify exactly how much of the picture to crop off. Click the OK button on the workpane when you're finished making changes. Again, if you change your mind, you can undo the change, but remember to save the file when you're certain about your choices.

Making Pictures Smaller

Next, let's look at resizing the picture. This is most useful when you want to reduce the size of your pictures before you email them to someone or upload them to a web page.

Click the Edit Pictures button again on the toolbar to get back to the main Edit Pictures workpane (refer back to Figure 4.18).

COMPRESS PICTURES

Let's do this the easy way. Click on the Compress Pictures link at the bottom of the workpane. Select one of the compress options such as Documents, press OK, save (Ctrl+S), and you're done (see Figure 4.20). To be honest, though, I rarely use this option because I want more control over the resize...which brings us to resizing.

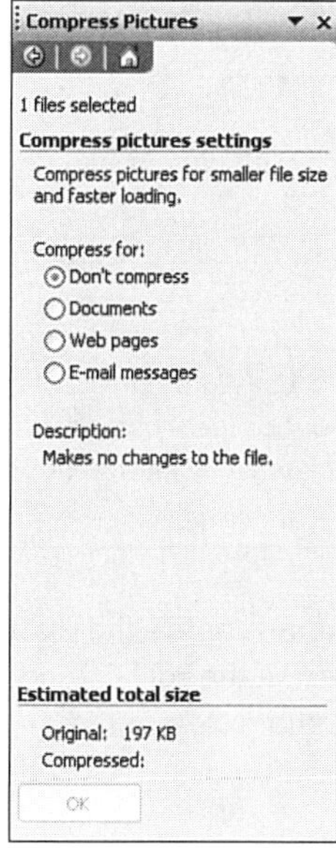

Figure 4.20

Compress Pictures workpane.

RESIZING

Go back to the main Edit Pictures workpane again by clicking the back button on the toolbar. This time, click the Resize link. Here, you get a myriad of picture resizing options for setting a custom picture size or a percentage of height and width (see Figure 4.21).

For example, enter 60% in the last text box to reduce the picture to 60% of its original size. Click the OK button at the bottom of the workpane. Again, you can undo the process if this didn't meet your expectations and save the picture when you're completely done. Usually, it takes me a few iterations of doing this before my pictures look exactly right.

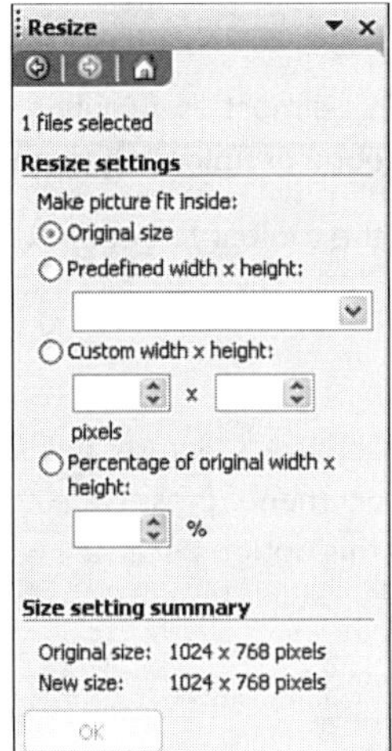

Figure 4.21

Resize workpane.

TIP

Picture corrections can be combined. Use Auto Correct first, crop the picture, and then resize it. Until you actually select File, Save, your original picture isn't affected, and you can undo changes you aren't happy with. This lets you experiment until you're sure that you like all your changes.

Auto Correct, cropping, and resizing/compressing are the most common uses I have for the Edit Pictures pane, but you can explore the rest of the Edit Pictures links for manual brightness/contrast corrections, color corrections, rotate/flip, and red eye removal.

Why Not Just Use PowerPoint?

"Aren't these in PowerPoint already?" you might ask? Features such as cropping, compressing, and brightening pictures are certainly available in PowerPoint itself, but Picture Manager allows you to make these edits outside of the context of a presentation.

Say that you want to resize and brighten a picture before you post it on your web page. Although PowerPoint 2007's new user interface is impressive, doing a pure picture task like this in Picture Manager is much faster than trying to do this in PowerPoint, which is focused more on presentation creation than picture editing.

Changing a Picture's Format

With a picture open in Picture Manager (see "Quick Edits in the Edit Pictures Workpane" in the previous section), select File, Export. This brings up the Export workpane (see Figure 4.22).

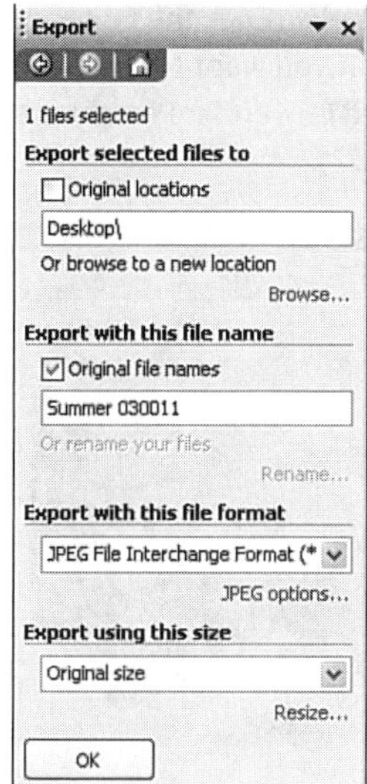

Figure 4.22

Export workpane.

Choose a different file type for the Export with this file format option. Then click OK to export the picture.

NOTE

In most Office applications, you change the format of the file by going to File, Save As and then changing the Save As Type. In Picture Manager, the Save As Type drop-down is grayed out. So remember to use Export when you want to change file types.

Batch Editing

Everything we've described so far affects one picture at a time, but one of Picture Manager's most powerful capabilities is managing large collections of pictures and editing them all at once. Perhaps you need to correct brightness on a few dozen product catalog photos before adding them to a presentation. Or maybe you need to crop the screenshots you took of your hot new website before including those in a presentation.

Instead of opening one picture through PowerPoint, let's now start Picture Manager normally. Click the Start Menu button and choose All Programs, Microsoft Office, Microsoft Office Tools, Microsoft Office Picture Manager.

In the left pane, choose a folder that contains a lot of photos, such as your My Pictures folder. In the middle pane, select a picture by clicking on it. Then hold down the Ctrl key and click other pictures until a few of them are selected. You can also press Ctrl+A or choose Edit, Select All to select all the pictures in the directory.

Now, you can apply what you learned earlier. Click the Edit Pictures button on the toolbar to bring up the Edit Pictures workpane. Let's say that you want to make all these selected pictures 60% smaller. Click the Resize link. Enter **60** in the third box under Percentage of Original Width × Height. Click the OK button at the bottom (see Figure 4.23).

Figure 4.23

Resize multiple pictures at one time.

This batch-editing feature works with all the editing features described in the previous sections on using the Picture Manager.

5

Diagrams and SmartArt

IN THIS CHAPTER

- What's so Smart About It?
- Inserting SmartArt
- Anatomy of a SmartArt Graphic
- The Power of SmartArt Graphics
- Working with SmartArt Layouts
- Using Styles and Themes
- Create Graphic Commands
- Formatting Nodes
- Creating Animations
- Placeholder Trick
- Photos and SmartArt—Frame Your Pictures

What we're about to show you is going to revolutionize how you create presentations. SmartArt is a new feature for Word, PowerPoint, and Excel; but of the three, PowerPoint is definitely the application in which SmartArt makes the most impact.

By now, you realize that the presentation of your content is essential. If your presentation is organized, aesthetically pleasing, and conveys what you want, all that is left is for you to do is figure out what you are going to say during the presentation. SmartArt can handle the first three objectives, allowing you more time to come up with the actual content and what you will say to accompany the presentation.

What's so Smart About It?

To label a SmartArt as just a diagram is like saying that Michael Jordan is just a basketball player. Instead, think of SmartArt as your first option when you want to display data in a way that will capture the attention of your audience.

The basic idea of SmartArt is that you have a set of data that you need to lay out graphically. Maybe it's a list, maybe it's a flow chart, maybe it's a table of contents, maybe it's a food pyramid; regardless of what type of relationship the data has, SmartArt makes it easy to convey it in a professional manner that will amaze your audience (see Figure 5.1).

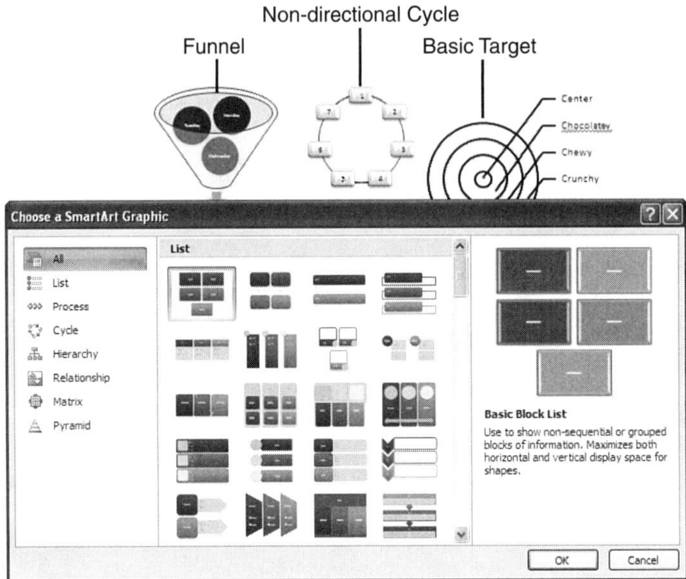

Figure 5.1

A few types of data that can be represented with SmartArt. From left to right, Funnel, Non-directional Cycle, Basic Target. Find all of these on the Insert SmartArt dialog or gallery.

The basic types of SmartArt are grouped together and include

- List
- Process
- Cycle
- Hierarchy
- Relationship
- Matrix
- Pyramid

Within each general type of SmartArt, you can use multiple layouts to display your data.

TIP

To get the most out of your data, the approach we recommend is to insert your SmartArt first, and then try out the various layouts to see what looks best in your presentation.

The real intelligence of a SmartArt graphic is in the ease with which you can display your data beautifully and also maintain it through changes and edits. This means that you can create an amazing graphic based on an original set of data; then add to or subtract from your data, and the graphic automatically reflects the changes in the data.

NOTE

For the rest of the chapter, we assume that you have created your data in PowerPoint (although it could come from anywhere), and it could be anything from a list of groceries to an executive plan of action to a food chain.

In a way, you can think of the graphic in terms of relying on the data, and when you modify existing data—whether you are adding or deleting— the graphic creates space for new nodes or removes a node and gives all other nodes more space to breathe.

In Figure 5.2, notice how the graphic has updated automatically simply by observing your changes to the data. Imagine trying to do this by hand and having to remove and resize all other nodes (shapes) when an insertion or deletion occurs.

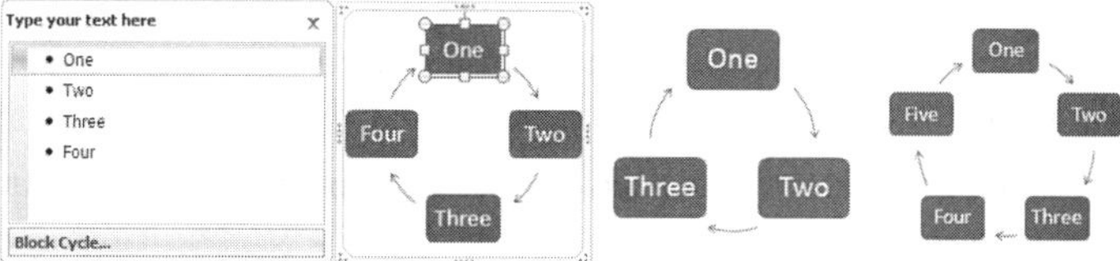

Figure 5.2

On the left is the original SmartArt; the middle has a piece of data removed; and the right has a piece of data added.

Inserting SmartArt

Depending on whether you have already created your data, you can insert SmartArt in one of two ways.

Using the Default

Without having any data, you can insert a default SmartArt, and it contains content placeholders with the words *[Text]* waiting for you to replace them with your actual data (see Figure 5.3). This is great for previewing how the data will look before you insert it, so you can focus on the formatting independently from the data creation.

To insert a default SmartArt graphic, do the following:

1. Select the Insert tab, and in the Illustrations group, click on the SmartArt icon.
2. Notice the three sections of the Choose a SmartArt Graphic dialog box: The left pane contains the basic types of SmartArt you can choose from, the middle pane shows icons that preview the look of the SmartArt, and the right pane contains a detailed description and a larger colored preview of the graphic. Figure 5.1 shows an example of how this looks.

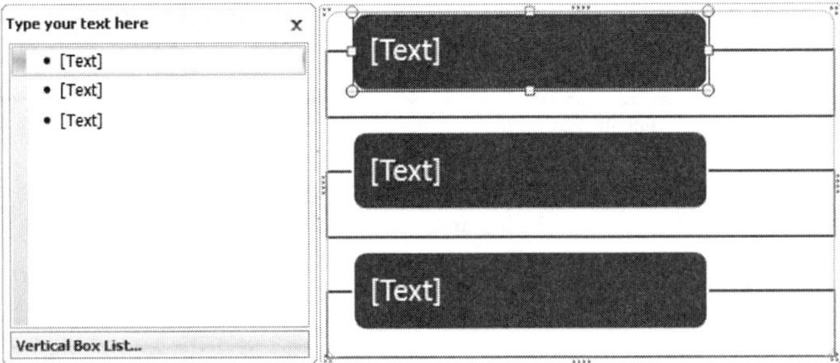

Figure 5.3

The default SmartArt has placeholders waiting for you to enter data marked [Text].

3. By default, the All category of SmartArt diagrams is selected in the left pane. If you want to narrow down the types of graphics previewed in the middle pane, select another type of SmartArt in the left pane.
4. Select a SmartArt graphic and notice that the preview pane on the right gives you a small summary and example of how the graphic will look.
5. When you're ready, click OK. You now have a SmartArt graphic in your presentation, ready for you to add data to and customize.

Convert Existing Content to SmartArt

An alternative way to insert a SmartArt graphic is to convert existing content to SmartArt. This is especially useful for presentations with existing data that needs to be spruced up, in addition to presentation authors who create their content first and then go back and make it look good visually. In fact, you can take all your presentations created in PowerPoint 2003 or older and convert all those boring bulleted lists into beautiful graphics.

The following types of content can be converted to SmartArt:

- Shapes
- Text boxes (Including WordArt)
- Placeholders

To convert one of these types of content to SmartArt, do the following:

1. Select the Home tab.
2. In the Paragraph group, click Convert to SmartArt to drop down a few of the layouts.

NOTE

This gallery is a great place to take advantage of Live Preview and hover over the layouts provided to see how the conversion would look.

3. Choose one of the 20 common layouts or click More SmartArt Graphics to find a different layout (see Figure 5.4).

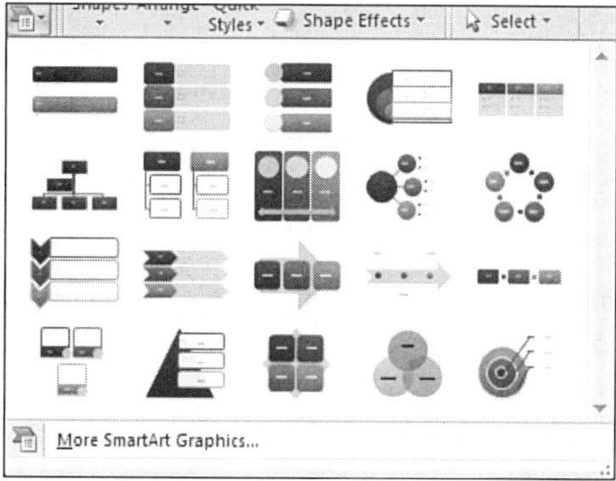

Figure 5.4

The Convert to SmartArt feature is a great tool that allows you to create content first using text boxes and bullets and then format it later.

Anatomy of a SmartArt Graphic

Before we delve too much into what you can do with SmartArt, let's look at the puzzle pieces you have to work with to create a SmartArt graphic.

Content Pane

The graphical representation of your data exists in the Content pane. With a SmartArt selected, this is the part on the right, as shown in Figure 5.5.

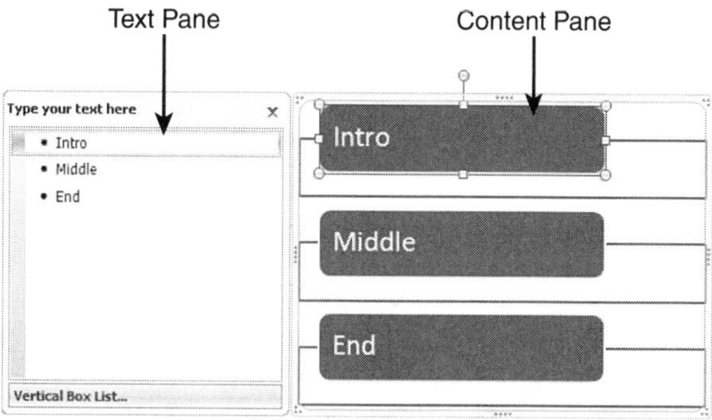

Figure 5.5

The anatomy of a Vertical Box List SmartArt. The left side is the Text pane; the right side is the Content pane.

When inserting a SmartArt graphic, the preview shows what the Content pane will contain. Note that the Text pane, described in the next section, is the same regardless of the type of SmartArt.

Text Pane

Fittingly named, the Text pane is the part of the SmartArt that, by default, is docked on its left side (but you can drag it around) and is titled Type Your Text Here (see Figure 5.5).

The body of the Text pane contains a bulleted outline of all the data you want the graphic to represent.

A great thing you can do with the Text pane is format your text. Imagine the words in your Text pane as just placeholders or links for the words in the Content pane. Select anything in the Text pane and apply formatting, such as changing the color, applying a style, or any other formatting you can do to text, as described in Chapter 2, "Everything You Need to Know About Text."

Although you can't see a difference in the text in the Text pane itself, look at the Content pane, where the text is modified. This is great for layouts that have rotated nodes, 3D nodes, or any hard-to-select shapes with text in them. In addition, you do not have to select each shape in the Content pane; rather, you have access to all the text in one place and can modify it there.

NOTE

Do not forget that you can move the Text pane around and it still remembers where it should be, even if you de-select the SmartArt.

From the SmartArt Tools Design tab, use the Promote and Demote buttons in the Create Graphic group to modify bullets and make them top-level bullets or child bullets (see Figure 5.6). This is also where you can toggle whether the Text pane will show up.

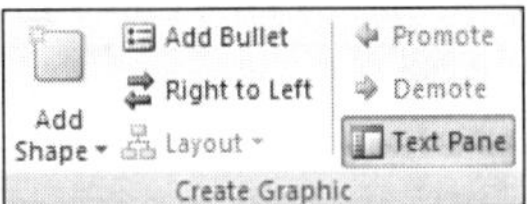

Figure 5.6

Create a hierarchy for your bullets by clicking the Promote and Demote buttons.

Nodes

The basic unit of the Content pane is a node. For many types of SmartArt, a bullet in your Text pane corresponds to a node in your graphic. If there's one thing we want you to remember, it's that **each node is just a shape**. Any formatting you can do to a shape (described in Chapter 12, "Formatting Shapes, Text, and More"), you can also do to a SmartArt Node. When a node is selected, the Format tab looks similar to the Format tab when a shape is selected.

Connectors

With some layouts, arrow shapes are added between nodes to convey the relationship between pieces of your data.

Again, these are simply shapes that are controlled by the layout engine. So, if you move a node, the connectors before and after it move to compensate for the change (see Figure 5.7).

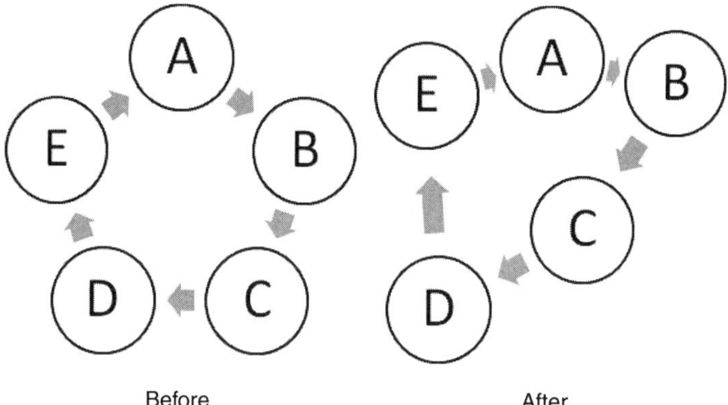

Figure 5.7

Before and after moving a node; notice the difference in the connectors.

The Power of SmartArt Graphics

When you insert a SmartArt graphic, notice the two separate panes described earlier. Why are there only two? The data (Text pane) is separated and decoupled from how it is displayed (Content pane).

This is the true genius of SmartArt in action; you are free to change the data independently of how it is represented visually. Let's think about this for a second because there are two main points we want to emphasize:

- If you modify your data, the graphics lay out again automatically. Why is this cool? Imagine trying to do this in another application—where you've created the graphics and data together—and then realizing that you need to add another item in your list. The amount of work required to do so would mean resizing every node, moving each one around to make room for a new one, and doing all the busy work yourself.
- You can modify or format your graphics without needing to change your data. The real power here lies in the fact that SmartArt diagrams are responsive to style and theme changes. Apply a design to your SmartArt or change the document theme, and watch all of your nodes change with respect to the new mode.

Now that the separation has been established, let's look at what exactly it is useful for. Compare using SmartArt versus creating a diagram in another application, creating all the pieces, and then attempting to do the following:

- **Repurpose data**—This is probably one of the most common occurrences, but moving data around in your set and mucking with the order is infinitely easier.
- **Add and Remove Nodes**—Data in a bulleted list is bound to be deleted and added to. Without SmartArt, you are left with adding and deleting nodes manually with no easy way of replicating nodes other than by doing a copy and paste.
- **Modify nodes**—Suppose that you want a node to be placed somewhere else in the SmartArt, but you still want the connecting arrows to point to it. All you need to do is drag the node. You do not need to change the rest of the SmartArt to match it, as the layout engine handles everything.

NOTE

Keep in mind that for some SmartArt layouts, there is a set number of bullets that you can have in your list before the data no longer fits. For example, try to insert the Gear SmartArt with a list of four or more bullets (not including sub-bullets), and notice that the fourth bullet and every one after that contains a red X for its bullet, which means that it won't show up in the display.

Working with SmartArt Layouts

Earlier, we gave you a list of data types that SmartArt can represent. Within each of those categories, there exist many layouts; for example, within the Process category, there are different ways in which the arrows convey data, how the nodes are arranged, and basically how the nodes show up.

Although layouts are more of a built-in attribute to a SmartArt graphic, it is important to understand how layouts affect the behavior of a SmartArt. Layouts affect only the Content pane and the location. Where your data shows up is a direct result of which layout is selected. The layout leaves your Text pane untouched, but modifies the look of your nodes; it might add connecting shapes between nodes, and—most of all—each layout changes *what form* your data is in and *where* your data ends up.

TIP

Some data works better with certain layouts but not with others. For lists, definitely use the List or Process types. We like to use Vertical Box List for tables of content or agendas in a presentation. Cycle is useful for displaying chains or pie charts and order. Hierarchy is a great organizational chart tool to show structure. Relationship, Matrix, and Pyramid fit many types of data, and you should try them out and see what fits.

You are forced to choose a layout when the SmartArt is first inserted, but do not worry—you can always change this later if you are not happy with how it looks.

To change the layout of an existing SmartArt, do the following:

1. Select a SmartArt, and then select the SmartArt Tools Design tab (see Figure 5.8).

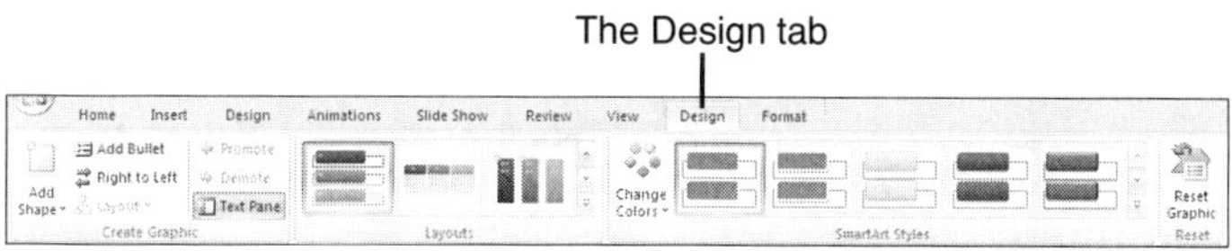

Figure 5.8

The SmartArt Tools Design tab.

2. Select one of the layouts you see, or click on the arrow to see more popular layouts. Figure 5.9 shows the Layouts gallery expanded.

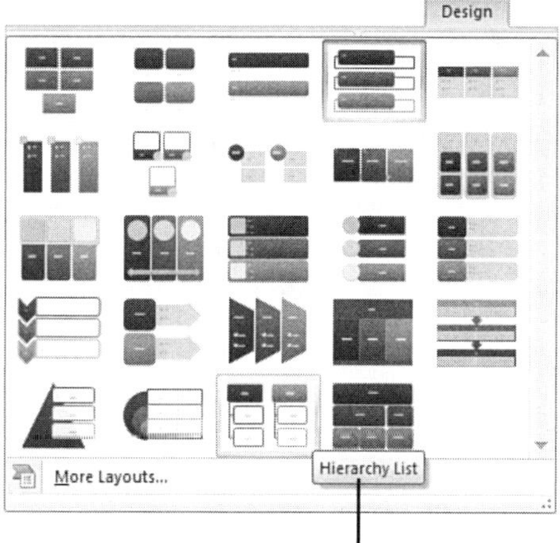

Figure 5.9

The Layouts gallery expanded.

NOTE

This is another perfect opportunity to use Live Preview to see what the new layout would look like before you apply it.

---

3. After you have chosen a layout you like, click on it to apply the layout to the SmartArt selected (see Figure 5.10).

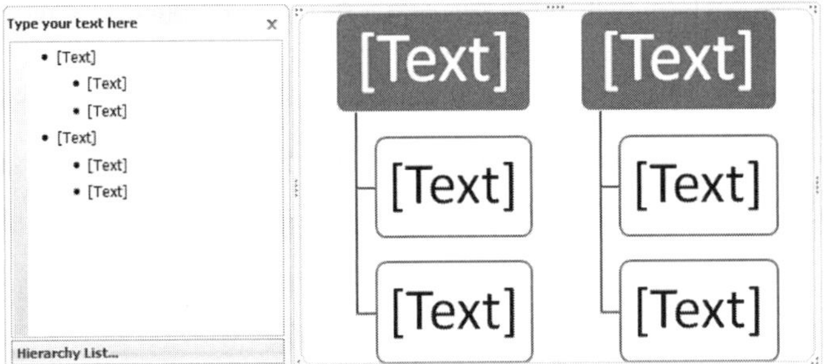

Figure 5.10

The end result of applying a Hierarchy List layout.

Using Styles and Themes

Because the contents of the Content pane consist of shapes (nodes), SmartArt is capable of handling style and theme changes.

SmartArt has out-of-the-box styles that can be applied (see Figure 5.11). Each style can change the 3D attributes, colors, gradient, or rotation of both the node itself and the text inside.

To view the nine different SmartArt specific styles, do the following:

1. Select a SmartArt diagram.
2. Select the SmartArt Tools Design tab on the ribbon.
3. View some of the Styles in the SmartArt Styles group of the ribbon. Hover over a style to activate Live Preview.
4. If none of those satisfy you, expand the gallery (which enables Live Preview) to expose all nine SmartArt Styles.

CAUTION

Don't forget that when you apply a style to your SmartArt, any previous formatting you have applied is lost!

Along the same lines of changing styles, SmartArt objects respect any changes to the document theme. When you change the theme for the document, the SmartArt diagram updates to the new theme as if each individual node were just another shape in the document. Chapter 11, "Dissecting Themes," contains more information about Office themes.

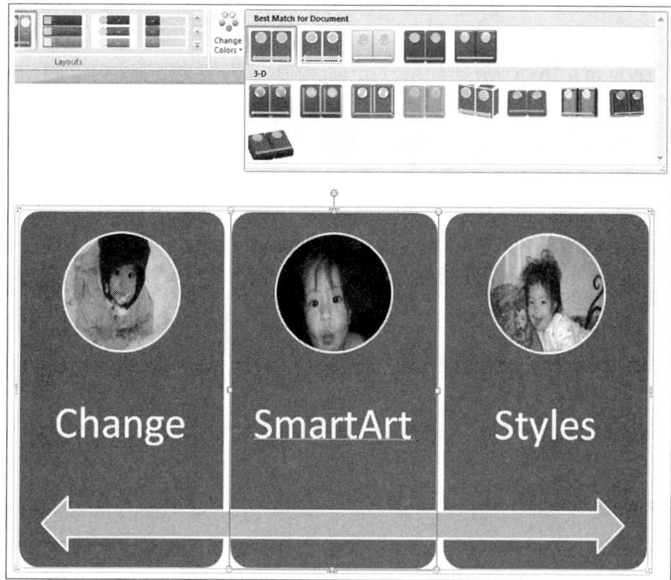

Figure 5.11

Change the Style of the SmartArt by selecting one of the preset styles from the gallery.

Create Graphic Commands

When a SmartArt is selected, the Design tab contains a Create Graphic group with useful commands that are specific to SmartArt (refer back to Figure 5.6).

The next few sections take you on a tour of the available options and how to use them.

Add Shape

Just as the name suggests, this option adds a new shape—at the end of the SmartArt if nothing is selected; otherwise, PowerPoint adds one where you have your cursor. Use the drop-down to specify exactly where you want the new shape added.

The newly inserted shape is exactly formatted as it should be according to the rest of the SmartArt. This is just like adding a new node.

NOTE

An additional feature called Add assistant is available from the Add Shape drop-down only if you have an Organization Chart type of SmartArt selected. It is used to add the next node that makes sense in the hierarchy.

Add Bullet

As noted earlier, a node in a SmartArt graphic corresponds only to top-level bullets. If you want sub-bullets, either press Tab while in the Text pane or click Add Bullet.

Right to Left

If you want to completely flip your SmartArt from right to left or left to right, use this command to do so. Do not attempt to try flipping a SmartArt graphic manually, as it will only cause you headaches. Not only does this option flip the connecting shapes for you, but also the order of the nodes.

This option doesn't change the order of the text in your text pane, only in the way that it is laid out.

Layout

This is not the same as the SmartArt Layout described earlier. This option is enabled only if you have an Organization Chart as your SmartArt. Use this option to decide how your nodes are organized—whether they hang off the left or the right, are standard, or both.

Make sure that you have a child node selected when trying to use this; otherwise, it is disabled.

Formatting Nodes

Remember that nodes are simply shapes. A great thing to do is select all (Ctrl+A) with the SmartArt selected, which chooses all the nodes. Now you can apply any formatting, such as the following cool tricks:

- **Rotation**—With all the nodes selected, drag one of the green rotation handles and rotate all the shapes together. This gives the SmartArt a cool effect.
- **Change Shape**—You are not constrained to the shape that comes with the layout. After you have applied a layout to your SmartArt data, simply select all and choose Change Shape from the SmartArt Tools Format tab. Use this to make it look as if you have your own Custom Layouts.
- **Edit in 2D**—Useful if you have 3D formatted nodes, especially if you have many nodes and selecting a 3D rotated node is not very easy. Not only is the text easier to edit, but the entire SmartArt becomes 2D again to make it easier to see what you have.

Creating Animations

One of the biggest time-savers included in this book involves applying animations to SmartArt. By now, you should understand that SmartArt consists of shapes, and shapes can be animated; therefore, SmartArt can be animated. But the really cool part is how SmartArt is animated:

1. Select a SmartArt graphic.
2. Select the Animations tab on the ribbon.

3. Choose an animation from the drop-down that treats each shape as an individual shape for things such as fly-in and other animations that have multiple steps. It gives each node a step.

NOTE

Live Preview works here, so preview your animations on-the-fly.

Now, watch as each of your nodes animates independently. All you had to do was apply one animation to the entire SmartArt, not each individual node (see Figure 5.12).

Figure 5.12

Animations applied to an entire SmartArt are applied to each individual node automatically.

NOTE

Not only do all the nodes animate independently, but each of the connector nodes that are automatically added, depending on the layout, gets animated too. Animations are covered in more depth in Chapter 15, "Going Beyond Slide-by-Slide."

Placeholder Trick

Earlier, we touched on how SmartArt can be inserted from placeholders. Because placeholders often contain bullets just as the Text pane does, the Convert to SmartArt action helps spruce up boring looking placeholders. Feel free to insert your data first into a placeholder. Then you can figure out how you would like it to be graphically represented by converting it to SmartArt and previewing the various layouts.

To convert a placeholder to a SmartArt graphic, do the following:

1. With a placeholder selected, enter data in each of the bullets or one per line.
2. Select the Home tab.
3. Select the Convert to SmartArt button.
4. Select a layout that fits your needs.

The final result is a much more visually appealing representation of the original, boring bullets (see Figure 5.13).

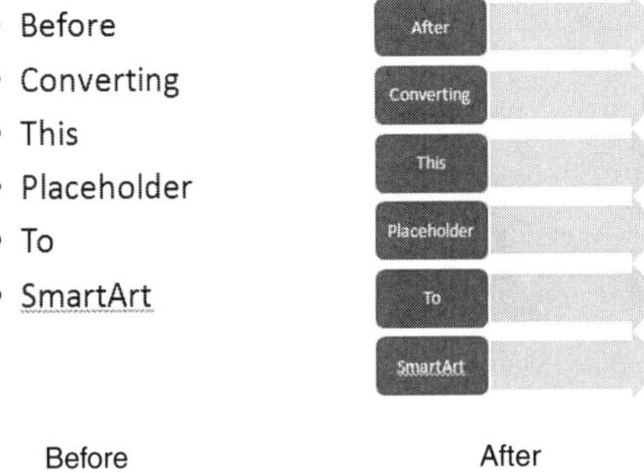

Figure 5.13

Convert to SmartArt on a placeholder.

Photos and SmartArt—Frame Your Pictures

One great use for a SmartArt graphic is to emphasize and accentuate a photo or image. For the types of SmartArt that have Picture in the name or a description of them—such as Bending Picture Accent List—a piece of the SmartArt has been reserved for a photo.

When you insert one of these SmartArt graphics, part of it resembles a picture icon, which brings up the Insert Picture dialog. When clicked, it lets you choose a photo or icon, as shown in Figure 5.14.

This is great for when you want to brand your SmartArt with the company logo or you have action shots to go along with your storyboard.

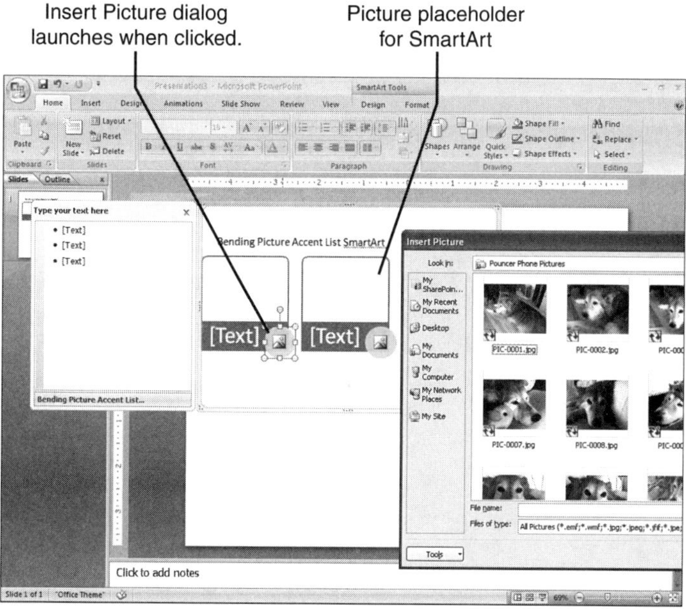

Figure 5.14

Notice the icon for the picture and the dialog that launches when you click on it.

6

Rediscover Charts

IN THIS CHAPTER

- Inserting Excel Charts into PowerPoint
- Getting Inside a Chart
- Understanding Chart Layouts
- Understanding Chart Styles
- Creating and Using Chart Templates
- Manipulating Data
- Dragging the Pie
- Working with Legacy Graphs and OLE Objects
- Converting to Office 2007 Format

Brand new to Office 2007 is the new version of Charts to replace the old Microsoft Graph Chart and the Microsoft Excel Graph—both of which were inserted as OLE objects in previous versions of Office. While you can still insert these OLE objects, you will be hard-pressed to find an opportunity to do so, given that the renovated charts in Office 2007 look amazing and function much better.

NOTE

OLE stands for object linking and embedding, a technology prevalent within Office to run one program inside another program. Microsoft Graph, the predecessor to Office 2007 Charts, used OLE. So, although graphs were technically part of PowerPoint, graph editing was actually done inside an entirely different program with menus and commands that are completely distinct from PowerPoint's. Office 2007 Charts do not use OLE and are just another feature that is seamlessly part of PowerPoint.

This isn't a tutorial on how to make pivot tables or economic regressions, or how to balance your company's finances. Instead, let us walk you through the new features that the reworked charts have to offer, and hopefully some of the tips and tricks we show you will enable you to do your job more efficiently.

Inserting Excel Charts into PowerPoint

There are a couple of important ways to get a chart into your presentation: You could use the commands found on the Ribbon to insert a generic chart with some default data, or you could copy and paste an existing chart from an Excel spreadsheet that contains the data you need.

Because charts are a graphical representation of data, and this data is usually in the form of tables or grids that you can find in Microsoft Excel, we're going to walk through copying and pasting charts from Excel first. Following that, we go into how to create a chart from scratch in PowerPoint.

Copying and Pasting

Charts are primarily a native Excel object. The data represented by the chart is contained within cells in a spreadsheet, but when you need to create a presentation, the best way to get a chart into PowerPoint from Excel is to copy and paste it.

Aside from the Copy and Paste buttons in the Clipboard group on the Home tab, you can use shortcut keys Ctrl+C and Ctrl+V to copy and paste, respectively. The default format in which the chart gets pasted is the Microsoft Office Graphic Object, which creates a native chart on the PowerPoint slide.

TIP

Charts can be pasted as other types, such as an OLE object or as a picture. Use Paste Special to see other formats, or use Ctrl+Alt+V as a shortcut.

After your chart is pasted, the Paste Options button appears in the lower right side of the chart (see Figure 6.1).

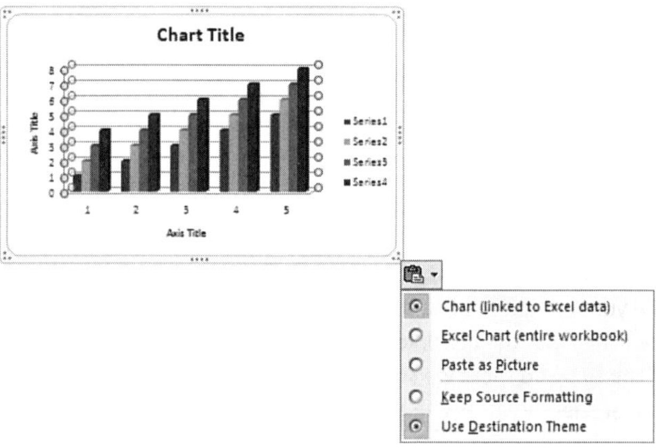

Figure 6.1

The Paste Options button allows you to specify certain paste options.

The following options are available after pasting a chart from Excel into PowerPoint:

- **Chart (Linked to Excel Data)**—The chart updates when the data is changed in Excel.
- **Excel Chart (Entire Workbook)**—The data is copied over to PowerPoint.
- **Paste as Picture**—An image of the chart is copied but cannot be changed further.

The following options relate to the presentation's theme and how the chart looks after it is pasted:

- Keep Source Formatting
- Use Destination Theme

By default, Chart (linked to Excel data) and Use Destination Theme are selected. In general, you want to leave your chart linked to Excel data in case the data in your Excel spreadsheet changes and you want the chart to update to reflect the changes. If you choose an option other than this, the chart does not change when the data in the cells change.

CAUTION

Keeping the Excel data inside your chart can have implications if you share the presentation with others because it can contain formulas or calculations that you might not want everyone to have access to. If this is a concern, choose the Paste as Picture option instead.

Inserting an Excel Chart from Within PowerPoint

To insert an Excel chart from scratch in PowerPoint, do the following:

1. Select the Insert tab.
2. Select Chart.
3. Choose a Chart Type (see Figure 6.2).
4. Click OK.

Notice that the following happens when you click OK:

1. Excel launches in a new window.
2. Both windows are resized to share the whole screen side by side (see Figure 6.3).
3. Fake sample data is created.

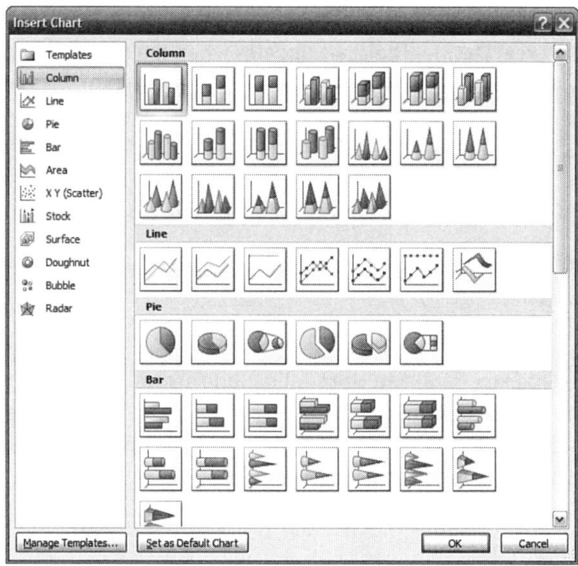

Figure 6.2

Insert a Chart from the Ribbon.

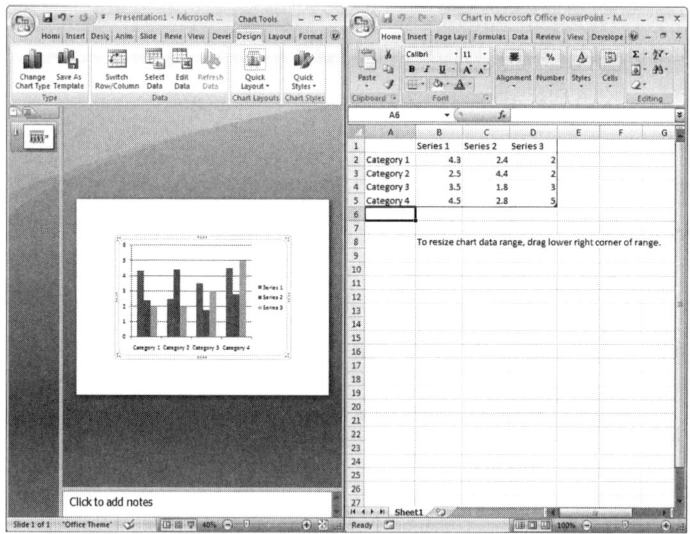

Figure 6.3

PowerPoint and Excel share the screen after inserting a new chart.

NOTE

As we explain later in this chapter, if you don't own Excel, Microsoft Graph appears instead of Excel.

Getting Inside a Chart

Charts are made up of the typical grids, legends, and other elements you would expect to find in a chart. The interesting part is how the meat of the chart is actually created: It uses shapes. This might sound familiar considering that SmartArt is made up of shapes, too.

Formatting

Because the contents of the chart are regular shapes, everything you can do to shapes can be done to the bars, pie pieces, lines, and any other chart piece you can find. (We discuss formatting shapes in Chapter 12, "Formatting Shapes, Text, and More.")

Let's walk through an example in which we format a series with some cool new effects. Start by inserting a default chart using the methods discussed in the earlier section.

1. Select a bar, series, or any piece of the chart.
2. Modify your selection using any of the Shape Styles commands from the Format tab to change the shape by adding effects, fills, and so on. Then click on Format, Format Selection.
3. Select the Fill option on the left of the Format Selection dialog (see Figure 6.4).

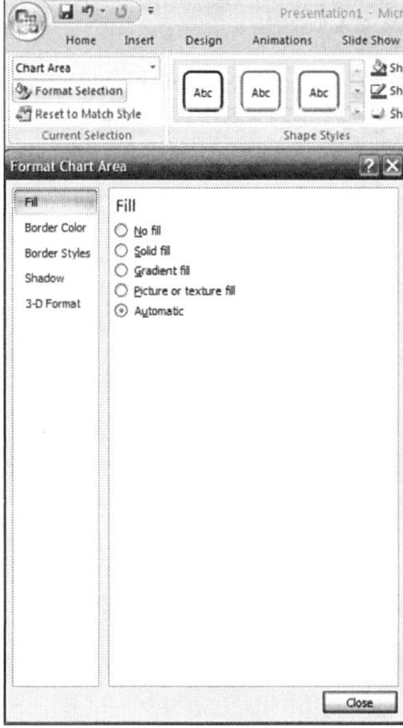

Figure 6.4

Click Format Selection to bring up the Format Chart Area dialog, where you can format portions of the chart.

4. Click on Gradient Fill and choose some nice colors. At this point, you can also apply a Border Style, Border Color, Shadow, or 3D Format. Try to avoid too much cluttering here. A simple shadow goes a long way (see Figure 6.5).

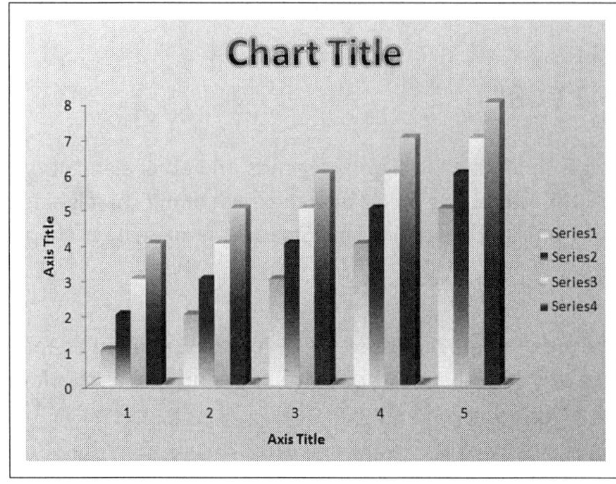

Figure 6.5

By applying a few fills and styles to pieces of a chart, you can end up with a pretty formatted chart series like this.

5. Repeat with the other series in your chart as needed.

Formatting a Specific Piece of a Chart

From the Current Selection group on the Format tab, you can select various parts of the chart, as well as use the Format Selection dialog to access additional options specific to each part of the chart (see Figure 6.6).

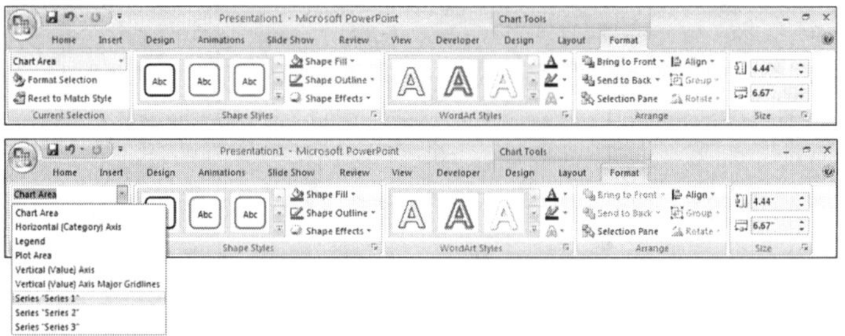

Figure 6.6

The Current Selection group and the Format Selection button.

Here's how you can discover these options:

1. Select a piece of the chart or use the drop-down list from the Current Selection group.
2. Click on Format Selection.

NOTE

The Format Selection dialog is modeless. This means that you can keep it open, continue working on your presentation, select a different part of the chart, and notice the dialog change, depending on what you have selected. This also means that if you click somewhere on your chart that you did not mean to, you can format it accidentally.

Now you can click around on various pieces of the chart with the Format Selection dialog open, and it adapts to what you have selected. Notice with an Axis selected, Axis Options is the first tab in the dialog from which you can modify the units, scale, tick types, and so on.

With this powerful tool, you can completely customize your chart to your liking. Experiment with the various menus in the Format Selection dialog to see how you can enhance your charts in ways other than what we've discussed here.

Inserting Objects into a Chart

Similar to the legacy charts feature, the new 2007 charts feature allows the insertion of Shapes, Pictures, ClipArt, Textboxes, and WordArt—all of which behave exactly as they would outside the chart.

The great thing about this is that the objects you draw into your chart remain there even if you move, resize, or modify your chart. You can also drag and drop objects into a chart.

This is especially useful when annotating your chart with arrows and text.

Understanding Chart Layouts

Within each chart type, there are various layouts that determine where pieces of the chart are located and how they look.

To change the layout of your chart, do the following:

1. Select a chart.
2. Select the Design tab under Chart Tools.
3. Click Chart Layouts to drop down the gallery of available layouts and see a small thumbnail of how it will look (see Figure 6.7).
4. Click the thumbnail to apply the layout.

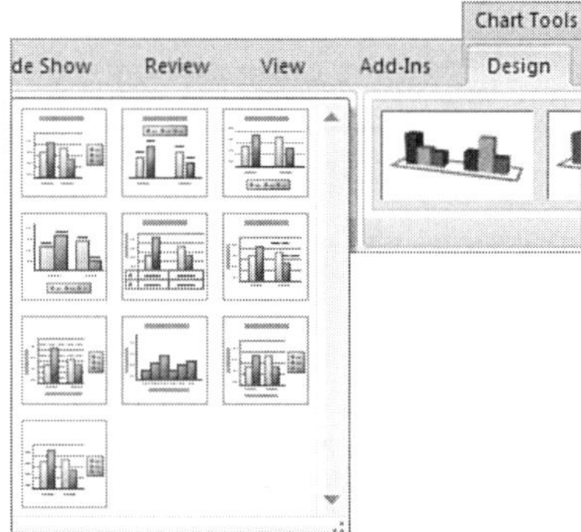

Figure 6.7

Change the layout of your chart type. Note that the number of layouts changes based on the type of chart you have selected.

Understanding Chart Styles

Forty-eight preset chart styles can be found on the Design tab under Chart Tools. These styles enable you to modify the colors and borders of the series and backgrounds of the chart.

Use these as a starting point, and then customize according to how you want your chart to look:

1. Select a chart. Figure 6.8 shows a chart with default styles.

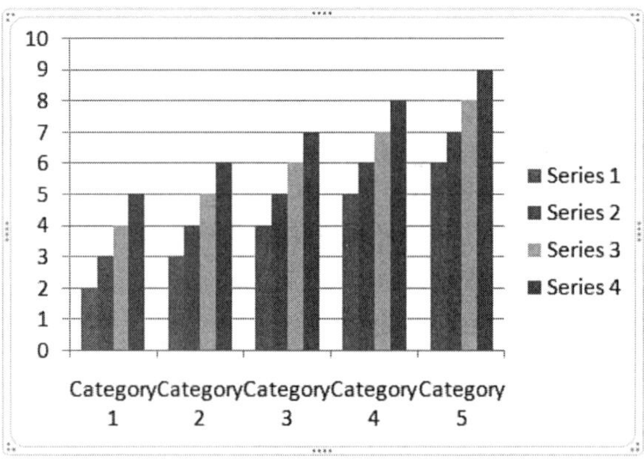

Figure 6.8

This is the default PowerPoint bar chart with only the data modified.

2. Select the Design Tab from the Chart Tools section.
3. From the Chart Styles group, click the drop-down arrow to open the gallery and see a full list of preset Styles (see Figure 6.9).

NOTE

Unfortunately, Live Preview does not work for Chart Styles.

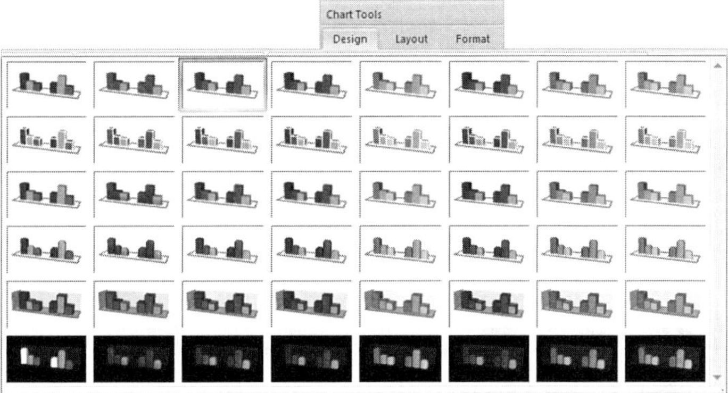

Figure 6.9

The gallery of styles you can apply to a Chart.

4. Select one of the styles.
5. Continue modifying your chart by adding effects to series and changing colors if necessary (see Figure 6.10).

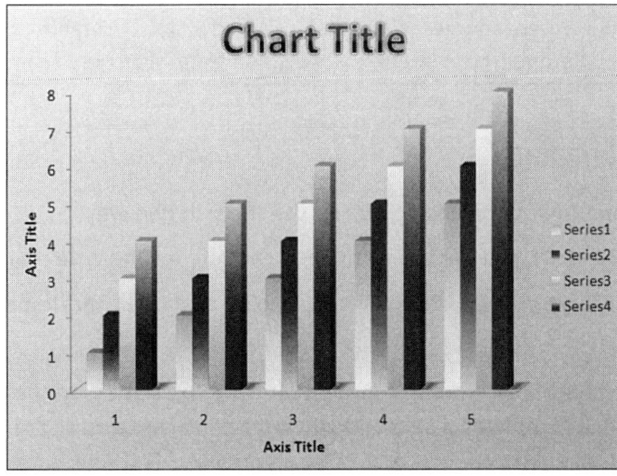

Figure 6.10

A chart created by using one of the Chart Styles and then modified more to suit our needs.

Creating and Using Chart Templates

Think of chart templates as saving your chart formatting in case you want to apply it to another chart.

A chart template is actually a file (`.crtx`) that is saved onto your hard drive. The format is a package containing XML that describes the content of the chart.

Creating a Template

To create a chart template, do the following:

1. Create a chart.
2. Format it any way that you want.
3. Select the Design tab under the Chart Tools area of the Ribbon.
4. Select the Save As Template option (see Figure 6.11).

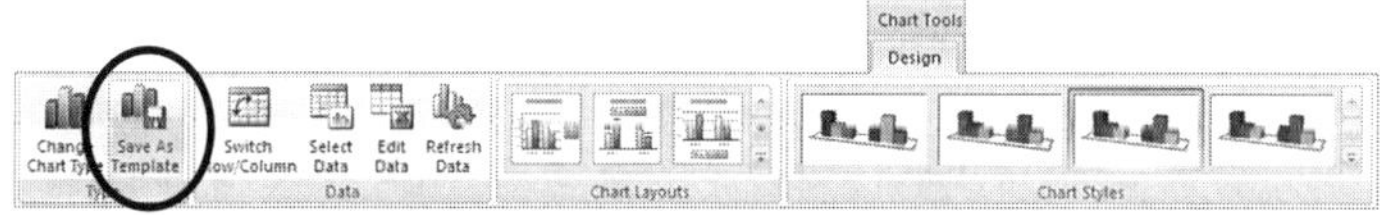

Figure 6.11

The Save As Template option allows you to save a chart template of your own and use it again later.

5. Choose a name and location to save the `.crtx` file.

NOTE

The default location where your templates will be saved will look something like this: C:\Documents and Settings\<*User Name*>\Application Data\Microsoft\Templates.

Using an Existing Template

After you have templates at your disposal, you can use them in two ways:

- After you create a chart, you can select a chart template for the type that it should be.
- With an existing chart, you can change its type to be that of a chart template.

When you first insert a chart from scratch in PowerPoint, the top option on the left pane is Templates (refer to Figure 6.2). When Templates is selected, the right pane contains all the chart templates located in the default Chart Template folder (C:\Documents and Settings\<*User Name*>\Application Data\Microsoft\Templates). Select one of the templates, and your newly inserted chart is given the same formatting and design as the template you saved.

Similarly, to change the type of an existing chart to that of one of your chart templates, do the following:

1. With the chart selected, click the Design tab under Chart Tools.
2. Select Change Chart Type from the Type group.
3. Select Templates from the left pane.
4. Select a template from the right pane.

The template's formatting is applied to the selected chart.

Managing Templates

This option is mostly for convenience, used for finding the folder in which templates are stored by default. It launches the directory containing the chart templates that is found by default at C:\Documents and Settings\<*User Name*>\Application Data\Microsoft\Templates. This happens in a separate Windows Explorer window for convenience.

You can access the Manage Templates feature from the Insert Chart dialog.

Manipulating Data

Charts are dependent on data. If no data exists, a set of default numbers is created in a table.

If you find yourself with a chart in PowerPoint and you want to modify the data that it is associated with, you can choose from a couple of methods.

First, you can modify the data by clicking the Select Data button (see Figure 6.12):

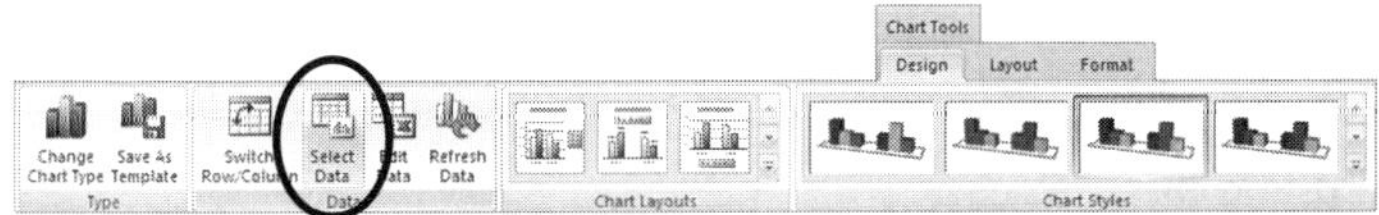

Figure 6.12

Use the Select Data feature to modify the data your Chart contains.

1. Select an existing chart.
2. From the Chart Tools section, select the Design tab.
3. Choose Select Data.
4. Notice now that Excel launches, if it was not already open, and the Select Data Source dialog opens with the data that your chart was created from selected (see Figure 6.13).

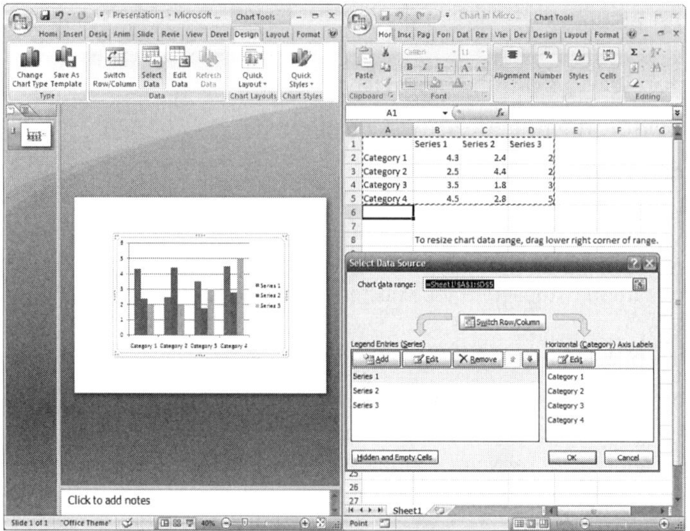

Figure 6.13

This is functionality that was never even dreamed of with the MS Graph Object that was the default chart type in previous versions of Office.

5. Modify the selection of cells or manually change the rows/columns using the dialog.

Optionally, you can modify the data directly by choosing the Edit Data option. Select Data allows you to modify the set of data, but by using Edit Data, you can actually change cells and manipulate the actual numbers. Because PowerPoint is not a spreadsheet tool, it makes sense that Edit Data launches Excel—if it is not already open—and resizes both PowerPoint and Excel to appear side by side, allowing you to work in both.

To use Edit Data, do the following:

1. Select an existing chart.
2. From the Chart Tools section, select the Design tab.
3. Choose Edit Data.
4. Notice that Excel launches (if it was not already open) and you're able to change the data that your chart uses.

TIP

Refresh Data is located on the same group as Select Data and Edit Data, and it is pretty straightforward. If you have pasted a chart and selected the Excel Chart (entire workbook) option with the Paste Options tag as described previously, Refresh Data is disabled because the chart is no longer linked to data within an Excel spreadsheet.

Dragging the Pie

New

Pie charts are a different breed. For instance, the default data provided with a pie chart is different from other charts. In addition, with pie charts, special rules are applied when pieces of the pie are dragged around. Instead of allowing you to move your pie all over the place while you drag, the pieces of the pie guide themselves away from the center of the pie but not anywhere else.

To see this in action, do the following:

1. Insert a pie chart.
2. Click once on a piece of a pie or select all the pieces (using the current selection list).
3. Click and hold to drag the pieces around.
4. Notice here that the pieces move toward and away from the center of the pie but not anywhere else.

TIP

You can also add commentary to your charts using text boxes and shapes.

When you want to emphasize a certain piece of the pie, drag it away from the others, as shown in Figure 6.14.

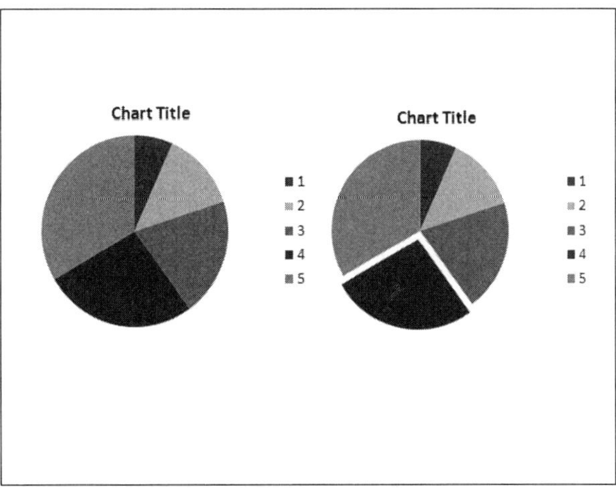

Figure 6.14

A piece of the pie emphasized.

TIP

Spruce up your charts by removing the plot area. This reduces clutter, and the chart it is still readable. Simply click on the background and press the Delete button.

Working with Legacy Graphs and OLE Objects

Advanced In this section, we travel back in time and explore the way in which we survived before SmartArt and the new charts came into existence.

We call these other objects legacy because they existed long before PowerPoint 2007. It is entirely possible that you might not be able to use the new SmartArt diagrams or charts with PowerPoint 2007. For instance, if your company has set a group policy that disables them, you are left with using only the legacy charts and graphs that exist as OLE objects.

In the following sections, we show you how to make full use of these OLE objects, including how to replace the ugly chart defaults that are unimpressive compared to the native, PowerPoint 2007, twenty-first century graphics.

Converting to Office 2007 Format

Let's take a look at what happens when you insert a legacy chart object and then double-click to activate it in PowerPoint 2007.

To insert a legacy chart, do the following:

1. Select the Insert tab.
2. Click on Object.
3. Select either Microsoft Graph Chart or Microsoft Office Excel Chart.
4. Now de-select the object you inserted by clicking somewhere else on the slide, and then select the chart again.

Each time you click on a legacy chart, you are prompted with the question, "Do you want to convert this chart to the new format?" (Figure 6.15 illustrates this.)

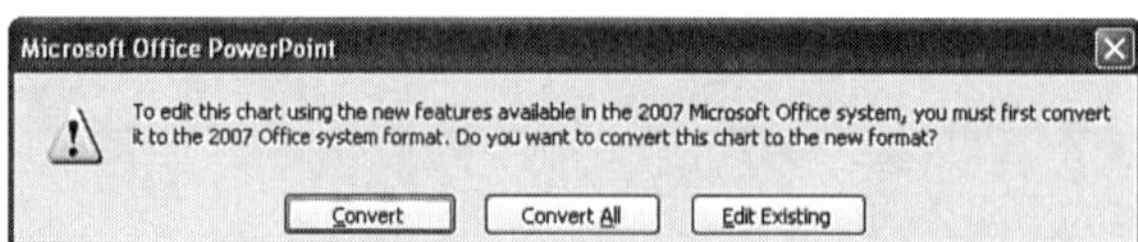

Figure 6.15

Decide whether you would like to convert your legacy chart OLE object into a native 2007 chart.

The decision here depends on whether you want to be able to fully use your chart with all the power of PowerPoint 2007, which is described in this chapter. The drawback to converting is that users of previous versions of PowerPoint are no longer be able to edit your chart.

OLE Facts

It's important to note a couple of random OLE facts here because somewhere down the line, you might have an OLE object in your presentation (such as a legacy chart) and might notice one or two quirks when working with them.

WHY CAN'T I UNDO INSIDE MY OLE?

While you're going along knocking out charts left and right, you might notice that something strange occurs when you try to undo an operation (Ctrl+Z) while the OLE object is activated. With a chart in edit mode or with any activated OLE object, if you try to undo many times, it's ineffective and probably only undoes the last thing you've done.

Although this might be a nuisance to those of us who make more mistakes than a first grader writing a book report, there is a simple, yet tedious workaround. When you make any set of changes while in an activated OLE object, double-click elsewhere to deactivate the chart. To you, nothing looks different, but internally PowerPoint logs it as an event it knows about. Now when you undo in deactivated mode, that event is undone as one operation.

To summarize: Enter edit mode, make your change, exit edit mode to let PowerPoint know what happened, and then you are able to undo in PowerPoint as much as you want.

This oddness exists because, technically, chart editing is happening inside a different program and not in PowerPoint. So, when you're making each individual chart edit, PowerPoint has no idea what's happening and can't save these operations for undo. By quickly exiting from editing the chart back to PowerPoint, PowerPoint gets control back and can save everything that's happened so far.

CORRUPTION

The format that your files are saved to in PowerPoint 2003 and earlier is binary, meaning that it's a bunch of 1s and 0s. This lends itself well to corruption of data because if just one of those 1s or 0s is flipped, your whole document could be ruined.

By adding an OLE object (such as the entire chart) inside your presentation, PowerPoint is adding a ton of new data in binary format that's a prime target for corruption. OLE data is fully editable, but because of that, it's complicated. Sometimes PowerPoint screws up, and you can lose your chart entirely.

For this reason, you will often find that a common paradigm to follow is to first use and edit your charts and OLE objects as OLE objects. When you're done editing and have finalized it, copy the chart and paste it as an image back into the desired spot. To do this, select the chart and copy (choose Home tab, and on the Clipboard group select Copy, or simply press Ctrl+V). Then, click on the Paste drop-down, select Paste Special (or press Ctrl+Alt+V), and select one of the picture formats, such as Picture (PNG).

After you've done this, the pasted chart image can't be edited, but the data there is much simpler and potentially smaller.

7

Working with Shapes

IN THIS CHAPTER

- Insertion Tricks
- Drawing Tools Format Tab
- Creating Custom Shapes
- Using Connectors to Save Time
- What Do Those Yellow Diamonds Do?
- The Brand New Selection Pane
- Embedding Objects from Other Applications
- Grouping Shapes and Objects

Most PowerPoint beginners rarely use them at all, but mastering the art of vector shapes is one of the keys to being a PowerPoint power user. Though shapes seem deceptively simple, there's a great deal of power under the covers.

Insertion Tricks

One of the first things you see when launching PowerPoint is the Shapes gallery or drop-down (see Figure 7.1) located on the Home ribbon in the Drawing group.

NOTE

Shapes show up as either a drop-down or gallery, depending on the width of the PowerPoint window.

It's easy to insert shapes from here. The Shapes gallery is also available on the Insert tab in the Illustrations group under Shapes, which is also where it lives in Word and Excel 2007.

NOTE

PowerPoint 2007 lets you choose from 18 shapes on the Ribbon, compared to the 4 that were on the old PowerPoint 2003 Drawing toolbar.

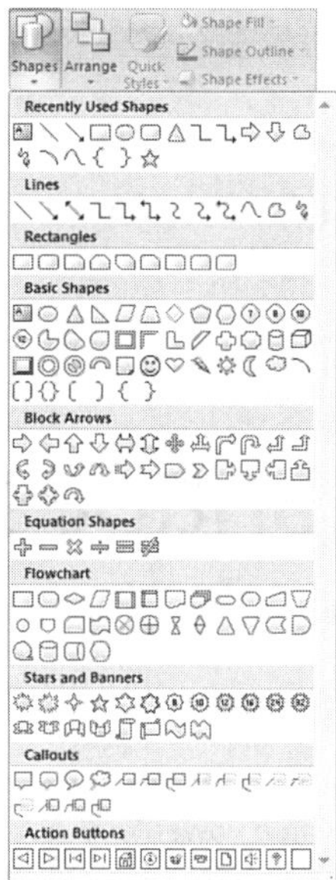

Figure 7.1

The Shapes group. The shapes in the Recently Used Shapes section at the top might look different, depending on which shapes you've used recently.

Expand the gallery, and hundreds of shapes wait for you to click them and create content. So far, you PowerPoint veterans might be rolling your eyes, but let's look at some shape-related tips that you might not know.

Who Knew There Were So Many Ways to Insert a Shape?

Click one of the many shapes in the gallery. You now have two options:

- Click one time somewhere on the slide. The shape appears at its default size, typically one inch by one inch.
- Click and drag on the slide. This lets you decide at the time of insertion how big you want the object to be.

Okay, that's easy; but suppose that you've been contracted to insert 10 shapes. (I know, work is tough nowadays.) You could click the icon, click or drag on the slide to insert the shape, click the icon, click or drag on the slide, click the icon, and so on. It would take forever, and let's be honest; you're smarter than that.

Instead, let's take advantage of some timesaving alternatives. Here are two tricks to quickly duplicate a bunch of shapes:

- Select the shapes you want to duplicate, hold down Ctrl, and drag any of the selected shapes to another spot on the slide.
- Select the shapes and press Ctrl+D.

After using Ctrl+D to duplicate a shape, the duplicate shape is offset slightly right and down of the previous shape. If the duplicated shape was in the exact same position, you probably wouldn't see it.

TIP

If you select a slide in the thumbnail pane, Ctrl+D duplicates slides, too.

Lock Drawing Mode

If you right-click a shape from the Shapes gallery, the option to Lock Drawing Mode is displayed (see Figure 7.2). When this option is selected, each time you click and drag on your presentation, a new instance of the shape you selected is created. This makes it easy to insert many shapes at the same time.

NOTE

Lock Drawing Mode only stays active for the shape you selected. Clicking just about anything on the Ribbon, such as clicking Bold or clicking another shape to insert, exits Lock Drawing Mode.

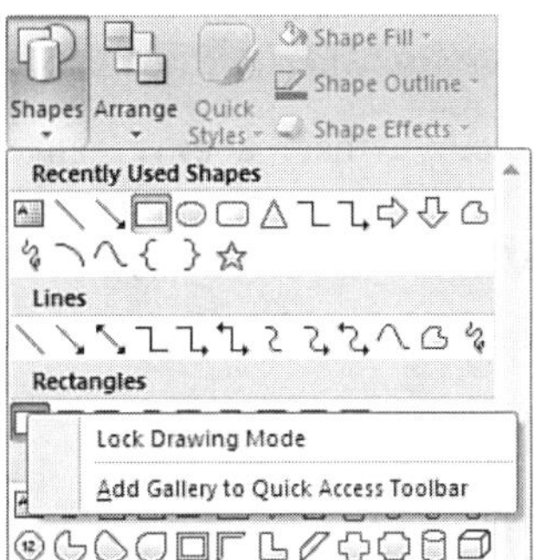

Figure 7.2

Right-click a shape in the gallery to use Lock Drawing Mode.

How can you tell whether you're in Lock Drawing Mode? Just look at the mouse pointer. If you have a crosshair mouse pointer, as shown in Figure 7.3, you're in Shape Insertion Mode. In this state, when you single-click, the default shape size is used (which is usually one inch by one inch). The most common thing to do is to click and drag the shape to a size you're happy with and then let go to create the shape. After creating the shape, if you still see the crosshair—waiting for you to insert another shape—you know that you're still in Lock Drawing Mode.

Figure 7.3

The mouse pointer becomes a crosshair during Shape Insertion Mode.

To turn off Lock Drawing Mode, simply select another shape, right-click the shape in the Shapes gallery again and uncheck Lock Drawing Mode, or press Esc on the keyboard.

NOTE

If you're familiar with previous versions of PowerPoint, Lock Drawing Mode is equivalent to double-clicking on a shape on the Drawing toolbar. Be careful though; if you double-click on a shape in PowerPoint 2007, you end up with nothing—literally. It sees your first click as selecting the shape, and then the next click is taken as a de-select.

Drawing Tools Format Tab

Immediately after inserting a shape, a Drawing Tools Format tab appears on the Ribbon to give you the ability to format your shapes. We explain contextual tabs such as this one in Chapter 1, "Introducing the Office 2007 User Interface," when describing the new user interface.

Let's dissect this new tab group by group so that it doesn't seem as overwhelming. As shown in Figure 7.4, from left to right on the Drawing Tools Format tab, we have the Insert Shapes group (mentioned briefly already), Shape Styles, WordArt Styles, Arrange, and Size.

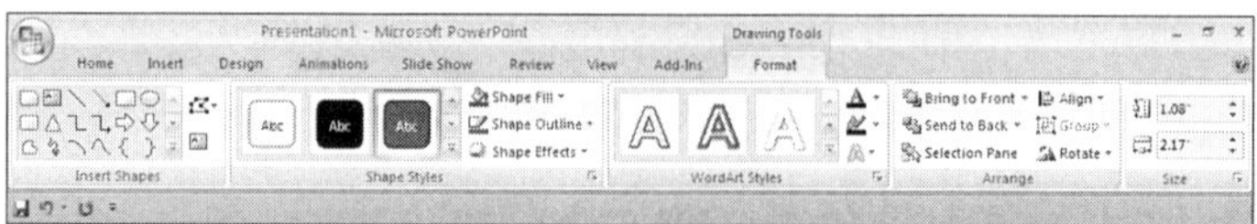

Figure 7.4

The Drawing Tools Format tab.

Using Shape Styles

This group is one of the coolest and most useful places to go to make your shapes look great. Right away, you can see previews for several shape styles. The exact number of styles you can see depends on the width of your window. There are many more to choose from if you expand the gallery by clicking on the button at the bottom right of the gallery (see Figure 7.5).

Hover over any of the shape styles, and Live Preview kicks in and gives you a little taste of what would happen if you actually clicked this style. If you want to apply a style to multiple objects, just select them first using Ctrl+click, or drag to marquee-select them.

The styles available to you can change anything from the shape fill to the shape outline to the text color, or you can add any of the cool new effects to the shape that we talk more about in Chapter 12, "Formatting Shapes, Text, and More."

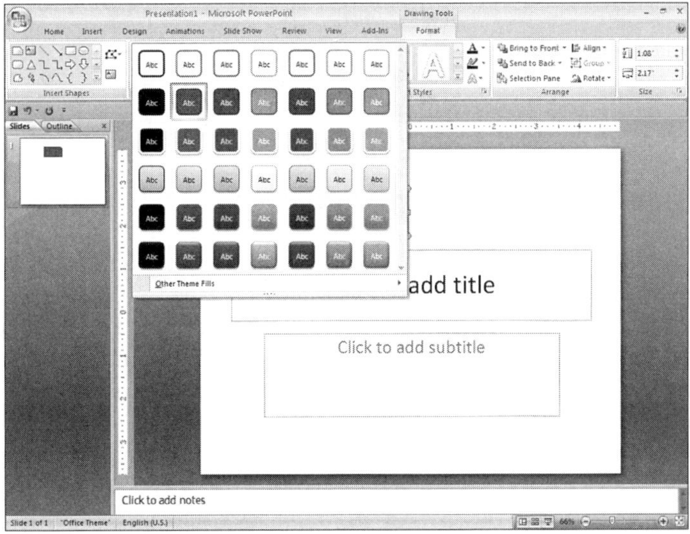

Figure 7.5

A ton of exciting new shape styles are available to format your shapes with a single click.

Applying a Shape Fill

If you're adventurous enough to pass on the preset shape styles offered in the gallery, you always have the option of changing different attributes of the shape yourself. Let's look at one quick way of using the Drawing Tools Format tab to add a fill. (Chapter 12 goes into much more detail on shape formatting.)

To customize the fill of your shape, first click on the Shape Fill button (see Figure 7.6) to the right of the styles gallery.

Just as color scheme colors were displayed prominently in previous versions of PowerPoint, the Theme Colors are located on the top row of the color picker. (Learn more about themes in Chapter 11, "Dissecting Themes.") The rest of the color picker contains tints of the theme colors. Located below this is a set of Standard Colors you might be interested in, followed by No Fill for when you want the shape to be filled with nothing. Clicking any of these sets the fill color on the shape.

We've only grazed the surface of fills here. You will learn much more about fills—including picture, gradient, and texture fills—in Chapter 12.

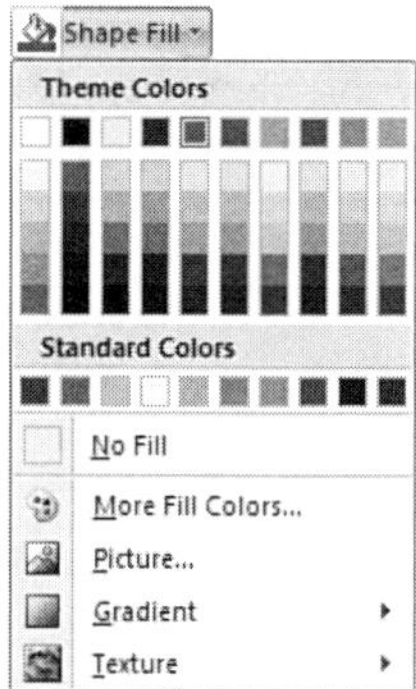

Figure 7.6

The Shape Fill button is your portal to modifying the innards of your shape.

New Shapes

Office users have requested that new shapes be added to the product, and in PowerPoint 2007, Microsoft listened. The shapes are still segmented into groups such as Lines, Basic Shapes, Block Arrows, Flowchart, Stars and Banners, Callouts, and Action Buttons. However, there's an increase in the number of shapes in each group between PowerPoint 2003 and PowerPoint 2007; there's a new Equation Shapes group, and you can notice subtle improvements in even classic shapes such as hearts and arrows.

NOTE

The shape improvements in PowerPoint 2007 are too massive to fully document in this book. But, we mention one subtle example here—block arrows. In PowerPoint 2003, if you stretched a block arrow very wide, the entire arrow grew proportionally; so for large arrows, you would get a very large arrowhead. Though this could be mitigated by manually adjusting the yellow diamond (more details later in this chapter), the process was not fun. In PowerPoint 2007, block arrows "limo stretch," meaning stretch like a limousine. If you stretch a PowerPoint 2007 block arrow very wide, the body of the arrow grows, but the arrowhead stays the same size, which is usually what you want.

Creating Custom Shapes

The cookie cutter shapes in the gallery aren't enough to satisfy your thirst for shapes? No problem. Create your own.

Choosing a Shape Tool

From the Drawing group on the Home tab, click the Shapes button and select Freeform or Scribble. These are the last two items in the Lines section in the large Shapes drop-down (see Figure 7.7).

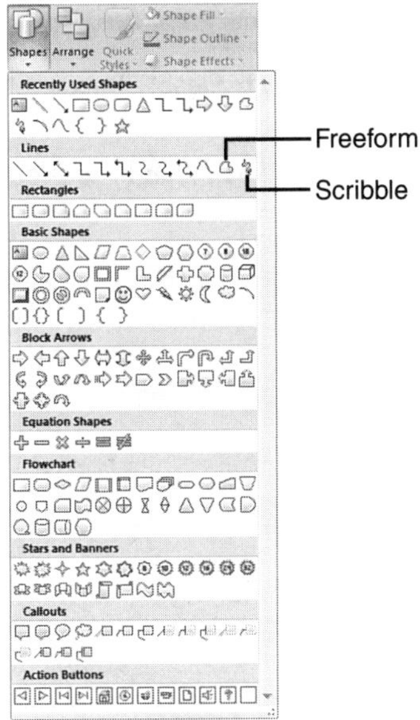

Figure 7.7

The Freeform and Scribble tools in the Shapes drop-down.

With the Freeform tool selected, click to create a point, move the mouse to a new location, and click. A new point is added and a line appears between the two points. Continue this process until you're finished creating your shape. Double-click or press Esc to stop creating new points. Figure 7.8 shows an example of something crazy we drew. Scribble is less structured and just lets you...well...scribble.

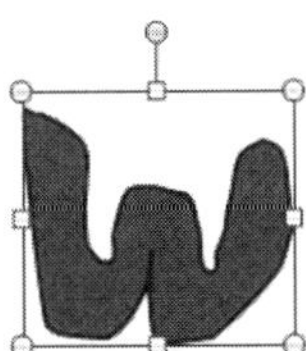

Figure 7.8

The Freeform and Scribble tools allow you to release your inner creative beast. This one was made with the Scribble tool.

NOTE

Similar to Freeform and Scribble, the Arc tool—which is near the two in the Shapes drop-down—can be used to create custom lines.

Editing Shapes

Once inserted, these shapes are infinitely malleable. Impossible, you say? There's no way they could be that flexible, you say? Let's edit some points:

1. Right-click on the shape you just created, and you should see the contextual menu shown in Figure 7.9. Select the Edit Points command.

Figure 7.9

You can find the Edit Points command when right-clicking a Freeform or Scribble shape.

2. When Edit Points is selected, you enter Edit Points mode, where you can move vertices of the shape and also drag pieces of an existing line to create a new point (see Figure 7.10).

Figure 7.10

Edit Points mode allows you to drag points on the shape to change it. The red line gives you a preview of how it will look.

EDITING LINE SEGMENTS AND POINTS

In this mode, if you right-click on a line segment, more options are available to create curved line segments, close off a path, and basically help you create a custom shape that isn't pasted in as a picture and will actually "act like a shape." Acting like a shape means that it is fully editable and themeable just like any of the premade shapes you can insert.

Similarly, right-clicking on an existing point gives you the option to create a smooth, straight, or corner point in addition to adding a new point or deleting the one selected.

TIP

When you're in Edit Points mode, the cursor looks different when you hover over a point compared to when you hover over a line segment. Make sure that you see the correct cursor before right-clicking, so you don't accidentally edit a point when you're trying to edit a line segment, or vice versa. The points cursor has a rectangle center with four arrows coming out of it, whereas the lines cursor looks like a cross with no arrows.

It can often be hard to manage all the points that are editable on one shape. Try zooming in using the zoom bar at the bottom-right corner of your PowerPoint window to make everything bigger.

HIDING PORTIONS OF PICTURES

Let's take a look at an interesting example of a use of Edit Points.

Suppose that your favorite photo and image editor is broken or too hard to use, and you would like to hide part of a picture.

1. Insert the picture into the Presentation.
2. Click the Freeform tool, as shown previously in Figure 7.7, to begin inserting a custom shape.
3. Draw a shape around the area you want to cover up (see Figure 7.11). This should be a simple shape, where you click, release, move, click, release, move, and so on. If you instead click and drag to draw the shape, PowerPoint adds many endpoints to your custom shape, which might be difficult to edit later.

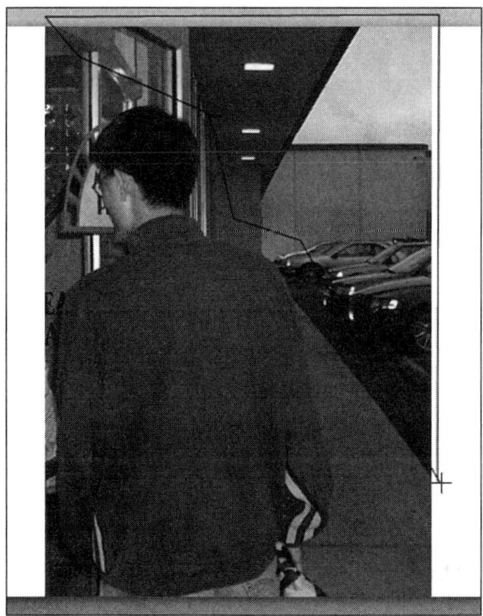

Figure 7.11

Let's hide the right side of this picture by covering it with a custom shape. You can be less precise in this step since step 6 will fix it up.

4. To remove the outline, go to the Drawing Tools Format tab's Shape Styles group and select Shape Outline, No Outline.
5. Fill the shape with the color of the background that you want to use to hide the picture by choosing the Drawing Tools Format tab, and then in the Shape Styles group, click Shape Fill (see Figure 7.12).

TIP

In Figure 7.12, we've simply filled the shape with a solid white color, but if you want the shape to take on the fill of the slide background, try using a slide background fill. See the "Background Fill" section in Chapter 12.

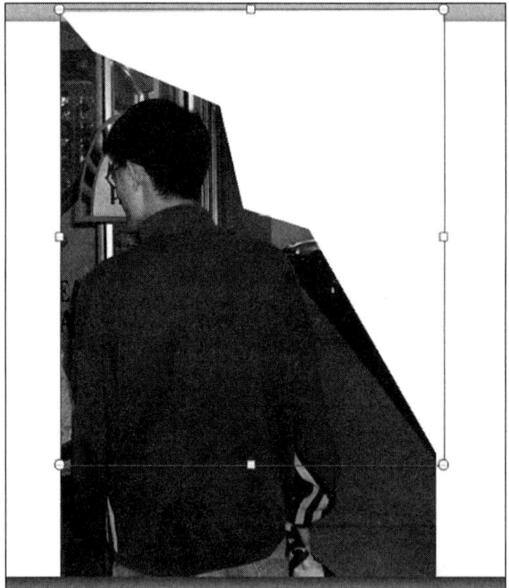

Figure 7.12

Fill the custom shape to hide the picture. Remember, this shape you just made is just like any other shape—you can do anything to it!

6. Modify the existing points, create new ones, and curve the lines to exactly fill up the space you want to cover.

Using Connectors to Save Time

Office lines are the smartest shapes you will ever meet. They're ideal for the perfectionist, the indecisive, and the lazy.

NOTE

In PowerPoint 97–2003, there were lines and there were connectors. Lines were...well...lines. Connectors had the special behavior described in this section, where the ends stuck to other shapes. In PowerPoint 2007, the two concepts are merged. Static, non-connectable lines are no more, and the combined concept is simply called a "line." To accommodate those who just want lines to work the way they always have, as well as to appease the crowd who never connected their lines to anything, the new lines were made slightly less sensitive than old school Office 2003 connectors.

The perfectionist creates a presentation full of shapes and inserts arrows and lines to represent relationships between ideas, and then realizes that he needs a few rectangles by a few pixels each, which requires manually updating all the lines (see Figure 7.13). For a more complicated diagram, repositioning all the shapes would take hours alone, not to mention updating all the arrows and relationships.

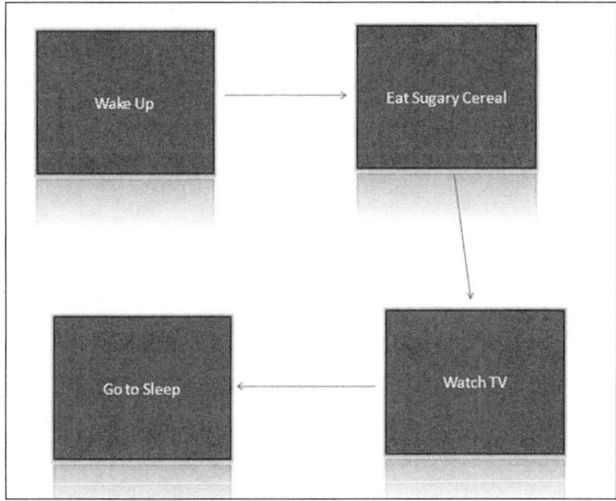

Figure 7.13

You would be hating life if you had to move this shape, along with all the lines attached to it, somewhere else. Each shape and line would have to be individually moved after moving the first shape.

TIP

For simpler diagrams, consider using a SmartArt diagram instead of creating your own from scratch. They usually look better than anything you can make yourself in a short amount of time. For more information about SmartArt, see Chapter 5, "Diagrams and SmartArt."

This is where using connected lines saves you time and makes it super easy to reposition everything later.

How to Connect

First, add a bunch of shapes to your slide. We need shapes so that we have something to connect.

Next, to insert a line, go to the Drawing group on the Home tab and click Shapes. Insert one of the first couple of lines in the Lines section.

To connect a line with something, simply

1. Move the end of a line close to another shape until you see the shape's red connection sites light up (see Figure 7.14). Make sure that you're dragging just the endpoint of the line and not the entire line, or this won't work.
2. Release the line end on top of one of the connection sites to dock it there. If the line end turns red, you know that you've successfully docked.

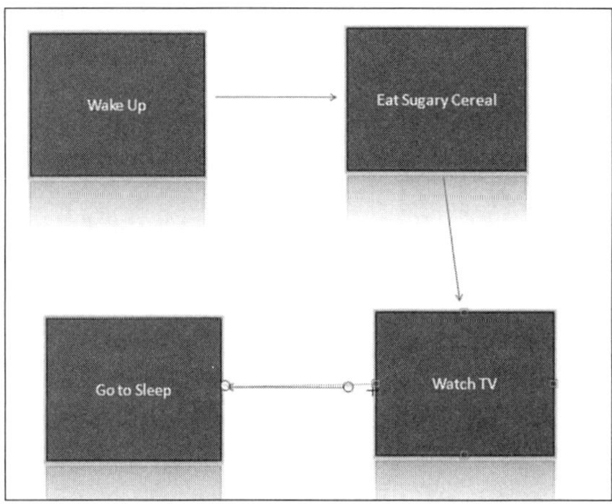

Figure 7.14

When you move the end of a line near another shape, the shape's connection sites will light up, showing you where you can dock the line.

By connecting lines with other shapes, the lines will remember what they're connected to and automatically reroute when those objects move. This happens whether the connections are moved, rotated, resized, or flipped (see Figure 7.15). How cool is that?

TIP

In addition to moving the ends of existing lines to connect them to objects, you can also create a connection when first creating a line. After choosing a line from the new Shapes drop-down, move the crosshairs cursor near a shape, and you should see the connection points light up in red.

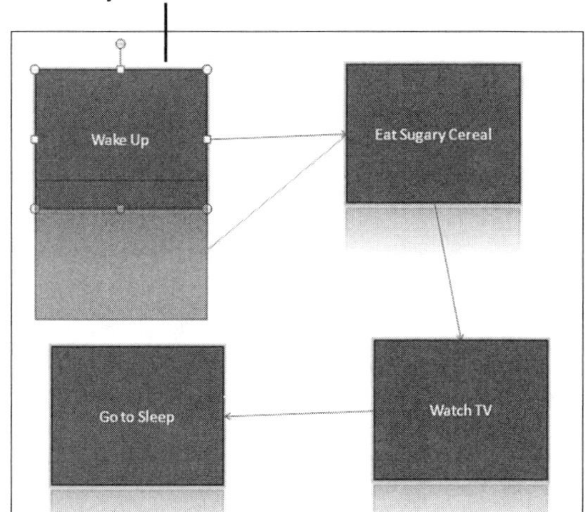

Figure 7.15

After being connected, the line moves when the shape moves.

Rerouting Lines

If you don't like how PowerPoint draws the line after you've docked the two line ends to different objects, you have the ability to reroute the line so that it goes where you want it to go. This command finds the closest connection sites between two objects and moves the line there. You can find the rerouting command by right-clicking a connector and choosing Reroute Connectors.

Alternatively, if you know exactly how you want the line to connect, just select the end of a line and manually drag the end to another connection spot.

NOTE

PowerPoint is inconsistent with its "line" and "connector" terminology. In the Ribbon, when you're inserting a line from the Home tab, Drawing group, Shapes gallery, you insert them from the section of the Shapes gallery. When you right-click a line, however, the contextual menu has both a Reroute Connectors and a Connector Types option. Rest assured, though, that although there was a difference in previous versions of Office, in 2007, there's no difference between a line and a connector.

Customizing Lines

Connectable lines are customizable and come in three main flavors: straight, elbow, and curved (see Figure 7.16). They are your be-all and end-all tools for creating any sort of organizational chart or diagram that involves any sort of flow, direction, or relationship among various components (well, except for SmartArt; see Chapter 5).

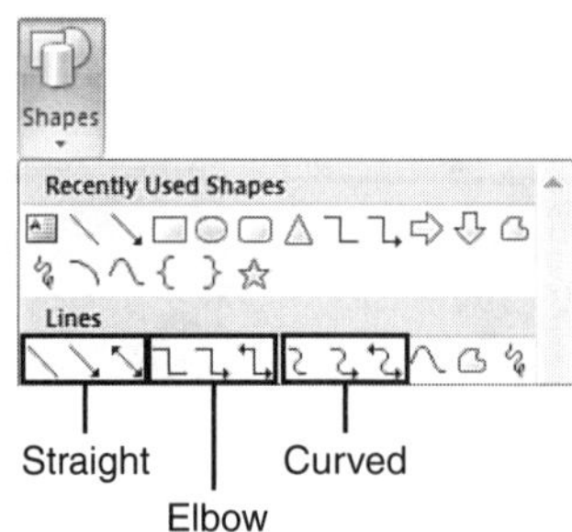

Figure 7.16

The three different types of connectable lines are straight, elbow, curved—each of which can have different end types: no arrow, arrow, and double arrowed.

Don't forget! Lines can be formatted with different widths, line styles, and colors, as well as arrows at one end, both ends, or none at all. Learn more about formatting in Chapter 12.

What Do Those Yellow Diamonds Do?

Some shapes have a yellow diamond adjust handle, which can modify how the shape looks by changing certain parts of its geometry. Notice how this smiley face shape has the yellow diamond in the middle of the mouth. This is called an adjust handle. You can drag the adjust handle up to make the shape sad or ambivalent (see Figure 7.17).

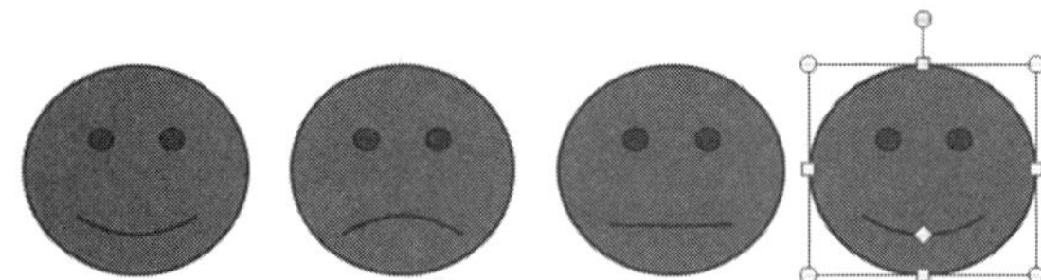

Figure 7.17

Here's a typical smiley face autoshape. Notice the yellow diamond indicating an adjust handle on its mouth. By dragging the diamond up, the smile inverts and is now a frown.

Watch for the yellow diamond whenever you insert a shape. It's just one more way to customize a shape so that it looks more the way you like. It also makes the number of possible shapes endless (see Figure 7.18). You can change any type of arrow, callout, or any other shape into exactly what you're looking for.

Most shapes have a stick at the top with a green circle. Clicking and dragging the circle lets you rotate the shape. You can find more tips about the rotation stick in Chapter 14 ("Positioning Slide Elements" in the "Rotate Shortcuts" section).

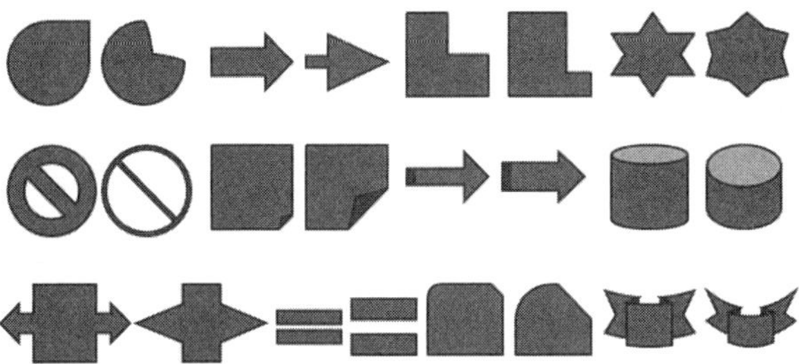

Figure 7.18

Here's a little taste of some of the variations on shapes when adjusted.

Like the yellow diamonds, WordArt with a text Transform effect also has a diamond-shaped adjust handle. These are purple instead of yellow. It seems weird that it's a different color, but it's so that you can have an adjustable shape that contains adjustable, transformed text and you won't be confused which handle controls what. You can find these text effects on the Format ribbon tab by going to the WordArt Styles group and clicking Text Effects, and then choosing Transform.

The Brand New Selection Pane

One of the trickiest part of having many objects and shapes on a slide is selecting one that is hidden by others or has only a small part visible because of other obstructions on your slide. To solve this, a new Selection pane was added to PowerPoint 2007 (see Figure 7.19).

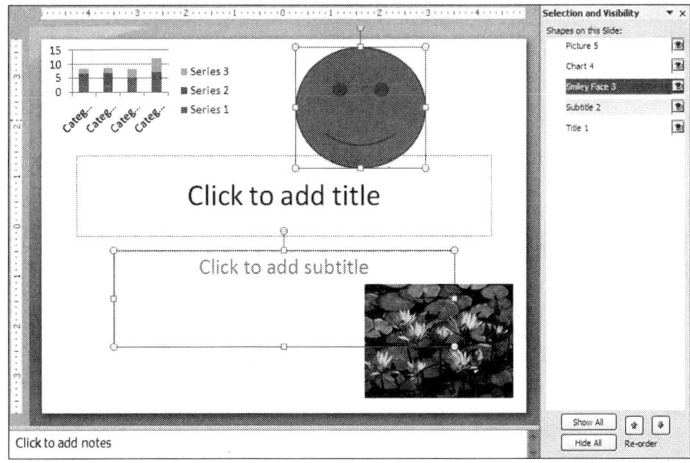

Figure 7.19

PowerPoint 2007's new Selection pane.

NOTE

PowerPoint 2003 had a similar Select Multiple Objects dialog. However, it was a hidden power user feature that was not accessible by default from any of the toolbars or menus.

To activate the Selection pane, go to the Home tab in the Editing group, and click Select. Then, choose Select Pane from the drop-down.

Now you can click on items in this pane, and it selects the corresponding object in your slide. Click on the text of the object to change its name for use later when you need to refer to this object, such as for Custom Animations or Action Settings. This is the best way to change the name of an object and to distinguish it from others.

If you hold down the Ctrl key and click on other items, they are also selected. However, not all selection behaviors apply. For example, the Shift+click operation does not select multiple objects.

The eyeball icon to the right of each item toggles the visibility of the object when clicked. An open eyeball means that the object is visible, but when clicked, it becomes a blank square; you will notice that the shape is no longer visible on the slide. If you hide a shape here, it is invisible throughout PowerPoint, including during a slideshow.

This is a great tool to help you select objects that are behind others, as well as change the depth level (z-order of the objects) because the Selection pane treats the objects on the top as the topmost objects in the slide. Use the Re-order up and down arrow buttons to change the order of the objects.

NOTE

PowerPoint objects, such as shapes, all have depth, or z-order. If you move one shape so that it overlaps with another, one of the two shapes always stays on top. The bottom shape is said to have greater "depth" and a lower "z-order." You can change which shape appears on top by right-clicking one of the shapes and using Bring to Front and Send to Back to change its depth. The Selection pane arrows also change the order.

TAKE A SHORTCUT WITH THE TAB KEY

Are you one of those people who hates to use the mouse? Then there's good news! You can still select shapes/objects and fill them with text without ever leaving the comfort of your keyboard.

Yes, we're talking about the Tab key. Pressing Tab cycles through the existing shapes and objects on the current slide so that you can save yourself a click or two and a potential carpel tunnel injury. If you don't have anything selected, Tab selects the placeholders in order and then any other objects on the slide.

After you have selected a placeholder, shape, or text box that you want to type into, press Enter to enter text mode and type whatever you want. When you're done, press Esc once to exit back out to the top level and resume tabbing to move around again.

Embedding Objects from Other Applications

One of our favorite things about Microsoft is that all its children play nicely together, and PowerPoint is a good citizen in the Microsoft application community. Insert Object is a perfect example of using OLE technologies to integrate objects from different applications into others.

NOTE

OLE stands for object linking and embedding, pronounced oh-*lay*, as in "Oil of Olay." OLE tries to accomplish a marriage between various applications, where parts of one application can be hosted inside another application. Think of it as being able to insert a Word document or an Excel spreadsheet inside your presentation. It's not just limited to Microsoft Office applications, though, and you can embed anything inside PowerPoint that obeys the OLE interfaces. The first version of Office to support OLE 2 was Office 95.

The entries in the Insert Object menu are created based on the applications installed on your computer that support exporting an OLE object. By default, most of the Office applications support this, so if you have a spectacular Visio diagram full of intricate flow charts and diagrams and want to use it in a presentation, Insert Object is the way to go.

On the Insert tab, go to the Text group and click Object. Choose an Object type to create something new (see Figure 7.20). For example, you can embed an Excel spreadsheet inside of PowerPoint by choosing Microsoft Office Excel Worksheet. Or, select the Create from File option and point to an existing file.

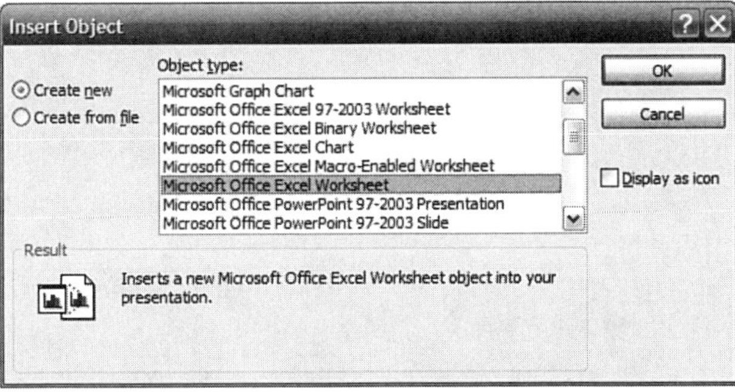

Figure 7.20

Choosing Object from the Insert tab opens the Insert Object dialog for creating OLE objects.

Suppose that you then want to edit this embedded object. Simply double-click on the object to "activate" it. It's actually running the other program, only inside of PowerPoint. Notice in Figure 7.21 that we're editing the Excel worksheet inside of PowerPoint. Even the Ribbon tabs are Excel specific.

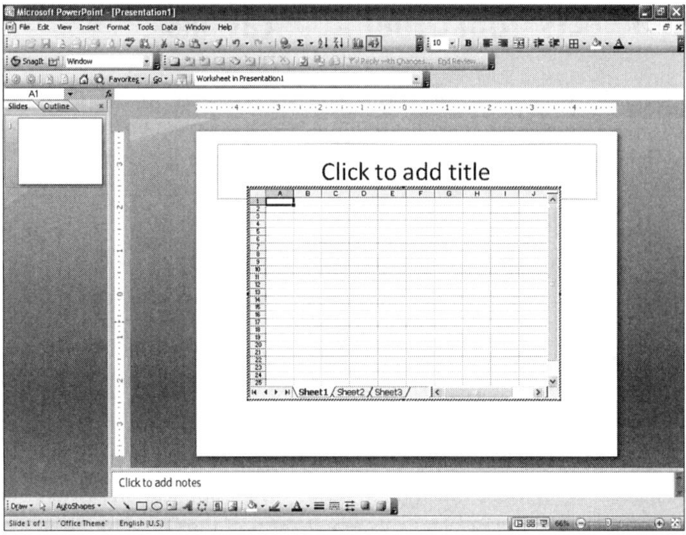

Figure 7.21

When activated, an OLE object acts just as it would in its native host application.

To return to normal PowerPoint editing mode, simply click outside your newly inserted object, and you will see a deactivated OLE object. When deactivated, an OLE object looks much like a picture or screenshot of the current state of the object.

THE ESC KEY

The Esc key—you know, the top-left button on your keyboard—lets you abort many operations in PowerPoint. It lets you easily change your mind when

- You're *dragging out a new shape* to insert, but you totally change your mind. Press Esc, and no shape is inserted.
- You're *resizing* something by dragging one of the resize dots on the side. Press Esc, and the object reverts to its original size.
- As long as you don't release the mouse button, it lets you easily change your mind while *moving* something. Press Esc, and the object returns to its original position.
- Pressing Esc lets you move out one level in a selection. For example, if you're *editing text inside a placeholder*, press Esc, and the placeholder is selected instead. Or if you're inside an OLE object, pressing Esc a few times will exit OLE editing and move you back out to the slide.
- No matter what you have selected, pressing Esc a few times lets you deselect everything on the slide.

Of course, after you've already done the insertion, resize, or move, if you change your mind, just press Ctrl+Z to undo the operation. But Esc can save you a few precious seconds.

Grouping Shapes and Objects

Grouping shapes and objects is an excellent way to maintain order in your festooned presentation.

After you have positioned shapes and objects in a manner you like, group them so that you won't have to modify each one individually. This is particularly useful when you combine shapes to create new ones.

To do so, select the shapes you want to group, right-click one of the selected shapes, select Group and then select Group again.

Now you're left with a set of selection handles surrounding the objects you grouped (see Figure 7.22). You can resize/move/flip/rotate and perform any operation on this group that you could on a shape. You can even group several groups!

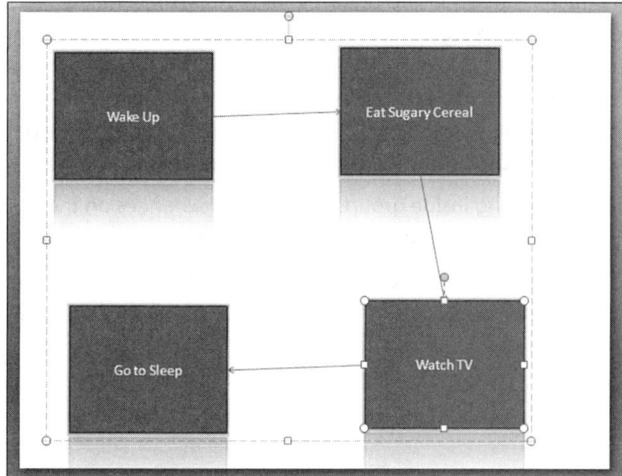

Figure 7.22

A group of shapes.

Ungrouping and Regroup

Say that you changed your mind and don't want a group after all. Simply ungroup by right-clicking the group and choosing Group, Ungroup, and the group is returned to individual objects and shapes. Then, perform whatever modifications you would like.

Oops, we changed our minds. We actually want a group after all. Instead of again going through all the trouble of figuring out what shapes belonged to your group, simply right-click that shape again and choose Regroup. PowerPoint is smart enough to remember what was grouped last and combines them into one group again.

Even if some of the shapes in your original shape are deleted, PowerPoint does its best to regroup any surviving shapes. If all but one shape is deleted, however, the Regroup command is disabled.

Also note that regroup information is not saved in the presentation, so if you ungroup, save a presentation, and reopen the presentation, you can no longer regroup. That group is lost.

Group Trivia

Now that we've covered the basics of groups, let's cover some more interesting trivia about PowerPoint groups:

- New to PowerPoint 2007, Ctrl+G groups items together, due to popular demand. In previous versions of PowerPoint, this brought up the Grids and Guides dialog (learn more about Grids and Guides in Chapter 14, which is about positioning). Ctrl+Shift+G ungroups an existing group.
- Before PowerPoint 2007, items inside groups could not be moved or resized. Ungrouping and regrouping was much more common in order to make last minute positioning tweaks. In PowerPoint 2007, objects inside groups can be moved to your heart's content, and the group updates its size to accommodate the changes. You can even remove items from a group without regrouping. But even in PowerPoint 2007, groups inside groups cannot be updated. Only the top-level group and the bottom-level shapes can be modified without ungrouping.
- Placeholders cannot belong inside groups. If something changes on the master, PowerPoint doesn't have to dive inside every group on every slide to look for placeholders to update.
- PowerPoint stashes information inside groups themselves. For example, if you apply an animation to a group, that information is stored on the group. If you ungroup, that destroys the group and the animation is lost.

8

Tables Like You've Never Seen Before

IN THIS CHAPTER

- Different Ways to Insert a Table
- Copying and Pasting Excel Tables
- Animating Table Cells
- Adding Style to Tables
- Applying Effects
- Advanced Table Facts

Another feature that has been completely revamped for the 2007 Office release is PowerPoint tables. Although the new tables differ quite a bit from the previous versions, you should find the new behavior to your liking. You might not know that tables in Word, Excel, and PowerPoint are all different. This chapter familiarizes you with the PowerPoint flavor.

Different Ways to Insert a Table

As with most objects, head to the Insert tab on the ribbon to find the Table button.

The Grid

From the Table button, a drop-down reveals a grid of 10 columns and 8 rows of boxes. At the bottom of the drop-down, you see the Insert Table, Draw Table, and Excel Spreadsheet options (see Figure 8.1).

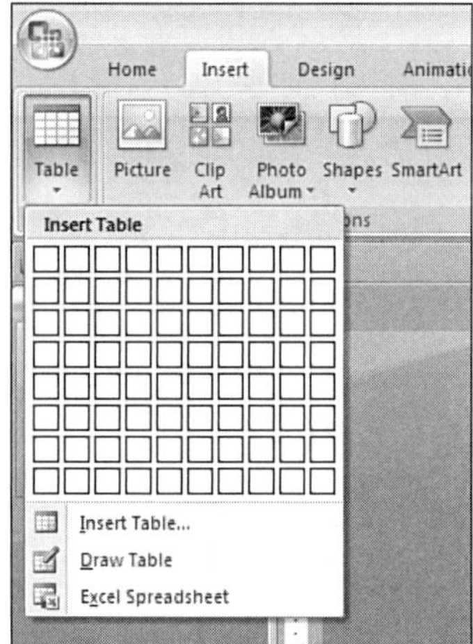

Figure 8.1

The drop-down revealed from clicking Insert Table.

This top part of the drop-down containing the set of boxes is pretty cool. You can choose the size of both the rows and columns by clicking and dragging with the mouse, rather than having to input exact rows and columns. It gives you a visual representation of the table rather than forcing you to calculate the size of your table in your head, visualizing how many rows and columns, and then entering that information. In addition, a preview of the table is shown as it would be inserted in your slide. Simply drag to select the desired size of the table and click to insert it (see Figure 8.2).

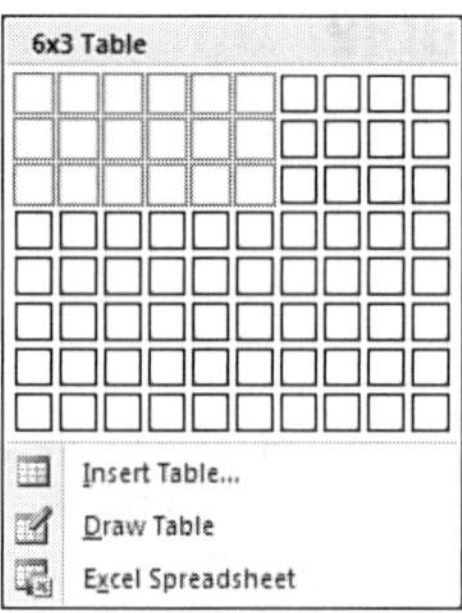

Figure 8.2

Insert a table by choosing its size via the mouse and a set of boxes.

Insert Table Dialog

However, if you want a table larger than the maximum 10x8 cell table that is allowed from the Table button drop-down, click the Insert Table option, as seen in Figure 8.1. This brings up the Insert Table dialog (see Figure 8.3).

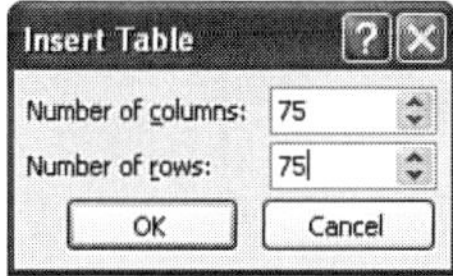

Figure 8.3

The Insert Table dialog enables you to customize the size of your table grid.

This will look familiar if you have ever inserted a table in previous versions of PowerPoint. Enter a number for the rows and columns or use the up and down arrows to increment and decrement.

NOTE

A subtle yet important difference here between PowerPoint 2007 and PowerPoint 2003 is that the maximum number of rows and columns has increased from 25x25 to 75x75 in PowerPoint 2007.

Draw Table

The Draw Table option is interesting in that it lets you click and drag to select a region that will become a table. The main advantage is that it lets you set the overall height and width of your table, which is useful if you know ahead of time what space you want the table to occupy.

But because it doesn't know how many rows or columns you want, the default is 1 and 1, so you end up with one cell in your table (see Figure 8.4). After this is done you can increase the number of rows and columns to create the rest of your table.

NOTE

A neat feature available now is the ability to specify a table's height and width on the ribbon. With a table or table cell selected, click on the Layout tab under Table Tools; then find the Table Size group and modify the Height and Width.

Excel Spreadsheet

The Excel Spreadsheet option is not as intuitive as you might think. Remember from Chapter 6, "Rediscover Charts," how inserting a chart would launch Excel and put the applications side by side? When Excel Spreadsheet is selected from the Table button, rather than launching the Excel application, an OLE object containing an Excel Spreadsheet is inserted (see Figure 8.5).

This lets you use the full power of Excel, including all the Excel ribbon tabs, all from inside PowerPoint. To return to PowerPoint when you're done, just click outside the Excel spreadsheet or press Esc on your keyboard.

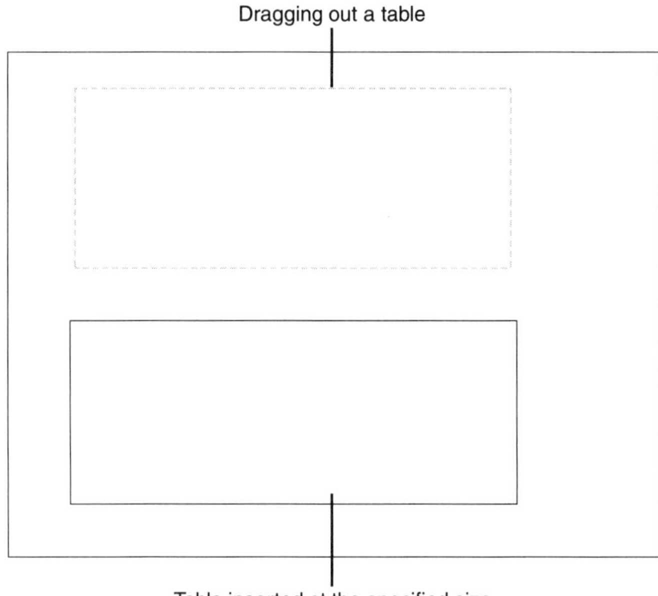

Figure 8.4

Use Draw Table to manually indicate an area that you would like to use for a table.

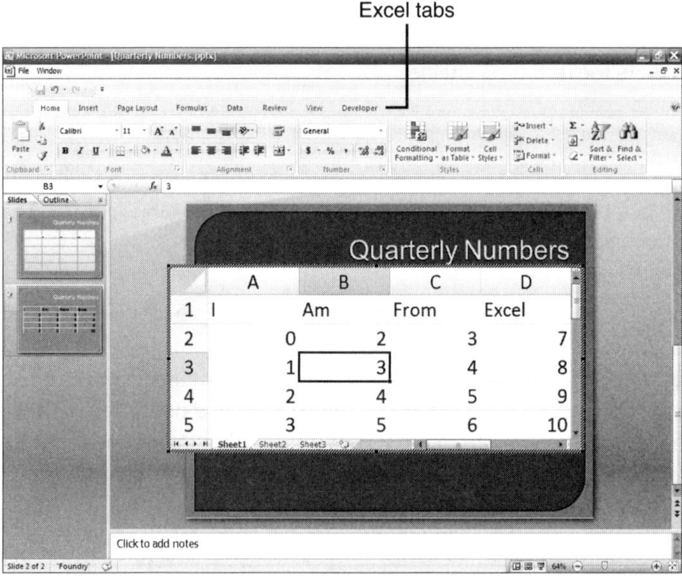

Figure 8.5

Excel Spreadsheet adds an Excel Spreadsheet OLE object into your presentation.

Copying and Pasting Excel Tables

Advanced Another easy way to create a table is to enter your data in Microsoft Excel and then copy and paste it into PowerPoint, as shown in Figure 8.6.

The column and row borders even get copied correctly into PowerPoint, just as they appeared in Excel. These become regular PowerPoint tables, which can be themed and edited in full fidelity inside PowerPoint.

If you feel more comfortable in Excel, you can instead paste the Excel data as Excel OLE data (see Figure 8.7). Although the tables look fairly similar, when you double-click the OLE version spreadsheet, you have access to the same Ribbon tabs that are in the Excel user interface, just as you saw in Figure 8.5. To paste as Excel OLE, go to the Home tab, click the arrow under Paste in the Clipboard group, choose Paste Special, and select Microsoft Office Excel Worksheet Object in the resulting dialog. The downside is OLE objects are a little clunky. Your formatting choices are more limited from within PowerPoint; you cannot format cells individually, for instance.

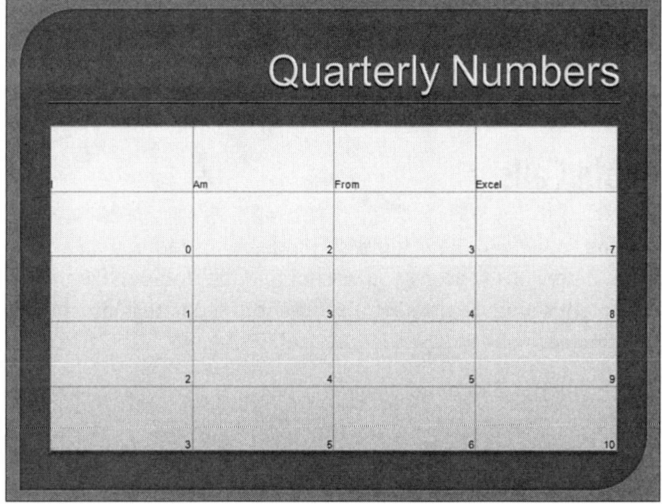

Figure 8.6

Pasting Excel data as a native PowerPoint table.

All this can also be applied to copying and pasting Word tables. Again, by default, a Word table is converted and pasted as a native PowerPoint table. You can use Paste Special to add it as a Word OLE object.

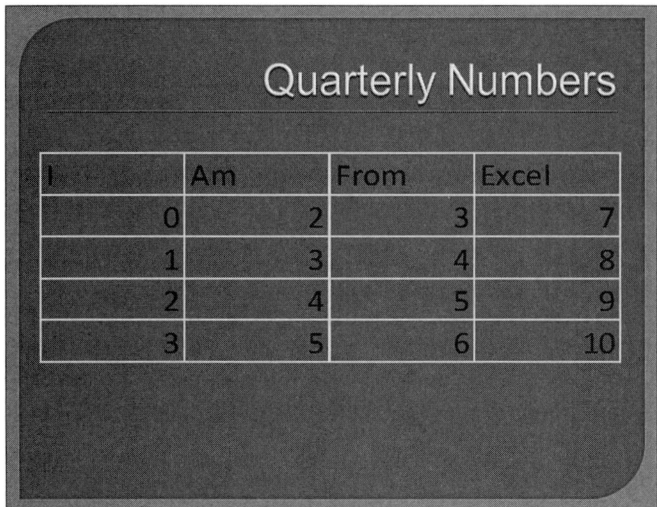

Figure 8.7

Pasting as a Microsoft Office Excel Worksheet Object results in an Excel OLE object.

Animating Table Cells

Advanced Because the PowerPoint 2007 table is a single object rather than a group of individual shapes as in previous versions, you will not find the Ungroup command as an option to use on the table. This might sound devastating if you want to separate it into individual cells for something like animating each one independently.

Fortunately, there's a common workaround that works just as well with a little extra effort. To convert a table into a group of individual shapes, do one of the following:

1. Select a PowerPoint table.
2. Copy the table.
3. Choose Paste Special. You can find this option on the Home tab, in the Clipboard group. (Click the arrow on the Paste button.)
4. Select Picture (Enhanced Metafile). You might have to scroll down in the dialog.
5. Click OK.
6. Now that you have converted the table to a metafile, you can right-click on it and choose Ungroup. You are prompted to make sure that you know what you're doing. Confirm the operation.
7. Now that you have a single group, you can right-click on it and choose Ungroup again.

Alternatively, you can use Save As Picture to achieve the same result:

1. Select the PowerPoint table.
2. Right-click and select Save As Picture.
3. Choose a folder where you want to save the picture and select Enhanced Windows Metafile (.EMF). You might have to scroll down in the dialog to see the option.
4. Click OK.
5. Now that you have saved the table as an enhanced metafile, click Insert Picture and choose the file you saved.
6. Right-click the table object and choose Ungroup.
7. Right-click the table object again and choose Ungroup again to get individual shapes for cells.

Both methods work equally well: The main difference is that the Paste Special method requires you to save the table as a file and then insert it into your presentation.

Now that you have individual shapes for each cell, use the Animations tab to animate them the way you want (see Figure 8.8).

A great thing to do here is select a row of table cells, add a custom animation, and then select all the text for that row and add a custom animation that starts after the cell animation ends. This will create a great-looking effect in which the table cells animate first, followed by the table cell text. Read more about PowerPoint animation in Chapter 15, "Going Beyond Slide-by-Slide."

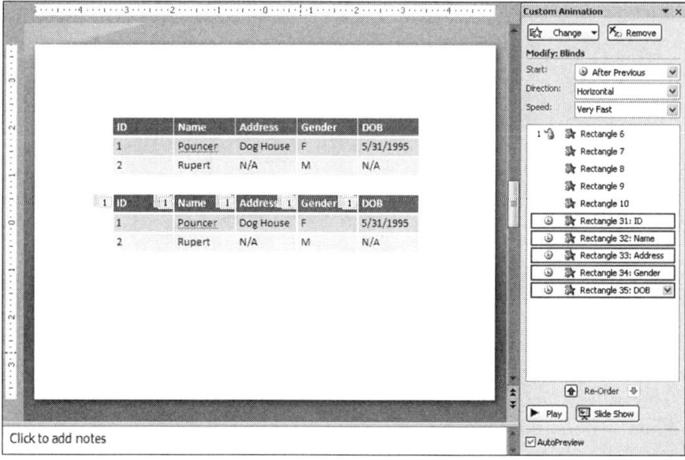

Figure 8.8

After you ungroup your metafile twice, you have a shape for each cell, which allows you to add individual-cell animations.

Adding Style to Tables

New Because tables are the latest addition to improved graphics in PowerPoint 2007, they inherit the ability to be styled. Like most PowerPoint objects, the easiest way to style a table is to select from a gallery of canned choices—this time from the Table Tools Design tab and then choosing from the choices in Table Styles. As you will read in Chapter 11, "Dissecting Themes," these are derived from the presentation's theme.

PowerPoint also makes it easy to apply these common customizations to a table:

- Header row
- Total row
- First column
- Last column
- Banded rows
- Banded columns

These pieces of the table inherit special styling from the current table style when a style is applied to the table. Notice that the Table Style Options group of the Table Tools Design tab has each of these options with a check box next to each (see Figure 8.9). When checked, each option changes the look of one or more columns or rows. Figure 8.10 shows which part of the table changes for each of these effects. Of course, these can be combined so that you get a table with a Total Row and Banded Columns, for instance.

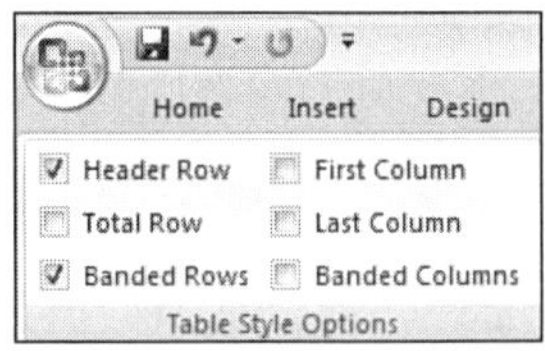

Figure 8.9

The Table Tools Design tab lets you choose which table style options to apply to the currently selected table.

NOTE

Depending on the current table style, checking these boxes might not appear to have any effect. For example, if the current table style is a plain table, checking Total Row won't appear to do anything. If you later change Table Styles to something that makes Total Row formatting visible, formatting for Total Row will appear. Essentially, you're requesting that PowerPoint add a Total Row, but the author of the theme is the final arbiter of whether your table will look good with that change.

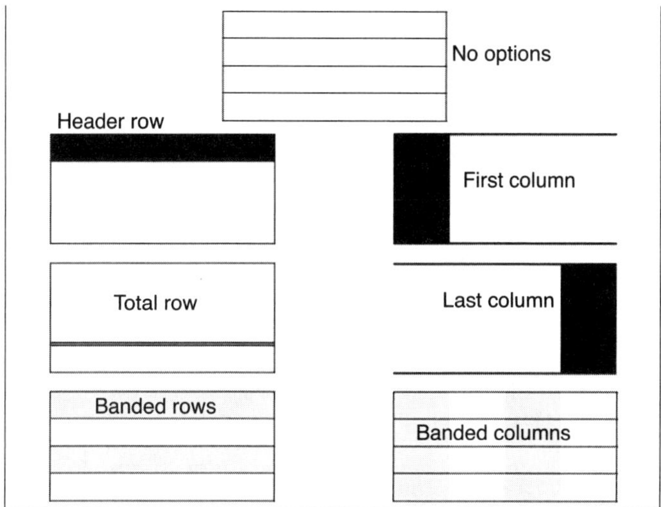

Figure 8.10

Checking each Table Style option applies one of the visual changes shown here. For example, Total Row creates a line right above the last row in the column.

To apply a style, do the following:

1. Select a table.
2. Click on the Table Tools Design tab.
3. Under the Table Styles group, select a Best Match for this Document style that is shown by default, or open the gallery and choose a style that you like (see Figure 8.11). Best Match isn't a specifically labeled style; it is the group of styles that is listed first because it best fits the current theme.

If you select the entire table and apply formatting, such as a fill, any changes you make are applied to each cell rather than to the table as a whole. For example, if you apply a picture fill, each cell in the table will contain that picture.

TIP

The advice here applies only to native PowerPoint tables. For Excel OLE tables, the entire table is treated as one object, and you can apply very limited formatting to the entire OLE object, such as a border around it or a picture or texture fill.

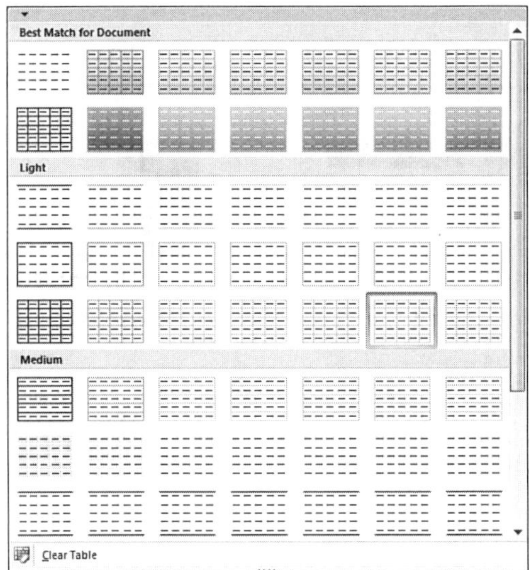

Figure 8.11

The Table Styles gallery.

Applying Effects

New effects in PowerPoint 2007 can also be applied to tables, although they are applied to the entire table for the most part, not individual cells. For example, Shadows and Reflections take effect on the entire table, but Cell Bevels apply on a per-cell basis.

To apply effects, do the following:

1. Select a table.
2. Click on the Design tab. Under the Table Styles group, find the Effects button to the right of the Styles gallery: It is at the bottom of the three buttons on the right.
3. Click the Effects button to open its drop-down list and apply Cell Bevel, Shadow, or Reflection.

To learn more about applying effects in PowerPoint, see Chapter 12, "Formatting Shapes, Text, and More."

Advanced Table Facts

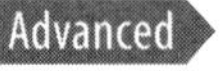

Now we have the basic functions of tables covered, but there are still a few unrelated quirks about how tables work.

Resize

Resizing a table is similar to resizing other objects in PowerPoint. When the table is selected, you see selection handles appear around the table (see Figure 8.12). Use your mouse to grab the middle of any of the four sides and drag your mouse to resize.

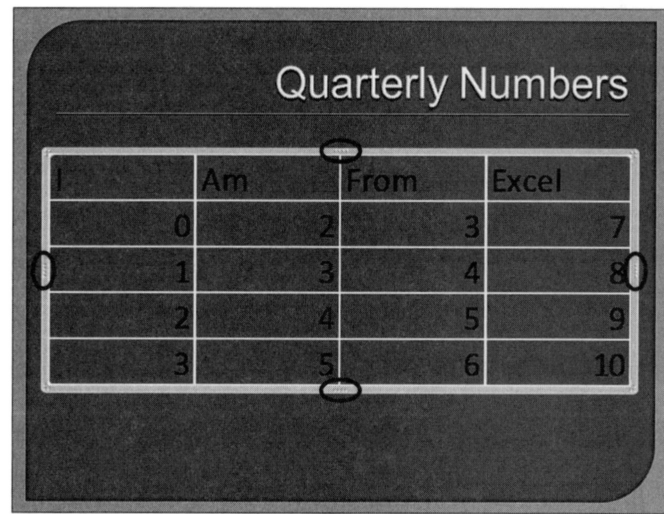

Figure 8.12

Drag the middle of the selection handles around the table to resize a table.

Notice that when you resize a table, the size of your text does not change with it, which might cause your table to have a lot of extra whitespace that you do not necessarily want. If you want your text to resize proportionally with your table, simply hold down the Shift key while you resize and the text font size will change when you resize the table (see Figure 8.13).

You can also modify the table height and width in the Table Size group on the Table Tools Layout tab.

Insert Rows and Columns

Insert a row by clicking the Table Tools Layout tab and then going to the Rows & Columns group. Here, you find commands such as Insert Above, Insert Below, Insert Left, and Insert Row.

When you insert a row, the table itself gets larger and the row is placed either above or below the cell currently selected. However, if you contrast this with what happens when you insert a column, the behavior is different. With a new column, the table width remains the same, but a new column is added, making the existing columns smaller (see Figure 8.14).

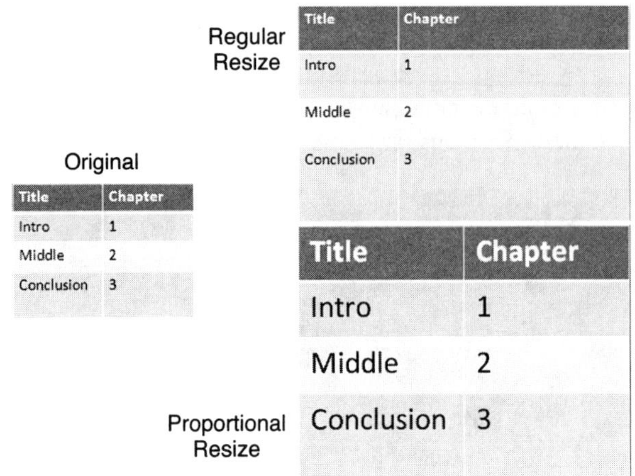

Figure 8.13

Proportional resize versus regular resize.

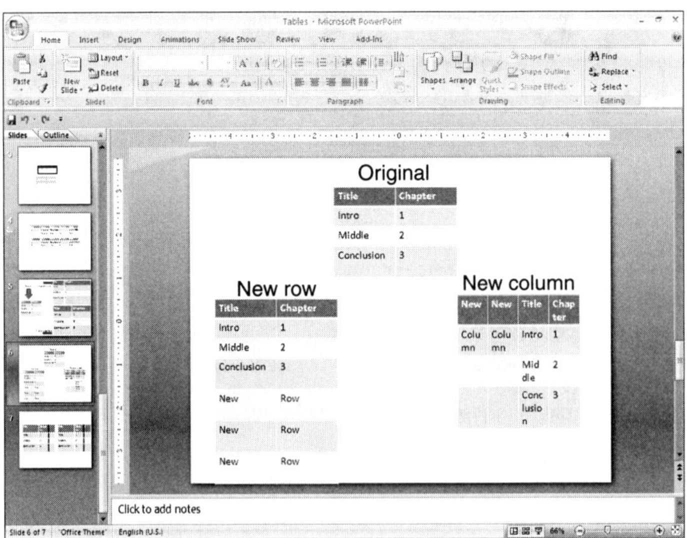

Figure 8.14

Inserting a row adds a new row and makes the table itself bigger in total area. Inserting a column does not increase the size of the table itself, but rather resizes all the existing columns, making them smaller to accommodate the new column.

Cell Sizes

The Cell Size group under the Table Tools Layout tab lets you specify an exact height and width for the current cell. A button to the right of each text box lets you distribute the heights evenly across the selected rows so that all your cells have the same height, or you can distribute widths across the selected columns so that all your cells have the same width.

Cell Margins

The Cell Margins drop-down under Table Tools Layout, Alignment lets you choose between four common margin choices: Normal, None, Narrow, or Wide. If that doesn't accommodate your needs, choose Custom Margins at the bottom, and you can set specific Left, Right, Top, and Bottom margin values.

Splitting and Merging Cells

To split one table cell into two table cells, simply select that cell, go to Table Tools Layout, Merge, and choose Split Cells.

To merge multiple cells into one, select multiple cells, and then click Merge Cells, also on the Merge group.

Draw Table

The Draw Table option inserts row and column dividers when it is applied to an existing table. This is useful when you don't want to go through the trouble of using the Ribbon to split a cell (see Figure 8.15).

You can find Draw Table on the Draw Borders group under Table Tools Design tab . After choosing Draw Table, your cursor turns into a pencil. Use the pencil with your mouse to draw internal borders inside an existing table.

You can also draw diagonally, but it will not create a new cell. Drawing diagonally creates a new table if you start at the corner of the existing table or just selects the content if you start anywhere else.

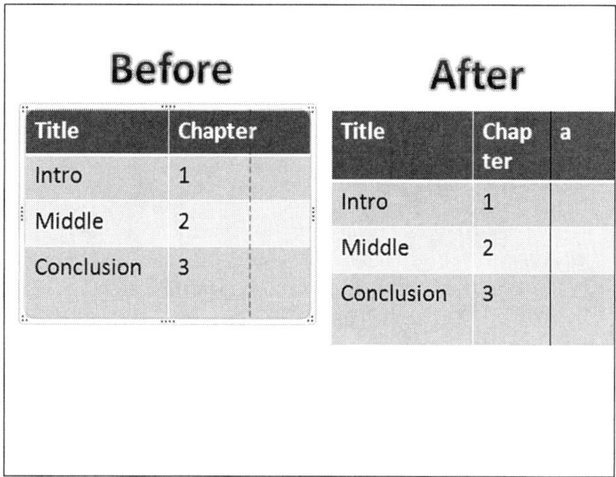

Figure 8.15

Draw Table lets you split rows and columns by drawing a line between existing cells. In the left table, we're using the Draw Table pencil to draw a vertical line down the right column. The table on the right shows how this created an additional column of table cells.

NOTE

Make sure that your cursor is inside an existing cell on the table you want to split cells on. Otherwise, Draw Table will create a new table in your presentation.

9

Inserting Content into PowerPoint

IN THIS CHAPTER

- Using Smart Tags to Customize Pasted Content
- Advanced Paste Techniques
- Reusing Slides
- Using Sounds and Videos Effectively
- Tablet PC Features in PowerPoint (Ink)
- Inserting Mathematical Equations Using Word

At this point, you should be familiar with much of the content you can create from within PowerPoint. This chapter explores the world outside PowerPoint, including pasting content from other applications, using the Slide Library with SharePoint, and inserting audio and video into a presentation.

Using Smart Tags to Customize Pasted Content

Advanced Smart Tags are helpful square menus that appear upon certain operations. Let's look at a few examples of Smart Tags in action.

Paste Smart Tag

Let's see these Smart Tags (also known as Paste Tags) in action:

1. Create a new presentation.
2. Go to the Design tab, Themes group and look at the available themes.
3. In the list of Design Templates, select one of the colorful ones. For this example, we use the Concourse Template.
4. Insert a shape, add some text, and copy it using the Home tab, Clipboard group by clicking Copy or pressing Ctrl+C. Note the color of the shape.

6. Create a new presentation by clicking the Office button and in the New options, choosing Blank Presentation and then Create (or by simply pressing Ctrl+N).
7. Paste the rectangle by navigating to the Home tab, looking at the Clipboard group, and then clicking on Paste (or pressing Ctrl+V). Notice the color is different from what you copied in step 5.

Figure 9.1 shows the progression of the process described in these steps.

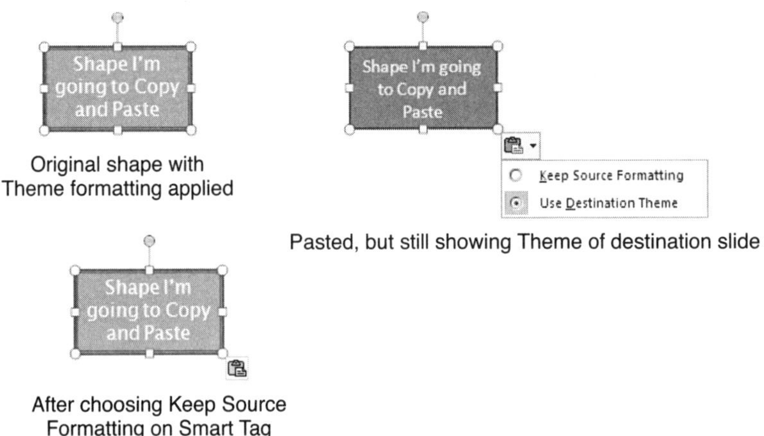

Figure 9.1

The pasted shape is a different color, matching the target presentation's theme until Keep Source Formatting is chosen from the Smart Tag menu.

Notice the little square icon that appeared next to the pasted shape. This is a Smart Tag. Click on it to get the menu to appear (as shown in Figure 9.1). Here are two options. What's currently selected is Use Destination Theme, which means that the shape is taking on the design from the current theme. This new presentation has a different theme from the previous presentation, which is why the shape looks different.

Click Keep Source Formatting. Notice how the shape now takes on the design from the source presentation. If you change your mind, you can easily undo or choose again from the Smart Tag menu.

AutoCorrect Smart Tag

Here's a simpler way to make a Smart Tag appear:

1. Start a new presentation.
2. In the title placeholder, type `teh` and press the spacebar. Notice how PowerPoint AutoCorrect made two corrections to the text. It corrected your spelling to *the* and capitalized the first letter automatically (*The*).
3. Notice the narrow blue line that appeared under The. Hover your mouse over the blue line, and the AutoCorrect Smart Tag will appear. Click the Smart Tag, and you will see what is shown in

Figure 9.2. Here, you have the option to undo what PowerPoint did automatically (choose Undo Automatic Corrections), as well as disable the particular rules that PowerPoint just applied to correct that text (choose Stop Auto-Capitalizing First Letter of Sentences and/or Stop Automatically Correcting "Teh").

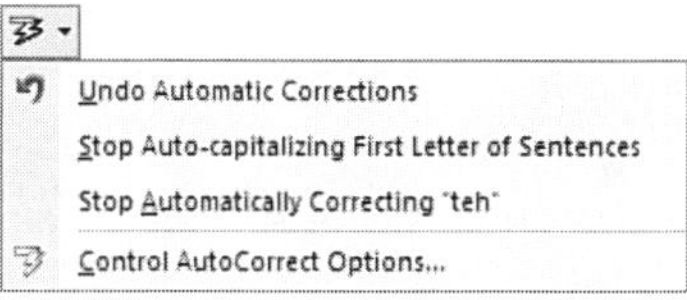

Figure 9.2

Smart Tag options for AutoCorrect.

NOTE

You will also see Paste and AutoCorrect Smart Tags in other Office applications such as Word and Excel.

Overflowing Text Smart Tag

Next, let's look at an entirely different Smart Tag:

1. Create a new presentation and insert a new slide (press Ctrl+M).
2. In the body placeholder, type nine or more bulleted points.
3. The Smart Tag appears in the lower left corner. There are two sets of choices here. The first section lets you choose whether the text should get smaller to stay inside the placeholder, or whether it should stay the same size but be allowed to go outside the placeholder (see Figure 9.3). By default, it's the former.

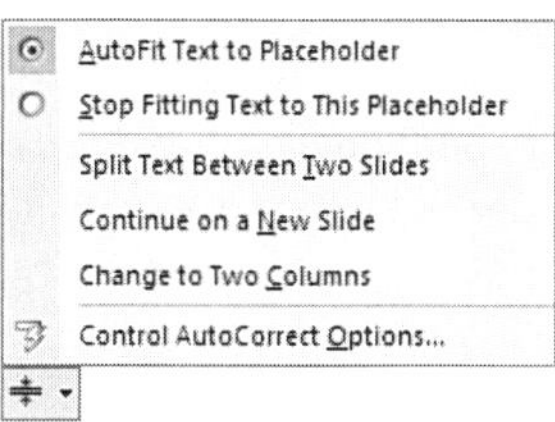

Figure 9.3

A Smart Tag appears when you type a lot of text into a placeholder.

4. The second set of options lets you format the text in various ways.
   - **Split Text Between Two Slides**—Choosing this option lets you take half the text from this placeholder and plop it onto the next slide.

- **Continue on a New Slide**—Choosing this option lets you leave this text as it is and just move to the next slide to continue typing.
- **Change to Two Columns**—Choosing this option lets you leave this text as it is, but converts this slide's layout into two columns so that subsequent text you type can still fit on this slide.

5. Let's do the last one. Click on Change to Two Columns. Now we can continue typing more, and everything will still fit. Notice how there are other options as well for splitting the text onto a second slide or continuing to type on the next slide.

Smart Tags Are Contextual

You will notice that these Smart Tag sections really don't have much to do with each other. One is about fine-tuning pastes; one is about AutoCorrect; and one is about overflowing text. That just goes to show you that Smart Tags aren't specific to any particular type of features. They appear whenever PowerPoint's making a best guess at what you want to do, but still wants to give you the option to tell it to do something different.

If you learn nothing else from this section, the key lesson here is that you should look out for these and click them when you see them because they add some useful options that you won't otherwise see.

TIP

If you know how to program and Smart Tags sound cool to you, Microsoft has a free Software Development Kit (SDK) for writing Smart Tags that work in Word, Excel, and PowerPoint. Download it here: www.microsoft.com/downloads/details.aspx?FamilyID=c6189658-d915-4140-908a-9a0114953721&displaylang=en.

Advanced Paste Techniques

Advanced Here's a little background about how the Windows clipboard works. When you copy something, the program decides what formatting it wants to put onto the clipboard. Say that you copy some fancy text in Word:

T^{hi}s *is* fancy **text**.

Word puts these six formats on the clipboard:

- **HTML**—Yep, this is the same language used to make web pages. Microsoft Office uses it to copy/paste text between different Office applications.
- **The native Word format (Microsoft Office Word Document Object)**—This guarantees that no data gets lost while copying from and pasting to Word.
- **A picture (WMF, EMF)**—This puts an image of the text on the clipboard. Learn more about these formats at http://en.wikipedia.org/wiki/Windows_Metafile.

- **Formatted text (RTF)**—This lets you paste to WordPad and other basic text editors. All the special formatting is preserved.
- **Unformatted text**—This lets you paste into Notepad and other basic text editors. You will lose the underlining and the bold because Notepad doesn't understand formatted text, but at least you get the text itself.
- **Unformatted Unicode Text**—This is similar to unformatted text but has a different encoding.

NOTE

In reality, Word just advertises that it can support these formats. To avoid doing unnecessary work, the data itself isn't pushed to the clipboard until the paste happens or Word is closed.

When you then paste in Word, or to some other program, that program decides which of these clipboard formats it wants to use. For example, if you paste into WordPad, WordPad looks at the six previous formats, picks formatted text as its favorite, and grabs that data from the clipboard.

If you were to paste into PowerPoint, PowerPoint supports all six of the preceding formats, but will pick the first one, HTML. Sometimes this is what you want; sometimes it isn't. Thankfully, if you use PowerPoint as the receiving program, you can tell PowerPoint that you know better and tell it exactly which format you want it to use.

1. First create some fancy text in Word and then copy it to the clipboard (press Ctrl+C).
2. In PowerPoint, go to the Home tab and click the arrow under Paste in the Clipboard group. Select Paste Special to get the Paste Special dialog (see Figure 9.4). You will see that the clipboard contains all six formats mentioned previously.

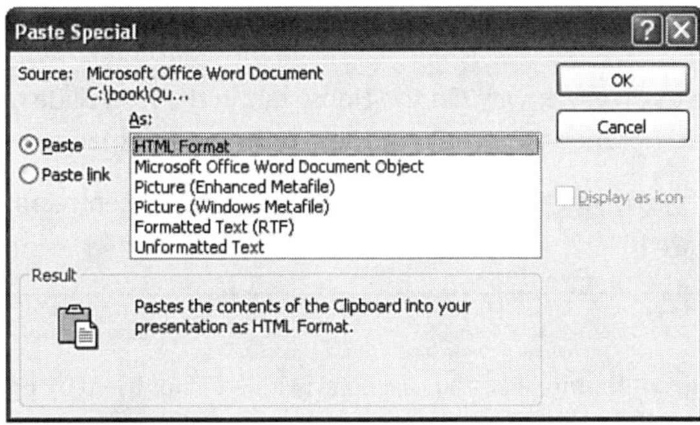

Figure 9.4

Select Paste Special in PowerPoint.

3. Let's say that for some reason I want it to paste as a picture so that I can apply some picture effects to it. I select one of the picture options and click OK.
4. Notice that it comes in as a picture instead of as text. You can verify this by trying to edit the text.

Most of our usage of this feature is very similar to our example in which we want to paste something as a picture:

- If we have a diagram from Visio that we want in our presentation, we can paste it as a picture. This puts the picture in our presentation but prevents it from being changed.
- Select a slide in the PowerPoint thumbnail pane and copy it. If you now paste it, PowerPoint will pick its native format (Microsoft PowerPoint Slide Object) and insert another slide.
- If you pick a picture format using Paste Special though, you can insert slide thumbnail images in your presentations. We've found this useful when creating summary or navigation slides in presentations.

TIP

Office 2007 has a new keyboard shortcut for Paste Special: Ctrl+Alt+V.

Reusing Slides

Advanced In today's world, we are all about recycling and reusing. In PowerPoint, you can do the same thing. Why re-create the same material, or even similar material, over and over again when you can simply reuse it from another source, such as an existing presentation that you or someone else has created?

Reusing a Slide from Another Presentation

Say that you remember having this great slide in another presentation that you want to reuse today. You might open that other presentation, find the slide, copy it, switch back to today's presentation, and then paste.

In PowerPoint 2007, there's an easier way. On the Home tab, in the New Slide group, click Reuse Slides at the bottom. Then click the Open a PowerPoint File link on the workpane.

After you select a file, it shows you thumbnails from the selected presentation, and you can quickly grab just the slides you want.

NOTE

After you see the list of thumbnails, you can quickly insert all of them by right-clicking one of them and choosing Insert All Slides.

If you work for a rich corporation that's deployed Microsoft Office SharePoint Server 2007, you can alternatively choose the Open a Slide Library link. This lets you grab slides from a Slide Library where others from your company might have saved slides that you can grab and reuse.

Reusing Slides with Slide Library

Slide Library is a brand new feature added to PowerPoint 2007 that integrates with Office Microsoft Office SharePoint Server (also known as MOSS).

NOTE

Slide Library only works with Office Enterprise or Office Ultimate, so if you don't have those versions and don't see Slide Library as an option, you know why.

It's an excellent way to reuse slides from various presentations and will help you collaborate with others without having to email around entire presentation files.

A slide library is exactly what it sounds like, a collection of individual slides that sit on a SharePoint server and can be added to by anybody with access to your site. After the library is populated with slides, creating a presentation using existing slides is extremely easy, as you can mix and match slides that other people have created without doing all the work. Say goodbye to the old-fashioned days when you were emailing presentations around, finding your way to the right slide you wanted, selecting all the content, pasting it, and realizing that something was lost in the copy and paste or that you need to do this for dozens of slides and begin to feel overwhelmed.

SETTING UP THE SLIDE LIBRARY

First things first: You must have Microsoft Office SharePoint Server 2007 installed to use with Microsoft Office PowerPoint 2007 Ultimate or Enterprise.

NOTE

After you have a MOSS site set up, make sure that you have given permission to enable Slide Library. This might have to happen on a per user scenario. Also, we don't go into how to set up a MOSS site in this book, but the resources should be available online, or you can ask your favorite IT professional.

After this is all set up and you are able to create your own site content, click on Site Actions and select Create as shown in Figure 9.5.

SHAREPOINT

SharePoint is Microsoft's server companion product to Office. The basic Windows SharePoint Services is free if you're running Windows Server 2003, but the deluxe variant, Office SharePoint Server, is a separate product you pay for. Usually, you will only find these deployed at corporations, so if you don't know what SharePoint is or don't use Office in a corporate environment, you're probably out of luck. Unfortunately, Slide Library is only available with Office SharePoint Server, the more expensive product. Read more about SharePoint at www.microsoft.com/sharepoint/.

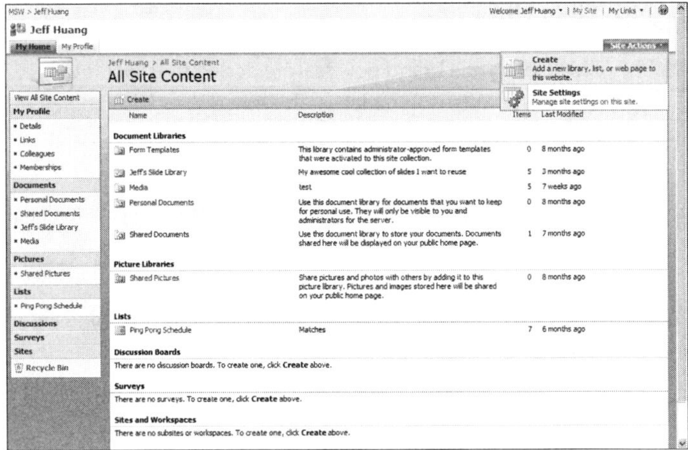

Figure 9.5

From the main SharePoint site, click on Site Actions and then Create in order to get to the option of inserting a Slide Library.

Now you will find yourself with a lot of options for content that you can create, and one of them happens to be a slide library, as shown in Figure 9.6.

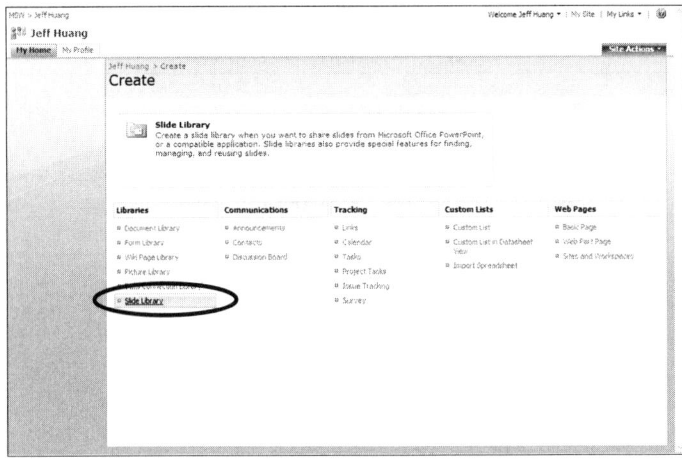

Figure 9.6

Under the Libraries section, select Slide Library. This must be enabled by an administrator.

You will be asked for a name and description of the slide library in addition to whether you want a shortcut made for it and whether you want to create versions of the library.

Now you should have something that looks like a blank slide library waiting for you to fill it with excellent slides.

ADDING TO YOUR LIBRARY

Two methods can be used to add slides to your library: Use PowerPoint to upload slides to the SharePoint site, and use the SharePoint site to grab slides from a PowerPoint presentation.

PUBLISHING FROM POWERPOINT

First, PowerPoint has the capability to publish slides to a SharePoint server, assuming that you know the URL of the site. To do this, first open the presentation that contains the slides you want to upload and make sure that the presentation is saved (otherwise, PowerPoint notifies you that you need to do so). Then click the Office button, select the arrow next to Publish, and then select Publish Slides (see Figure 9.7).

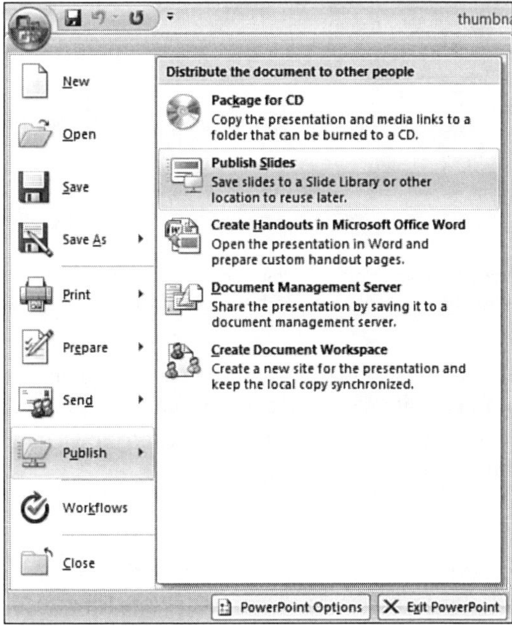

Figure 9.7

The Publish Slides option from the Office button allows you to upload Slides from your presentation to a SharePoint site.

Now you will notice a dialog that looks like the one shown in Figure 9.8 that presents you with all the slides in this presentation. Click the check boxes next to slides to select them or use the Select All button. If you click on the File Name or Description fields, you can edit them; that information will be published along with the slide. Select Show Only Selected Slides if you have many slides and do not care about the ones you are not going to publish. This will give you a better idea of what content is going to end up on your site.

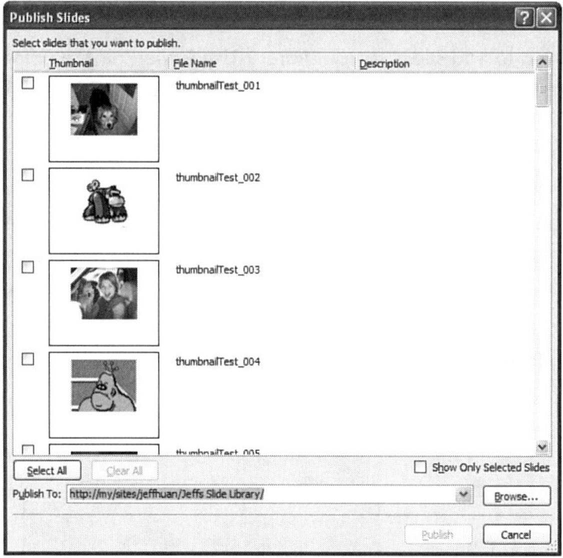

Figure 9.8

The dialog to Publish Slides lets you customize pieces of the slide that will end up on the SharePoint site. Click on the fields under File Name and Description in order to modify that information for a specific slide.

Make sure that only the slides you want to upload are checked and then select Publish. Notice that the dialog has gone away. You might be puzzled at first if you already have your SharePoint site open in a web browser because the site does not automatically refresh and it might look like nothing has happened. Press F5 to refresh your browser to see the changes.

ADDING SLIDES FROM SHAREPOINT

Now we will show you how to grab slides from the SharePoint site and add them to the library. From the SharePoint site, select Upload and click on Publish Slides (see Figure 9.9).

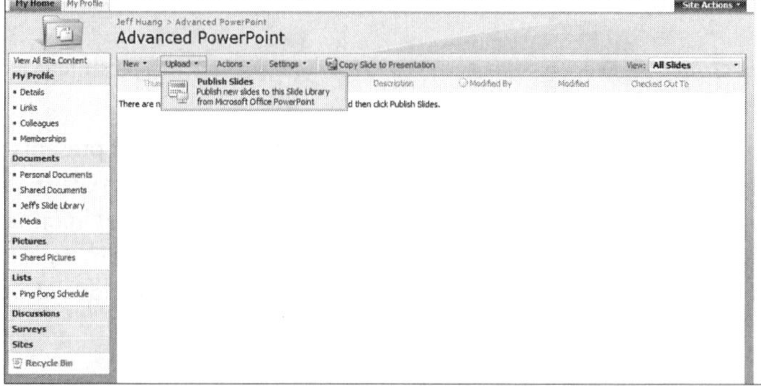

Figure 9.9

Click the Upload button on the SharePoint site to insert new slides into the library.

CAUTION

If the Windows Explorer interface is used to access the library, it might corrupt the slide library. This seems to be a bug in the current version that might be fixed, but be warned.

If it isn't already open, PowerPoint launches and brings up the Open File dialog. Find a presentation you want to use slides from and select it. You are presented with the same dialog as shown back in Figure 9.7 that shows all the slides in the presentation and lets you customize them before uploading them to the site.

Now continue the previous steps to complete the uploading process, and refresh your SharePoint site to see the new slides in action. (Refresh the browser using F5 or the Refresh button.)

NOTE

We don't actually mean *action* here because the preview of the slide in the library does not preview any animations or transitions.

USING THE SLIDE LIBRARY

Now that you have a populated library of excellent slides you want to reuse, we can show you how to take advantage of this great resource and save yourself and your team some time.

From the main Slide Library page, you will notice that the list of slides has corresponding check boxes next to them. Select the ones you want to include in a presentation, and then click Copy Slide to Presentation (see Figure 9.10).

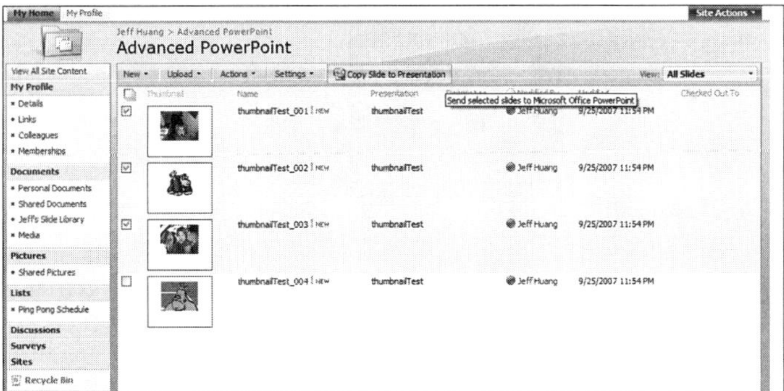

Figure 9.10

Choose slides to copy.

PowerPoint will launch if it hasn't already, and the Copy Slides to PowerPoint dialog appears. From this dialog, you can select the destination for the slides—either an open presentation or a new presentation—and also a couple of options.

The first option has to do with the design theme that the slides have after they are incorporated into the new presentation; check the Keep the Source Presentation Format box if you want the slides to look as they did when they were created, or leave it unchecked to match the slide's content with the rest of the slides in the presentation.

The next check box, Tell Me When This Slide Changes, is sort of like data binding, or, in other words, the slide on the server will notify this presentation that it has changed if somebody makes modifications to it. That way, you can ensure that you always have the latest copy of this slide and are notified to update it when it changes on the SharePoint server.

Tell Me When This Slide Changes

If this check box is selected when importing a slide from a slide library, you will notice an icon on the thumbnail of this slide in the Thumbnail pane (see Figure 9.11).

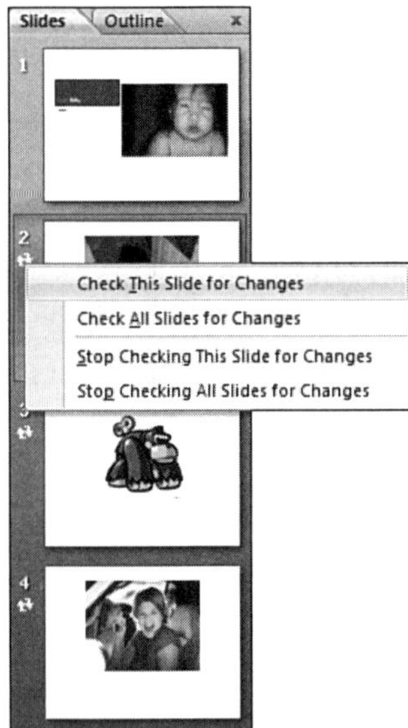

Figure 9.11

The thumbnail of slides that can be synchronized with the SharePoint site contains a small icon that looks like two arrows in sync.

Click on this icon and look at the four options:

- Check This Slide for Changes
- Check All Slides for Changes
- Stop Checking This Slide for Changes
- Stop Checking All Slides for Changes

When the Check This Slide for Changes option is selected, you are presented with the Confirm Slide Update dialog shown in Figure 9.12.

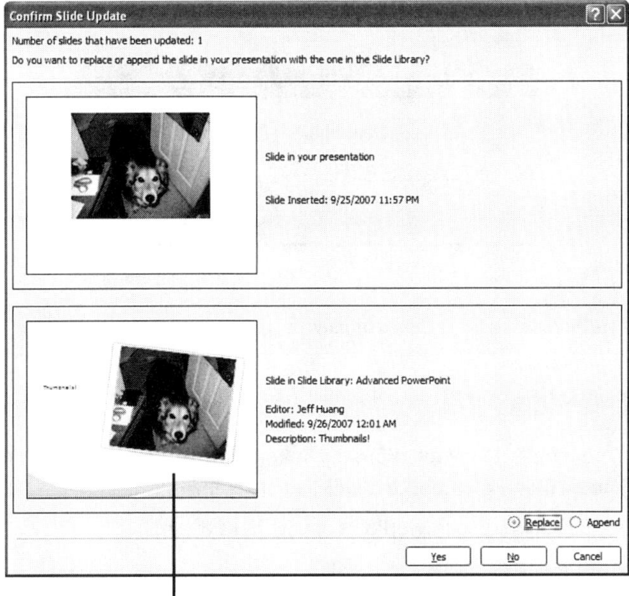

This slide has been updated after it was copied from the library.

Figure 9.12

Synchronizing a slide means comparing the version on the SharePoint site with the one you have in your presentation and deciding whether you want to replace or append the version on the site with the one in your presentation.

This shows you a preview of the two slides and lets you decide whether you want to replace the slide in your presentation with the one on the SharePoint site or whether you want to just append the modified slide into your presentation and use it that way.

If the two slides are exactly the same, a dialog tells you that there are no updates at this time.

Using Sounds and Videos Effectively

Advanced Sounds and videos can play an important part of presentations whether it's part of a demo or you have content created in other programs. It's important to know how to use them and what pitfalls to avoid.

TIP

Always copy movies and sounds to that same folder before you reference them in PowerPoint. This avoids broken links, which we talk about next.

Inserting multimedia is very easy. Go to Media Clips group on the Insert tab, and choose Movie. Select a file that you want to play. Then, in the dialog that pops up, decide whether you want the movie/sound to play automatically when you get to that slide during the slideshow or whether you want to click it to activate it (see Figure 9.13).

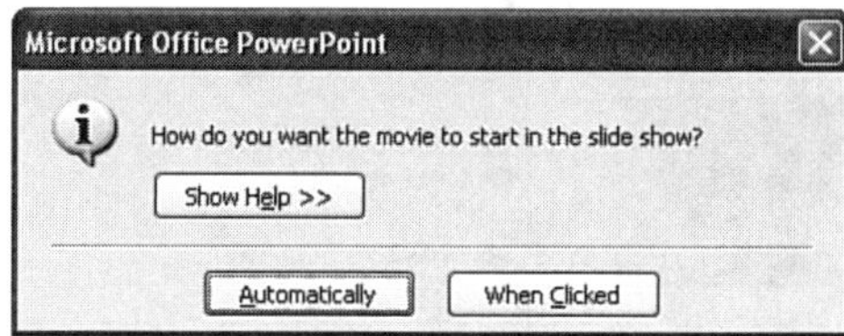

Figure 9.13

Insert a video, and you are prompted when it should be played.

Linking Versus Embedding

Sounds and movies are handled by PowerPoint by linking and embedding. Here's how PowerPoint decides what multimedia files are embedded and which are linked:

- Movies files are usually big, so PowerPoint always links them.
- All sounds except for `.wav` files are always linked.
- For `.wav` files, the rules are a little more complicated. If the `.wav` file is larger than 50MB, it is automatically linked. If it's less than 50MB, the cut off is determined by the user. You can configure this setting by going to the Office button and clicking PowerPoint Options. Choose the Advanced tab in the Save section and click Link Sounds with File Size Greater Than ____ Kb. By default, this is set to 100Kb, which means that all files 100Kb and smaller are embedded and all files larger than 100Kb get linked.

LINKING

Linking means that PowerPoint remembers where the multimedia is, and when asked, goes to that exact location on your computer and plays it. But, when you save the presentation, the multimedia is never saved as part of the `.pptx` file.

So, say that you have a link in spiffy.pptx to a sound on your hard drive and send spiffy.pptx to your friend Bob, who saves it on his home machine. When he goes to Slide Show to try to play the sound, PowerPoint tries to find the sound file on Bob's hard drive, can't find it because it isn't at the same documents folder path, and fails to play it.

The main advantage to linking is that your presentation size stays low. With linking, you can have a few dozen sounds playing inside your presentation, and the file still stays slim.

EMBEDDING

Embedding means the opposite. That is, the file is actually saved inside the `.pptx` file. So, for the previous example, if the sound had been embedded inside the file, Bob could open spiffy.pptx and you'd have less fear that the sound wouldn't play because the actual sound file is embedded inside spiffy.pptx that you sent Bob.

The advantage to embedding is obvious; you don't have to worry about broken links. The downside is that it can quickly bloat files if you have a few embedded sounds.

Distributing a Presentation That Contains Movies or Large Sounds

PowerPoint doesn't give you the power to embed at will, but mostly to keep `.pptx` file sizes reasonable. This means that you can't send included movies and large sounds inside a `.pptx` file. There are a couple of ways to send a presentation with included movies or large sounds, though.

The first option is to package the presentation to be burned on a CD. Assuming that you have a CD burner on your computer, you can easily burn the presentation, along with any included multimedia files, to a CD, which you can hand deliver to the recipient. You can read a little more about Package for CD in Chapter 18, "Publishing Your Presentation to Any Format."

If you click on the Copy to Folder button on the Package for CD dialog instead of clicking Copy to CD, your files are copied to a folder on your hard drive rather than to a CD. You can then zip up the contents of this folder to send on its way. In Windows XP and Windows Vista, you can do this by right-clicking the folder that Package for CD created, select Send To, and then select Compressed (Zipped) Folder (see Figure 9.14). This packages all the presentation files, including multimedia, to a single `.zip` file, which the recipient needs to unzip, but can then use. This `.zip` file can be sent to the recipient attached to an email, on a USB thumb drive, or any other way that you'd normally send someone a file.

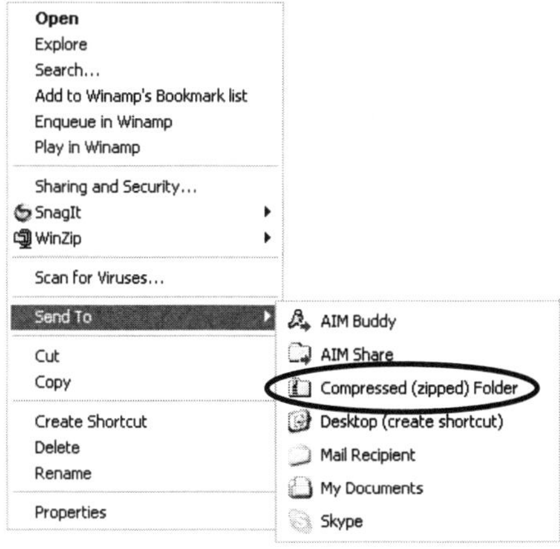

Figure 9.14

Combine and compress the files PowerPoint dumped out into one `.zip` file.

TIP

Package for CD adds some other random files to the folder, such as the PowerPoint Viewer, which you might not want. To avoid the Package for CD feature, stick your presentation file (`.pptx` file) in a folder. When you're done, compress (zip) that folder as described previously. PowerPoint presents fewer surprises when you reference movies and sounds that are in the same folder as the presentation.

Another option for emailing your presentation, or enabling others to view it online, is to use the Single File Web Page save option.

Click the Office button and click Save As to open the Save As dialog. In the Save As Type drop-down at the bottom of the dialog, choose Single File Web Page (`*.mht; *.mhtml`). This spits out one single `.mht` file that includes any multimedia files. The presentation can then be viewed in Internet Explorer or reopened using PowerPoint.

Looping Sounds

After you've inserted a sound and you select it, PowerPoint displays the Sound Tools Options ribbon tab. On the Sound Tools Options tab, Sounds Options group, check the Loop Until Stopped box, and the sound will repeat over and over.

Sounds Spanning Multiple Slides

New

By default, sounds are limited to the current slide. In Slide Show, your sound starts playing, but if you move on to the next slide, the sound stops playing. To make a sound play across multiple slides, go to the Sound Tools Options tab, Sounds Options group and change the Play Sound value to Play Across Slides.

NOTE

Before PowerPoint 2007, getting a sound to span multiple slides was much more involved. The new, simpler method of just changing the value of Play Sound on the Sound Tools Options ribbon tab takes care of the complicated process of setting options that you had to choose in PowerPoint 2003. PowerPoint 2007's new user interface simplifies this down to two simple clicks.

Playlists

PowerPoint might just call them sounds, but it can actually open many kinds of Windows Media content, including `.m3u` playlists. Yep, this means that, combined with the last technique, you can have a list of songs playing in the background of your presentation. This is particularly great to complement a picture slideshow created with the Photo Album feature, described in Chapter 4, "Working with Pictures."

CREATING A PLAYLIST

`.m3u` playlists can be created easily in music players such as Winamp, as well as even exported from iTunes with a little work, but we walk through a quick example of creating one using Windows Media Player because just about everyone has that on their machines. We're using the latest version, Windows Media Player 11, so your mileage might vary if you're using an older or newer version of Windows Media Player.

1. Launch Windows Media Player (from the Start button select All Programs, and then choose Windows Media Player).
2. Click the Now Playing tab at the top and find the tall, thin pane on the right. It reads, Drag Items Here to Create a Playlist.
3. Drag music songs you like from your desktop or other folders into that pane. After you're done, a list of a few songs should show up in there.

NOTE

Because we're using Windows Media Player for this example, you need to use files that Windows Media Player can play, such as MP3 or WMA files. Songs purchased from the iTunes Music Store won't work because Windows Media Player cannot play them.

---

4. Click the Now Playing List button above the list you created, and select Save Playlist As.
5. At the bottom of the Save As dialog, find the Save As Type drop-down and choose the M3U Playlist value (see Figure 9.15).

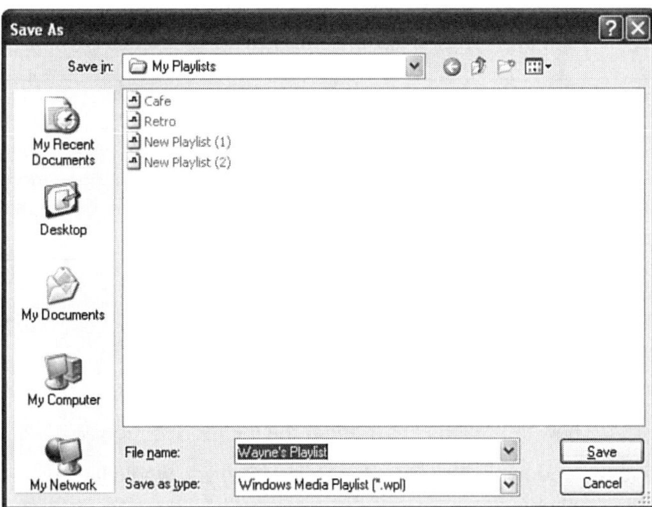

Figure 9.15

Save a playlist in Windows Media Player as a M3U playlist.

6. Then, just save the playlist somewhere on your hard drive, preferably in the same folder as your PowerPoint file.

NOTE

If you're more technical, it's possible to create your own M3U playlists using a text editor, such as Notepad, or the Command Prompt. Check out this KB article for details: http://support.microsoft.com/default.aspx?scid=kb;en-us;249234.

USING PLAYLIST IN POWERPOINT

Now that you have a playlist, let's use it in PowerPoint. It's actually very simple. In PowerPoint, go to the Insert tab, Media Clips group, and choose Sound. Then, navigate to the playlist you saved earlier. PowerPoint treats the playlist exactly like a sound file, so you can do the same techniques we walked through before, such as looping the playlist or playing it across multiple slides.

Tablet PC Features in PowerPoint (Ink)

Advanced One of the new additions in PowerPoint 2003 was native Ink support for Tablet PC users. Ink is useful for jotting down notes and feedback.

How to Ink

If you are using a Tablet PC, the Review tab will look a little different than if you were using a non-Tablet PC—there is the addition of the Ink group with a button called Start Inking.

NOTE

Ink is only available to users using Tablet PC hardware running Windows XP Tablet PC Edition or Windows Vista Home Premium, Business, or Ultimate editions. If you don't meet those requirements, you can still do some limited inking in Slide Show (see Chapter 16, "Running Slide Show Like a Pro").

Although it seems more natural for Ink to be on the Insert tab, the idea is that Ink is primarily used for taking notes. To use the Inking mode, do the following:

1. First click on the Start Inking button from the Review tab.
2. Notice now that a new tab called Pens is under the Ink Tools section.
3. Here you have the option of choosing what type of Pen you would like to use: Ballpoint Pen, Felt Tip Pen, or Highlighter.
4. Under the Format group, select the Color drop-down and choose a color. Select the Weight drop-down to choose the thickness of the line you want the pen to use.
5. Now start inking away using your stylus.

When you are done creating the lines and want to format them or move them around, simply click on the Select Objects button from the Select group, and this returns you to the regular mouse cursor instead of the pen you were using before.

TIP

PowerPoint doesn't support true inking; you cannot add content to a PowerPoint placeholder by selecting it and writing, as with other inking programs. The ink is added as a separate object on the slide.

TIP

Although taking notes and jotting down quick handwritten comments are a great application of Ink, don't forget that Ink is just another tool you can use to create content. After you have enabled the Ink following the instructions just given, you can create hand-drawn graphics just as you would on a blank canvas with a set of pens or pencils.

Limitations of Ink

You will notice that once Ink has been inserted, it appears to look and feel just like any other shape in that you can resize it, move it around, copy and paste it, and so on. However, notice that you cannot rotate the Ink.

Also, despite giving Ink colors that belong to the Theme color section, they do not update when the design is changed.

NOTE

Ctrl+A (select all) does not select ink objects.

Inserting Mathematical Equations Using Word

Advanced PowerPoint doesn't have native equation support, but Word does. First, create your equation in Word:

1. Launch Word and create a new `.docx` file.
2. On Word's Insert tab, Symbols group, choose Equation. This plops an equation onto the page and brings up the Equation Tools Design ribbon (see Figure 9.16).
3. Click around on the ribbon to create an equation.
4. Click the little handle on the top left of the equation. This selects the entire equation.
5. Copy it (press Ctrl+C).
6. Launch PowerPoint and paste (Ctrl+V), and bam; you have an equation in PowerPoint.

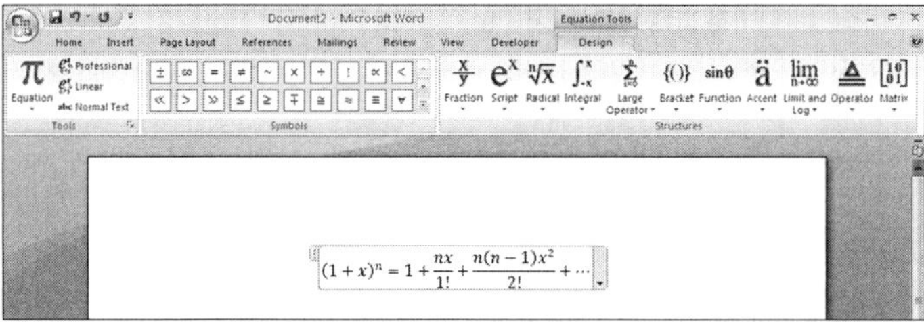

Figure 9.16

Equation tools come up after inserting an equation.

This just pastes a picture of an equation, so to edit the equation, you have to go back to Word and re-paste it into PowerPoint.

The previous chapters walked through different types of PowerPoint data you can create. Now that you have a plethora of content, these next few chapters show what you can do with it.

Manipulating Content

10 Formatting Your Presentation 173

11 Dissecting Themes 199

12 Formatting Shapes, Text, and More 217

13 Demystifying 3D 245

14 Positioning Slide Elements 265

10

Formatting Your Presentation

IN THIS CHAPTER

- Uses of the PowerPoint Thumbnail Pane
- Adding a Slide Background
- Understanding Slide Masters
- Introducing Brand New Slide Layout Options
- Using the PowerPoint Outline Pane
- Placeholders Explained
- Customized Headers and Footers
- Presenter Notes
- Printed Handouts
- Color Modes
- Programming PowerPoint with Macros

Up until now, we have taught you how to make individual objects look amazing. In this chapter, we delve into easy ways to format your presentation as a whole.

In addition, we will show you some neat, timesaving features that will help change the look and feel of the presentation independent of what the content might be.

Uses of the PowerPoint Thumbnail Pane

Advanced The Thumbnail pane—also known as the Slide Miniature pane, found on the left side of the PowerPoint window—is one of the easier ways to arrange slides (see Figure 10.1).

NOTE

Another way to arrange slides is via the Slide Sorter view, where you can see all slides at once.

If you don't see a list of thumbnails on the left side, go to the View tab, Presentation Views group and click Normal to switch back to Normal view.

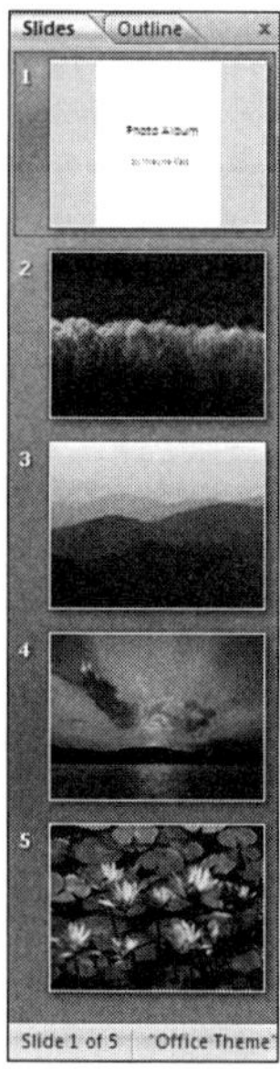

Figure 10.1

The Thumbnail pane.

NOTE

The Thumbnail pane was new to PowerPoint 2002 (Office XP). Before that, only the Outline option was available in the left pane.

Reordering Slides

Reordering slides is easy with the Thumbnail pane. Just drag slides up and down to change where they appear in the slide order. You can right-click a slide (see Figure 10.2) and choose to cut, copy, or paste it elsewhere in the slide order, or you can even copy it and then paste it into another presentation. Options for duplicating or deleting slides also exist.

NOTE

Not very well-known is the ability to change the layout of a specific slide or slides (if many are selected) by right-clicking and choosing a new layout from the contextual menu.

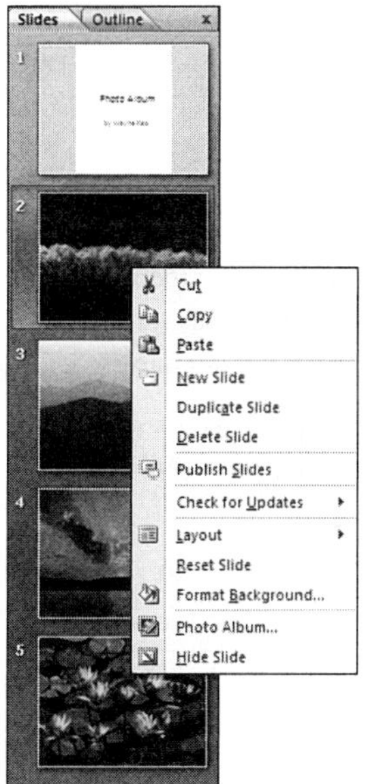

Figure 10.2

Slide contextual menu.

Apply to Many Slides

It's easy to select multiple slides. Just click on one slide to select it, hold down Ctrl or Shift, and click other slides to add to the slide selection. (As with text, pressing Ctrl adds a particular slide to the selection, whereas pressing Shift adds all slides within the range of the first selected slide to the one you Shift+click on.) Then, all the commands described previously will apply to all the selected slides.

TIP

The Slide Sorter view also makes it easy to manipulate many slides at once. Select it by going to the View tab, Presentation Views group and choosing Slide Sorter.

Adding a Slide Background

Advanced Inserting a background for a slide is easier than ever. To select from the options available in the current theme, go to the Design tab, Background group and choose Background Style. You will learn more about how Office comes up with these options in Chapter 11, "Dissecting Themes."

To have more control over the options for backgrounds, you can right-click the slide and choose Format Background. PowerPoint treats the slide background as one giant shape, so you get the most power of shape formatting right here. For example, you can set a gradient or picture fill. Refer to Chapter 12, "Formatting Shapes, Text, and More," to learn about the specific shape formatting options.

Understanding Slide Masters

Advanced A great way to save a lot of time is to learn and understand how the Slide Master works. It will save you redundant work by allowing you to change how the Master looks, and each slide following that Master will reflect those changes.

For example, if you want the company logo to appear in the corner of every slide, change it on the Master one time rather than copying and pasting it onto each slide.

NOTE

By default, every presentation contains a Slide Master.

To modify the Slide Master and affect all slides under that Master, do the following:

1. Go to the View tab, Presentation Views group and choose Slide Master.
2. In the Thumbnail pane (far left, under the ribbon), the topmost item in the list is the first Slide Master. Below it are the Slide Layouts used in this presentation. Select the Master.
3. Modify the first Master slide in the list. For example, in Figure 10.3, we've added a logo to the top right. Watch as your changes appear on all the slides in the Thumbnail pane. Now you can close Master view.

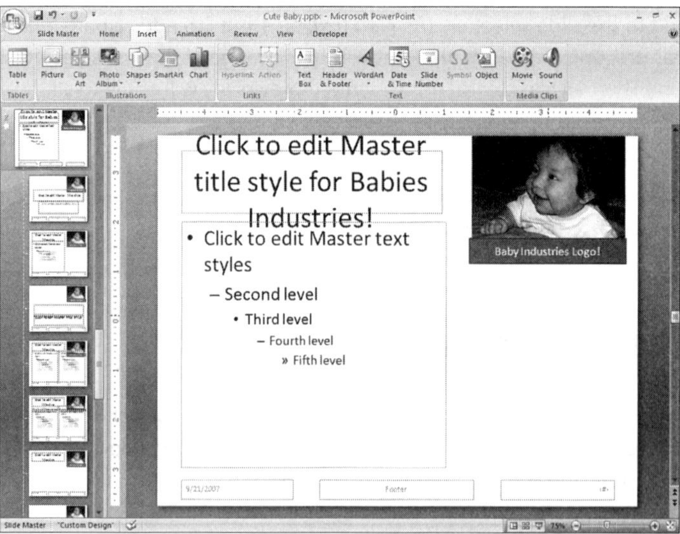

Figure 10.3

The Slide Master will affect all slides that use this Master in your presentation.

This is useful not only for inserting content, but also for formatting slides—any formatting changes on the Master also apply to child slides. Try changing the background, fonts, colors, and more and notice the changes on slides that inherit from the Master. To see the changes, close Master view and return to editing mode.

Additional Masters

Just as in previous versions of PowerPoint, it is possible to create multiple Slide Masters. The difference in this version is that with each new Master created, a new set of layouts is created and associated with that Master (see Figure 10.4). We talk more about layouts later in this chapter.

NOTE

The multiple Masters feature was first introduced in PowerPoint 2002 (Office XP). Before that, each presentation could contain one Slide Master at most. Multiple Masters was a highly requested feature, but it was a very difficult feature to add since previous versions of PowerPoint allowed only one Master. Since they shared the same file format, versions of PowerPoint prior to 2002 still needed to be able to open and edit PowerPoint 2002 files.

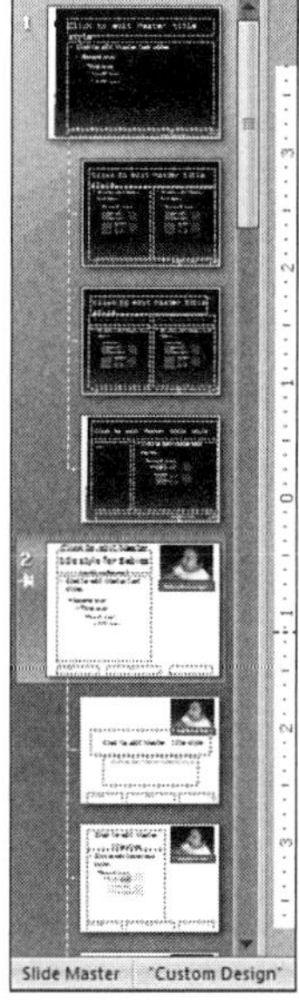

Figure 10.4

Each new Master creates a set of new layouts. New Masters are placed after the currently selected Master, not at the end of the list.

To create a new Master, do the following:

1. If you are still in Slide Master view, skip to step 2. Otherwise, select the View tab and choose Slide Master.
2. On the Slide Master tab, Edit Master group, click on Insert Master.

With each new Master, you can apply new layouts to slides corresponding to that Master. To apply a layout from the new slide Master to a Slide Master, do the following:

1. Return to Normal view by going to the Slide master tab, Close group and choosing Close Master View.
2. Right-click a slide in the Thumbnail pane and choose Layout from the contextual menu.

Hide Background Graphics

This is a relatively obscure feature, but we feel obligated to mention it to you in case you see the little check box with the option and get confused.

NOTE

Experts might not find this feature obscure, as they tend to use it in combination with the new layouts to allow you to set up a slide so that you can use a layout without worrying about which background objects will come with the placeholders. It's also useful if you have navigation elements on a slide layout or Master, but do not want those elements to be carried over to a specific slide.

Basically, this feature tells the current slide to ignore any pictures/graphics on the Master slide's background. Usually if you are editing the Slide Master and you insert pictures, and then go back to your slides, each one inherits those Master pictures as part of the background. If you don't want these graphics to show up on a slide, go to the Design tab, Background group and check Hide Background Graphics. Then, the background pictures on the Master slide won't appear on this slide. Or, to apply this to all the slides in the presentation, do the following:

1. Right-click on a background of any slide, and select Format Background.
2. From the Fill table, you will notice the check box mentioned earlier that says Hide Background Graphics is unchecked by default.
3. Check the box and click Apply to All Slides, depending on what you want.

NOTE

This feature was very confusing in previous versions of PowerPoint. Not only was it labeled Omit Background Graphics from Master, but also the check box was checked by default, meaning that any new pictures added to the Master would not show up on all slides.

Introducing Brand New Slide Layout Options

While Slide masters are not new to PowerPoint 2007, customizable Slide Layouts certainly are, and each Master can now have a series of layouts. This differs from previous versions in which layouts were hard-coded, and you were stuck with the few canned layouts preprogrammed by Microsoft.

Layouts 101

Let's revisit some layout basics. For the uninitiated, layouts are templates to help you create certain types of slides by putting placeholders in some preprogrammed positions. Layouts define how and what content can be added to the slide by defining placeholders. Placeholders are explained later in this chapter briefly; they define a spot where an object can be added and can contain formatting, including effects, color, animations, and more. These save you enormous amounts of time and energy, as you can insert a slide with a certain layout that has placeholders ready to help you create content tailored for that type of slide.

The various layouts are similar to the ones found in previous versions of PowerPoint:

- Title Slide
- Title and Content
- Section Header
- Two Content
- Comparison
- Title Only
- Blank
- Content with Caption
- Picture with Caption
- Custom Layout

To create a new slide that follows a layout, use the drop-down from the Home tab's Slides group in the New Slide gallery (see Figure 10.5).

New Slide

If you simply click on the New Slide button without dropping down the gallery (clicking on the top part of the button), the default layout used is the same as the one inserted above it or the one selected. An alternative way to insert a new slide is to click in the Thumbnail pane on a slide where you want to insert a slide after, and then press Enter. Also if you click between slides in the Thumbnail pane and press Enter, a new slide is inserted.

Change a Slide's Layout

If you want to change the layout of an existing slide, either because you just want to change it or because you do not like the default layout, do the following:

1. On the Home tab, Slides group, click the Layout button to open the gallery.
2. Select a layout (see Figure 10.6).

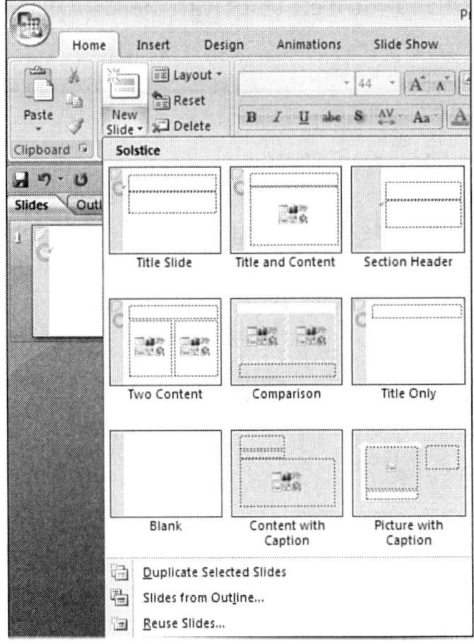

Figure 10.5

Drop down the New Slide gallery to choose a layout for your new slide.

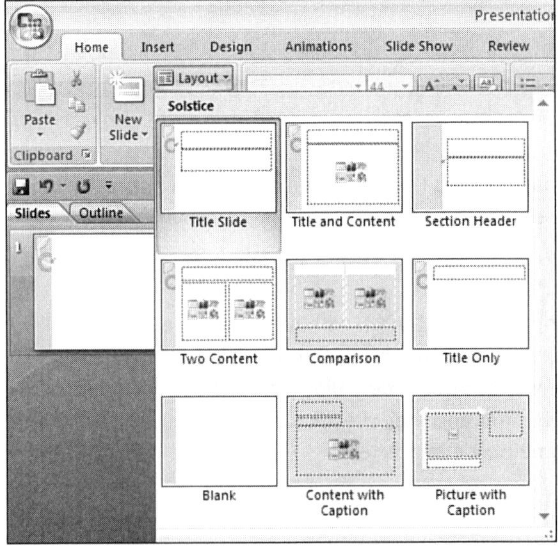

Figure 10.6

Change the layout of an existing slide.

Alternatively, you can right-click a slide in the Thumbnail pane and choose Layout on the contextual menu.

Customize a Layout

If the out-of-the-box layouts do not suit your needs, you have the ability to create your own type of layout. This is new to Office 2007. Layouts follow the master, meaning that they inherit all the contents of the Master Slide, but they can contain placeholders you add.

To create your own layout, do the following:

1. Enter Slide Master view by clicking on the View tab, and selecting Slide Master.
2. Click on Insert Layout.
3. Notice a new thumbnail in your Thumbnail pane corresponding to your new layout. If you hover your mouse over it, the name will be Custom Layout Layout (see Figure 10.7).

NOTE

The newly inserted layout is added below an existing layout if one is selected or between layouts if you have clicked between two. If a Master Slide is selected, the new layout is added to the end of the list.

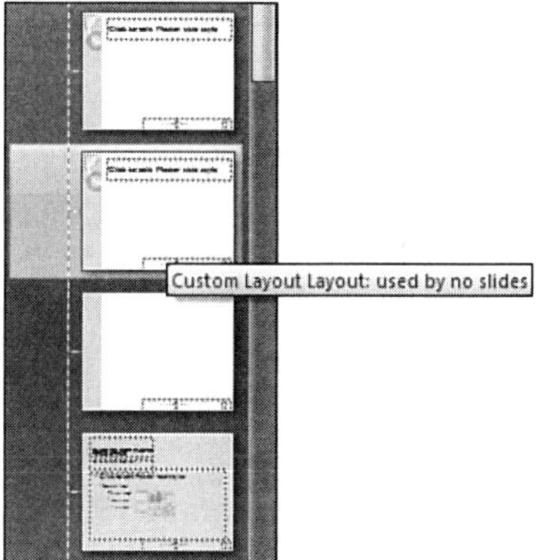

Figure 10.7

A newly created custom layout.

4. Now that you have this new layout, insert new placeholders by going to the Slide Master tab, Master Layout group and choosing Insert Placeholder. Move content around and modify the slide in a way that you want any slide to be when set to follow this layout. This is covered in more detail in the next section.

NOTE

As with all masters, layouts can contain content that you want to show up on all slides that follow the layout. For example, you can give a background to all slides that follow the Comparison layout.

5. To rename the layout you have created, click the Slide Master, Edit Master, Rename button. It is a lot easier to keep track of them after they are named to describe what the layout actually looks like.
6. After you exit Slide Master view (Slide Master tab, go to Close Master View, and then Close), go to the Layout gallery again on the Home tab, and you will see the layout you created in the gallery.

NOTE

Layouts can be swapped with other layouts, and your slide will not lose its content. With a slide selected, insert content into placeholders and then click on Layout from the Home tab and select a different layout. Notice that your content is still there, but it has been moved around to fit the new layout.

Using the PowerPoint Outline Pane

Advanced When you're first whipping up a presentation, you're usually really focused on content and not so much on how it's going to look. You're just putting down thoughts for topics you're planning to cover. That's where the PowerPoint Outline pane can come in handy.

Creating a Quick Presentation Outline

To begin, switch to the Outline pane by clicking the Outline tab at the top of the slide thumbnails (see Figure 10.8).

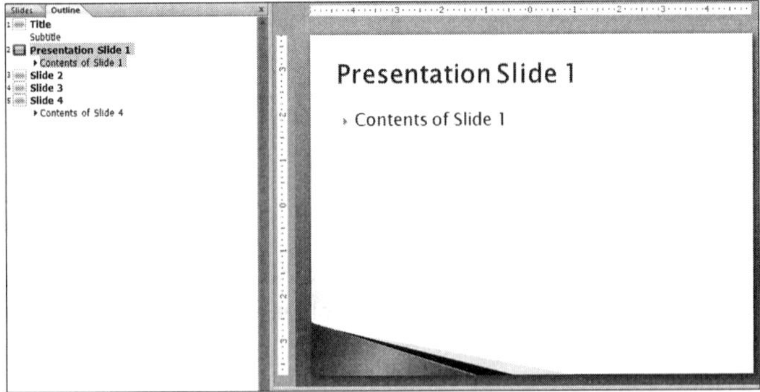

Figure 10.8

There are Slide and Outline tabs above the Thumbnail pane to help you manipulate the text more easily.

Using the Outline pane is similar to working in most outlining programs, or using Word's outlining feature. See Table 10.1 for some basic guidelines for working in the Outline pane.

Table 10.1 Using the Outline Pane

Action	Result in the Outline	Result on the Slide
Enter	New line	A new slide if you are on the top level of a slide; in general, Enter gives you a new line at the same level.
Tab	Demote one level	None
Shift+Tab	Promote one level	Puts the text into the body placeholder or if the text is already in a placeholder, promotes one level in the body placeholder text
Double-click the rectangular slide icon	Collapses or expands that item	None
Drag	Drag an item up or down in the outline	Changes order of the slides or text

If you can't remember all of those, they're also available on the contextual menu, which you can trigger by right-clicking on the outline.

In addition to the commands we described in Table 10.1 that have keyboard equivalents, the contextual menu also lets you show or hide formatting. You may have formatted the text to have crazy sizes or colors or other text formatting like bold, italic, or underline. By default the Outline pane doesn't show you this to encourage you to focus on the text. This option lets you decide whether you want to show text formatting in the outline.

Creating Slides from the Outline

PowerPoint is great for creating and presenting a presentation, but despite what we wrote previously, you might not feel comfortable organizing your thoughts or writing text using the Outline pane. Some PowerPoint users prefer organizing text in Microsoft Word or Notepad, where they can focus on the text without worrying how it looks.

Here's a simple outline we created in Notepad. Note that we used tabs to indicate different outline levels:

```
Wayne's Favorite Shows
Star Trek
	Enterprise isn't so good, though
	The O.C.
	Joan of Arcadia
	Law and Order
	The West Wing

Jeff's Favorite Shows
	Survivor
	Entourage
	Family Guy
```

It's now easy to import this text into PowerPoint when I'm ready to create my presentation.

Start up PowerPoint and go to the Home tab, New Slide group and click the arrow on the bottom half of Add Slide. Choose Slides from Outline at the bottom of the gallery (see Figure 10.9). Or, you can just click the Office button and from the Open options, you can open the Notepad file directly.

NOTE

You might have to change the file type to outline. Also note that you don't get a title slide in the new presentation; you only get content slides. This is a change from previous versions.

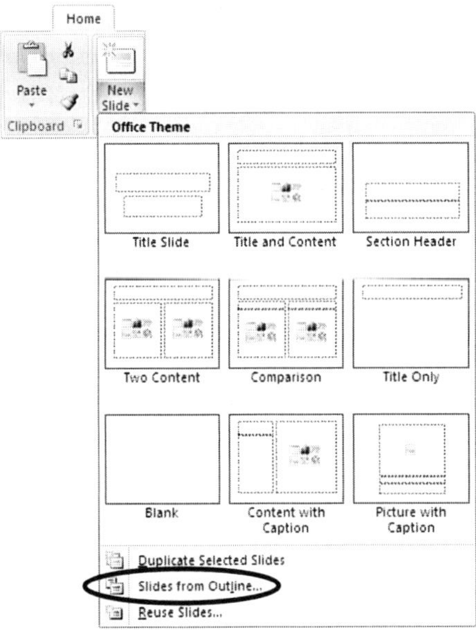

Figure 10.9

Insert slides from an existing outline; in this case we've added the outline to an existing presentation so it looks a little different than if you started from scratch.

Then just apply a design template to make it pretty. This works most successfully with

- Plain text files that are tab delimited
- WordPerfect files
- Word files that have headings created in Outline View

Placeholders Explained

Advanced Placeholders are the hints at what should be added to a specific layout. They contain positions and content type (SmartArt, shape, table, and so on) suggestions that appear by default on the slide, depending on the layout. Placeholders do not show up during Slide Show mode unless they have content. In addition, they can contain formatting options such as effects, colors, animations, fonts, and more. This is a great time-saving opportunity when you know that there will be multiple slides of a given type and that they should all follow the same layout. Decorate this layout using placeholders, and you're set.

Standard Placeholders

While the name may not ring a bell, you have definitely seen a placeholder and have most likely used one. By default, a new presentation opens to a Title Slide containing a Click to Add Title text box placeholder whose sole job is help you create content (see Figure 10.10). Notice that when you click inside a placeholder, the default text goes away and you can add your own title or subtitle.

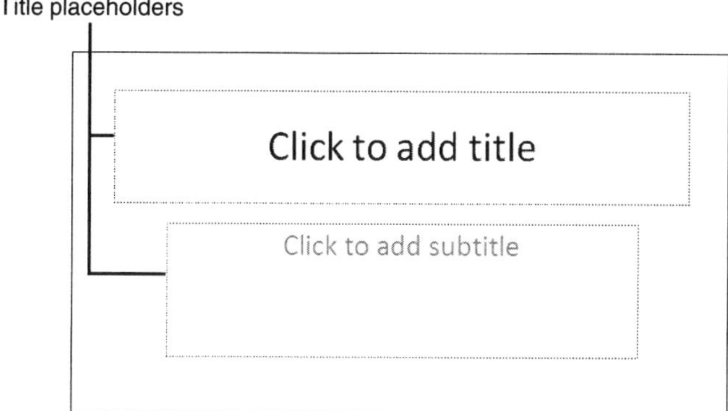

Figure 10.10

The default Title Slide and Title Placeholders.

Text is not the only type of placeholder; in fact, many placeholders allow you to insert any type of content, including tables, SmartArt, charts, pictures, Clip Art, and media (see Figure 10.11). You are able to insert the following types of placeholders:

- Content—Allows you insert text, tables, SmartArt, charts, pictures, Clip Art, and media
- Text
- Picture
- Chart
- Table
- SmartArt

- Media
- Clip Art

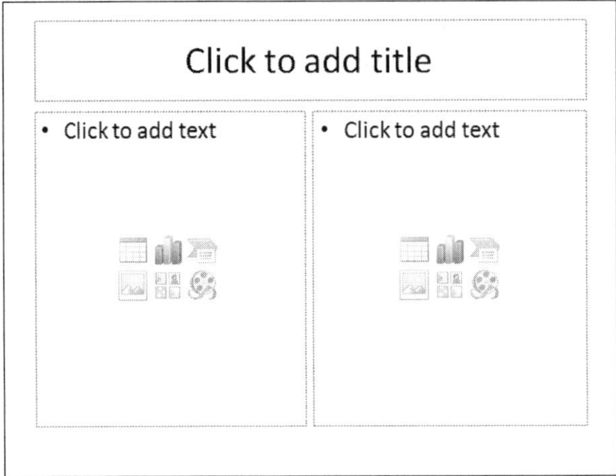

Figure 10.11

The Content placeholder helps you save time by giving you an easy way to insert various types of objects.

NOTE

Have you ever noticed how the outline of placeholders is a dashed black and white line? This isn't an accident; it's so the outline is visible regardless of what color the background is. If it were a solid black outline, a black background would render the outline invisible.

The type of placeholder that exists on a slide depends on what type of slide is created. By default, the various types of Slide Layouts (described earlier) contain different placeholders corresponding to their type. Picture with Caption contains exactly what it should: a picture placeholder and two text placeholders (see Figure 10.12).

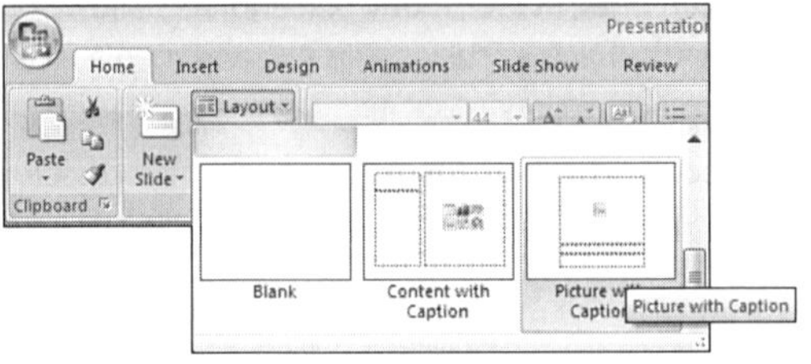

Figure 10.12

The Picture with Caption layout contains placeholders for a picture and a caption.

If you are familiar with the Placeholder icons that existed in previous versions of PowerPoint, you know that these little icons are shortcuts (the small images found inside the placeholder) to help you create content, going along with the theme that placeholders exist to make inserting or creating content easier. Simply click on an icon corresponding to the type of content you want to insert to save yourself a trip to the Insert tab.

JUMPING BETWEEN PLACEHOLDERS

Ctrl+Enter is a neat shortcut you can use to quickly jump between placeholders in a presentation. Let's see it in action:

1. To start, create a new presentation and make sure that you have a slide selected, not a slide thumbnail.
2. Press Ctrl+Enter. You're now in the title placeholder, which is the top placeholder.
3. Type some text in the title placeholder.
4. Press Ctrl+Enter again. Now you're in the subtitle placeholder, the bottom of the two placeholders.
5. Again, type some text, this time in the subtitle placeholder.
6. Press Ctrl+Enter a few more times. Note that each time you press the shortcut keys, selection moves to the next available placeholder on the slide. Or, if you're on the last placeholder on a slide, PowerPoint creates a new slide.

One other thing to try is to go back to the first slide in the presentation. If you press Ctrl+Enter, the first placeholder is selected, in addition to all the text inside. Press Ctrl+Enter again, and the same thing happens with the next placeholder.

Getting the hang of it? For power users, this is a fast way to jump between placeholders and type in text without having to tediously select slides one at a time and then select all the text inside that placeholder.

This works for text-based placeholders. For graphic or media placeholders, you can't use this tip.

Custom Placeholders

New to this version of PowerPoint is the ability to create your own placeholders. First you have to enter Master view so that you can edit one of the Slide Layouts.

1. Get into Master view (as we did in the previous section) by selecting the View tab and then selecting Slide Master.
2. In the Thumbnail pane, notice that one Slide Master has many Slide Layout slides branching from it (see the "Layouts 101" section earlier in this chapter). Select a layout you want to modify by clicking on any slide except the top one in the Thumbnail pane. We will choose the first layout right under the Master.
3. Click the Slide Master tab and go to the Master Layout group. Click Insert Placeholder to create a default Text Placeholder, or drop down the gallery to see what other types of placeholders can be inserted (see Figure 10.13). This would be useful if you need to add a text box to every title slide in the presentation.

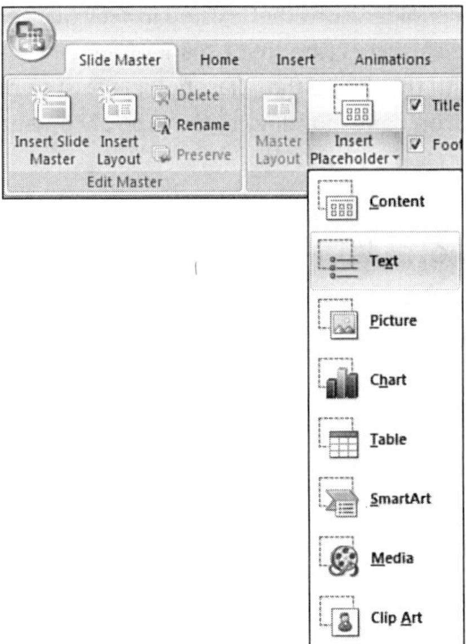

Figure 10.13

The Insert Placeholder gallery allows you to create your own placeholders.

4. After you exit Slide Master view (Slide Master, Close Master View, Close), go to the Home tab's Slides group and click Layout to open the gallery again, and you will see that layout now contains the placeholder you added (see Figure 10.14).

NOTE

A shortcut for getting back to the tripane view (normal view) is to simply click on the left-most view button on the Status Bar. Learn more about the View Indicator shortcuts in Chapter 16, "Running Slide Show Like a Pro."

You can also decide the position of placeholders by clicking and dragging them around after step 3 in the previous example.

CAUTION

Be careful! If you edit the text inside the placeholder, you're only editing the prompt text. This means that the Edit mode text you see is changed, but the Slide Show mode text doesn't change. If you want a real text box with text inside to show up on the layout, insert a text box, not a placeholder.

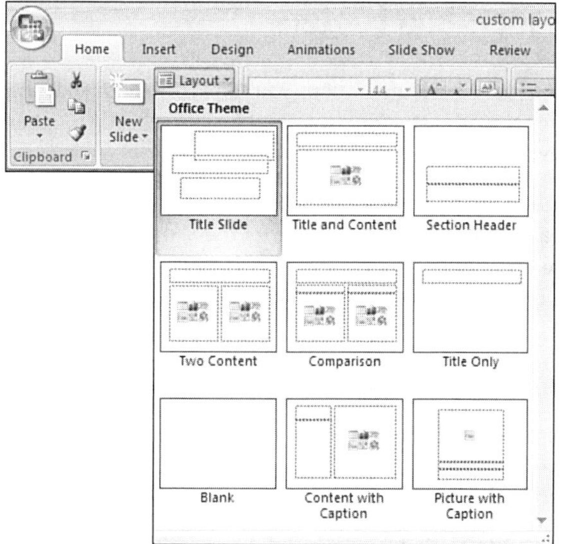

Figure 10.14

The layout you modified now contains that placeholder.

USING FORMAT PAINTER

We talk much more about the abilities of Format Painter in Chapter 12, but we want to point out one of its uses here—helping you make one slide take on the formatting of another slide.

As you might know, Format Painter takes formatting from a source and applies it to a destination. One nice use of this is on slides as a whole:

1. Select the slide you like in the Thumbnail pane.
2. Click the Home tab and in the Clipboard group, click Format Painter. Format Painter is the button that looks like a paintbrush. Notice how your cursor turns into a paintbrush.
3. Click another slide in the Thumbnail pane where you want that formatting applied.

Now you have two similar looking slides with the same theme, colors, fonts, and so on.

NOTE

The painter does not paint the layout, only the design-based items. If an element is on the layout but not on the Master, it is not painted on.

Customized Headers and Footers

Advanced Headers and footers are annotations you can add to each slide that convey more information. They can be useful for displaying the current slide number, the date, a custom message, logo, and so on.

To bring up the Header and Footers dialog, select the Insert tab and in the Text group, click Header & Footer. You should see a dialog with two tabs—one for the Slide and another for the Notes and Handouts pages in case you want different information printed out for notes and handouts versus regular slides.

NOTE

This dialog also contains helpful settings, such as updating automatically for date and time. Also, it's often helpful to not show headers and footers on the title slide, so there's an option to Don't Show on the Title Slide.

Adding header and footer information to all the slides is easy: Simply get the settings the way you want and click Apply to All from the Header and Footer dialog. This propagates the settings to all the slides.

By default, the formatting of the header and footer will follow the Slide Master. To change that, simply change the Master, and all the children follow:

1. Select the View tab and click on Slide Master.
2. Edit the styles and formatting of `<#>` or `<footer>`, but be careful not edit their values, or you might break the "header-ness" of it and cause it to no longer be a header value. Feel free to add additional text to these fields, though.
3. Close Master View.

Presenter Notes

Advanced Presentations are not just about what the audience sees; there is a whole side to it specific to you, the presenter. Notice that an entire pane is dedicated to writing notes about a slide, and a specific view can be used to print out or just see what notes go with which slides.

Using the Notes Pane

The Notes pane is a great place to jot down some thoughts or ideas or even some prompts you have about a specific slide. It's the pane located below your slide, and it can handle the text inputs and editing (see Figure 10.15).

NOTE

The Notes pane can only contain text, no graphics, or anything else. Also, the formatting is stripped on the text so that it looks black, but it can contain bullets.

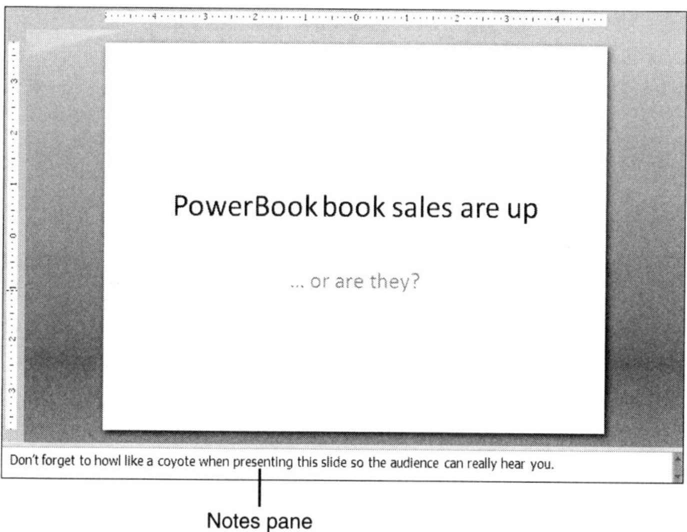

Figure 10.15

The Notes pane, although small, is useful for keeping track of information corresponding to a specific slide.

The Notes pane is available from the Normal view, which is the default view when opening a presentation.

Using the Notes Page

You can display the contents of the Notes pane in a format that's better suited to viewing the slide and the notes side by side, where the slide and the notes are presented on one page called the Notes Page.

NOTE

These are the same notes as in the Notes pane. If you edit them here, it changes the notes in the Notes pane and vice versa. This only holds true for the text box you see. The Notes Page is different in that you can add other objects such as shapes and pictures, but these do not appear in the Notes pane because it can only contain text.

To access the Notes Page, do the following:

1. Select the View tab and go to the Presentation Views group. Click Notes Page.
2. Notice a page for each slide with a picture of the slide on the top and the contents of the Notes Pane on the bottom in a text box (see Figure 10.16). The slide picture can be moved around but not edited, whereas the text box containing the notes can be edited.

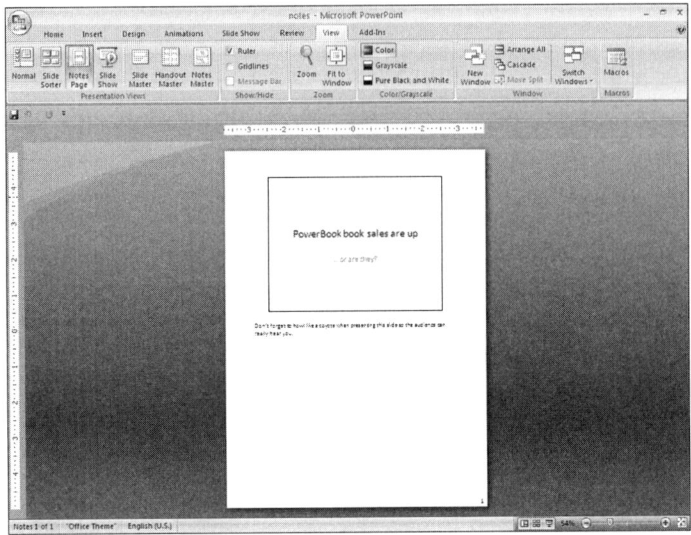

Figure 10.16

The same information on the Notes Page.

When to Use Notes

We've noticed two distinct uses for PowerPoint notes.

One set of users exercises the ability to annotate a slide and display notes during Presenter View (see Chapter 16). This lets a presenter see notes for each slide as she presents, and the notes can be used as prompts for the speaker. In addition, while the presentation is going on, if a discussion occurs and the presenter wants to augment the annotations to the slide, Presenter View allows the presenter to change the notes during the presentation.

The other camp sees the Notes Page as more of a script view, where each slide is more like a picture and the notes can facilitate the telling of a story. The presentation in Notes Page format can be distributed in this format when printed.

One difference between the Notes Page over the Notes pane is that your notes can be richly formatted on the Notes Page. Just select some text in the notes, and go crazy with the Format tab on the ribbon. You can apply effects, fills, and outlines. If you then return to Normal view (on the View tab, go to the Presentation Views group and choose Normal), you will see that PowerPoint only shows bold, italic, and underline formatting.

Printed Handouts

Along the lines of distributing presentations, there is another mode specifically designed for such a thing: Handouts.

Handouts are a great way to distribute your presentation in a way that conveys many slides on one page, especially if the level of detail is not necessary when viewing each slide.

To print a presentation as handouts, click the Office button and click the arrow next to Print. Under the Print What drop-down, select Handouts and then change the Handout options, such as how many slides are on each page and the orientation (see Figure 10.17).

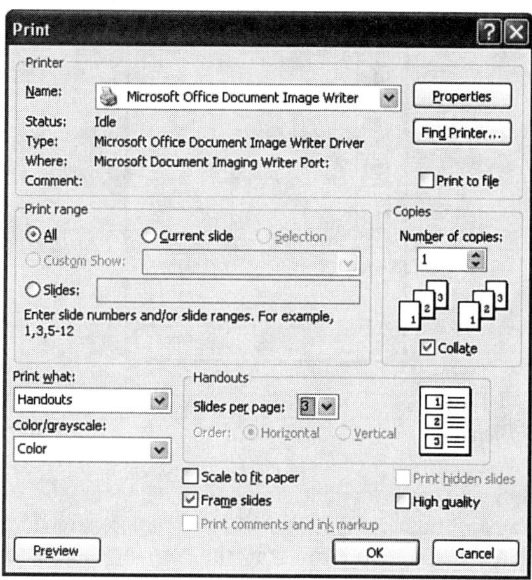

Figure 10.17

The Print Handouts option is found on the Print dialog.

Handout Master

An entire Master is dedicated to how handouts look when printed. To access it, select the View tab and click Handout Master.

Now you can make modifications which will be propagated to all handouts such as the date, the orientation, styling, colors and so on. This is a handy way to modify the handouts all at once.

WORD HANDOUTS

If you feel more comfortable customizing your handouts in Word, Office makes it easy to export your data to a Word document.

This feature requires that you have Microsoft Office Word installed, which will most likely be the case unless you only have PowerPoint installed on your machine.

1. Go to the Publish tab and choose Create Handouts in Microsoft Office Word.

Continues...

2. Choose the layout you think your audience will like (see Figure 10.18). Our favorite is the second choice, Blank Lines Next to Slides, which gets plenty of slides on each page and leaves room for the audience members to take notes about your brilliant presentation.

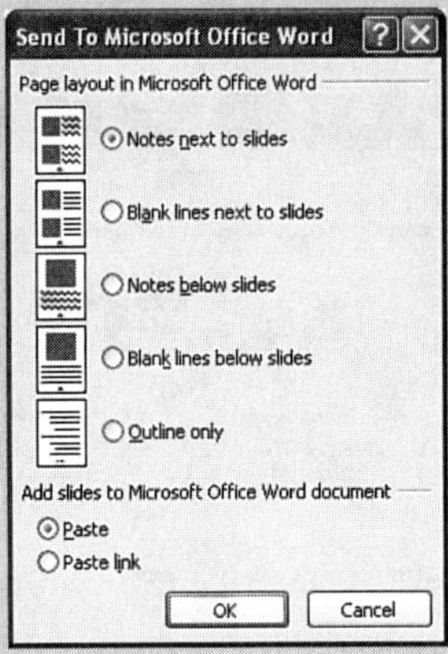

Figure 10.18

Choose a format for your Word handouts.

3. Finally, choose whether to paste the slides into the Word document or to just paste a link to the slides. Just pasting the slides is a little safer, as links are known to get corrupted. But pasting a link is a handy option if you think that you might update the slides later and want the Word document to automatically update itself.
4. Voilà! You have Word handouts (see Figure 10.19). You work with them in Word as needed, and then print them out.

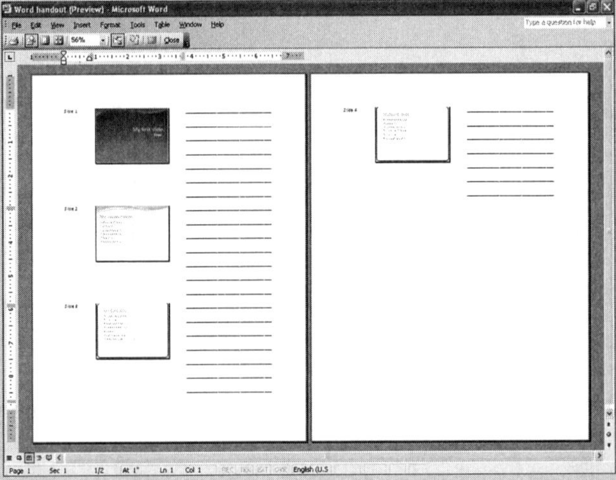

Figure 10.19

The resulting Word handouts are created.

Color Modes

This next feature is really helpful for previewing a presentation for printing, yet still allowing you to edit the presentation.

Essentially four different color modes exist: Color, Grayscale, Pure Black and White, and High Contrast Mode. The first three are accessible by default from the View tab's Color/Grayscale group (see Figure 10.20).

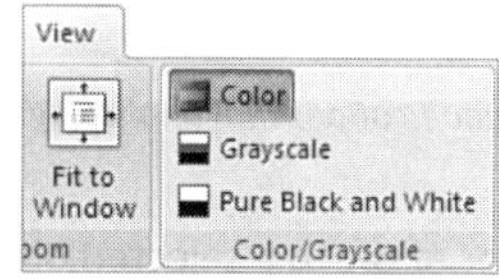

Figure 10.20

Access different color modes from the View tab.

Viewing the Presentation Color Mode

Color is selected on the View tab by default, and your presentation in displayed in...well...color. Choosing Pure Black and White recolors all objects in your presentation to be either white or black. Similarly, choosing Grayscale changes all colors to a shade of gray. After the View Color Mode is changed, you can continue to edit the presentation normally, but view it as it would look like when printed to a black and white printer.

NOTE

These same color mode options appear in the Print dialog and in Print Preview.

Choosing a Per-Object Color Mode

After a different color mode is selected, a new tab is inserted in front of the Home tab. The tab name is different, depending on which color mode you selected. It contains another set of options, which we now describe.

In addition to having the ability to change whether a presentation is seen in color or one of the black and white modes, you can also set how each object is viewed. For example, if you want everything to be in grayscale except for one chart because it's too hard to distinguish parts of the chart, you can set the Per-Object Color Mode to be black and white.

NOTE

High Contrast Mode is only available when Windows itself is in High Contrast mode. This is usually accessible from the Control Panel's Accessibility option.

The options on the tab are shown in Figure 10.21. Settings chosen here also take effect when printing and are useful if you want a certain object to look differently when it is printed in black and white or grayscale mode.

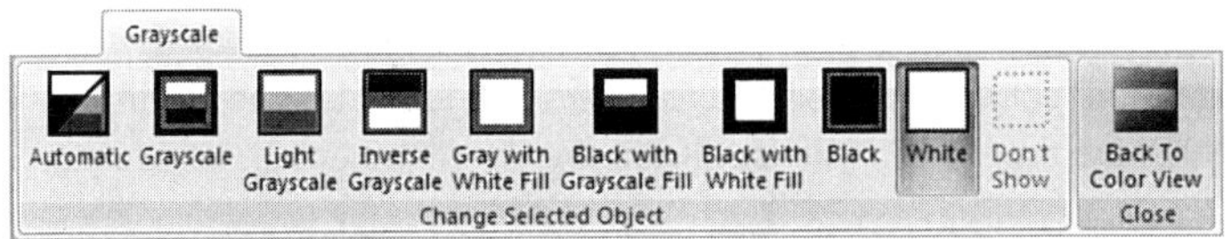

Figure 10.21

The Per-Object Color Mode tab allows color modifications that apply only to the selected object.

It's important to note that these options apply to a selected object. If nothing is selected, these options take effect on the slide background. This is one of the most confusing parts of the feature.

NOTE

This is useful in cases in which objects should not show up when printed or need to show up differently.

Programming PowerPoint with Macros

One advanced feature in PowerPoint is the ability for software programmers to create macros, small computer programs that run inside PowerPoint.

For Experts Only

Previous versions of PowerPoint included a macro recorder, which let you click a record button, do a bunch of regular PowerPoint operations, and PowerPoint automatically generated a macro for you. This let even nonprogrammers create macros.

Unfortunately this functionality was dropped in PowerPoint 2007. So, only the truly advanced and curious will find this section interesting. If you end up programming PowerPoint, we officially deem you an expert.

Creating a Macro

Entire books are written about writing macros and Microsoft Office extensions, so we won't try to do that here. Macros are programmatic actions that can be associated with an object when clicked or otherwise. They encompass just about anything you can do with PowerPoint by exposing an Object Model that you can use to program. We will take you quickly through creating one macro and give you some tools to create some of your own:

1. Enable the Developer toolbar. Go to the Office button, click PowerPoint Options, and then click the Show Developer tab in the Ribbon. Click OK.

2. Create a new presentation (Ctrl+N).
3. Go to Code group in the Developer tab the and click Macros.
4. Type in **`FirstMacro`** for the macro name and click Create.
5. Add the code snippet that follows, into the Sub. This code changes the title placeholder text on the first slide and also adds a rectangle shape. The result should be as shown in Figure 10.22.

```
Set firstSlide = ActivePresentation.Slides(1)
firstSlide.Shapes.Title.TextFrame.TextRange.Text = "PowerPoint rocks!"
firstSlide.Shapes.AddShape msoShapeRectangle, 20, 20, 200, 100
```

NOTE

This program crashes if you don't have any slides in the presentation.

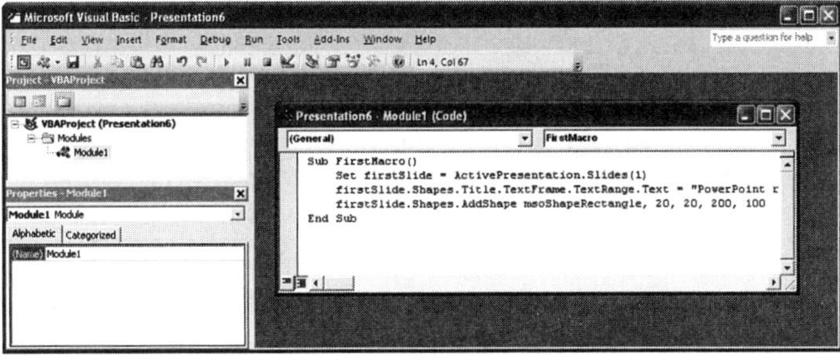

Figure 10.22

Some macro code added to the PowerPoint Visual Basic editor.

6. To run the macro, go to the Run menu and choose Run Sub/UserForm (or just press F5). If you close the Microsoft Visual Basic window and return to PowerPoint, you will notice that the first slide has changed.

TIP

You can add your newly created macro to the Quick Access Toolbar. Go to Office button and click the PowerPoint Options button. In the Customize section, under the Choose Commands From drop-down, select Macros. Then select your macro, click Add, and then click OK. Make sure that the macro is generic; otherwise, if you try to use it on a presentation that it isn't meant for, it might fail.

Learn More

We barely scratched the surface when it comes to writing programs for PowerPoint. Here are some additional resources so that you can learn more:

- A reference of the complete PowerPoint object model is available on MSDN here: http://msdn2.microsoft.com/en-us/library/aa644701.aspx. This covers all the programmable objects in PowerPoint, describing their properties and methods.
- If you're like us, you're more comfortable programming with C#, C++, or even Visual Basic using the latest version of Microsoft Visual Studio, rather than using Office's weird VBA language and its ancient code editor. Here's an example of automating PowerPoint using Visual Studio: http://support.microsoft.com/kb/303718.
- To make it even easier, Microsoft's Visual Studio Tools for Office 2005 Second Edition product (VSTO 2005 SE) supports PowerPoint starting with its 2005 release (even though SE came out in November 2006), so you can buy yourself a copy from your favorite retailer.

NOTE

Visual Studio Tools for Office 2005 does not support PowerPoint; Visual Studio Tools for Office Second Edition (VSTO 2005 SE) does provide add-in solution support for PowerPoint. VSTO 2005 SE is a free add-on to Visual Studio 2005 Professional.

- After you're comfortable writing macros for yourself, the next step is creating PowerPoint add-ins that can be distributed to others. Learn more about add-ins here: http://skp.mvps.org/ppafaq.htm. Another great site is http://pptfaq.com/index.html#name_PROGRAMMING_POWERPOINT.
- You can customize the Ribbon, including creating your own Ribbon tabs. Read more here: http://msdn2.microsoft.com/en-us/library/ms406046.aspx. Another helpful site is http://pschmid.net/index.php.

11

Dissecting Themes

Themes are essential tools used to create visually stunning PowerPoint presentations. In PowerPoint 2007, themes are a completely new beast from what you've been used to in the past.

We start with some simple exercises to familiarize you with using themes. Then, in the second half of this chapter, we dig deep and teach you more than you ever wanted know about themes.

We can't teach you aesthetics or good taste in this chapter, but we will arm you with tools that can help you make even the ugliest presentation just a little nicer.

IN THIS CHAPTER

- Making Unique and Beautiful Presentations
- Example of Using a Theme
- Different Types of Theme Files
- Core Parts of an Office Theme
- Creating a Theme

Making Unique and Beautiful Presentations

New People have complained about how PowerPoint looks for nearly a decade. In this section, we discuss how to use PowerPoint 2007's new themes to quickly make your presentations look stunning, yet unique.

Your Presentation Shouldn't Look Like You Stole It

The main complaint people have had for years is that most PowerPoint presentations look the same. Previous versions of PowerPoint shipped with a decent number of design templates, but the problem was they got dated rather quickly. After a few months of looking at various PowerPoint presentations, you had pretty much seen every design template in existence unless you devoted significant time searching for templates. If you deviated from canned design templates, you were on your own, which usually meant that your presentation wouldn't be as pretty unless you were a great artist and could create your own beautiful templates.

The new 2007 themes make it easy for non-artists to pick and choose parts from various designs and incorporate them into their presentations. This gives many more design combinations than PowerPoint 2003, which only let you use the entire design template or none of it. It also becomes easy to use professionally designed designs while customizing small portions of your presentation, so you aren't stuck trying to be a designer. Speaking of designers, the responsibility of matching colors, creating backgrounds, and positioning data in the themes was left for a set of professional designers who were hired by Microsoft.

NOTE

Old-timers might remember the AutoContent Wizard that existed in previous versions of PowerPoint. It walked you through a few steps and churned out a styled presentation for you at the end. The new Office themes replace the AutoContent Wizard and address its one major shortcoming: Most AutoContent Wizard presentations look very similar to one another.

It's Easy to Change Your Presentation's Look

Applying themes in PowerPoint 2007 is easier than ever. Microsoft hired designers to create some styles that are coordinated and look great. Even if you can't match your socks with your belt, you can find some great default themes to apply to your vanilla presentation so that you can automatically transform it into a great looking work of art. Applying a theme and making a few customizations requires just a few quick clicks.

Themes Across Office

One major difference between design templates in PowerPoint 2003 and the new Office themes is that 2007 themes can be used in Word, Excel, and Outlook emails, in addition to PowerPoint. Themes are applied to shapes, text, tables, diagrams, charts, slide layouts, and much more.

This is great if you have a company logo or color theme because you can create a theme to stylistically coordinate your spreadsheets, documents, presentations, and emails.

Example of Using a Theme

Let's walk through a quick example of using a theme in PowerPoint.

Apply an Entire Theme

We start by changing the entire presentation theme:

1. Start PowerPoint with a blank presentation.
2. Click the Design tab.
3. To the right of the gallery in the Themes section, click the bottom of the three buttons to expand the gallery.

4. Hover over different themes in the gallery (see Figure 11.1) and watch the presentation change. When you see one you like, click the theme to change your presentation. You can also use a theme you got off the Internet or one you created by choosing Browse for Themes at the bottom of the Themes gallery.

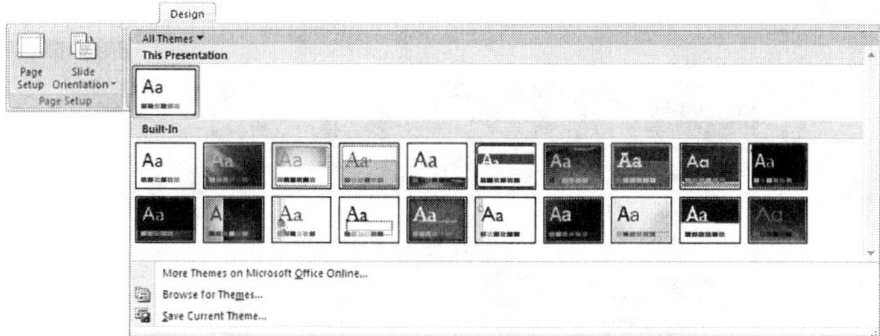

Figure 11.1

The Themes gallery expanded.

5. Now type some text into the title placeholder, and then select part of it.
6. Go to the Format tab. In the WordArt Styles group, click Text Fill (the top of the three drop-downs on the right side). Choose one of the Theme Colors in the top portion. Note that the color choices you're given here are specific to the theme you chose earlier, so unless you try really hard to make it ugly, it probably won't look horrible.
7. Go to the Format tab's Shapes Styles group and choose a pretty shape style from the gallery. Now you have a colored text box with some colored text. What we have is in Figure 11.2; your results will vary depending on the theme and colors you've chosen.

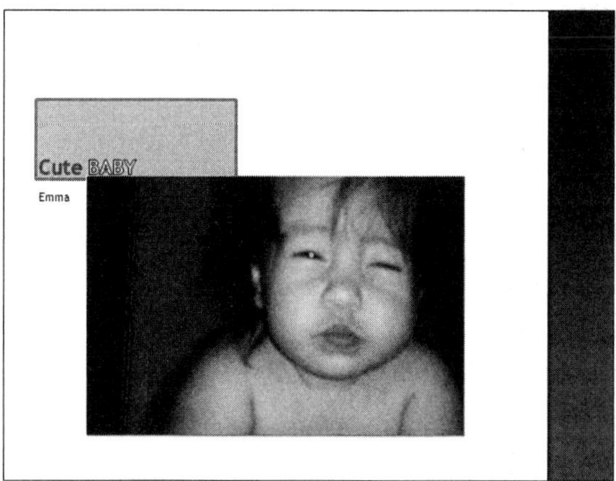

Figure 11.2

An example of some theme choices made to text and shapes after applying the Opulent theme. Compare this with Figure 11.3.

8. Finally, let's change themes again. On the Design tab, go to Themes and change the theme to your second favorite in the gallery. Everything changes—including the color and effect customization you made, which is still slightly different from the other shapes in this presentation—but everything looks good because the style comes from this new theme. Compare the result (ours is seen in Figure 11.3) with what you had before (ours is shown in Figure 11.2) and see how easy it was to change the layouts and the colors with a couple of clicks.

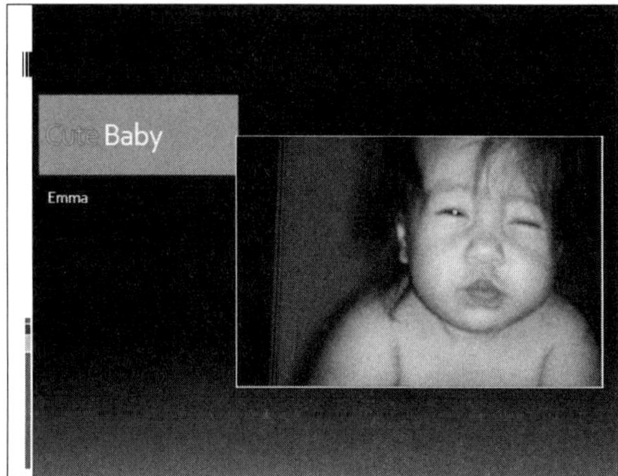

Figure 11.3

The result of changing the design theme to Metro. After one click, you have a different text box color and text color, and the layout is different.

This example shows how you can make very specific changes to your presentations that still follow the theme. This ensures that these customizations look good and update appropriately after you change themes. You can easily make changes to text fills, lines, effects and shape fills, lines, and effects in the same way, resulting in aesthetically pleasing and good looking objects that all follow the theme.

CAUTION

Despite PowerPoint 2007 making style choices easier, you can still occasionally create something visually displeasing, whether on purpose or by accident. For example, if the text color you chose happens to be the same as your chosen shape background color, it's possible that the text will disappear. Or, you might end up with some color choices that simply don't look great together. Don't be disheartened; just apply different colors or themes until you create something you like.

Apply Different Parts of Themes

We've now played with changing the theme of the entire presentation. What if we like part of one theme and part of another theme?

Whereas PowerPoint 2003 had one monolithic theme concept called a design template, PowerPoint 2007 splits themes into five different components that you can use independently:

- **Color scheme**—Used by Word, Excel, and PowerPoint 2007
- **Font scheme**—Used by Word, Excel, and PowerPoint 2007
- **Effect scheme**—Used by Word, Excel, and PowerPoint 2007
- **Slide masters**—Used by PowerPoint 2007
- **Slide layouts**—Used by PowerPoint 2007

Let's say that we're happy with the fonts and effects in our current presentation, but we want to use a different set of colors. That's easy enough to accomplish:

1. Go to the Design tab, Themes group and click the arrow to open the gallery. Choose a theme from the gallery that is appropriate for your presentation.
2. Back on the Design tab, go to the Themes group. This time, click the Colors button and choose a different set of colors that go with your chosen theme.

Now you're using colors from one theme and everything else from another theme. PowerPoint comes with 20 or so themes. By mixing and matching fonts, colors, and effects, you get a lot of combinations. This number doesn't even include background styles, which we discuss later in the chapter.

Different Types of Theme Files

Advanced Themes, effect schemes, font schemes, color schemes, presentations, and templates can all be pretty overwhelming. What's the difference between all of these? We explain it all in this section.

Theme Versus Effect Scheme Versus Font Scheme Versus Color Scheme

In the previous section, we showed everything inside a theme. The core parts are an effect scheme, a font scheme, and a color scheme. In addition to being inside a theme `.thmx` file, each of these three schemes also have their own file format (see Table 11.1).

Table 11.1 There Are Many Types of Theme Files

File Type	Extension	Format	Description
Theme	`.thmx`	binary ZIP	Contains a copied effect scheme, a font scheme, a color scheme, and other data like PowerPoint layouts. The gory details are in the previous section.
Effect Scheme	`.eftx`	binary ZIP	Contains multiple fill, lines, effects, and background styles.
Font Scheme	`.xml`	text XML	Contains names of two fonts.
Color Scheme	`.xml`	text XML	Contains 12 colors.

In the previous section, we discussed how to choose from a list of schemes and change your color scheme. When Office is displaying this list of color schemes, it isn't actually looking through your list of themes and parsing out the color information. It just looks through the color scheme `.xml` files that came with Office and shows colors from those.

NOTE

The effect, font, and color schemes that come with Office 2007 can be found in x:\Program Files\Microsoft Office\Document Themes 12. When you create your own as described in the previous section—such as a custom color scheme—they are saved in x:\Users\BillGates\AppData\Roaming\Microsoft\Templates\Document Themes on Windows Vista or x:\Documents and Settings\BillGates\Application Data\Microsoft\Templates\Document Themes on Windows XP.

What's more confusing is that these color schemes mostly have the same name as themes. For example, one of the themes that comes with Office is Apex. When you buy Office 2007, you get Apex.thmx, which is applied when you click on the Apex theme using the Themes gallery on the Design tab. It also changes the color, font, and effect schemes in your presentation to the ones stored inside Apex.thmx.

But, let's say that you want to apply a custom font scheme using the Fonts drop-down on the Design tab in the Themes group. Now you're looking at the list of font schemes, which are `.xml` files. If you choose Metro as your font scheme, it pulls the fonts from Metro.xml, not from Metro.thmx. Metro.thmx and the Metro theme aren't involved at all. It works similarly when you apply a color or effect scheme; these won't involve the theme file but just the respective color scheme (`.xml`) or effect scheme files (`.eftx`).

Theme Versus Presentation Versus Template

Now that you have schemes and themes straight, how do these relate to presentations (`.pptx`) and template (`.potx`) files? This is more confusing since themes replace templates, which were the primary way of styling your document in previous versions of PowerPoint:

- Themes (`.thmx`) are standalone files shared across Word, Excel, and PowerPoint 2007. We've explained all the gory details of themes in the previous few sections of this chapter. They contain an effect scheme, a font scheme, a color scheme, and PowerPoint layouts and masters.
- Presentations (`.pptx`, `.pptm`) contain slides, masters, formatting, and all the core parts you'd expect in a presentation. They also contain style information copied from a theme, including theme colors, theme fonts, and theme effects. Remember, you can mix and match so that a slide in a presentation might contain a background from one theme, theme colors from a second theme, and theme fonts from yet another theme. And one shape in the same presentation can glow from a different effect scheme from a completely different theme.
- Templates (`.potx`, `.potm`) were more like themes in previous versions of PowerPoint, but in PowerPoint 2007, they're essentially just an example presentation and contain everything you'd find inside a presentation file.

Core Parts of an Office Theme

Now that we've talked about using themes, this section goes more in depth about what's in a theme that so you have a better understanding of how themes work.

Themes are intentionally designed to contain a small amount of abstract style information. This is for two reasons:

- **Content reuse**—Originally, the designers of Office themes tried to be specific, embedding specific font sizes, for instance. This doesn't work well across applications though because PowerPoint's font sizes are generally much larger than Word's. By staying abstract, the theme can be applied to mean something slightly different in each Office application.
- **More theme-based choices**—Many visual styles can be derived from each theme. For example, a theme contains only a handful of text colors, but the application can derive a slew of them from that core set. This is very important because although it's good that you can ignore the theme entirely and set your own custom colors, PowerPoint wants you to follow something derived from the theme whenever possible so that your changes are restyled if the theme changes. So, you have a lot of colors to choose from—many more than were stored in the actual theme—yet all of them are ultimately theme colors.

Let's look at everything that's physically inside a `.thmx` theme file.

NOTE

If you're a techie and want to follow along, a `.thmx` file is similar to other Office 2007 files such as a `.pptx` file. Take your favorite `.thmx` file and rename it to `.zip`—for example, take Apex.thmx and rename it Apex.zip. Then, you can use Windows Explorer, WinZip, or another Zip program to take a closer look at what's inside (as shown in Figure 11.4). Most of what's discussed here is found inside the theme1.xml file.

Font Scheme

Part of a theme is the Font Scheme. Let's take a look at what this actually is.

NOTE

The PowerPoint user interface calls these Theme Font, Theme Color, and Theme Effect. The file format calls them Font Scheme, Color Scheme, and Effect Scheme. We use them somewhat interchangeably in this section of the book, but don't be confused: The names are completely synonymous.

A theme contains two fonts:

- **Major font**—Used mostly for headers
- **Minor font**—Used mostly for body text

These two fonts can different or the same. The default Office theme sets both to Calibri.

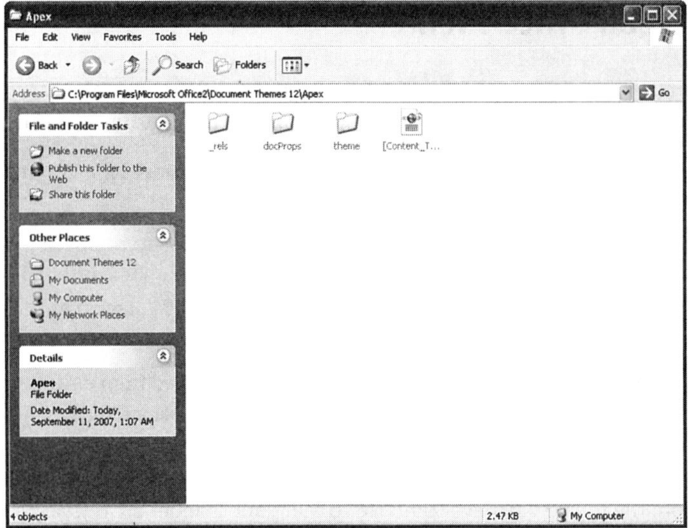

Figure 11.4

A listing of files inside a theme using Windows Explorer in Vista.

In comparison, PowerPoint 2003 design templates could specify fonts for placeholders by setting fonts on the master. But, text boxes and shapes that weren't based on master objects could never change fonts based on the template. It was up to individual users to make sure that they looked good and to manually change them after changing design templates.

NOTE

In reality, many more than two fonts are stored because each theme that ships with Office contains one major font and one minor font for each locale/language that Office ships in.

USING A THEME FONT

Let's see these in action:

1. Start a new presentation.
2. Type some text into a placeholder and select it.
3. Drop down the font selector on the Home tab, Font group (see Figure 11.5). Notice how the first two choices are listed under Theme Fonts. If you set the font as one of these, your text automatically changes fonts if you change themes or font schemes.

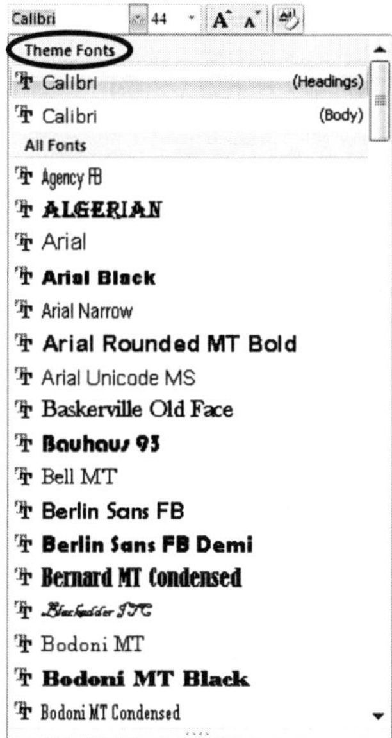

Figure 11.5

Display available fonts. Notice how the first two choices are theme fonts.

TIP

Changing theme fonts can seriously change the layout of text you've carefully positioned throughout your presentation. For most presentations, you should feel free to experiment by applying different font themes. But, if text layout is extremely important to you, your best bet is to apply a theme or a theme font before adding a whole bunch of text to your presentation. Learn more about font schemes and new Office 2007 fonts in Chapter 2, "Everything You Need to Know About Text."

CHANGING AND ADDING FONT SCHEMES

To change a font scheme, go to the Design tab, Themes group and click the Fonts drop-down. Choose from the list of font schemes that come with Office (see Figure 11.6).

You can add your own font schemes to the list by going to the Design tab, Themes group, clicking the Fonts drop-down, and choosing Create New Theme Fonts (seen at the bottom of Figure 11.6). In the dialog (Figure 11.7), you can specify the two fonts, give it a name, and then it's added to the list whenever you use Office.

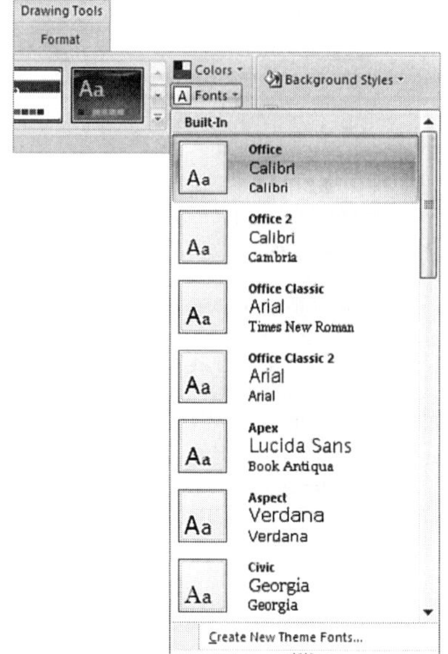

Figure 11.6

Choose from a list of font schemes.

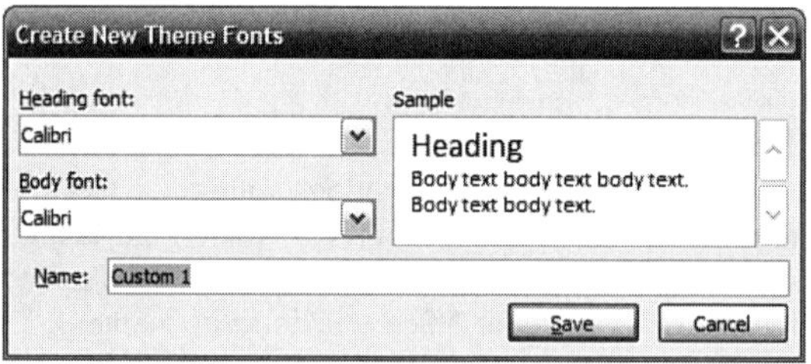

Figure 11.7

Dialog to create new theme fonts.

Color Scheme

A theme contains 12 different colors:

- Four colors are for text and backgrounds. There are two light colors and two dark ones, and Office's design guidelines say that the two dark colors must each be visible on the two light backgrounds, and vice versa.
- Six are accent colors. The design guidelines say that they must be visible when placed on top of the previous four colors.
- Two of the colors are for the hyperlink and followed hyperlink colors.

Some additional notes about using color are

- Each color may be a simple RGB (for example, 30% red, 30% green, and 40% blue) or named color (for example, I want it to be "magenta"), but PowerPoint supports more exotic options such as a reference to a system color, like the current window text color. Colors that aren't RGB or names can't be set inside PowerPoint, and theme makers have to set them by manually editing the theme in XML.
- PowerPoint 2003 design templates each contained a smaller set of eight colors that worked just for that template. It had one color each for background, text, shadow, title text, fills, accent, hyperlink, and followed hyperlink. Because 2007 themes need to work in Word and Excel, the eight colors weren't enough since Word documents and Excel spreadsheets nearly always have white backgrounds, and colors that looked good on the theme background color wouldn't necessarily look good on white. So, in addition to carrying over the main color scheme colors from PowerPoint 2003 to 2007, each PowerPoint 2007 theme contains more colors that are guaranteed to work on dark backgrounds and some that work on light backgrounds.

To apply a Theme Color, do the following:

1. Start a new presentation.
2. Select one of the placeholders.
3. Go to the Home tab, Drawing group and choose Shape Fill (see Figure 11.8) to view the Office color picker.

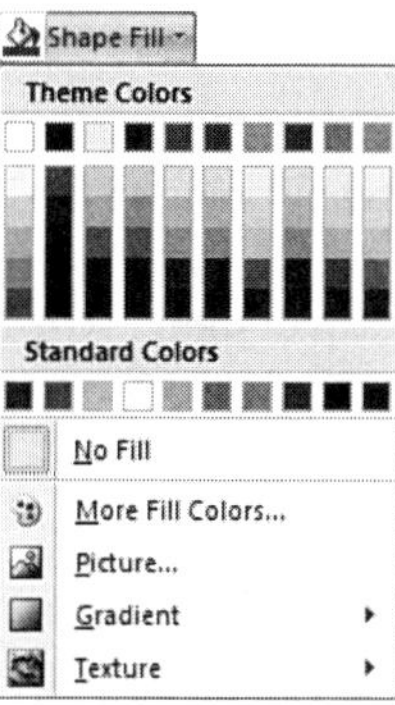

Figure 11.8

The Office color picker.

Of the theme colors, notice how there are 10 columns, corresponding to the 10 colors in the color scheme. Below each of the 10 colors are subtle tints of the color that Office derives automatically from each scheme color.

Scheme colors are also subtly woven into other formatting menus. For example, if you use the shape gallery (select a shape and then go to Format tab, Shape Styles group and choose from the gallery on the left) or apply an effect like a glow (on the Format tab, Shape Styles group, choose Shape Effects and then Glow), these change your shape to use a scheme color.

Change color schemes by going to the Design tab, Themes group and click the Colors button. Choose from the list of color schemes that come with Office (see Figure 11.9).

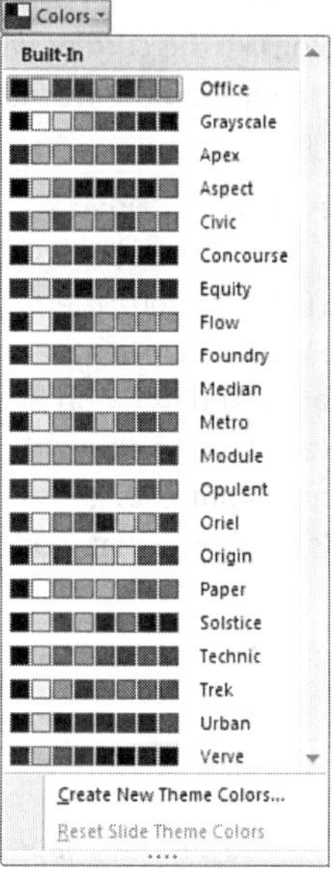

Figure 11.9

Choose from the list of Office color schemes.

Again, you can add your own color scheme by going to the Design tab, Themes group, clicking the Colors button, and choosing Create New Theme Colors (shown at the bottom of Figure 11.9). In the dialog (Figure 11.10), choose a color for each of the 12 scheme colors, give it a name, and save it for future use throughout Microsoft Office.

Effect Scheme

Finally, the effect scheme is part of a theme that determines which fill, line, effect, and backgrounds are used.

An effect scheme contains four sets of three items each:

- Fill styles
- Line styles
- Effect styles (shadow, 3D, glow, blur, and so on)
- Background fill styles

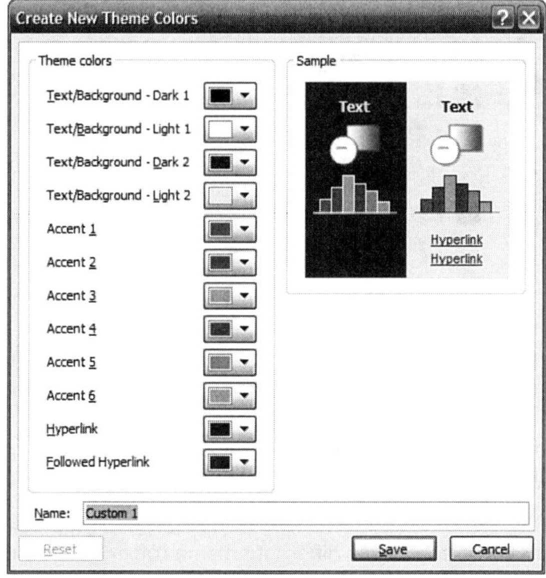

Figure 11.10

Dialog used to create new theme colors.

There are three variations for each component here, one for

- A subtle variation
- A moderate variation
- An intense variation

Any of the styles might contain references to an image—in which case, the image file would be stored inside the effect scheme. For example, a theme might have a picture fill of a sunset as one of the three fill styles. In that situation, the picture of the sunset would be stored in the effect scheme.

USING A THEME EFFECT

Effect schemes are used to create many of the PowerPoint galleries that let you quickly change the look of text or shapes:

1. Start a new presentation.
2. Select one of the placeholders.
3. Go to the Format tab. In the Shape Styles group, click the bottom arrow to the right of the gallery (see Figure 11.11).

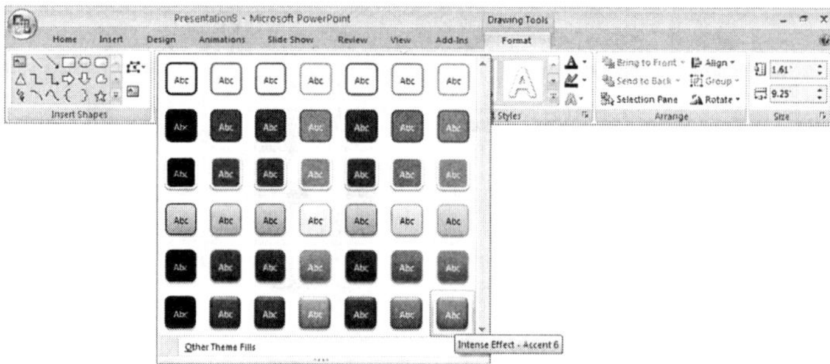

Figure 11.11

View 49 styles you can quickly apply in the Shape Styles gallery.

Note how there are 7 columns and 7 rows, providing 49 options altogether. These 49 options aren't stored in the theme. Rather, Office generates these automatically from the abstract color and effect scheme information:

- The seven columns come from seven different scheme colors. Note how the text colors look good on the fill colors because of the color rules mentioned earlier.
- The seven rows come from combining the subtle, moderator, and intense variations of fill, line, and effect styles with each other.

CHANGING OR ADDING A EFFECT SCHEME

As with the color or font scheme, changing effect schemes is as easy as going to the Design tab, Themes group and clicking Effects, and then choosing from the list (see Figure 11.12).

NOTE

Ready to add your own effect scheme? Unfortunately, it's not as easy as it was with colors and fonts. PowerPoint doesn't provide a user interface for creating an effect scheme, so you have to edit the theme file directly, which is beyond the scope of this book. We're sure that someone will eventually write a tool to make this easier.

Object Defaults and Extra Color Schema List

The theme can contain information that specifies what style new shapes take on and provides some space to store extra color schema used by other Office applications. Themes that ship with Office don't specify values for either of these, so just ignore them.

Thumbnails

The theme contains a few canned thumbnails, which are used to display a preview of your theme viewed from the Windows Explorer or from the Office Themes gallery. You can edit these with any image editor, and you will see the changes when you preview the theme in Explorer or Office.

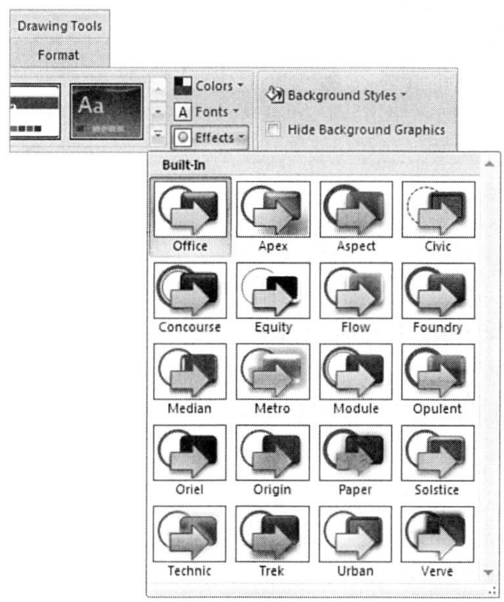

Figure 11.12

Choose from the list of Office effect schemes.

- **Shell**—thumbnail.jpeg is used to show a quick preview of the theme in Windows Explorer. When you select a theme in Windows, this will be displayed in the preview box.
- **Gallery**—themeThumbnail.jpeg and auxiliaryThemeThumbnail.jpeg are used to preview the theme in the Office gallery. It's essentially the little square icon that appears when you view a theme in the Office Themes gallery.

Slide Layouts and Masters

Finally, themes contain PowerPoint slide layouts and slide masters. That's why when you switch themes, the layout of your slides changes too:

- A slide layout contains a definition for a slide. This includes the positions of every shape and placeholder that appears on the slide, along with the formatting of each of these objects, such as colors, effects, and fonts.
- A slide master merely has a list of layouts associated with that master, and any additional shapes that the theme authors want to appear on every layout associated with that master.

We don't want to rehash layouts and masters here, so for a refresher, read Chapter 10, "Formatting Your Presentation," where we discuss creating custom layouts.

That's it. You now know everything inside a theme.

NOTE

Previous versions of PowerPoint had animation schemes—animations that were supposed to look good with a particular presentation. Animation schemes no longer exist and are not part of PowerPoint 2007 themes.

Creating a Theme

We've explained in previous sections how to make your own quick-and-dirty color and font schemes. Real PowerPoint power users make entire themes though, so let's construct a quickie:

NOTE

If you're a professional Office theme maker, these instructions aren't for you. The Office user interface only exposes a small fraction of the customizability available in the file format and to create the best themes—comparable to the themes that come with Office—you need to learn to learn XML and the file formats to edit a `.thmx` file directly.

---

1. Start with a blank presentation.
2. Add some master slides, a notes master, a handout master, and a title master. Chapter 10 details how to do this. Don't forget to add some special bullets, a header and footer, and maybe even some annoying animation sounds to your master slides.
3. Create a custom color and font scheme and select them (on the Design tab, Themes group, choose Color or choose Font). You can't create a custom effect scheme or background style using the PowerPoint user interface, but you can select an existing one to use for your theme by going to the Design tab, Background group and choosing Background Style or to the Themes group and click Effects).
4. Save your creation by going to the Design tab, Themes group, dropping down the gallery, and choosing Save Current Theme at the bottom (see Figure 11.13).

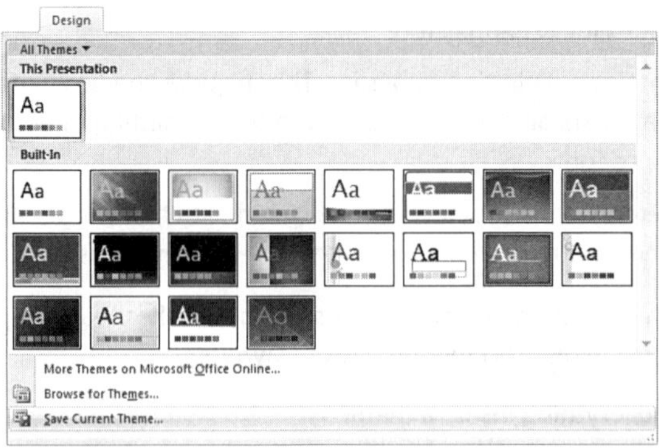

Figure 11.13

Choose the Save Current Theme option to save the current styles as an Office theme.

Voilà! You've got a theme.

To use your theme, open a blank presentation or a presentation you want to restyle. Go the same place under the Design tab, Themes group, open the gallery, but instead choose Browse for Themes. (You can see it in Figure 11.13 above Save Current Theme.) Then find the theme you saved on disk and apply it. If you really like your theme and want it to appear in the gallery for everyone using your computer, you can add it to the built-in list at x:\Program Files\Microsoft Office\Document Themes 12, assuming that your IT administrator has given you permission to do so.

12

Formatting Shapes, Text, and More

IN THIS CHAPTER

- What Can I Format?
- Three Ways to Apply Formatting
- Impressive Fills
- Advanced Line Styles
- Brand New Effects
- Transparent Overlay
- Customize the Default Shape
- The Mysterious Paintbrush Icon (Format Painter)
- Using Repeat Can Save You Time
- Mastering Multiple Undo
- Change Shape

Now that we've shown you how to create excellent content, let's journey into some tips on making it prettier.

When most people think Microsoft Office graphics, the first thing that comes to mind is Clip Art, WordArt, or something equally ugly and tacky. That obviously isn't acceptable for *your* presentation, so often you'd spend hours deciphering Adobe Photoshop to perform a simple operation such as adding a soft shadow or a glow on some text because such tasks were impossible to do in previous versions of PowerPoint. Though that might have been representative of Office graphics for the last decade or so, that assumption is no longer true.

For the PowerPoint 2007 release, an entirely new feature set was created to support amazing graphics. This means it's easy to create twenty-first century visuals that are easy to create and aesthetically mind-blowing. If you want to jazz up some shapes, spiff up your text, or make a nice graphic for your next marketing stunt, Office 2007 makes it very easy to do so. Formatting a presentation also helps your audience read slides easily and understand the message you are trying to convey.

What Can I Format?

We're going to focus on formatting a simple rectangle shape, but the formatting described in much of this chapter is applicable to a plethora of objects, whether they are

- Shapes
- SmartArt diagrams
- Charts
- Text
- Tables
- Or even parts of these objects, such as one bar in a chart

After an object is selected, go to the Format tab to see what changes can be made to the object.

NOTE

If you have a shape selected, this is the Drawing Tools Format tab. If you have SmartArt selected, it's the SmartArt Tool Format tab you want. Whatever you select, the tab is labeled Format.

Three Ways to Apply Formatting

There are three ways to apply formatting in PowerPoint. You can use gallery styles, do specific formats from the gallery, or use the Format Shape dialog.

Let's walk through an example. Insert a rectangle by going to the Home tab's Drawing group and opening the Shapes gallery. Click one of the rectangles, and then click on the slide to insert the rectangle. (More information about inserting shapes can be found in Chapter 7, "Working with Shapes.") Now let's discuss the different ways you can customize this rectangle.

Gallery Styles

The easiest way to format is to choose from the style gallery. With the rectangle you inserted earlier selected, go to the Drawing Tools Format tab's Shape Styles group and choose from the gallery of shapes. Whatever you select is applied to the shape, changing everything about it—including its fill and its outline—and often applying fancy effects such as a shadow or a reflection. You can click the bottom of the three buttons to the right of the gallery to fully expand the style gallery and see the available choices (see Figure 12.1).

You can make similar text formats by going to the Drawing Tools Format tab, and then the WordArt Styles group, and choosing from the gallery of formatted text. You learned in Chapter 11, "Dissecting Themes," about how Office uses themes to determine what styles end up in both the shape and text galleries.

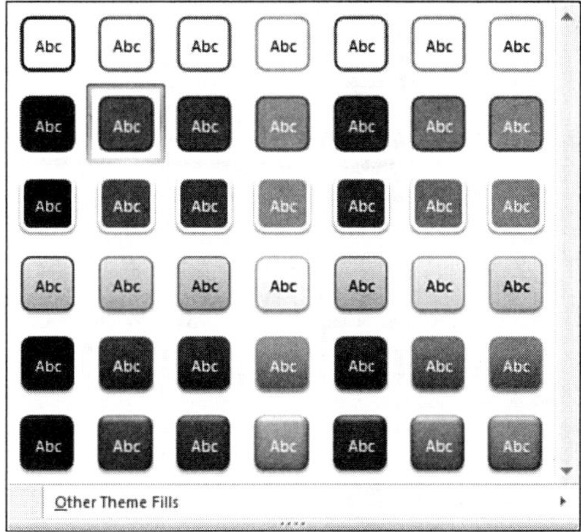

Figure 12.1

Expand the style gallery to see some styles that can be applied to a shape.

NOTE

To quickly format when you have a shape handy, just double-click the shape, and PowerPoint switches you over to the Drawing Tools Format tab.

Formatting from the Ribbon

Most gallery formats look nice enough, but they're overkill if we just want to make one very specific change, such as change a rectangle's fill to red.

Making a single edit, such as changing the fill color, is easy enough to do: Go to the Drawing Tools Format tab, the Shape Styles group, and click Shape Fill. Select your favorite fill (see Figure 12.2). For text, you'd use the Drawing Tools Format tab, go to the WordArt Styles group, and choose Text Fill. If you look on the Shape Styles and Text Styles groups, you will see other drop-downs that let you change the outline or apply effects. For example, going to Drawing Tools Format tab, Shape Styles group, clicking Shape Effects, and choosing Glow lets you apply a glow to a shape.

Format Shape Dialog

Finally, for super power users, there's the Format Shape dialog. For this example, let's say that we want to be very specific about the type of outline for our rectangle:

1. Select the rectangle again.
2. Go to the Drawing Tools Format tab, Shape Styles group, and click the box launcher (the little rectangle at the bottom right of the group). Alternatively, right-click your rectangle and select Format Shape. Either command brings up the Format Shape dialog, which lets you customize all aspects of a shape in great detail.

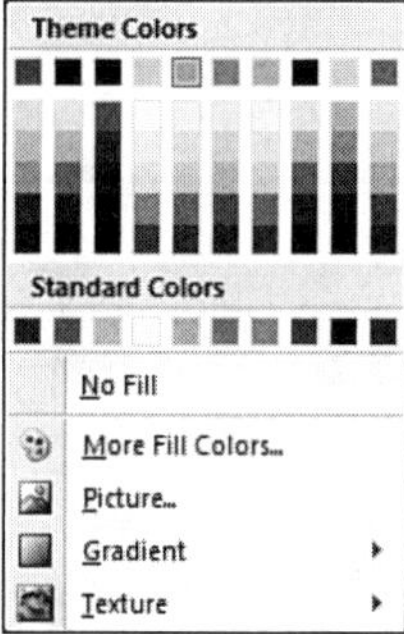

Figure 12.2

Choose a shape fill.

NOTE

Read more about the Ribbon's dialog box launcher in Chapter 1, "Introducing the Office 2007 User Interface."

---

3. Select Line Style on the left and set a new dash type for the outline. We will discuss each of these line options in greater detail later in this chapter. Notice how the change is applied right away.
4. Close the Format Shape box.

Again, the same effect can be applied to text by clicking the expand rectangle in the Drawing Tools Format tab's WordArt Styles group or by selecting text, right-clicking, and choosing Format Text Effects.

Impressive Fills

There's more to life than just plain, solid fills. In this section, we talk about the different ways you can fill an object.

Solid Fills

We already talked about super simple solid fills in this chapter. With your favorite items selected, go to the Drawing Tools Format tab, the Shape Styles group, and then click Shape Fill to choose your favorite fill color. You can learn more about the two types of colors, Theme Colors and Standard Colors, in Chapter 11.

Gradient Fills

A gradient fill is actually very similar to a solid fill, only with more than one color. A solid fill uses one color for the entire fill. A gradient uses several set colors and smoothly transitions between them. For example, Figure 12.3 shows a gradient from black to white to gray.

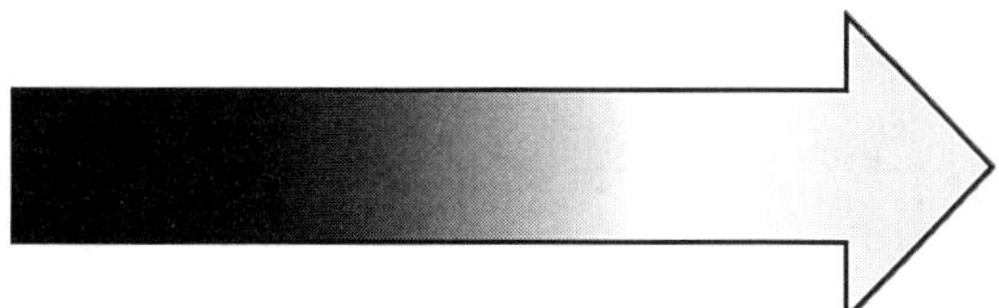

Figure 12.3

This gradient goes from black to white to gray.

APPLYING A SIMPLE GRADIENT

Applying a basic gradient fill is easy. With something selected, go to the Drawing Tools Format tab and then the Shape Styles group. Click Shape Fill, Gradient to choose from the canned variations shown in Figure 12.4. These gradients all involve colors pulled from the current theme that your presentation is using (again, more on themes in Chapter 11).

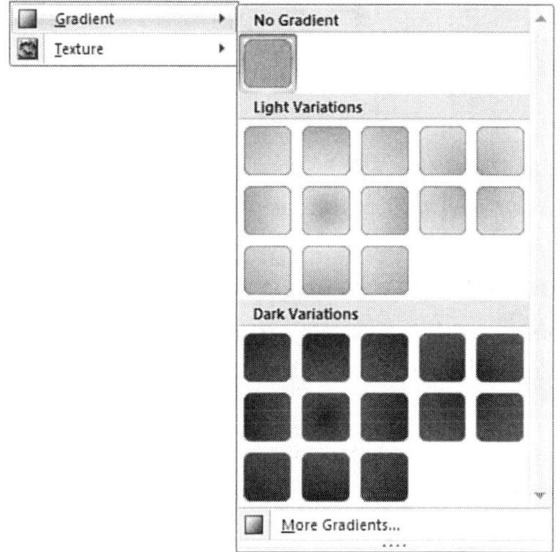

Figure 12.4

Choose from the canned gradient in the Gradient menu.

CREATING CUSTOM GRADIENTS

To do something more custom, do the following:

1. Go to the Drawing Tools Format tab and then to the Shape Style group and click Shape Fill.
2. Click Gradient. Click the More Gradients button at the bottom of the drop-down. Choose Gradient Fill if it isn't already chosen. Make sure that the dialog doesn't cover up the shape you're formatting because as you change things in the dialog, the shape changes immediately. Move the dialog off to the side if you need to.

3. Choose the Gradient Fill option. You get a very complex set of options shown in Figure 12.5.

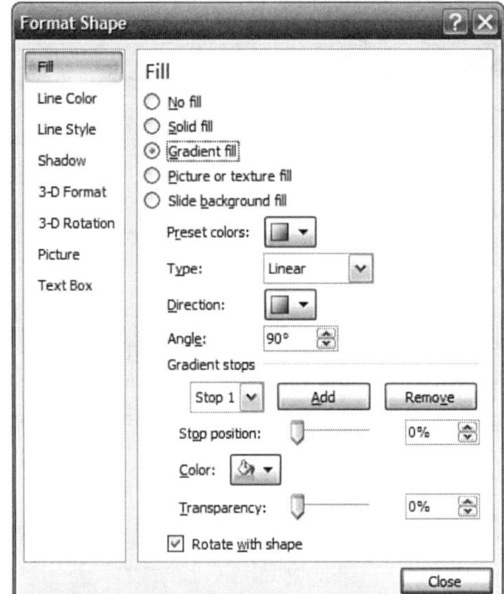

Figure 12.5

Advanced gradient options. Your settings might look different depending on the gradient you selected.

A few drop-downs on this dialog box let you change things about the gradient:

- **Preset Colors**—Lets you select from some canned gradients. They have been here since older versions of PowerPoint had them, but they're honestly pretty ugly so we suggest skipping over them.
- **Type**—Describes how PowerPoint transitions between different colors in the gradient. See Figure 12.6 to see what the different gradient types look like.
- **Linear**—The color band between colors looks like a line (hence the name "linear").

TIP

The number of bands is independent of the number of stops. Placing many stops very close to one another can be used to visually produce one smooth band.

- **Radial**—Has a circular color band between colors.
- **Rectangular**—The color band looks like a rectangle.
- **Path**—The gradient's color band depends on the shape that you're applying the gradient to. For a star shape, for example, the path gradient's boundary is star shaped.

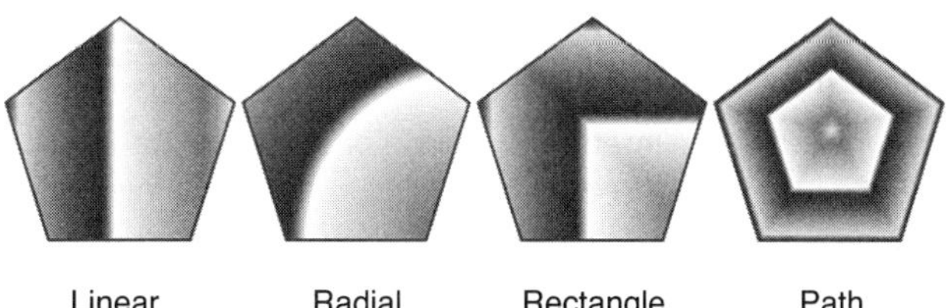

Figure 12.6
The four gradient types applied to a rectangle shape.

- **Direction and Angle**—These actually do the same thing by letting you choose what direction the boundary between colors faces. For example, a 0° linear gradient has colors changing from left to right, whereas a 90° gradient goes from top to bottom. The Direction drop-down lets you choose from some preset choices, whereas the Angle text box lets you type in an exact number. These are grayed out if you set the Type as Path because the direction is determined by the type of shape you have.
- **Rotate with Shape**—This check box at the bottom of the dialog lets you choose whether the colors rotate when you rotate the shape. You will learn more about rotation in Chapter 14, "Positioning Slide Elements."

The dialog also lets you add and remove colors in the gradient. Each of these color points is called a *gradient stop*.

The Gradient stop drop-down lets you choose which stop in the gradient (Stop 1, Stop 2, and so on) you want to edit. When you choose a value, the Stop position, Color, and Transparency values change to show you what their values are for the current stop. To add more stops, click Add. To delete the selected stop, click Remove.

Here's what the values within each stop mean:

- **Stop position**—Lets you determine how important this stop/color is in the gradient. The stops define when gradient changes from one color to the next with the stop order determined by the stop number. For example, if you want Stop 3 to stand out a lot in your gradient (for example, you want the blue in your red, white, and blue gradient to stand out the most), select Stop 3 in the drop-down and increase the Stop position percentage. Similarly, if you want the color to have less prominence, decrease the percentage.
- **Color**—This sets the color for this gradient stop.
- **Transparency**—Choose how transparent that stop is. This means that part of your shape can be more transparent than other parts.

Creating Gradient Overlays

Advanced Overlaying transparent, gradient-filled shapes on top of existing objects creates a stunning, yet very professional effect. It's fairly easy to create and can be applied to any object you have in your presentation.

Let's walk through an example. We have a picture of a mountain, and we want the left side to represent day and the right side to represent night.

1. Insert a picture by going to the Insert tab's Illustrations group and choosing Picture. If you have Windows XP, you can find this exact picture (see Figure 12.7) at `C:\Documents and Settings\All Users\Documents\My Pictures\Sample Pictures\Winter.jpg`, but any picture will do.

Figure 12.7

Insert a large picture.

2. For this overlay, you need three rectangles. To insert these shapes, go to the Home tab's Drawing group, select Shapes, and choose a rectangle. Drag out the first rectangle so that it covers up the left half of the picture, and then create two more rectangles that each cover up a quarter of the remaining area on the right side, as shown in Figure 12.8.
3. Shift-click to select all three rectangles and set the line style to No Line. To do this, go to the Drawing Tools Format tab, find the Shape Styles group, click the Shape Outline drop-down, and choose No Outline.
4. Now it gets more hard-core. Select just the big rectangle on the left side. Right-click it and choose Format Shape to bring up the Format Shape dialog.
5. Click Fill on the left, and then choose the Gradient fill option.
6. PowerPoint creates three gradient stops automatically, so there are three choices. You want to play with the middle gradient stop. So, change the Gradient Stops drop-down from Stop 1 to Stop 2. Then change the Transparency value from 0% to 100%, which sets the transparency of the middle gradient stop.

   Three stops are set, and we're making the middle stop see-through; this means that you will be able to see through the middle of the rectangle completely, as shown in Figure 12.9.

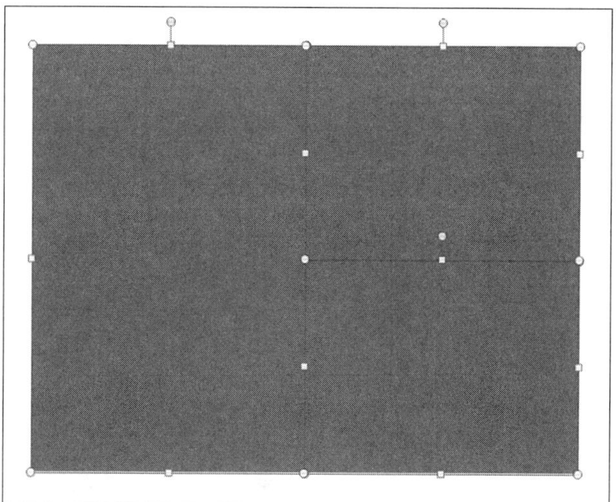

Figure 12.8

Cover the picture up with rectangles.

Figure 12.9

Make the middle of the big rectangle see-through.

Okay, now that the left side of the picture looks spiffy, let's work on the right side:

1. With the Format Shape dialog still open, select the top-right rectangle. (You might need to reposition the dialog so that it doesn't block the rectangle.)
2. In the dialog, click Fill on the left, and then choose Gradient Fill. Choose black as the color for the first gradient stop.

3. In the Gradient Stops drop-down, switch to Stop 2. Verify that the Transparency is set to 100%, or set it to 100% if it isn't.
4. Switch to Stop 3 in the Gradient Stops list and click Remove to delete it. We only want two gradient stops for this rectangle.
5. Finally, select the bottom-right rectangle. In the Format Shape dialog, click Fill on the left and set it to Gradient Fill as well. Stop 1 should already be selected, so we're manipulating the first gradient stop. Set the Transparency to 100% so that we can see-through the first stop. Switch to Stop 2 and change the transparency back to 0%.

Close the dialog, and bam; you get the cool looking effect pictured in Figure 12.10. Neat, huh?

Figure 12.10

Final results of our gradient overlay recipe.

This technique of overlaying partially transparent shapes on top of pictures or other objects is effective for making subtle color changes to stuff that's underneath. Experiment with shapes other than rectangles, with different gradient colors, and with different transparencies, and see what you can come up with.

Picture Fills

Want to use a picture as your shape background? That's easy enough.

Once again, start with your basic rectangle. Go to the Home tab and in the Drawing group, click Shapes. Choose a rectangle, and then click on the slide to insert it. To apply a simple picture fill to your rectangle, select the rectangle, and then go to the Drawing Tools Format tab. In the Shape Styles group, click the Shape Fill button and choose Picture. Then browse to a folder in which you keep your pictures and choose a picture to use.

NOTE

After the picture is inserted, notice how the Picture Tools Format tab appears. This lets you apply picture-based effects to your picture-filled shape. Details on using pictures in your presentations can be found in Chapter 4, "Working with Pictures."

Textures and Picture Fills

Of course there's more to picture fills than just that simple case. Insert a new rectangle, right-click it, and select Format Shape. Choose the Picture or Texture Fill option in the main pane on the right, shown in Figure 12.11.

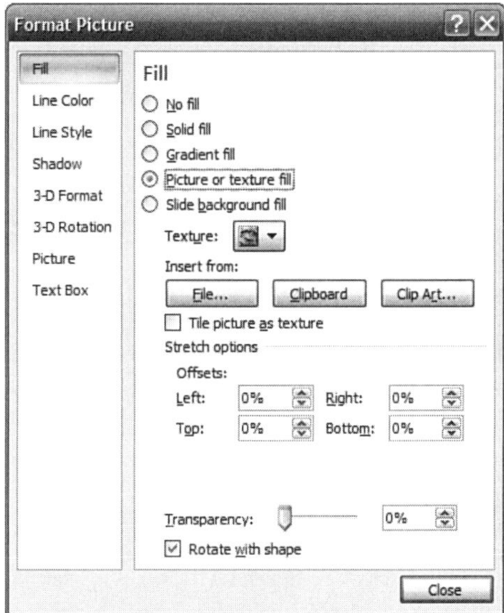

Figure 12.11
Picture Fill dialog.

Let's briefly walk through the options found on this dialog:

- **Texture**—Lets you choose from a canned set of textures that have come with PowerPoint for several versions.
- **Insert From**—Most likely, you want to insert a picture from a file you have. But, PowerPoint also lets you insert something you copied to the clipboard or use some Clip Art.
- **Tile Picture as Texture**—If you check this box, the image is tiled, meaning that it keeps repeating to completely fill up the shape. If it's unchecked, the image you choose is stretched to fit the shape.
- **Stretch Options**—These options appear if the Tile Picture as Texture box was unchecked. The four percentages let you adjust where the edges of the image touch the edges of the shape.

For example, if you make the Left percentage negative, the left border of the image will spill a little outside the left border of the shape. Similarly, making it positive means that there will be a slight gap between the left border of the shape and the left border of the image.

- **Tiling options**—These options appear if the Tile Picture as Texture box is checked (see Figure 12.12). The Offset values let you choose where to begin tiling the image. You might want to start with half a tile, for instance, rather than have the first tile begin at the left border of the image. The Scale values let you reduce the size of the image so that you can tile more of them. Alignment lets you choose where to start tiling from, and the Mirror type lets you choose whether the second tile is a mirror image of the first tile or whether it just appears normally.

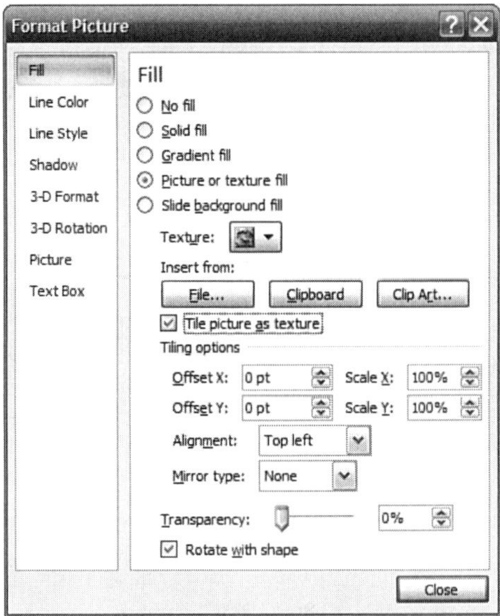

Figure 12.12

Picture Fill dialog when Tile Picture as Texture is checked.

- **Transparency**—Choose how transparent the picture should be.
- **Rotate with Shape**—Decide whether you want the picture to rotate when the shape rotates.

NOTE

Previous versions of PowerPoint also supported pattern fills. For this, you'd select between 64 different colorless patterns. This was useful in the days before color monitors and color printers were as prevalent as they are now. PowerPoint 2007 no longer supports pattern fills, and if you open an older presentation with one, PowerPoint converts it to a picture fill.

Background Fill

One special type of PowerPoint fill is a slide background fill. You will find the other fills (solid, gradient, and picture) in other Office applications such as Excel, but Slide Background Fill is unique to PowerPoint.

Say you have a rectangle that you give a background fill. The rectangle gets the same fill as the background, even if you have a few other shapes underneath the rectangle. You can think of it as using a hole punch: You're cutting a hole in everything that lies between your shape and the background.

Here's how to set one up:

1. In a new presentation, change the slide background to a picture. To do this, right-click the slide background and choose Format Background. Click the Gradient Fill option to fill the slide background with a gradient.
2. Insert a shape of some sort (use the Shapes gallery on the Home tab). A rectangle will do just fine.
2. Right-click the shape and choose Format Shape.
3. Choose the Slide background fill option.

Note that this didn't simply copy the background's fill type, which is set to a two color gradient, and plop it on the rectangle. If we apply the same two color gradients directly to the rectangle, it looks different (see Figure 12.13).

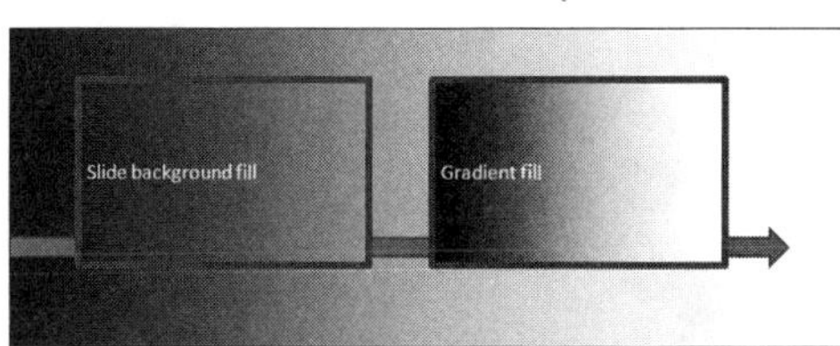

Figure 12.13

Setting a gradient fill isn't the same as a background fill. Notice how the left side of the gradient-filled rectangle on the right is dark, whereas the background at that part of the slide isn't nearly as dark.

A background fill is actually equivalent to punching a hole all the way through and the shape picking up the fill from the background.

INTERESTING USES OF BACKGROUND FILLS

This section gives a brief overview of two creative uses for a background fill.

Say that you want to put a link to slide 1 on every slide in your presentation. So, you go to the Slide Master, and you stick an Action button to the first slide on there. (Read Chapter 15, "Going Beyond Slide-by-Slide," for more on Action Buttons.)

Awesome! But that button shows up on the first slide, too. And it's sort of silly to have a link on the first slide to the first slide.

Now, this is certainly fixable. We could, for instance, use a different master or a different layout for the first slide; you learned about those in Chapter 10, "Formatting Your Presentation." Those aren't perfect though, because if we ever update the master we would have to remember to also update the special master or layout we created for the first slide. We're probably not going to remember to do that.

This is where background fills come in handy. All we have to do is cover up the link on the first page with a background filled shape. In Figure 12.14, we've inserted a rectangle shape on top of the Action Button, removed the line (selected the button, went to the Drawing Tools Format tab, went to the Shape Styles group, and chose No Outline), and given it a background fill. Best of all, our first slide still follows the same master as the rest of the slides, but that special Action button we added on the master won't show on the first slide because we've covered it up.

NOTE

Another way to accomplish this task would be to add the Action button just on the layouts in which it made sense. This means that you wouldn't have to hide the button on the other layouts. The downside is that you would have to add the button multiple times if you wanted the button on most of your layouts.

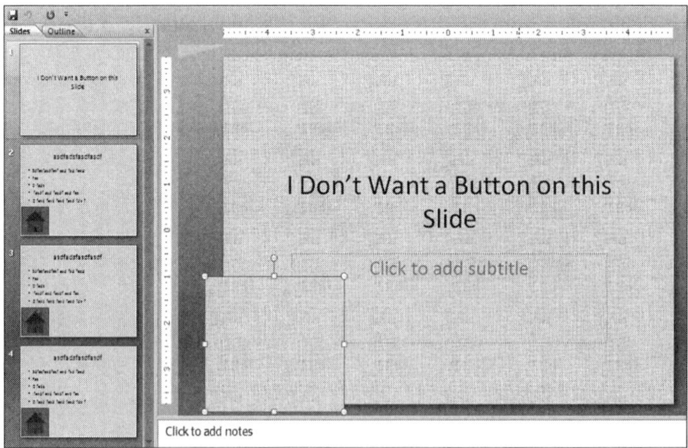

Figure 12.14

Putting a background filled shape on top of the Action button hides the Action button on the front page, while still allowing that slide to follow the same master as our other slides.

Just as a background-filled object can be used to hide a button on the master, background fills can be used to punch holes through parts of pictures. This lets you create nonrectangular pictures in a totally custom shape that you determine.

TIP

If you don't need something too custom and just want your picture in a simple shape such as a star, a circle, or a heart, insert a shape and then apply a picture fill to it, as described earlier in this chapter.

1. Insert a picture.
2. Go to the Home tab and in the Drawing group, click Shapes. Choose Scribble in the Lines section; it's the last item in the Lines section.
3. Use the pencil to circle the area of the picture you want to hide.
4. Right-click the shape you created and choose Format Shape.
5. Choose Line Color on the left and then select No Line.
6. Click Fill on the left, and then choose Slide Background Fill.
7. Click OK, and voilà! You've punched a hole through part of the picture (see Figure 12.15).

Figure 12.15

The result of a background-filled freeform on top of a picture is a partially hidden picture.

Advanced Line Styles

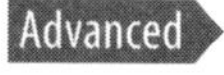

Shapes, text, diagrams, and charts have outlines. PowerPoint allows you to format them in a pretty rich way.

Line Color

If you're comfortable with fills from the previous section, setting a line color is just as easy.

- To use the gallery, go to the Drawing Tools Format tab, Shape Styles group and click Shape Outline to select an outline color.
- Alternatively, you can use the Format Shape dialog to select a line color, which lets you apply gradient colors. Just right-click the shape and choose Format Shape. Choose Line Color on the left, and you can select No Line, which can be hard to find there under the Line Color section. But, usually you would select Solid Line or Gradient Line. The gradient line options may look complicated at first, but you will quickly notice that they're identical to the gradient fill options described earlier in this chapter.

NOTE

A gradient line might not appear to do anything if the line itself or the outline around a shape is too narrow. Gradient-colored lines are new to PowerPoint 2007 and weren't available in previous versions of PowerPoint. Previous versions of PowerPoint allowed setting patterned lines; however, they aren't available in PowerPoint 2007. It's all give and take.

Line Style

Colors aren't the only changes you can make to a line or an outline. To explore PowerPoint line styles, let's walk through an example:

1. Insert a line from the Shapes gallery (on the Home tab's Drawing group). Choose one of the lines in the Lines section and click the slide to insert it.
2. Right-click the line and choose Format Shape to bring up the Format Shape dialog.
3. In the left section of the dialog, choose Line Style. You will see the options shown in Figure 12.16.
4. Let's make our line thicker. For illustration purposes, make the width 15 pt so that it's very large and you can easily see it.
5. A compound line describes how many parallel lines your line is composed of. If we choose the second option, notice how our line becomes two lines running alongside one another.
6. A dash type chops up the line in the other direction so that the line becomes a series of shorter segments instead of one continuous line. If we choose the third option (Square dot) for Dash type, look at how the line is no longer continuous but broken into smaller pieces.
7. Change the Cap type to Round. Notice how each segment is rounded now rather than having sharp corners as it did before.
8. Let's skip to the arrow settings at the bottom. These let you decide whether to have arrow heads and the ends of the line (Begin Type, End Type) and how big the arrowheads should be (Begin Size, End Size). Steps 4–7 are visually shown in Figure 12.17.

Figure 12.16

Line styles in the Format Shape dialog.

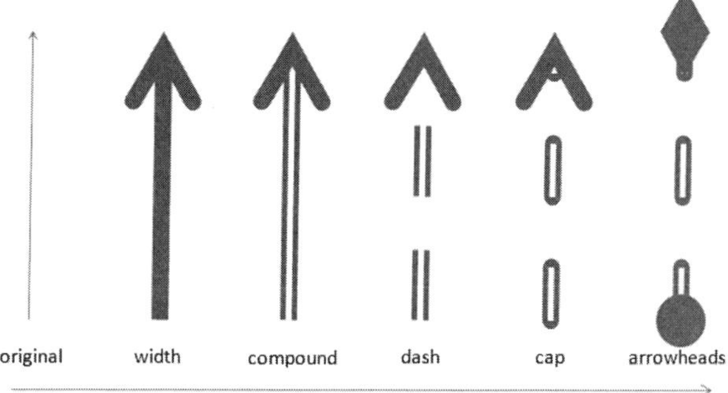

Figure 12.17

Customize each line style attribute one at a time.

Join type determines how two lines should join in a corner. For example, if you have a rectangle shape and choose Miter for the join type, the rectangle corners are sharp. A round join type gives rounded corners, and bevel is the compromise between the two (see Figure 12.18). A join type isn't applicable to our example, which uses a simple line because the line never joins another line.

TIP

Remember, like most tricks in this chapter, lines are not specific to rectangles or even to shapes. Try customizing lines on text, pictures, diagrams, and charts.

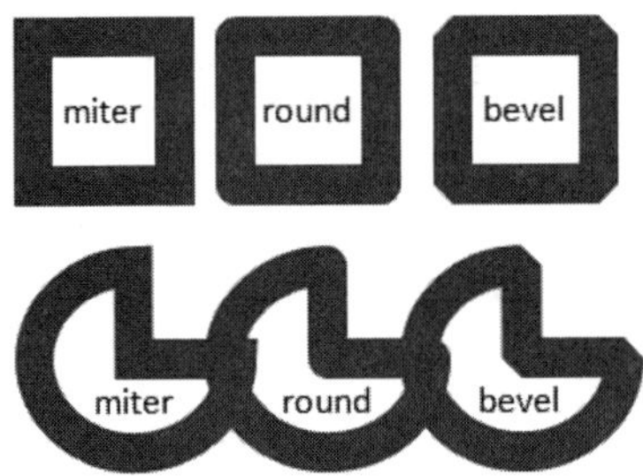

Figure 12.18

The three join types on both a rectangle and a partial circle shape.

DRAWING ELLIPSIS...

Let's walk through a more concrete usage of lines: An ellipsis, also known as "dot dot dot," can be useful to have in a diagram. For example, say that we actually have 100 blocks. Instead of drawing all 100, we just draw a few and have an ellipsis there to represent the rest.

We've been asked on several occasions how to make one of these, so we thought that we'd publish the steps we use:

1. Create a line. On the Home tab's Drawing group, click Shapes and choose the plain, normal leftmost line in the Lines section and click the slide to insert it.
2. Change the dash style to dots by selecting the line and going to the Drawing Tools Format tab. In the Shape Styles group, click Shape Outline. Choose Dashes, and then choose the second, Round Dot option. You can probably see that the line now has many tiny little dots.
3. Let's increase the thickness so that we can actually see the dots. Use the Drawing Tools Format tab and go to the Shape Styles group, click Shape Outline, click Weight, and then choose 6 pt.
4. Change the length of the line as necessary either by dragging the ends of the line or using the Size drop-down list on the Drawing Tools Format tab.
5. Voilà! Figure 12.19 shows the result.

TIP

If you prefer rounded dots for your ellipsis, set a rounded Cap type in the Format Shape dialog. You learned about this in the "Line Style" section earlier in this chapter.

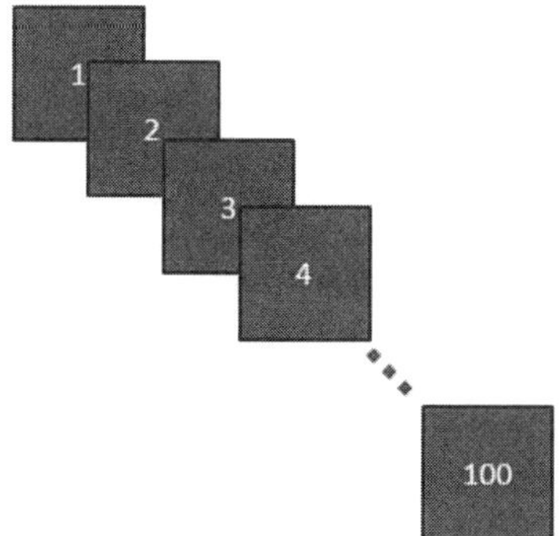

Figure 12.19

An ellipsis created with a PowerPoint line.

Brand New Effects

Now that we've looked at fills and lines, we explore some of the fancier effects in PowerPoint. Look at examples of all these in Figure 12.20. Again, these can be applied to all sorts of objects such as text and charts; don't limit yourself to shapes.

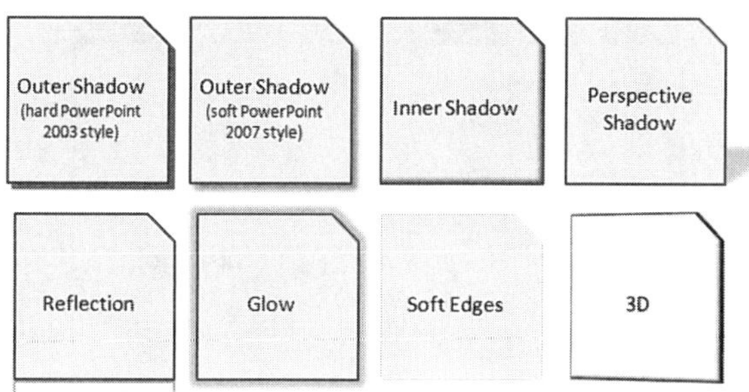

Figure 12.20

PowerPoint 2007 introduces a variety of effects.

Shadow

Everyone's seen a shadow. Let's explore the many types of shadows in PowerPoint.

SOFT VERSUS HARD

Shadows have been around in PowerPoint for a long time, but previous versions of PowerPoint only let you set "hard" shadows in which the entire shadow was one solid color.

PowerPoint 2007 supports the more popular and realistic-looking "soft" shadow. With these, the edges of the shadow fade away and get softer around the edges.

EXOTIC SHADOW TYPES

PowerPoint calls a traditional shadow an Outer Shadow, but PowerPoint 2007 also supports more exotic shadow types:

- **Inner Shadow**—The shadow is inside the subject.
- **Perspective Shadow**—The shadow floats beneath or falls behind the subject.

SETTING A SHADOW

Setting a shadow is pretty easy. Just select a shape, diagram, chart, or picture, and go to the Drawing Tools Format tab. In the Shape Styles group, click Shape Effects. Select Shadow, and then choose from the available options.

TIP

Text can similarly be shadowed in the Drawing Tools Format tab by going to the WordArt Styles group, clicking Text Effects, and then choosing Shadow.

If you choose Shadow Options, the Format Shape dialog gives you more control over the color, transparency, size, blur amount, angle, and distance of the shadow (see Figure 12.21). This is a big step up over previous versions of PowerPoint, which only gave control over the shadow distance and color.

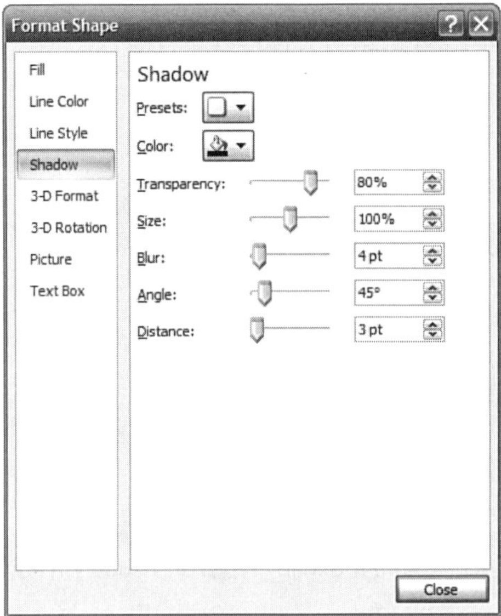

Figure 12.21

Customize the shadow in the Format Shape dialog.

Reflection

Forget copying your shapes, rotating them upside down, flipping them, stretching them, and trying to make a reflection yourself. Two clicks of a button, and you end up with a beautiful reflection.

Select whichever object you want to reflect, and look at the Drawing Tools Format tab. For shapes, go to the Shape Styles group, click Shape Effects, and choose Reflection. For a text reflection, go to the WordArt Styles group, click Text Effects, and choose Reflection. You will find your object looking back at itself like a reflection in water in no time.

HIDDEN EFFECT CUSTOMIZATIONS

The PowerPoint 2007 file format supports more customization options than the simple choices presented in the Reflection gallery. It lets you customize a reflection's position, direction, and alignment, as well as whether the reflection should rotate with the shape. Unfortunately, there's no advanced reflection control in the Format Shape dialog, so there's no real control of these options inside PowerPoint.

The same is true for glows and soft edges. There are simple galleries, but nothing inside PowerPoint itself that lets you view or change the power hidden in the file format.

If you're feeling brave, Chapter 18, "Publishing Your Presentation to Any Format," introduces you to the file format, and you can try editing these directly yourself. If you wait a few years, it's possible that Microsoft will one day add these options to the PowerPoint user interface.

Glow

What better way to brighten your day than with a little glow? Glow is another new Office 2007 effect that can be applied using a gallery. Select something, go to the Format tab's Shape Styles group, open the Shape Effects drop-down, and choose Glow to try it out.

Soft Edges

Finally, there's the new soft edges effect, which cuts off part of the edges of an object and makes them...well...soft. To be honest, it doesn't look that great except on photos. But, if you have a object that you want to give a "feathered edge" to, go to the Format tab's Shape Styles group, click Shape Effects, and then choose Soft Edges.

CAUTION

You've likely seen an incredibly tacky WordArt in a restaurant indicating where the bathroom is or a sign advertising the Catch of the Day. Remember that the next generation of these overused signs are just around the corner by overusing the effects just discussed. So, don't just settle for the default values they apply. Be creative and mix and match effects to see if you can create a unique look.

Bevel, 3D Rotation

Tired of living in two dimensions? Well you shouldn't be because you don't—you live in three, and so should your graphics. Three dimensional effects like Bevel and 3D Rotation are described in Chapter 13, "Demystifying 3D."

Transparent Overlay

Advanced One pretty effect is to overlay a semitransparent object over the slide.

1. After you have some content on your slide, insert a rectangle that covers the entire slide. Or create a few rectangles that cover large portions of the slide. You can experiment with other shapes as well.
2. Select the shape, choose the Drawing Tools Format tab, and go to the Shape Styles group. Click Shape Fill, and then choose a fill of some kind. A solid color or a picture fill will do fine.
3. Right-click the shape and choose Format Shape. Go to the Fill section on the left if it's not already selected. For the Transparency slider near the bottom, set it to 65% or so.
4. Get rid of the line around the shape. Click Line Color in the left pane of the dialog and choose No Line to get rid of the line.
5. Click Close. The result is a pretty overlay that filters your existing content (see Figure 12.22). The overlay will also look nice even if you change themes because the shape uses a color from the theme.

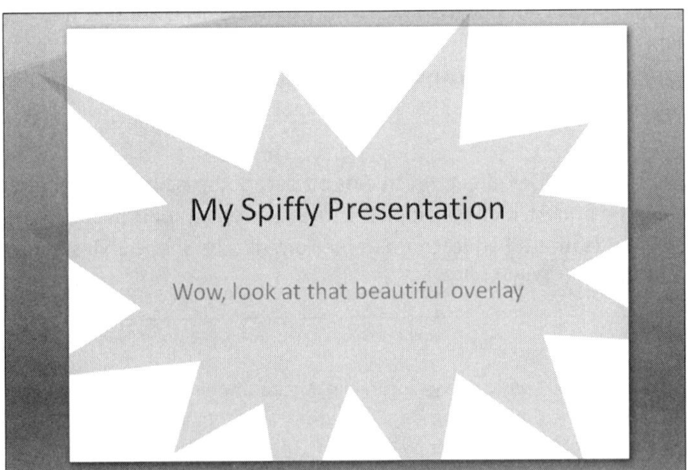

Figure 12.22

Placing a semitransparent shape over the slide creates a nice-looking effect.

Customize the Default Shape

Advanced Maybe you went to Berkeley like we did (Go Bears!), and you wish that all the shapes you inserted would have gold fills and blue lines. Or you're loud and wish that all the text you typed was size 72 and bold. Fear not! That's what defaults are for.

Insert a rectangle shape by going to the Home tab, going to the Drawing group, clicking the rectangle in the Shapes section, and clicking somewhere on the slide to insert it.

Now go crazy on it. Give the rectangle a gradient or picture fill (on the Drawing Tools Format tab, go to the Shape Styles group, and click Shape Fill); give it a crazy line. (On the Drawing Tools Format tab's Shape Styles group, click Shape Outline.) Type some text into the rectangle. Format the text by changing the font size and making it bold and underlined. (Go to the Home tab and look in the Font group.)

When you're done, right-click the rectangle and click Set as Default Shape. Now, whenever you insert a new shape or a new text box, it defaults to whatever formatting you just used.

These defaults are saved into the presentation, so they work if you copy the presentation to another machine. But, you need to set them again if you start a new presentation.

NOTE

In previous versions of Office, you could also go into the Format AutoShape dialog and check the Default for New Objects check box at the bottom to have all the changes you made set as the default on that computer. In Office 2007, there's no OK button on the Format Shape dialog, and all changes you make are applied to the selected items immediately. So, this check box no longer exists.

The Mysterious Paintbrush Icon (Format Painter)

Advanced Often you've formatted something only to want to format something else exactly the same way. Maybe you typed a few words, made them pretty by applying some colors and styling, and now want to make another word look exactly the same. Maybe you got a picture looking picture-perfect, and you want another picture to look exactly the same. Enter Format Painter. This tool allows you to copy the formatting only, from one object to another. This means that if you have several different shapes to be formatted in the same way, you don't have to choose each one individually and set the formatting. For example, say that your presentation contains a slide with a star, one with an oval, and one with a square to which you want to apply the formatting from a rectangle on another slide. You can simply copy all the formatting applied to the rectangle and "paint" it onto your other shapes. This feature works the same way with text.

Format Painter Example Using Shapes

To use Format Painter to copy the formatting from one shape to another, do the following:

1. Insert two pictures and select the first picture.
2. Format the picture by going to the Picture Tools Format tab, going to the Picture Styles group, and choosing something pretty from the gallery. Feel free to apply other edits to the picture, such as recoloring it, changing the picture shape, giving it a border, or changing brightness/contrast (see Chapter 4 to learn a lot about formatting pictures).
3. With the formatted picture still selected, go to the Home tab's Clipboard group and click the Format Painter button. The button looks like a paintbrush (see Figure 12.23).

Figure 12.23

Format Painter button.

4. Note how your cursor mouse now has a paintbrush next to it.
5. Click the second picture you inserted in step 1. Now it is formatted with all the formatting you applied to the first picture.

Format Painter Works on Other Things Too!

It's not like we haven't repeated ourselves enough times already, but we say it again: This doesn't only works on shapes. Try Format Painter on text, pictures, tables, diagrams, and charts too.

In the Thumbnail pane and Slide Sorter view, you can even pick up the formatting from one slide and apply it to another slide. It will take the theme colors and background from one slide and apply it to another.

Format Painter Tips

Here are random facts for you Format Painter power users:

- There are shortcut keys for Format Painter. Use Ctrl+Shift+C to pick up and Ctrl+Shift+V to apply. After you get accustomed to using the shortcuts, you will find yourself using Format Painter more often.
- Format Painter never saves shape geometries. You will never be able to pick up the "circle-ness" of a circle, apply it to a rectangle, and have it turn into a circle. Similarly, Format Painter doesn't pick up or apply shape sizes.

- Format Painter does respect colors coming from an Office theme. If you use Format Painter to pick up a theme color from one item and apply it to another item, the color will update correctly and still be a theme color. Similarly, if you pick up a theme color from one place and apply it to an object on another slide that follows colors from a different theme, the target object will visually have a different color from the original color and will match the target object's theme. More information about theme colors is discussed in Chapter 11.
- Shapes formatted using Format Painter lose their links to the Master. Say that you have a placeholder on the slide that derives its formatting from a Master placeholder. Say that you use Format Painter to pick up that placeholder's formatting and apply it to a star shape. If you then change the formatting on the Master placeholder, the star shape won't get the new formatting.
- Format Painter doesn't work on Excel text. So, the next time your Excel-wielding, rich, financial buddies try to impress you with their Excel prowess, demonstrate text Format Painter for them and make them cry (or not).
- Though most Office users these days don't use Format Painter, Format Painter is one of the oldest features in Microsoft Office—found even in the earliest versions of Word.

Using Repeat Can Save You Time

Advanced If you've been using Windows for a while, you're undoubtedly familiar with Undo and Redo. You probably even use the Ctrl+Z and Ctrl+Y keyboard shortcuts.

Repeat is their unloved step brother. It's pretty easy to use. Here's an example:

1. Insert a rectangle anywhere on the slide.
2. Do step 1 again to insert a second rectangle.
3. Select one of the rectangles and change its line style (using the Drawing Tools Format tab, as shown in previous sections of this chapter). PowerPoint remembers the last command you applied.
4. Select the other rectangle.
5. Press Ctrl+Y to repeat the procedure. This applies the line change to the second rectangle.

Redo and Repeat are not found anywhere on the Ribbon. By default though, it's the rightmost button on the Quick Access Toolbar to the right of the Office button (see Figure 12.24).

NOTE

If you ever remove the Redo button from the QAT on accident, you need to re-add it by clicking the Office button, clicking PowerPoint Options at the bottom, and clicking Customize in the left pane.

Figure 12.24

Repeat/Redo on the Quick Access Toolbar.

You might be slightly confused why Ctrl+Y is the shortcut for this when you usually associate Ctrl+Y with Redo. It's simpler than you think: If you've just undone something, Ctrl+Y does Redo. If you've just performed an action, Ctrl+Y does Repeat. At any one time, either Redo or Repeat is available, but never both.

Mastering Multiple Undo

Advanced Sometimes you want to undo just the last operation. That's easy; just press Ctrl+Z. Other times, you want to undo the last 10 operations. There's an easier way to do it than pressing Ctrl+Z 10 times:

1. Find the Undo icon on the Quick Access Toolbar. It looks like a blue arrow pointing to the left.
2. Click the little down arrow to the right of it. This drops down a menu that lists all the possible actions that can be undone. You can pick as many items as you want to undo (see Figure 12.25).

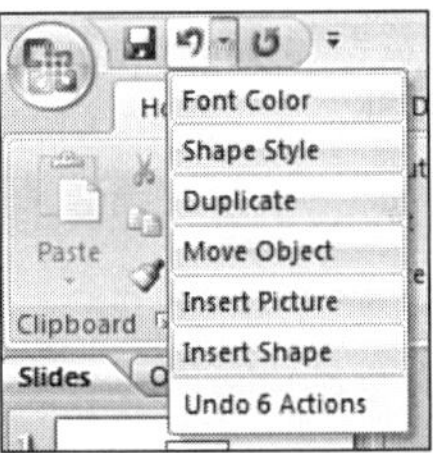

Figure 12.25

Undo multiple undo operations.

TIP

You can't undo an unlimited number of operations; by default, PowerPoint only stores the last 20 operations. To store more, click the Office button, select PowerPoint Options at the bottom, click Advanced in the left pane of the PowerPoint Options dialog, and then change Maximum Number of Undos in the first section.

Change Shape

Say that you inserted a rectangle, made a whole bunch of changes to it, and then realized that you really wanted an oval. It's easy enough to change your mind. Just select the shape, go to the Drawing Tools Format tab, the Insert Shapes group, and click Edit Shape. (Of the two buttons, it's the one on top.) Click Change Shape and choose an oval (see Figure 12.26).

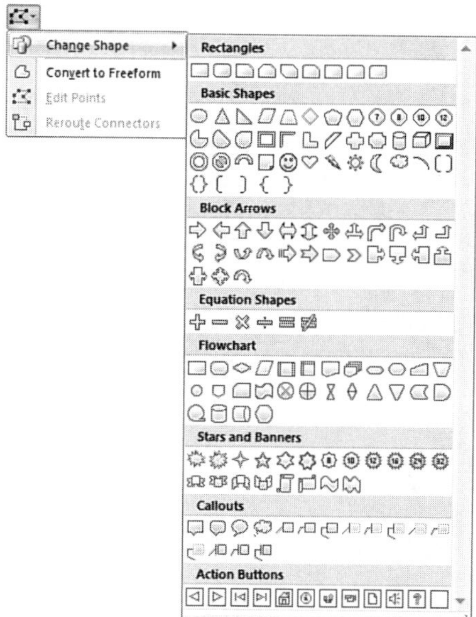

Figure 12.26

Change Shape in the Ribbon.

This works on SmartArt shapes as well. Select any shape within the SmartArt, choose the SmartArt Tools Format tab, go to the Shapes group, and click Change Shape.

13

Demystifying 3D

IN THIS CHAPTER

- 3D Example
- What Can Be 3D?
- 3D Rotation Explained
- Using 3D Formatting Effectively
- Be Careful!

Welcome to a release of Office with amazing 3D support.

The PowerPoint team at Microsoft spent a great deal of time and effort trying to establish PowerPoint 2007 with twenty-first century graphics, and allowing for 3D effects is a large step in the right direction. With this chapter, we show you how to make vivid, immersive content that depicts your information in a new eye-popping manner.

First, we provide you with a short example of how powerful this is just to give you a little taste of how easy it is. Then take a look at our list of what you can and cannot apply 3D effects to. We then go on to show you how to rotate your content so that any 3D effects you apply can actually be seen because the default view of the 3D objects might not be taken from the best angle. And finally, you'll get a tour through the various formatting you can use to add that third dimension and make your content more realistic.

3D Example

Let's jump right in and walk through an example of making a sphere—something that could easily impress, yet takes little effort.

First things first: We're going to make a sphere out of a circle by adding the third dimension.

1. Insert a circle into your presentation. To make the math easier, make sure that the circle is 4" by 4" by going to the Drawing Tools Format tab and entering **4** into the height and width fields, as shown in Figure 13.1.

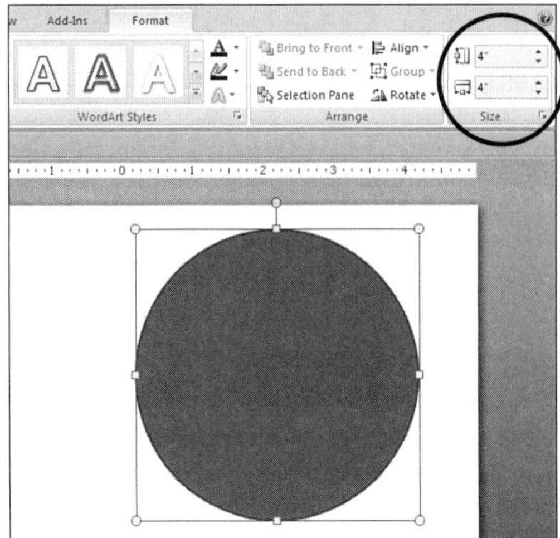

Figure 13.1

We have inserted a circle of size 4" by 4"—you will see why later when we create a sphere.

2. Next, open the Format Shape dialog by right-clicking on the circle and choosing Format Shape.
3. Then, click on the 3D Rotation button on the left side. We're trying to change the rotation of the object so that when we change it and make it 3D, we can actually see the results.
4. Click the Presets button and click on an example that you think will give you a good view of the object. We like Off Axis 1 Top (on the third row, middle column of our Parallel section of the presets, as shown in Figure 13.2) because it enables you to see the side of an object.
5. Now let's actually make this circle 3D. Click on the 3D Format button on the left of the Format Shape dialog, and then click on the drop-down next to Top. Select the first row and first column entry from the gallery under Bevel, which is labeled Circle, as shown in Figure 13.3. Repeat the process for the Bottom selection.
6. Enter **150** into the Top and the Bottom settings' Width and Height boxes. This is a number we came up with using trial and error. A lot of times, you can depend on this to work best.

NOTE

At this point, don't worry if your sphere is moved down in the workspace, as shown in Figure 13.4. This is supposed to happen because a bottom was added to the shape. We will move it back up in the next few steps.

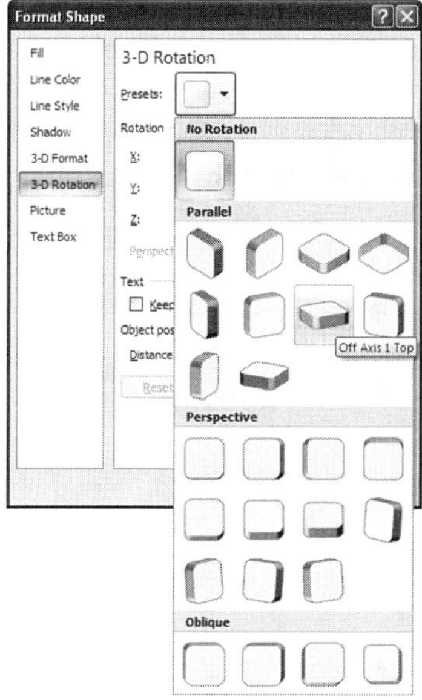

Figure 13.2

Rotation is key when dealing with 3D objects because you need to be able to see what your changes do. Off Axis 1 Top enables you to see the side of an object, which is helpful when you're trying to make a sphere.

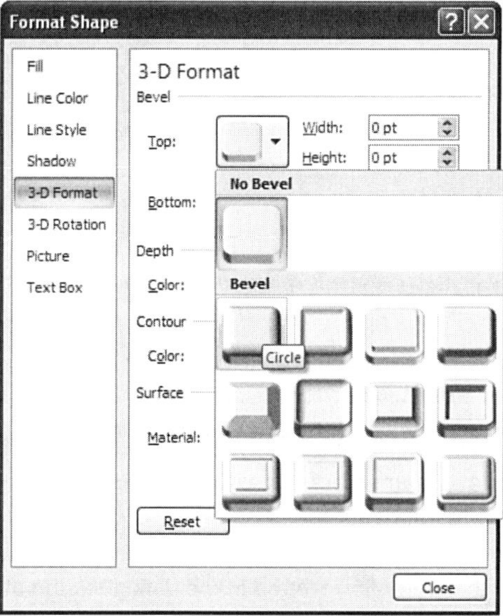

Figure 13.3

Add a Bevel to the top and bottom of a circle to make it a sphere.

We still have a couple of problems to deal with. For one thing, you can see a band in the middle of the shape because, by default, when you insert a circle, it has a blue fill with a darker blue outline. When you take this, rotate it, and then add 3D as we just did, the outline is still there. So let's get rid of it and make the sphere all one color (unless you want a band of color going around your sphere).

1. Click on Line Color on the left side of the Format Shape dialog.
2. From the Color drop-down, select the same color as your shape fill. By default, you want Blue, Accent 1, as shown in Figure 13.4.

TIP

Alternatively, you could click on No Fill from the Line Color options in the Format Shape dialog.

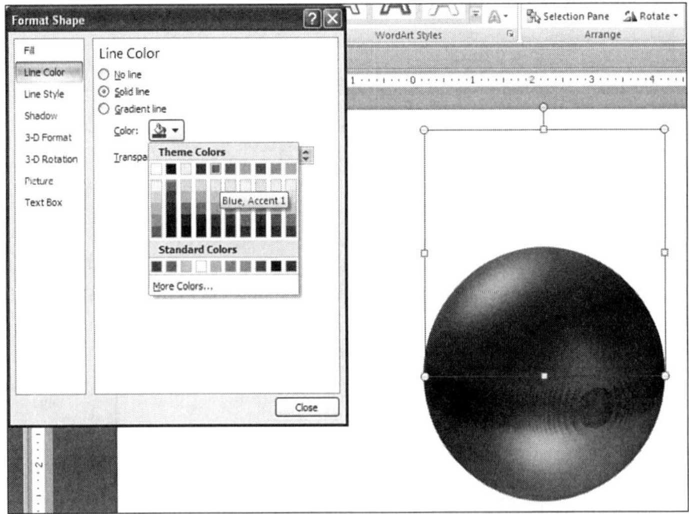

Figure 13.4

Remove the outline of your shape, or it will cause your sphere to look strange.

You can notice that the sphere is shifted down a bit, so to raise it up, go to the 3D Rotation options in the Format Shape dialog and enter `150` into the Distance from Ground box at the bottom. Doing so makes your sphere centered and similar to the one shown in Figure 13.5.

And that's it! While it might have seemed difficult at first, it definitely gets easier with time. Remember, use trial and error to figure out the exact details of the height and width of the top and bottom of your 3D object, and also take advantage of the presets because you can actually see what those might look like rather than fumbling around in the dark guessing at sizes.

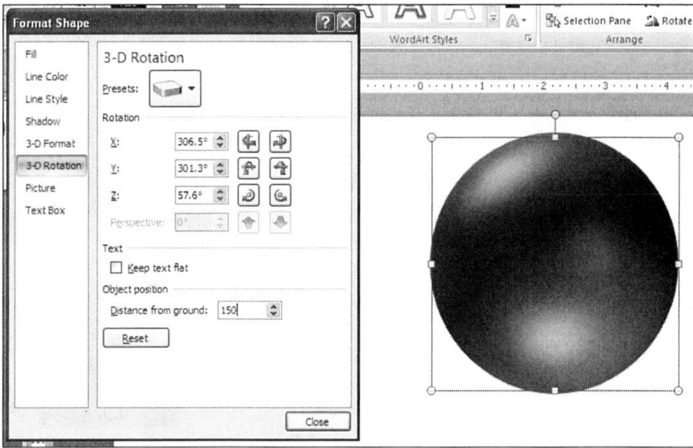

Figure 13.5

A finished sphere.

What Can Be 3D?

Now that you have seen an example of 3D in action, you need to know what types of objects can be affected by your 3D effects and rotations. If you find yourself wanting to add a little flare to your objects, consider sending it on a trip down the 3D rendering pipeline. This list might show you that you can add 3D effects to objects that you never thought possible.

You can add 3D effects to the following (see Figure 13.6):

- Shapes
- Grouped Shapes
- Pictures
- Charts (and elements)
- SmartArt (and elements)
- Text and WordArt

The following must remain in 2D (see Figure 13.6):

- OLE objects
- Tables
- Movies

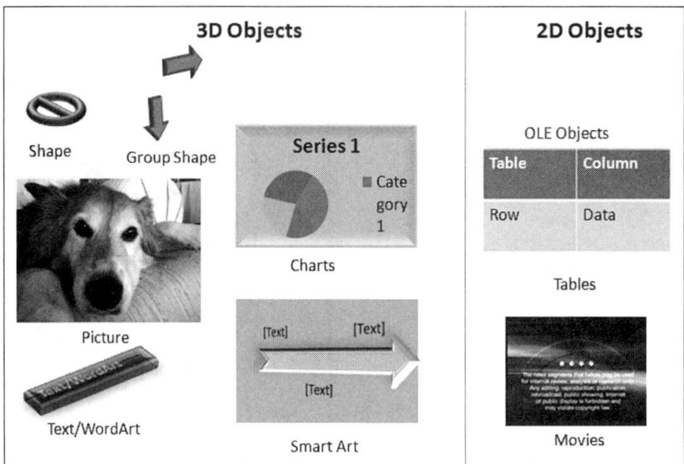

Figure 13.6

Examples of 3D objects and objects that must remain in 2D.

3D Rotation Explained

Now that we have walked you through a simple example, let's discuss in depth the two tools you have that apply to 3D: Rotation and Formatting.

Typically, we would explain in detail the 3D Formatting tab in the Format Shape dialog first because it appears on top of the 3D Rotation tab (see Figure 13.7), but things are a little different in this case.

Imagine trying to shave your name on the back of your head without using any mirrors. That's the same feeling you get when applying 3D Formatting by using the default 3D Rotation. Sure, you might notice a slight change here or there, but the default view is from a bird's-eye top-down view, which shows you nothing if you modify the bottom of your shape.

After you rotate your object, seeing the effects of applying 3D Formatting will help you immensely.

Preset Rotations

Twenty-five preset rotations exist to help you get an idea of some good rotations. These presets should cover most of the common scenarios you will need to view your 3D objects; if not, you can certainly customize the rotations yourself later on.

For now, let's take a look at the presets, which are split up into three different categories: Parallel, Perspective, and Oblique (refer to Figure 13.2).

The best uses of the presets are to experiment and take advantage of Live Preview to see what works for you. The presets are meant to give you a breadth of options to choose from without making you specify the exact rotation you want. Providing a custom rotation is explained in the next section.

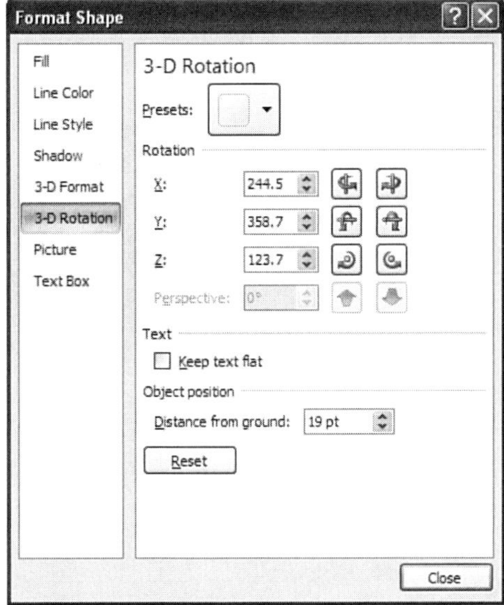

Figure 13.7

The 3D Rotation tab in the Format Shape dialog. Refer back to this when reading the rest of this section.

NOTE

Notice that the icon shows you graphically what the rotation will do, but for a more detailed description, you can hover your mouse over the icon.

Custom Rotations

If you are not satisfied with the preset 3D rotations, here is your chance to customize the rotation yourself.

Notice that there are two ways to enter a rotation: You can enter a number into the degrees box or you can click on the two opposing rotators to the right of them. Now notice that there is a rotation angle for each axis, allowing for full 3D rotation.

NOTE

The rotation only happens once; it is not like an animation that will keep spinning.

Rotation in each of the three axes results in a different view. Let's see how each axis affects a shape.

1. First, insert a shape and type some text so that we can distinguish the front from the back of the shape; we used a cloud in Figure 13.8.

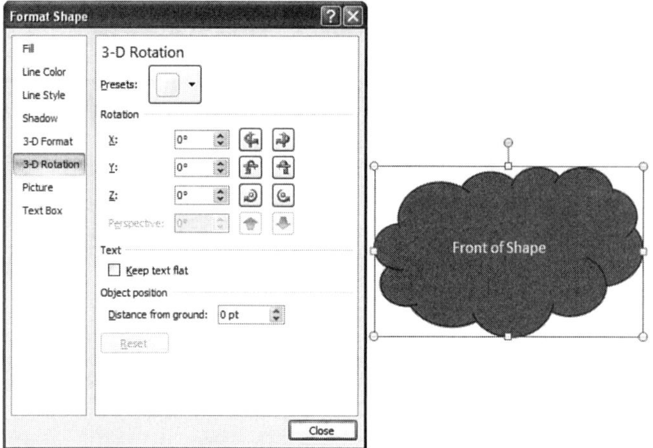

Figure 13.8

A brand new cloud shape ready to be rotated in 3D.

2. Next, let's play with the x-axis rotation. Enter **180** degrees and notice that the text has flipped on the x-axis (see Figure 13.9). Feel free to click on the Left and Right buttons next to the x-axis rotation input to incrementally rotate the object and get an idea of what kind of rotation this actually is.

NOTE

We are using terminology located at http://en.wikipedia.org/wiki/Three-dimensional_space, which describes Cartesian geometry and the Coordinate axes: x, y, and z.

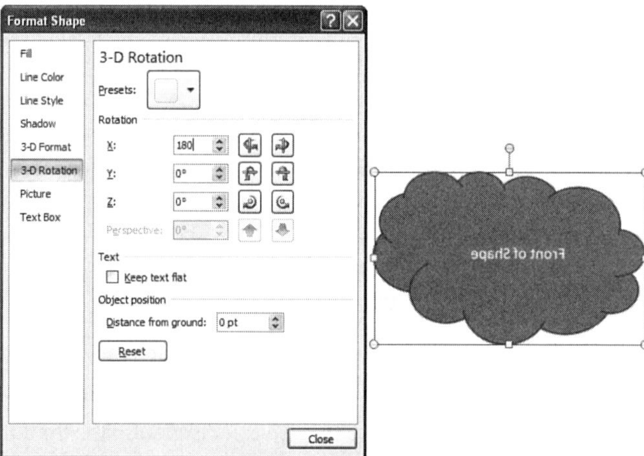

Figure 13.9

The cloud is rotated on the x-axis (left to right) 180 degrees, resulting in flipped text.

3. Now, reset your shape either by clicking on the Reset button or by entering **0** in the x-axis rotation field again. Next, we play with the y-axis rotation—again by entering **180** into the field and noticing that the shape and text have flipped upside down on the y-axis. The key thing to remember is the axis you enter the number into determines which axis the shape is rotated on. See Figure 13.10 for the result of the flipped shape and text on the y-axis.

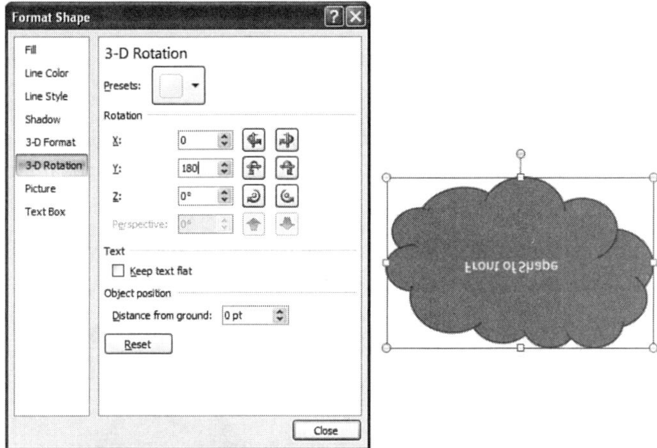

Figure 13.10

The cloud is rotated on the y-axis (up to down) 180 degrees, resulting in upside down text.

4. Again, reset your shape so that there is no rotation, and let's see what the z-axis rotation looks like. Enter **180** degrees into the field next to Z (see what it looks like in Figure 13.11). This shows text flipped and upside down, but another way to look at this is to see it as a clockwise rotation because the z-axis is clockwise/counterclockwise.

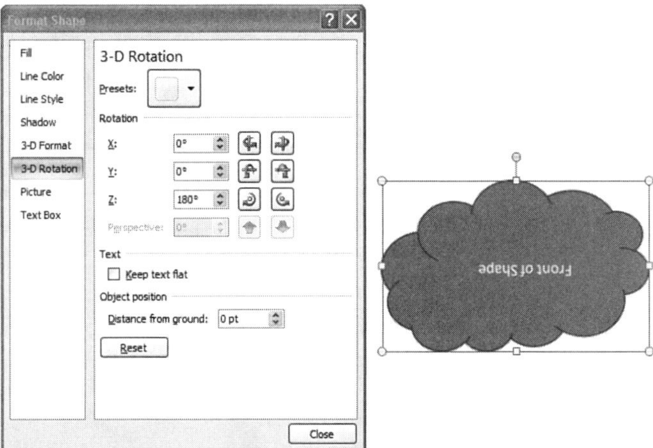

Figure 13.11

The cloud is rotated on the z-axis (clockwise, counterclockwise) 180 degrees, resulting in upside down and flipped text.

NOTE

For more information regarding rotation about the three axes, read about the 4x4 Transformation Matrix here: http://en.wikipedia.org/wiki/Transformation_matrix.

Text and 3D Objects

By default, the text on your objects gets rotated with the rest of the shape, as if it were written on the actual surface.

For example, in Figure 13.12, we have a sphere that has been rotated 305, 4.2, 36.6 degrees in the x, y, and z axes, respectively; as you can see, the text cannot be seen because of the rotation we have on the sphere.

If you don't want this to happen and would rather see the text in 2D as it was before any 3D formatting, check the Keep Text Flat box (seen in Figure 13.12), and it separates the text from the object.

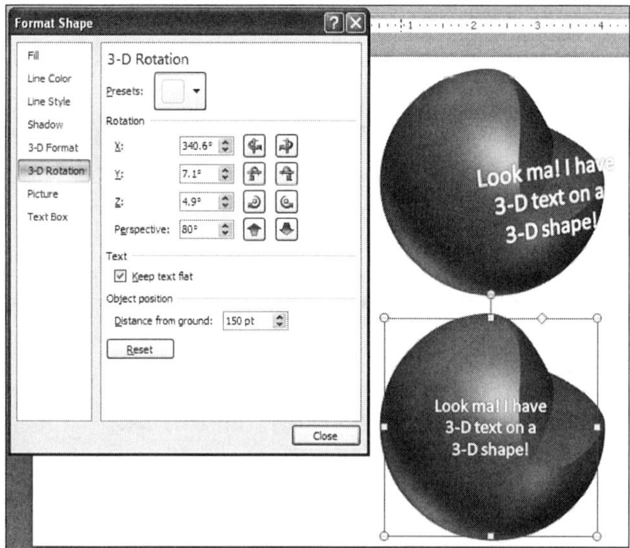

Figure 13.12

The Keep Text Flat option reverts your text back to its second dimension in case it becomes unreadable, as in this example, where the rotation causes the text to move to the other side of the shape.

This is a good idea, especially when you want the bottom or side of a 3D object to be shown, but you want the text to remain visible.

Object Position

This is another complicated one. In the 3D world, there is a concept of a "ground." By default, with no rotation applied, you are looking top down on the object, which is sitting on the ground.

The complicated part is when you apply a rotation. You need to either keep track of the new ground yourself, or just increase the Distance from Ground setting in the 3D Rotation section of the Format Shape dialog and see what happens to your object.

We used this setting previously (shown in Figure 13.5) to center our object after having added top and bottom halves to our circle, which was lying flat on the ground.

Reset

If you find that you don't like the rotation you've applied and you want to start from scratch, click Reset, and you are sent back to the 2D shape with the original fill and line.

Using 3D Formatting Effectively

Now that you can actually see the changes you can make, let's see what you can do to your shapes to bring them into the third dimension.

Figure 13.13 shows you how the dialog is laid out for the next few sections, so refer back to it if you need help remembering what parts of the dialog look like.

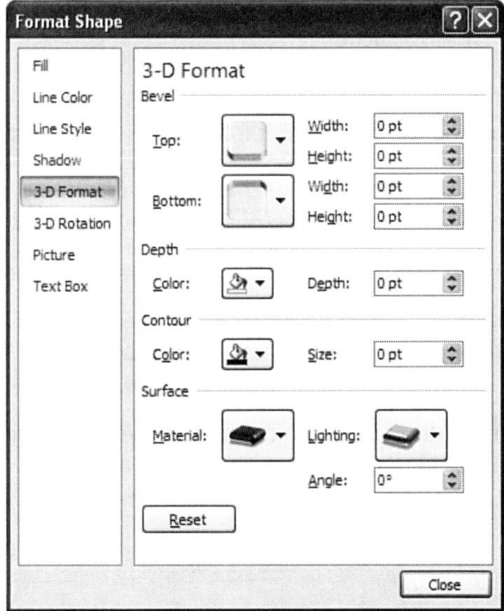

Figure 13.13

The 3-D Format dialog.

Let's walk through a few examples showing what each part of the dialog actually does.

First, let's start with a plain shape, as seen in Figure 13.14; then we will apply different formatting in each of the following sections. Assume that we reset the shape in between each section.

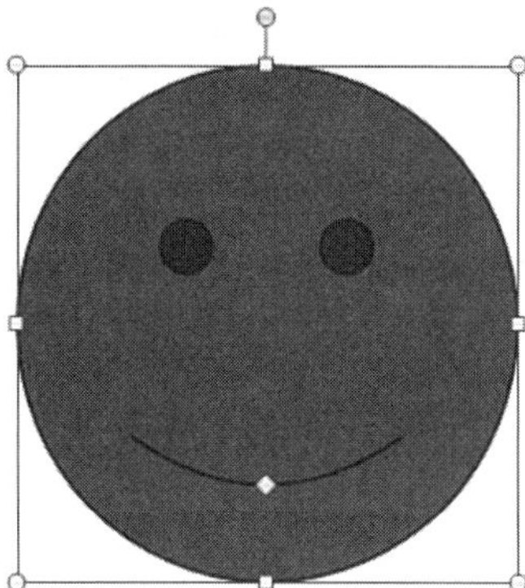

Figure 13.14

The guinea pig shape we will use to experiment with different 3D formatting elements.

How do you take a 2D shape and make it 3D? Well, it's not that easy. One way to do it is to split it up into the top and bottom parts. This is how the dialog is split up.

This means that your shape is still there, but all you are doing is adding stuff on top of it and below it.

Bevel

The bevel you select will determine what "body" you add—meaning that if you select a certain bevel, the shape of the 3D body you add will be different from others and will be made of diverse materials.

A set of 12 preset bevel types are offered to sculpt your shape. After you have a bevel applied, you can modify the height and width of the bevel by using the modifiers on the right.

With our original shape in Figure 13.14, let's first apply a 3D rotation so that we can see what Bevel actually does.

1. From the 3-D Rotation section of the Format Shape dialog, click on Presets, select Isometric Right Up, and the result should be similar to what's shown in Figure 13.15.
2. Next, let's add a top and bottom bevel (Circle Bevel is the top left bevel in the presets) and change the height and width of both top and bottom to be `40`. The result is shown in Figure 13.16.

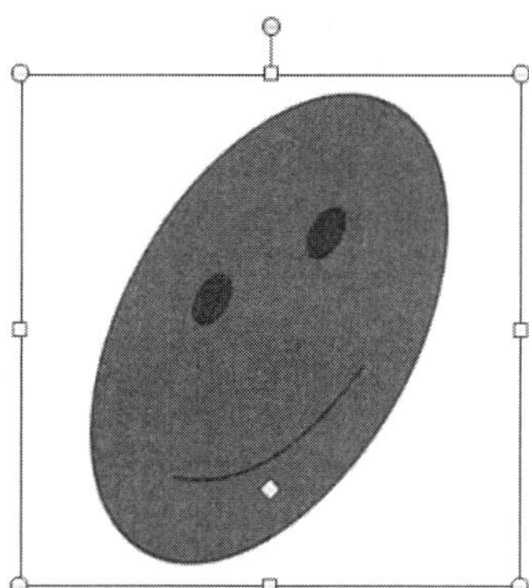

Figure 13.15

Our example from 13.14 with a rotation applied so that we can play with Bevel.

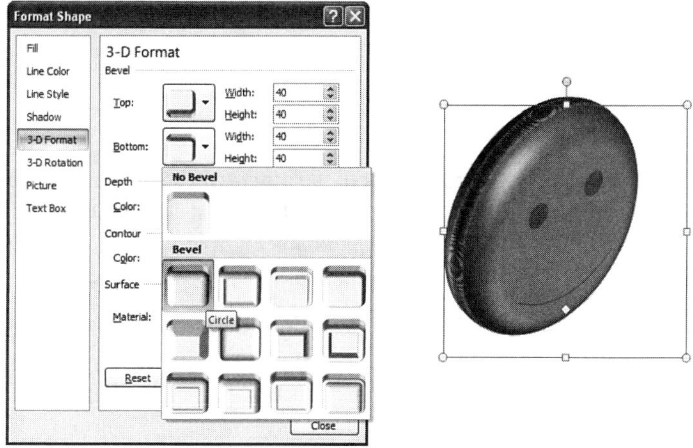

Figure 13.16

The result of adding bevel to our sample shape in Figure 13.15.

Depth

If you want to add a little girth to your object, consider adding some depth by increasing the Depth value. Select a color; you automatically add a 6-point depth. Notice that the area between the top and bottom of your 3D object has increased.

This is the area between the top and bottom of your 3D object.

For example, if we start with our rotated shape in Figure 13.15 and apply a depth of `40`, Figure 13.17 shows what we get.

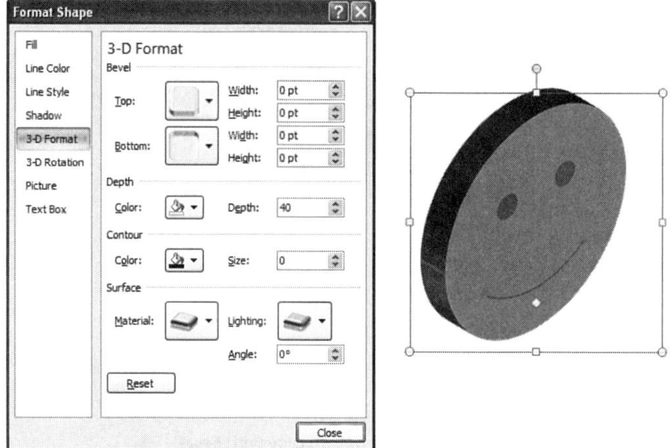

Figure 13.17

The result of adding depth to our sample shape in Figure 13.16.

Contour

You can think of the contour as the 3D equivalent of the outline. If you have added a depth to your 3D object, adding a contour modifies the outline on the depth. Just like the Depth dialog, you have a choice of color and an extent. By selecting a color, a default point of 1 will be applied, which looks small. The larger contour you add, the thicker the outline of the depth will be.

Continuing with our previous example from "Depth," if we keep our shape that has some depth and add a contour of size 5, the resulting shape looks like Figure 13.18.

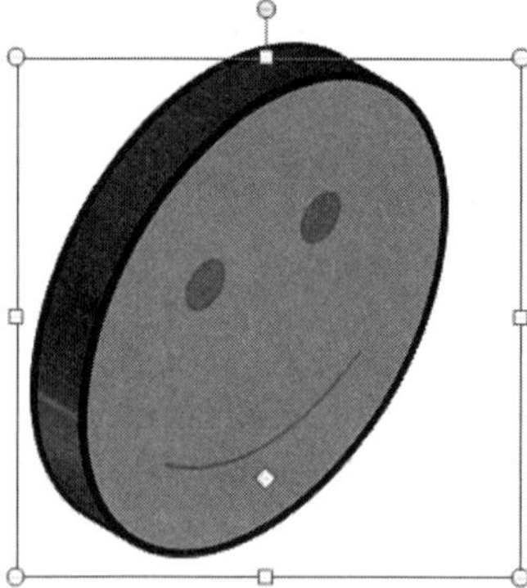

Figure 13.18

The result of adding contour (outline of the depth) to our sample shape in Figure 13.17.

Surface

Now that the physical attributes of the 3D object have been set, let's take a look at some more fine-grained customizations you can add, such as changing the material or lighting.

MATERIAL

Eleven different materials can make up your 3D objects (see Figure 13.19). We suggest playing around with them to see what looks good with your presentation. Also, a good strategy is to try something out, and then click Undo if you do not like it. Because the Format Shape dialog is modeless, you don't have to worry about bringing it back up each time you do and undo.

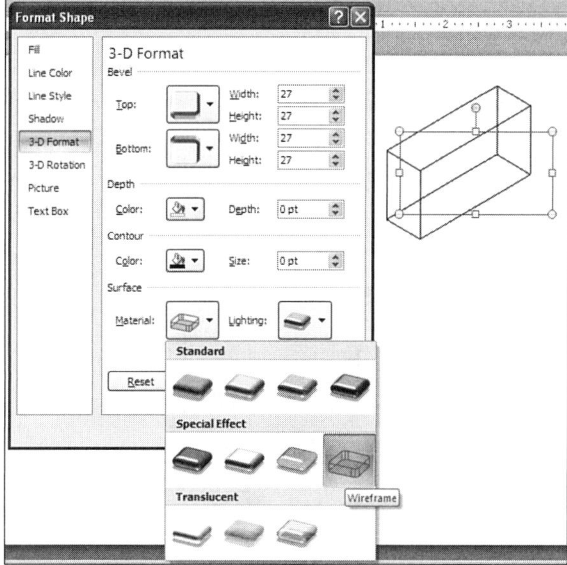

Figure 13.19

Try applying some various materials and seeing what you like. Our favorite is the Wireframe, which makes all objects look pretty neat.

To continue with our example, let's add a Clear Material to our shape from the "Contour" example in Figure 13.19. The result is what you see in Figure 13.20.

LIGHTING

The preset lightings are useful for putting your 3D objects into a real scene and making them look as though they exist in the real world.

It really adds the shimmer on the objects that you see because of the reflection of the light that bounces off the object.

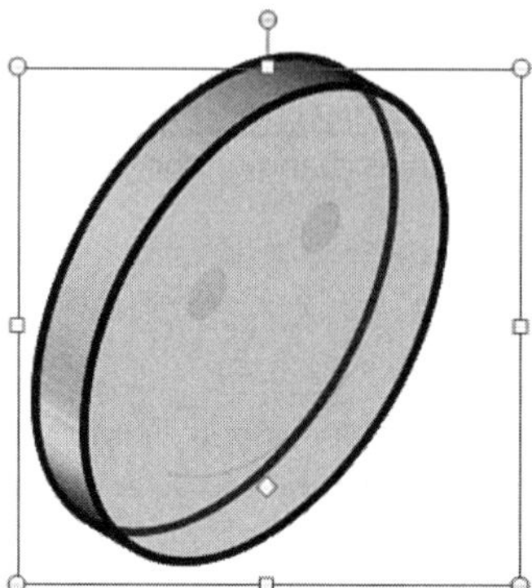

Figure 13.20

The Clear Material applied to our contoured shape from Figure 13.19. The surface changes to be semitransparent.

The lightings are separated into Neutral, Warm, Cool, and Special (see Figure 13.21); once again, we cannot tell you which will look good in your presentation. Just try a few out, and undo if you find yourself looking at something really ugly.

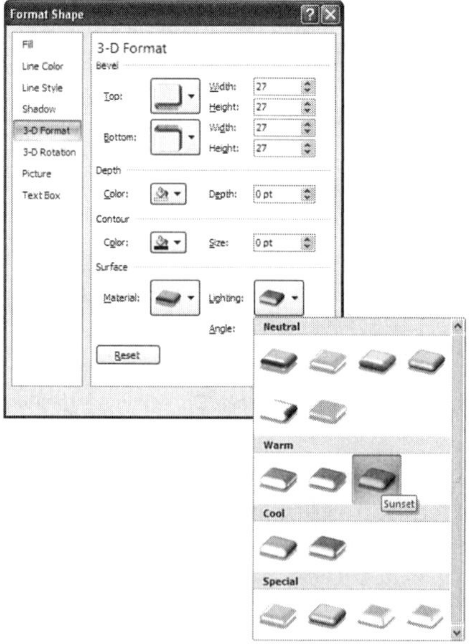

Figure 13.21

The various lighting schemes.

Continuing with our example, let's add the Flat Lighting to our shape with the Clear Material from the preceding exercise and also give it a 200 degree angle. Notice in Figure 13.22 that there's a bright spot on the depth of the shape because of the lighting.

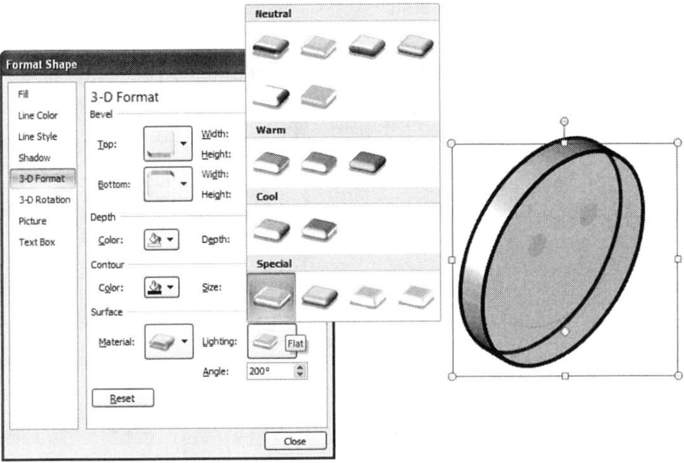

Figure 13.22

Lighting is applied to our shape with depth and a Clear Material from Figure 13.20. Notice the bright spot that can be controlled via the angle of the lighting.

ANGLE

Although this is entirely obvious, we have to note that the angle is associated with the lighting and determines where the light comes from. The example shown in Figure 13.22 displays what the lighting controls, and it can be helpful when moving bright spots on the shape.

Here's what happens when the angle is changed to 270: Notice how the bright spot on the depth of the shape has changed, and also the face of the smiley is now very bright and reflecting the light into your view of the shape in Figure 13.23.

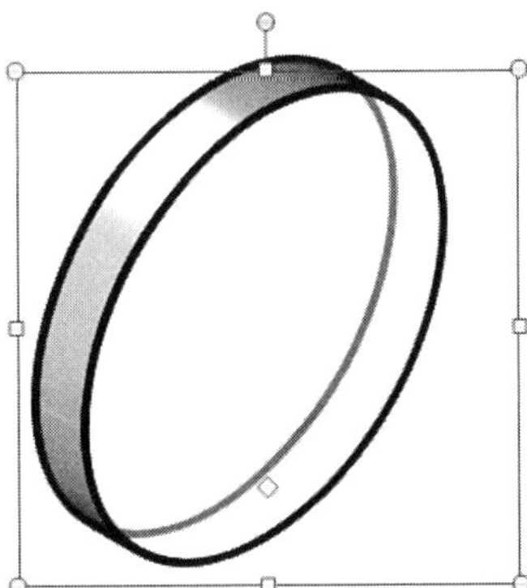

Figure 13.23

Changing the angle from Figure 13.22 results in the shape having a different bright spot, as well as the face of the shape changing to be bright, as if it were reflecting the lighting directly into our eyes.

Reset

If you're unhappy with what you've done and want to revert back to your original 2D object, click the Reset button.

CAUTION

Be careful: If you click the Reset button, you lose your 3D rotation in addition to any 3D formatting, because it is set back to the 2D shape.

Be Careful!

It is very easy to go overboard with 3D. Please take time and evaluate whether you need to add 3D to objects before you go making use of your new abilities.

Why? It Looks So Pretty!

An individual object made 3D might look good, but when mixed with other objects that are not 3D, it might clash and stand out like a sore thumb. Look at Figure 13.24 and see how a perfectly normal slide was ruined by making one object 3D and going overboard with adding additional shapes.

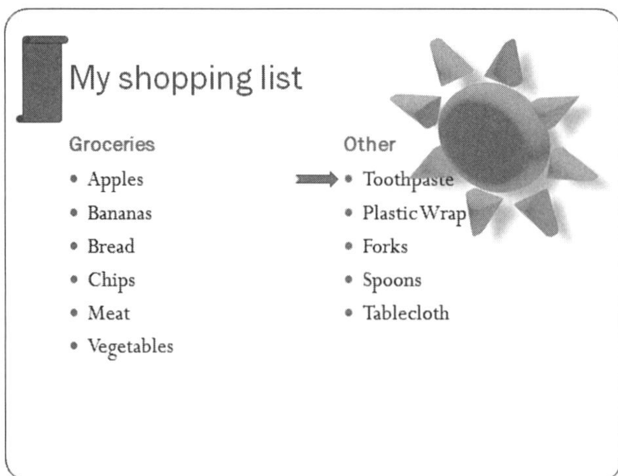

Figure 13.24

Choose wisely when you want to use 3D.

In this example, because the sun is 3D but other shapes are not, something looks amiss. Why don't the other shapes have shadows? Where is the light coming from? These are questions confused viewers notice.

Be Consistent

In addition to being consistent within one slide, you must also consider *all* slides in your presentation. If you are giving a presentation that is all 2D except for one slide, it will definitely stand out, but maybe not in a good way. It might just look tacky.

At the end of the day, you must consider all factors before deciding to use 3D. Some presentations will benefit from it, but many will not. It's important to use good style judgment.

NOTE

If you're familiar with graphics, it's also important to consider the vanishing point when introducing 3D into a scene. If the shadows don't match up, or the 3D objects do not look as though they could physically exist in the real world, then chances are it won't look good in your presentation.

14

Positioning Slide Elements

IN THIS CHAPTER

- Exact Positioning Using the Size and Position Dialog
- The Hidden Ruler
- Snapping to Grids and Guides
- Precise Positioning
- Combining Positioning Tricks

Now that you are proficient in creating amazing content, how can it be positioned so that it looks good? This chapter introduces you to tips and tricks to help you move content to suitable locations. These advanced features will certainly be a surprise if you thought that content could only be dragged around using the mouse.

Exact Positioning Using the Size and Position Dialog

Advanced Whereas some people prefer hands-on activities and would rather click on a shape and drag or resize it by hand using the mouse, others prefer a more precise method. This is where the Size and Position dialog comes into play.

This dialog, shown in Figure 14.1, has three main tabs: Size, Position, and Alt Text. All three are pretty self-explanatory, except maybe Alt Text, which is used when you choose Save as HTML and then open the presentation in a web page and mouse over the object. Kind of subtle, huh?

Notice that some fields on each tab are disabled. These are enabled if the selection is a picture. They let you crop a picture with great precision, optimize a picture for slideshow viewing, reset a picture back to its original size, and set a picture size based on the dimensions of the original picture. We talk more about these options in the next few sections.

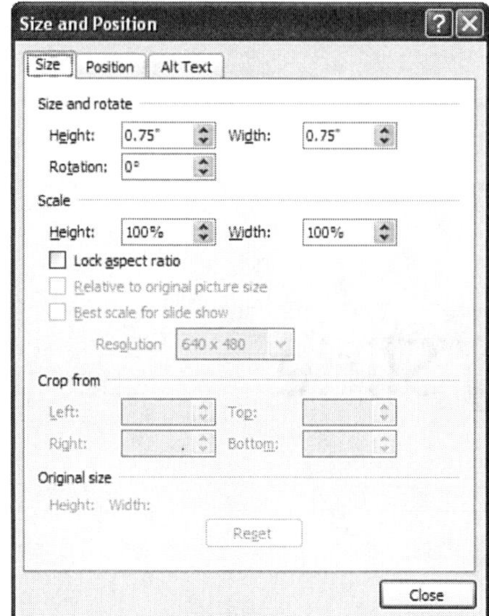

Figure 14.1

The main contents of the Size and Position dialog.

Using the Dialog

The two main ways to access the Size and Position dialog are as follows:

- Right-click on an object and select Size and Position.
- Go to the Format tab in the Size group and click the dialog launcher at the lower right.

One cool thing about this dialog is that it is modeless. In case you missed it in an earlier chapter, this means that the dialog can remain open, and it does not prevent you from continuing your work. That might not mean anything to you if you just jumped into the book in this chapter, so let's look at an example:

1. Click on a shape.
2. Launch the dialog.
3. Click on another object on the slide.
4. Notice that the dialog updates itself to reflect the new object selected.

Sizing Pictures

If you decide that you need to modify a picture, this dialog offers even more fine-grained control. First, by default, a picture has the Lock Aspect Ratio and Relative to Original Picture Size check boxes selected. This means that however you resize it, the height and the width are changed in equal amounts. If this means nothing to you, try the following:

1. Insert a picture.
2. Uncheck both the Lock Aspect Ratio and Relative to Original Picture Size check boxes.
3. Resize the picture to make the width much larger than it was originally.
4. Now zoom in on the picture using the zoom slider at the bottom right corner of the PowerPoint window. You can see the picture distortion.

Notice how ugly the picture looks now that it is resized. You have changed the picture from its original size, so now the picture looks pixellated because PowerPoint has to make up new pixels for the space you have created. When you keep the Lock Aspect Ratio and Relative to Original Picture Size options selected as you resize the picture, the actual pixels that exist in the photo are used to increase the size. Keep in mind that you can only resize it to a certain point and still retain its original clarity. If you resize to larger than the original picture size, PowerPoint has to eventually guess which pixels to use again, and your picture won't look good.

If you are unable get the result you want by using the picture's cropping handles, you can specify an exact cropping area in the Crop From section of the Size tab (see Figure 14.2). Chapter 4, "Working with Pictures," discusses other ways to crop and change the shape of a picture.

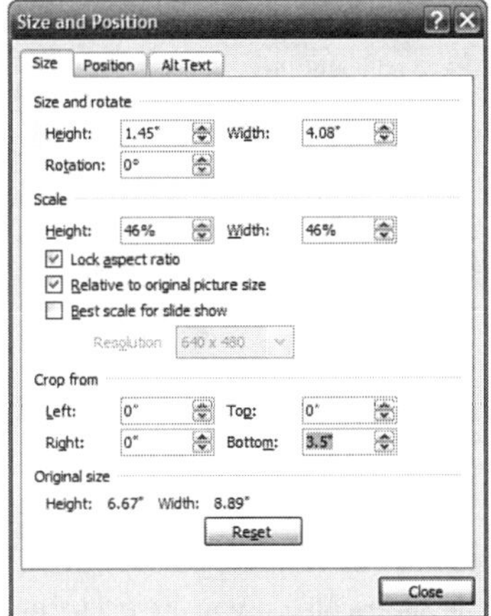

Figure 14.2

The Size and Position dialog lets you control precisely how much to crop. The top image is uncropped and the bottom image is cropped 3.5 inches at the bottom.

The Hidden Ruler

Advanced How many times have you seen people pull out a ruler and hold it up to the screen in order to measure some shape to make sure that it's aligned or the right size when printed out?

Okay, probably not that often, but you will be hard-pressed to find someone with the ruler enabled in PowerPoint because it's hidden by default.

To enable the ruler, simply click the View tab, go to the Show/Hide group, and check the Ruler check box (see Figure 14.3).

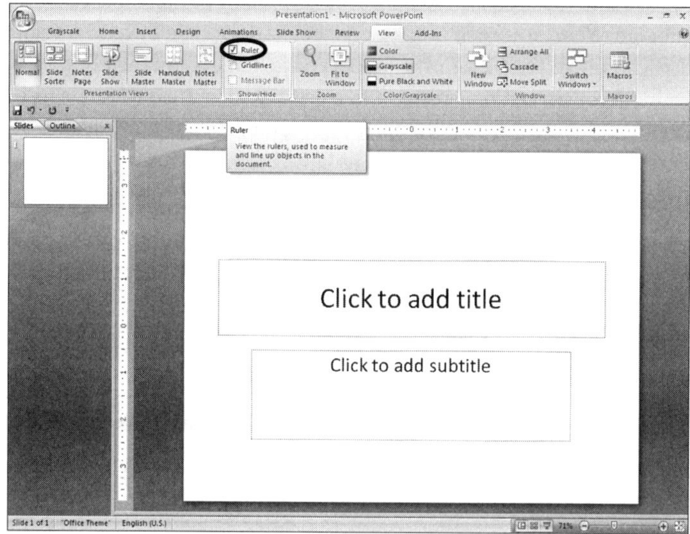

Figure 14.3

Find the Ruler check box on the View tab. Notice the rulers that are visible at the top and left of the workspace after the option is checked.

This is particularly helpful when you need objects to print at certain sizes (say, in inches). It is also useful for placing objects in the same places on multiple slides. Also, if you are accustomed to working in Microsoft Word, you might find it comforting that you can have the same ruler show up in PowerPoint.

Aligning Objects

Another useful application of the ruler is to align objects. You can select an object, go to the Format tab in the Arrange group, and select Align, but sometimes you need to just do it yourself, and having the ruler makes this manual alignment process easier.

Adjusting the Unit of Measure

By default, PowerPoint displays the ruler in units of inches. But, if you're from a locale where metric is the measurement system, you do not have to learn how to convert from inches to centimeters in order to use it. All you have to do is change a Windows setting, and the ruler automatically changes to centimeters instead of inches.

To change the units of measurement in Windows XP, close any open applications, including PowerPoint, and do the following:

1. Click the Start button and then click Control Panel. Assuming that your Control Panel is set to Category view, click the Date, Time, Language, and Regional Language Options.
2. Click the Change the Format of Numbers, Dates, and Times task.
3. Assuming that you're using English, click the Customize button.
4. Change Measurement System from U.S. to Metric.
5. Click OK until you return to the desktop. Your unit of measure in all applications (not just PowerPoint) is now set to metric.

To switch back to inches, just follow theses steps again and choose U.S. in step 4.

In Windows Vista, the instructions are a little different:

1. Close any open applications, and then click Start.
2. Click on Control Panel.
3. Click on Clock, Language, and Region.
4. Under Regional and Language options, click the Change the Date, Time, or Number format task.
5. On the Formats tab, click the Customize This Format button.
6. Now select Metric under Measurement system. Click OK until you return to your desktop. Your unit of measure in all applications is now metric.

Now restart PowerPoint, and notice your brand new ruler measurement.

Snapping to Grids and Guides

Advanced Snapping is a feature that constrains your mouse movements while you drag, making it easier to line up objects. By default, Snapping is turned on with the spacing between the grid lines set to 0.083 inches.

In previous versions of PowerPoint, this information was more readily available with the Grids and Guides command in the View menu. However, in PowerPoint 2007, this feature is somewhat hidden: To access the Grid and Guides dialog, on the Home tab in the Drawing group, click Arrange, Align, and then Grid Settings.

Enabling Grids and Guides

After you open the Grid and Guides dialog,

1. Check Display Grid on Screen and Display Drawing Guides on Screen.
2. Notice that dotted lines appear in the workspace, as shown in Figure 14.4. These are the grid lines being drawn on the screen.

CAUTION

Setting a low number for the grid spacing can make the grid very hard to see. Either choose a spacing 0.25 inches or greater, or zoom in on the slide a little, or you might not be able to see the small grid marks.

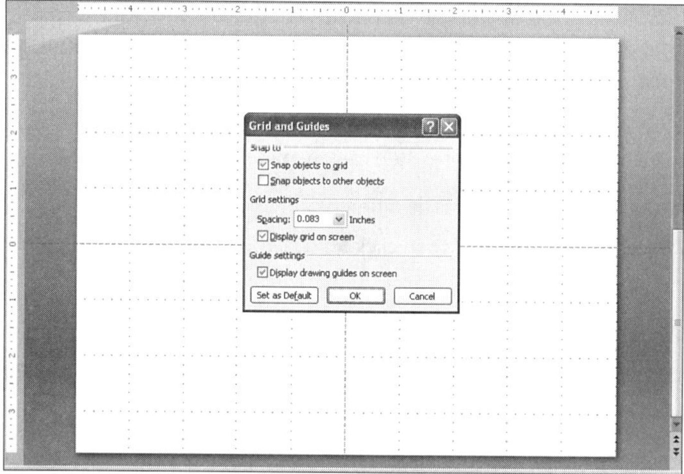

Figure 14.4

Grids appear when the Display Grid on Screen check box is selected.

Try inserting a shape and dragging it around. Notice how it's easier to get the shape to line up with those dotted lines. It's almost as if the grid lines are magnetic, and the shape sticks to it as you go by. You can notice the same stickiness when dragging to resize a shape.

You can control how wide each cell in the grid is in the Grid and Guides dialog shown in Figure 14.4.

The drawing guides are the two thicker dotted lines going through the middle of the slide. They serve a similar purpose as the grid, but you have control over where these are positioned. You can

- Drag them around to move them somewhere else.
- Hold down Ctrl while dragging to create a new guide.
- To delete a guide, drag it off the slide.

Grid and Guides settings are saved per user in Windows; they are not saved in the presentation. The nice thing is you can set these once, and they always apply whenever you're using that computer.

TIP

Guides can be toggled on and off by pressing Alt+F9. Grids toggle with Shift+F9.

Precise Positioning

Need to move a shape or a picture into an *exact* position, but can't get it positioned just right? Read on to see some helpful tips and strategies that you can use to solve your problem.

Using the Mouse

When you're just dragging around with the mouse, it sometimes feels as if the object is jerking around. PowerPoint is actually trying to help you by snapping the object to the grid or any guides that it knows about. As described in the previous section, grids and guides are available to make positioning objects in precise locations easier. But, even if the Grid and Guides feature isn't turned on, this snapping still occurs when you use the mouse to position objects.

To avoid this, press the Alt key while you're dragging the object around with your mouse. This modifier key causes PowerPoint to ignore the grid and guides and lets you position content more precisely, not snapped to a certain metric.

NOTE

If you don't think that you will have a need for the grid or guides, you can turn them off by opening the Grid and Guides dialog. Go to the Home tab's Drawing group, click the Arrange button. Choose Align, Grid Settings, and then uncheck everything in the Snap To section.

Using Zoom

Another handy feature we use for precise positioning in general, not just in PowerPoint, is zoom because it gives you greater precision when moving content around in your presentation.

New Notice the new zoom slider on the Status bar in the lower right corner of the window (see Figure 14.5). This is another welcome change from previous versions of PowerPoint. Now, instead of having a drop-down to select from, or entering in a zoom percentage of your own, you can actually drag the slider around to find the zoom percentage you want with just a move of your mouse. It is rare that you know exactly what zoom level you would like, and trying out all the options from the drop-down is a great deal more effort than dragging the slider.

Figure 14.5

The zoom slider.

Another way to use the zoom slider is to click on the slider at the percentage you want, and the slider moves directly there. You can figure out where to click based on the facts that 10% is the smallest zoom, 400% is the largest, and 100% is right in the middle.

The square button to the right of the zoom slider that has the four little arrows is a smart zoom tool. When you click on it, PowerPoint uses its "smarts" to change the zoom so that the entire slide fits into view.

Zoom is particularly useful for positioning or editing small objects, but keep in mind that if you have to zoom in to see objects in your presentation, it will be tough for those who sit in the back of your audience to see them, too.

ZOOMING IN JUST ONE PANE

In previous versions of PowerPoint, you can click on one specific pane, such as the thumbnail pane, and change the zoom, and it affects only the thumbnails in that pane, not the main slide content pane. This no longer applies when using the zoom slider in PowerPoint 2007, which always zooms in on the main slide.

But, you can still accomplish pane-specific zooming using the mouse wheel. For example, click on the thumbnail pane, hold down the Ctrl key, and then scroll your mouse wheel. Only the thumbnail pane zooms.

Using the Keyboard

If you are a keyboard person, like we are, and try to avoid using the mouse as much as possible, nudging lets you move something a tiny distance so that you can get it positioned precisely the way you want without leaving the keyboard.

How do you nudge an object?

1. Click the object (the shape, picture, SmartArt, chart, and so on) once (or press Tab until the object you want is selected).
2. On your keyboard, press an arrow key to move it up, down, left, or right. Doing so moves the object a certain amount based on the current grid and zoom. For more precision, hold down Ctrl while you're pressing the arrow keys, and you can move pixel by pixel. Similarly, holding down Alt while pressing the arrow keys moves twice the normal amount.

Some exceptions:

- This works in PowerPoint, in Excel, for floating shapes in Word, and for shapes inside a Word canvas. It doesn't work on Word shapes that are inline with the text because in those cases, Word controls the placement of the shape. But, you're a PowerPoint user, so you don't have to worry.
- Certain shapes have their positions locked, so you can't nudge them. For example, you can't select bars inside a chart and start nudging them around.

As mentioned previously, if you have enabled the snapping to the grid feature, this affects your nudges, so turn that off first to get more precise movement.

NOTE

In previous versions of PowerPoint, Nudge menu items used to be on the Drawing toolbar (View, Toolbars, Drawing to turn on the toolbar, then choose Draw, Nudge), but they no longer exist and with good reason—if you're going to go to the trouble of clicking that, you might as well just drag the shape into position.

Combining Positioning Tricks

You can perform certain operations together that are easy and save you time. The following can help you move and position your content with ease.

Resize Tricks

NOTE

The tips in this section do not apply to lines.

Everyone knows how to resize an object—just select one of the selection handles on an edge of the object and start dragging. But how many people know about special side effects that happen when a key is held down during the drag operation?

Remember, you can start dragging, and then press the modifier keys (Ctrl, Alt, and Shift) and release them as much as you like, and you will see a preview of what the effects will be. So, start dragging away and holding down different modifier keys to experiment with what happens. These keys cause a different resize behavior when pressed during resizing.

CTRL

Holding down Ctrl while dragging an object to resize it causes the resize to apply to both the side that you're dragging, in addition to the opposite side (see Figure 14.6). This results in a resize centered on the original center of the object. Notice the difference between that and a normal resize, which only stretches one side of the shape (see Figure 14.7).

This is a great way to increase the size of an object without having to re-center it.

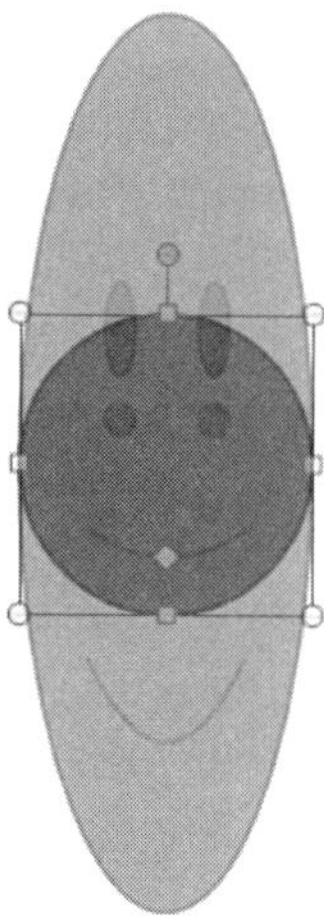

Figure 14.6

When Ctrl is pressed during resize, the opposite site of the object is resized accordingly, too.

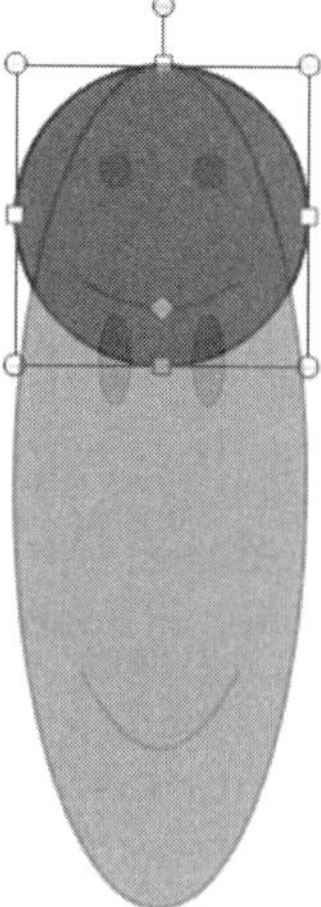

Figure 14.7

During normal resizes, only one side of the shape stretches.

SHIFT

This is a cool trick that is useful if proportion is important to you, and you like things to be uniform.

You really only notice the effects of holding Shift down while resizing if you drag from a corner of an object or an end of a line or connector. Why? Because it causes your resize to be proportional in both width and height (see Figure 14.8). Notice how this differs when you don't hold down Shift and resize a shape by dragging the corner (see Figure 14.9).

Holding down Shift while resizing from one of the non-corners (the top, bottom, or one of the sides) does nothing, and resizes won't be proportional.

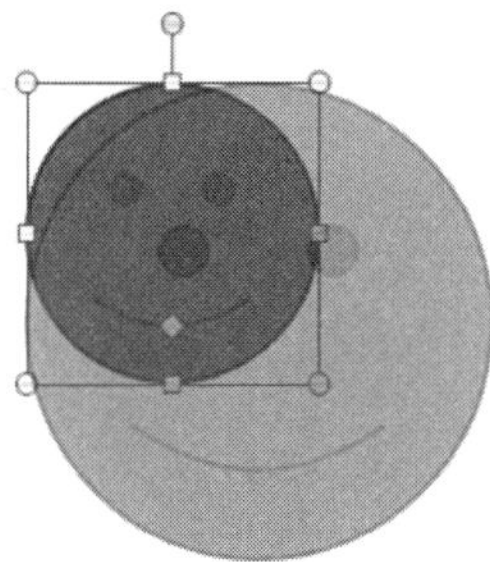

Figure 14.8

We were resizing the circle by dragging from the corner. When Shift is held during resize, the height and width are modified by the same amount, as shown here.

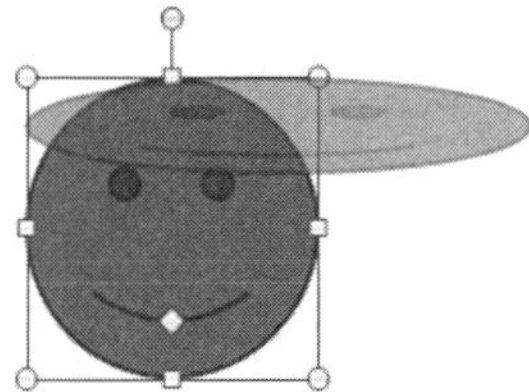

Figure 14.9

Resizing the circle by dragging from the corner normally does not maintain the circle's aspect ratio, and the whole circle stretches.

As always, if you are not convinced, just start a drag and then press the Shift key to see how it resizes your object. If you do not like what you see, simply let go of the Shift key, and the normal resize occurs.

ALT

As we mentioned earlier in this chapter, when the Alt key is pressed while resizing an object, it prevents snapping from occurring so that the resize is smoother and more precise.

TIP

You can use any and all these keyboard combinations together! Hold down both Ctrl and Shift and, yep...you guessed it, the resize is proportional and also occurs on both sides of the shape, causing it to be centered around the middle of the object. Add Alt to the mix, and the resize does not snap to any grids and is even more precise.

Rotate Shortcuts

We know that you are an advanced user and that you know the little green handle means a rotation of the object occurs when you click and drag it around (see Figure 14.10). But did you know that certain keys can enhance your rotating experience?

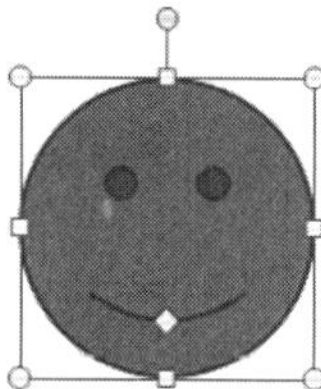

Figure 14.10

The rotation handle, easily identified by its green appearance. In this figure, it appears to stick out of the top of the smiley face.

Once again, we will walk through what effects the modifier keys have when held down during a drag operation—this time, we concentrate on what happens when you rotate an object.

CTRL

Ctrl no longer does anything. As you might have noticed, dragging the rotation handle rotates an object around the object's center. In other words, the object rotates around its center point just as a bicycle wheel spins around the axle in the middle.

In previous versions of PowerPoint, holding down Ctrl while rotating would cause rotation to occur around the bottom center of the object instead of the middle. This was equivalent to a default rotation, plus a move operation, and is similar to moving the bike wheel's axle to the very bottom edge of the wheel and spinning the wheel around that. This behavior is no longer present in PowerPoint 2007.

SHIFT

Rotation, by default, is at its most precise setting in that it does not snap to any grid while you're moving your mouse with the rotation handle selected.

If you want to rotate in less specific increments, simply hold down Shift, and the rotation snaps to the nearest 15 degrees.

ALT

As we mentioned already in this section, rotation does not snap to any grid by default, so holding down Alt—which typically prevents any snapping—has no effect while rotating.

ROTATION OPTIONS

If you select a shape and then go to the Home tab, the Drawing group, the Arrange menu, and then the Rotate menu, you can see these rotation options: Rotate Right 90°, Rotate Left 90°, Flip Vertical, and Flip Horizontal. Though fancy sounding, these options simply change the rotation value and are equivalent to using the green rotation handle.

For fine-grained control, you can also choose More Rotation Options at the bottom of the Rotate menu, which brings up the Size and Position dialog and lets you specify in degrees exactly how much to rotate.

Move Shortcuts

Perhaps the most common modification to an object regarding positioning is Move. We guarantee that you will move some objects during your presentation creation. Here are some tricks that help those of us with unsteady hands.

CTRL

Moving an object while holding down Ctrl creates a copy of the object rather than moving the object. It's a quick way to create many copies of something and quickly place each copy in your desired location.

TIP

Using Ctrl+D is another fast way to duplicate an object. It creates a copy of whatever object(s) you have selected and offsets them by a small amount to let you know they're actually there.

SHIFT

Holding down Shift while dragging snaps your object to the nearest axis (see Figure 14.11). In other words, it only moves horizontally or vertically along the x and y axes—useful if you cannot draw straight lines very well. If you don't hold down Shift, the shape just moves to wherever you drag it (see Figure 14.12).

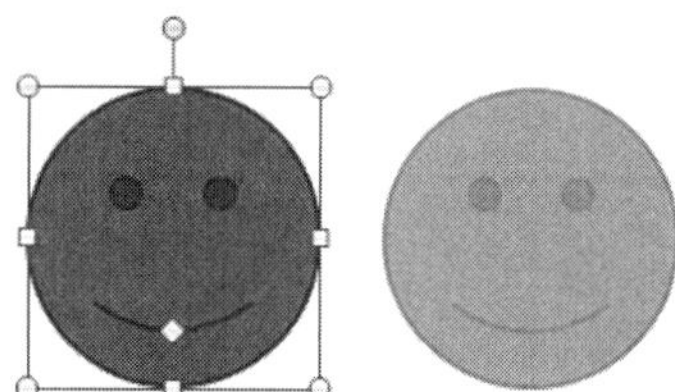

Figure 14.11

Hold down Shift and snap objects to the nearest axis.

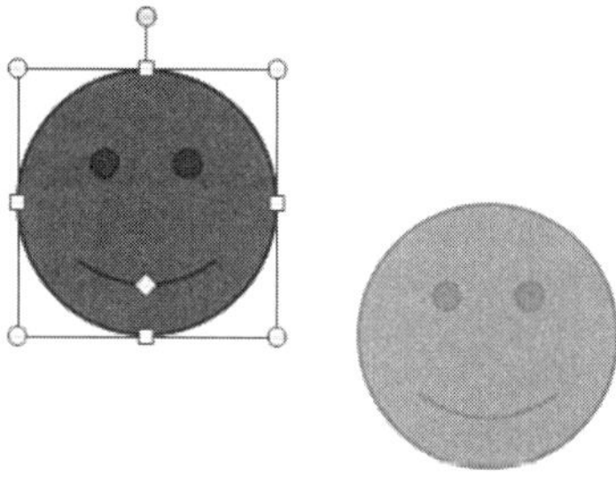

Figure 14.12

Compare that to a normal drag, which just moves the shape where you want to move it.

ALT

Alt does nothing during a move.

Align and Distribute Tips

If you have multiple objects selected and you want to line them up, simply visit the Format tab from the Drawing Tools ribbon, and you will find an entire set of operations under the Align button dedicated to what you need.

The Align drop-down has six different options: Left, Center, Right, Top, Middle, and Bottom. Whatever you have selected on the slide automatically lines up according to the option you choose.

Distribute is an interesting feature that spaces your objects equally apart. You need to select more than two objects, and then select either Distribute Horizontally or Distribute Vertically, and the objects become evenly spaced.

At the bottom, you see two choices: Align to Slide and Align Selected Objects:

- If Align to Slide is checked when you align or distribute, the objects are aligned or distributed using the entire slide as the bounds. So, if you align right, for instance, the selected shapes are shoved to the right side of the slide.

- If Align Selected Objects is checked when you align or distribute, the objects are aligned or distributed using the bounds of selection, which is typically smaller than the bounds of the entire slide. So, if you align right, for instance, the selected shapes are shoved as far right as the rightmost selected shape.

NOTE

In PowerPoint 2003 and earlier, there was simply a Relative to Slide check box. If unchecked, it implied that the distribute or align action should happen relative to the selection.

Figure 14.13 shows examples for align and distribute in action when combined with Align to Slide and Align Selected Objects.

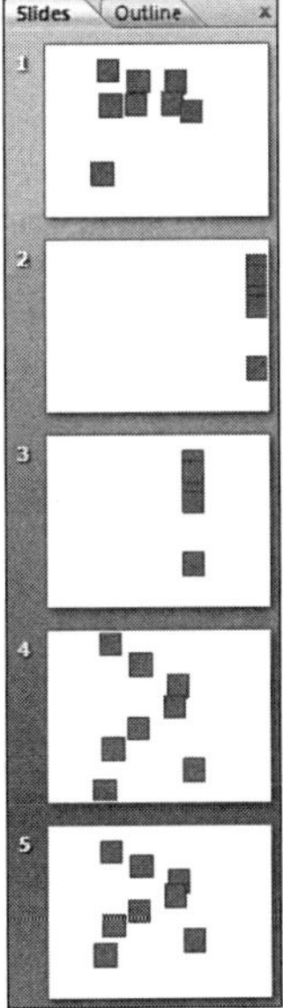

Figure 14.13

Align options used in combination to create interesting results.

The first slide shows some shapes arbitrarily placed on a slide. The second slide shows what happens if you align right with Align to Slide chosen. The third slide shows what happens if you align right with Align Selected Objects selected. The fourth slide shows Distribute Vertically with Align to Slide chosen. Finally, the last slide shows Distribute Vertically with Align to Selected Objects chosen.

By now you can create and manipulate beautiful and impressive content in your presentations, but that isn't all there is to a presentation. The chapters in this part cover advanced techniques using animations, in addition to delving into some pre-presentation work you can do to help you when you're actually delivering your content. In general, this section helps you make your audience say "Wow!" at your beautiful animations and polished slideshows.

IV

Wowing Your Audience

15 Going Beyond Slide-by-Slide 283

16 Running Slide Show Like a Pro 317

15

Going Beyond Slide-By-Slide

IN THIS CHAPTER

- Using Animations
- Custom Animation Types
- Adding Transitions
- Creating Custom Shows
- Hyperlinks
- Set Off Actions During Your Presentation
- Presenting Tools

There is more to a presentation than just slides. We want you to be able to create a presentation that blows away the competition. Some PowerPoint books we've read have silly tips telling you not to put black text on a black background. We won't treat you like you're an idiot, and this chapter take you much further than that.

First, you will learn how to create presentation animations. Having a presentation full of text and static, unmoving objects is not the best way to "wow" your audience, and while many animations these days can make a presentation look hokey, it is possible to create impressive animations and transitions that give your presentation kick. If you think about the most beautiful presentation ever, there's a good chance that it involved an animation of one object or another, in addition to some nice slide transitions.

Next, there are things you can do to improve your presentation before you even stand up in front of a crowd. It's easy to step through each slide and go through the motions, but it's even better if you can rehearse timings, save them, and use them during your actual presentation. Not only can you save rehearsed timings, but also you can actually use a microphone to practice a presentation and remember exactly what you said and when you changed slides so that you can just press Play and rewatch an entire presentation.

Using Animations

Advanced Animations come in two flavors:

- Preset, which are just point and click
- Custom, for the more adventurous presentation

Preset Animations

Let's talk about the standard animations for objects, which are one size fits all and come prepackaged for you so that all you have to do is decide what you want them to do.

Take a look at the Animations tab shown in Figure 15.1. This tab contains both the animations that correspond to individual objects, which this section is about, and the transitions from one slide to the next.

Figure 15.1

The Animations tab contains animations that are applied to whole slides and also to individual objects.

If you have an object selected, the Animate drop-down becomes enabled (see Figure 15.2) and allows you to choose one of five options:

- No Animation
- Fade
- Wipe
- Fly In
- Custom Animation

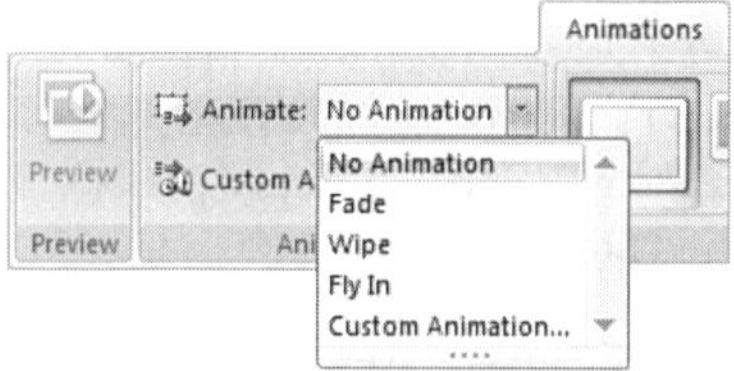

Figure 15.2

Click the Animate drop-down to reveal a set of preset animations.

NOTE

Keep in mind that the preset animations shown depend on what you have selected, so don't be surprised if you see something different from this figure if you have selected multiple lines, bars, shapes, and so on.

By default, No Animation is selected and causes your object to do nothing when slideshow is run. Fade, Wipe, and Fly In perform various effects to your object, which are pretty self-explanatory. It gets interesting when you select the last choice, Custom Animation, which is the same as clicking the Custom Animation button below the drop-down in the Animations group (see Figure 15.3).

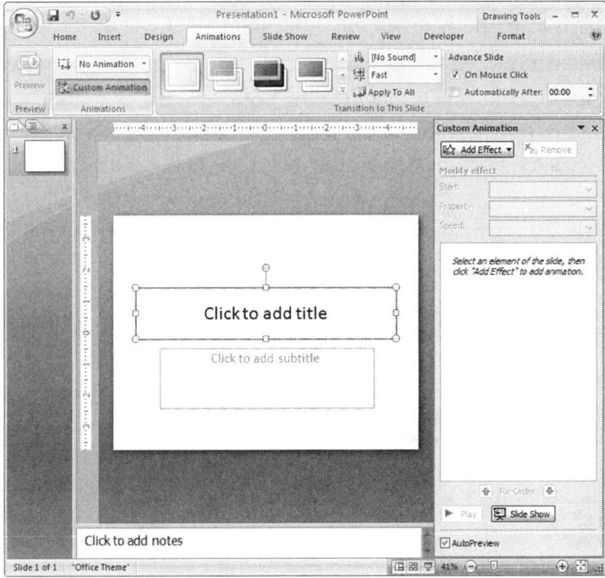

Figure 15.3

The Custom Animation button toggles the Custom Animation pane and does the same thing as selecting Custom Animation from the Animate drop-down.

Custom Animations

As of the Office XP release of PowerPoint, the ability to create custom animations has been included to help you think outside of the box. This is where the many PowerPoint experts claim their fame. Custom animations are very customizable and allow you to specify what you want the animation to look like, when it should occur, and what it should affect.

EXPLORING THE CUSTOM ANIMATION PANE

Take a look at the Custom Animation pane that appears when the Custom Animation button is selected on the Animations tab's Animations group:

- The top section allows you to add, change, and remove effects from the currently selected object.
- The middle area shows you what animations exist on the current slide. The order they appear in determines the order in which they will play during the slideshow.
- The bottom area allows you to play all the animations one by one to preview what they all look like. After Play is clicked, an Animation status bar appears next to each animation showing how far along the animation it currently is, while the slide itself will actually animate the object (see Figure 15.4). This is a great way to test what the animations will do rather than having to enter Slide Show mode every time.
- When Play is clicked, a timeline is shown at the bottom of the animation area that displays how long the animations occur for the whole slide, whereas the Animation status bar (which appears next to each Animation) shows the length for only one Animation.

NOTE

When Play is clicked, the Animation status bar and timeline are shown only while the animations are previewed and disappear if the preview is stopped.

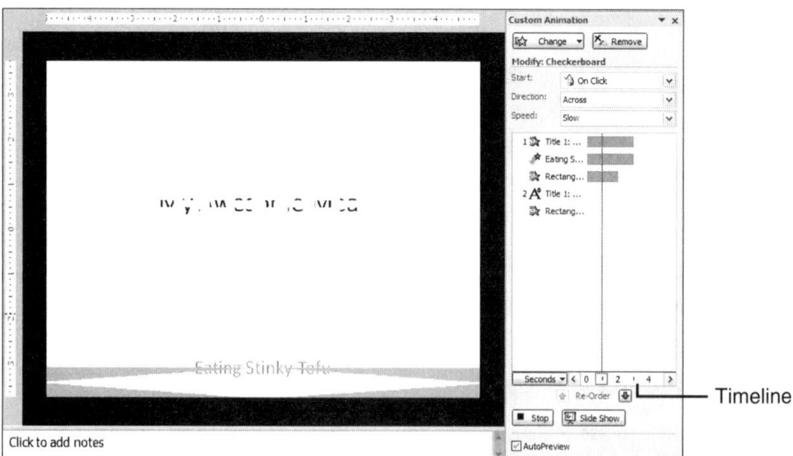

Figure 15.4

After clicking the Play button, the Animation status bar next to each animation displays the current progress and is a nice way to see relative lengths of animations compared to one another.

Another way to view this timeline is via the Show Advanced Timeline, which is an option under any of the animations drop-downs (see Figure 15.5).

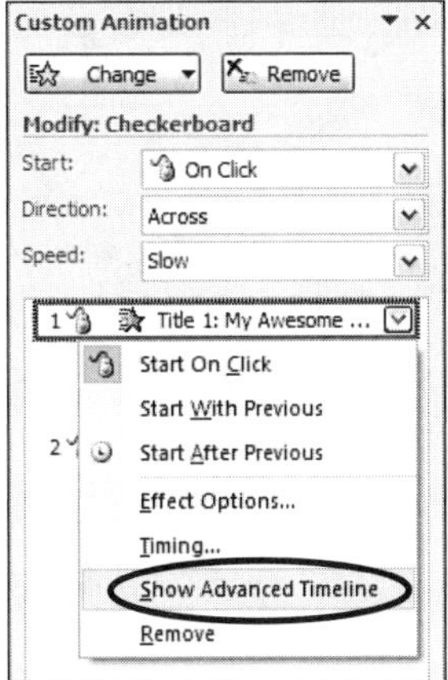

Figure 15.5

Selecting Show Advanced Timeline allows you to see how long each animation will take. The timeline shown will look like the one in Figure 15.4, except that it will not go away.

NOTE

One of the cooler things about the Custom Animation pane is its ability to be dragged to the top, bottom, left, or right of the application, and it will dock there, unlike many of the other panes in PowerPoint. This is helpful if you have very descriptive animations and want more space to be taken up on the tops and bottoms of your windows. In addition, when you view the advanced timeline, you can see more about it, such as how many seconds it will last. You can also zoom in and out of the timeline to focus on specific pieces of your animations.

USING THE SELECTION PANE WITH CUSTOM ANIMATIONS

Remember when we mentioned the Selection pane in Chapter 7, "Working with Shapes," and how it's useful to rename objects for use later? Well here's one of those times. Custom animations use the same name as the Selection pane to identify objects, so if you want to really know what object you're animating—such as the `BlueSquareWithFadeAnimation`—go ahead and rename your object to something unique via the Selection pane. Here's how:

1. Launch the Selection pane by going to the Editing group in the Home tab and choosing the Select drop-down and then the Selection Pane button (see Figure 15.6).

NOTE

At this point, you will have the task panes open side by side because task panes no longer stack on top of each other. If you want more screen space, you can close the Custom Animation pane if it makes things easier.

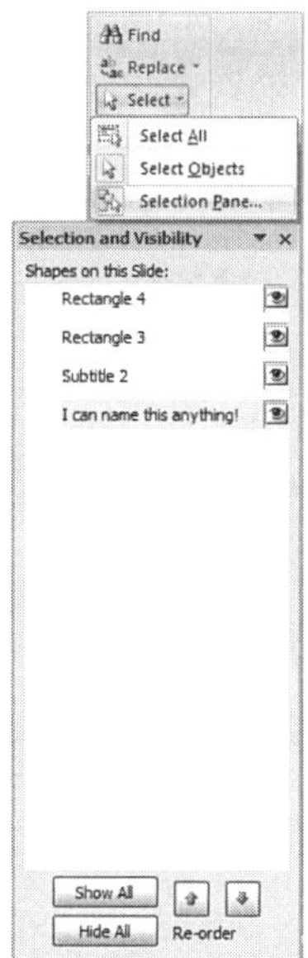

Figure 15.6

Open the Selection pane from the Home tab.

2. With the Selection pane open, select an object, click its name in the Shapes on this Slide list, and enter the name you want your object to have. The new name appears immediately in the Custom Animation task pane after changing it in the Selection pane. Also, at this point, you might want to close the Selection pane because you're done with it and it might just get in your way.

Custom Animation Types

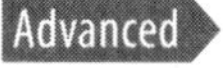

Custom Animation types can really make a presentation stand out. Let's explore the main types of Custom Animations, go into Motion Paths, and also look at Triggers.

Using Entrance, Emphasis, Exit

These three types of custom animations are grouped together only because they are separate from Motion Paths and are very similar to each other. The following sections regarding adding animations, previewing animations, and customizing their options apply to all types of Custom Animations.

ADDING AN ANIMATION

After you select something on your slide and click Add Effect in the Custom Animation pane, the top three options are similar (see Figure 15.7):

- **Entrance**—Specifies effects that change how the object first appears
- **Emphasis**—Changes the behavior of an object that has already appeared
- **Exit**—Removes the object from the slide in a certain fashion

Go ahead and try this as an example. Click Add Effect from the Custom Animation pane and then select Entrance and then Blinds.

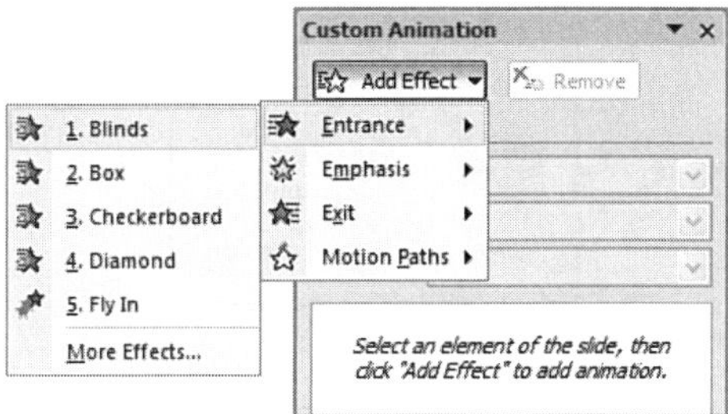

Figure 15.7

Three of the custom animations are very similar: Entrance, Emphasis, and Exit. All affect a certain part of the timeline of an object's animation. This is another case in which the list can look different depending on what type of animation is selected.

NOTE

These all have a More Effects option in the drop-down to reveal more custom animations. Be sure to check these out, as you might not have noticed how many there are.

ANIMATION OPTIONS

Now that you have an existing effect, open the animation's drop-down list by clicking the arrow on the right side of the animation in the list (see Figure 15.8).

Let's look at some of the things you can do with a custom animation from the options in the drop-down.

The top section of the drop-down affects when the animation takes place. These variations determine when the animation starts:

- **Start On Click**—Starts the animation as soon as the mouse is clicked.
- **Start With Previous**—Causes animations to begin at the same time as the immediately previous animation. If it is the first animation, it starts automatically.
- **Start After Previous**—Waits for the immediately previous animation to finish, and then it begins. Again, if it is the first animation, it starts automatically.

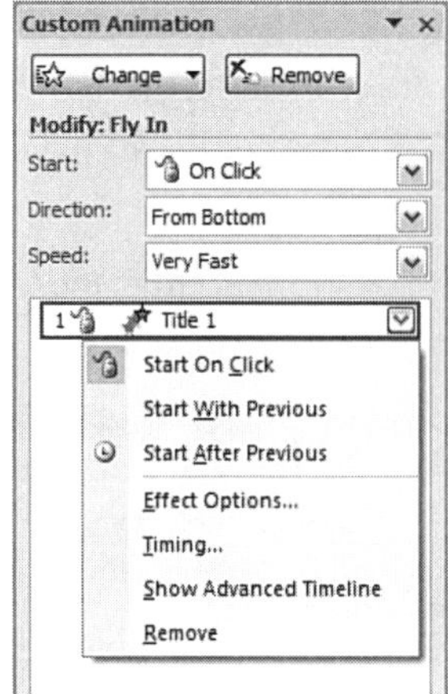

Figure 15.8

The drop-down next to each animation effect lets you customize options specific to that animation.

The bottom portion of the list is specific to this effect. Choose from Effect options (seen in Figure 15.9); Timing options, which include a toggle for the Show Advanced Timeline (mentioned before); and Remove, which you can also do by clicking the button at the top-right of the Custom Animation pane.

Figure 15.9

Effect options dialog.

If you choose Effect options, the dialog box that contains options specific to the selected effect is displayed. (The Fly In effect was the chosen animation in Figure 15.9.) You see a tab for Effect, which includes some of the options that you can also change directly in the Custom Animation pane, such as the Direction setting. The Timing tab (see Figure 15.10) offers additional options for perfecting the timing of the animation. The Text Animation tab (see Figure 15.11) is specific to the animation being created in our example, as we had text selected when the Effect options command was chosen. This tab will not be present if text is not selected.

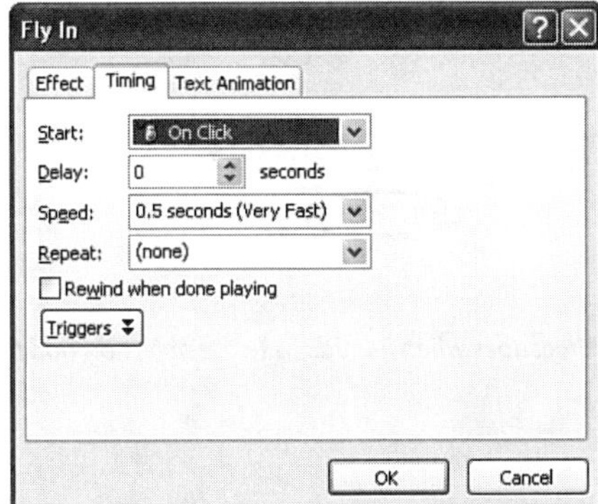

Figure 15.10

Timing options dialog.

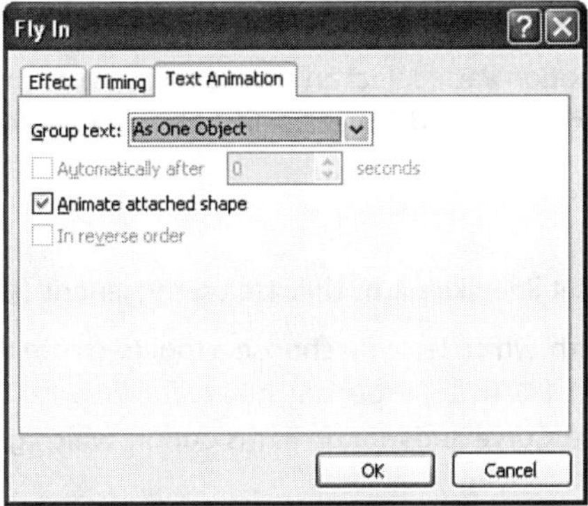

Figure 15.11

Text Animations from the Effect options dialog. We discuss this in more detail later in this chapter.

NOTE

Clicking on Effect options and Timing brings up the same dialog but defaults to different tabs of the dialog.

Although we won't go through every option under the Effect options because various effects have different options, we will advise you to explore all the options and all the different types of effects, as well as figure out what's customizable and what exactly you want the animation to look like. It's a good rule of thumb to imagine the animation you want and then try to create it.

PREVIEWING ONE ANIMATION

Clicking Play in the Custom Animation pane list with an animation selected shows you a preview of what it will look like during Slide Show mode. Also, if the AutoPreview box is checked at the bottom of the Custom Animation pane (see Figure 15.12), the animation will be previewed when it is added or changed.

Figure 15.12

AutoPreview will display what the Effect does when it is added to the object or modified.

Motion Paths

To add additional animations related to movement in the presentation, you will want to understand and use Motion Paths. A Motion Path allows you to specify a movement for the object, which you can then customize.

CREATING A MOTION PATH

First things first: To create a Motion Path, select an object you want to move around on the slide during the presentation, and then click on Add Effect, Select Motion Path from the list to reveal the options.

You can

- Choose one of the preset line-like paths that are pretty generic (see Figure 15.13).
- Select Draw Custom Path, which lets you choose a tool to create the path yourself using freeforms (see Figure 15.14). This is especially handy for use with Tablet PCs. The recommended option is to use the Line, Curve and Motion Paths option, which gives you many more preset options.

NOTE

It can be hard to create freeform custom paths unless you have a very steady hand and perhaps a Tablet PC. The alternative is using curves and lines in addition to Edit Points.

- Choose More Motion Paths to select from 64 more paths, which actually appear as shapes and other interesting paths (see Figure 15.15).

As with other animations, Motion Paths can be customized via the Effect options selection from the drop-down in the Custom Animation pane. From this dialog, you can lock the path, which can pin a path to a place on the slide background even if the object moves and also smooth the start or end. And, of course, choose the Timing tab and customize when this animation will occur, as well as any delays or events it needs to be aware of.

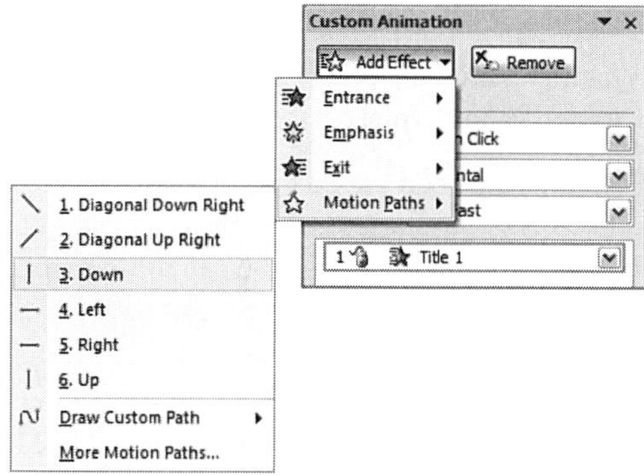

Figure 15.13

The preset Motion Paths you can choose from.

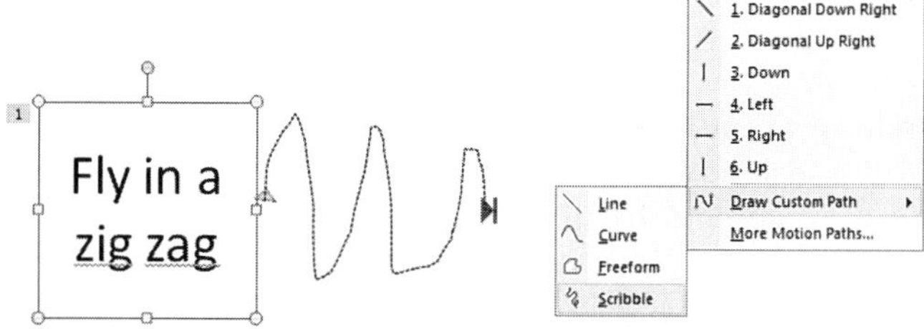

Figure 15.14

Choose Draw Custom Path to create your own path and specify where you want your object to go.

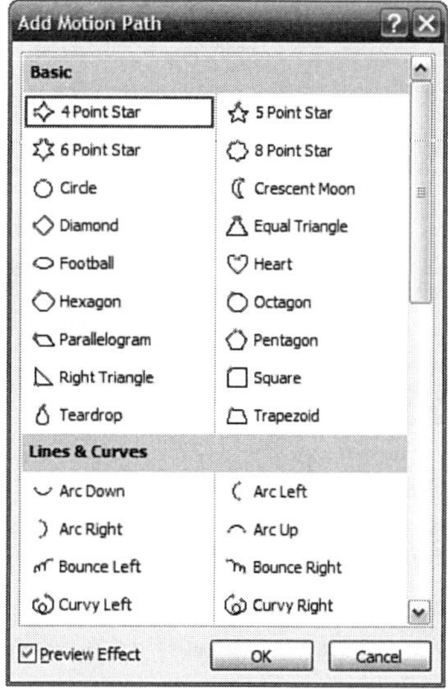

Figure 15.15

The other Motion Paths are numerous and contain very cool paths, which would be difficult to re-create.

EDITING MOTION PATHS AND THE RETURN OF EDIT POINTS

One really useful animation feature is after a Motion Path is created, it becomes editable so that you can change the rotation or drag the ends to make it larger or smaller.

You can be a real master of Motion Paths and use Edit points to adjust the path. Right-click the motion path and choose Edit Points to get started. If you aren't familiar with using Edit points to work with freeform shapes, revisit Chapter 7 and learn how you can move points around, add points, change the line segment types, and basically create any type of path you can imagine.

TIP

You can also right-click a Motion Path and choose Reverse Path Direction if you originally drew the path backward. Similarly, if you use Autoreverse, an option on the Effect options dialog, you can create half of the animation and have it loop back to the origin.

Animating with Text

Remember when we showed you the Animate drop-down on the Animations tab in the Animations group? Well, it changes when you have text on your objects. If you have text that supports multiple paragraphs (Title Placeholders do not support this), the Animate drop-down is augmented to contain more options. Notice in Figure 15.16 that the same five options are available as in Figure 15.2, but now there are two options for each: All At Once and By 1st Level Paragraphs.

NOTE

These options also exist when animating SmartArt and Charts.

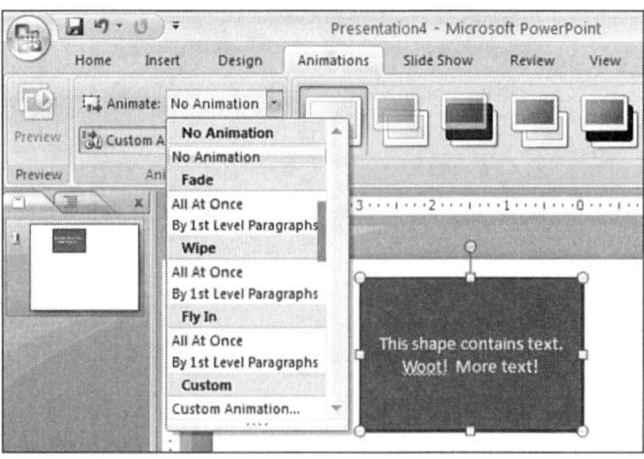

Figure 15.16

When text is available on your objects and supports paragraphs, the animation options expand to allow you to customize the animation on the text as All At Once or By 1st Level Paragraphs.

This is a great way to animate bulleted lists and nested lists. Try it out for yourself, and notice that it is a great way to group text together and also have a smooth animation apply to each group.

In addition to the standard animations, you can customize a Custom Animation for Text by clicking on Effect options from the Custom Animation drop-down and then selecting the Text Animation tab from that dialog. From here, you can change how "grouped text" (that is, several paragraphs) is animated, whether the shape that houses the text should be animated, and when the animation should start.

While playing around with custom animations, we found a pretty cool text effect you can create, which emphasizes your text and captures audiences' attention. We've actually used this animation and received feedback from people, who couldn't stop looking at it; it distracted people from the presentation. (So be careful when you use it.)

To get text that animates like Figure 15.17, do the following:

NOTE

The images don't do this animation justice; you need to try it for yourself!

---

1. Create a new presentation (Ctrl+N), type some text into the title placeholder, and select the placeholder.
2. Launch the Custom Animation pane by choosing the Animations tab, and then in the Animations group, choose Custom Animation.
3. Click on Add Effect, Emphasis, Grow/Shrink.
4. Right-click the new animation that appears in the Custom Animations list to make the drop-down visible. Or click on the drop-down arrow to the animation's right.
5. Select Effect options.
6. Make the Size larger than 150%. (We chose "Larger.")

NOTE

To do this faster, there's already a drop-down in the Custom Animations pane labeled Size, where you can change the size.

---

7. Check all three check boxes: Smooth Start, Smooth End, and Auto Reverse.
8. Choose to Animate Text: By Letter.
9. Select a 9% Delay between letters.
10. Under the Timing tab, choose Speed: 0.5 Seconds (Very Fast).
11. Set Repeat: Until End of Slide.
12. Click OK to save everything.
13. Click the Play button at the bottom of the Custom Animation pane to preview your creation (see Figure 15.17). This is the quick way to preview the animation, but it does not account for delays, so definitely test your animations with timing and clicks, with prev, after prev, and so on, in Slide Show mode.

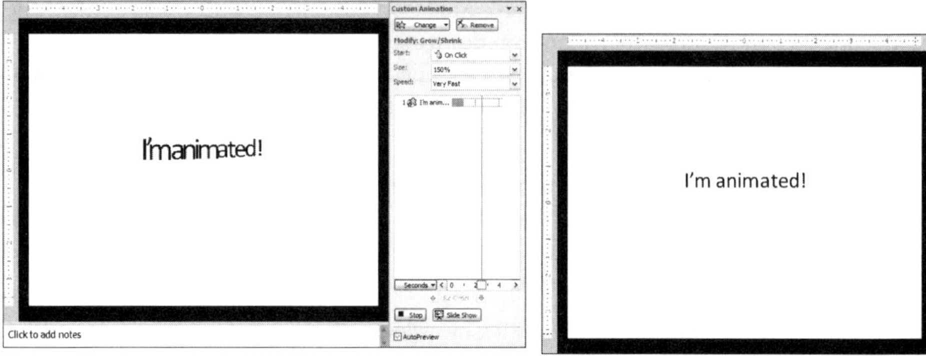

Figure 15.17

Sample text animation.

As usual, you should play around with the settings and tweak it how you want it, but this is a start.

Triggers

Now that you're an expert in the use of custom animations, let's take it a step further and give you the power to start animations when an object is "triggered," which means clicked on in this case. We are about to show you how to start an animation when another object on your slide is clicked.

To set a trigger, right-click an animation in the Custom Animation pane and choose Timing. Click on the Triggers drop-down, which has an interesting double arrow symbol (see Figure 15.18).

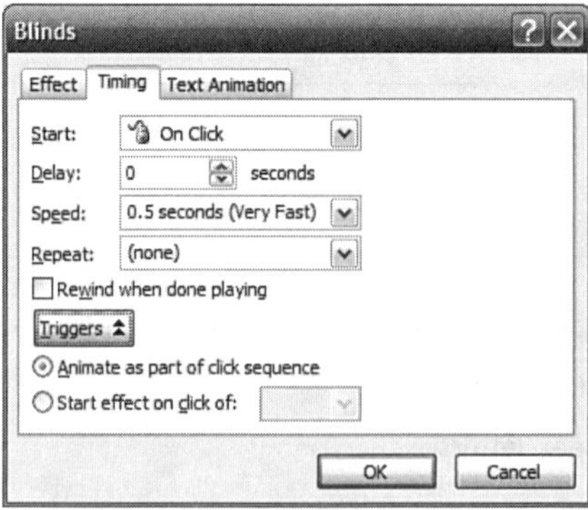

Figure 15.18

The Triggers button from the Timing drop-down from a Custom Animation drop-down on the Custom Animation pane.

Note that, by default, the Animate As Part of Click Sequence is selected, and after the other Start Effect On Click Of option is selected, the topmost drop-down on the Custom Animation pane will be set to On Click because what we are about to do requires clicking.

To specify which object needs to be clicked in order to start the Custom Animation, click on the drop-down and select an object based on its name. Remember, this is the same name you set via the Selection pane earlier this chapter.

Adding Transitions

Advanced Can you remember the last great presentation you saw that did not include any transitions between slides? Transitions are used in order to make a presentation run smoother and mitigate the sudden change between one slide and the next. Although it might seem as though transitions should be operations that occur between slides, to create one you must choose a slide and apply a transition that will occur *before* this slide is viewed in Slide Show mode. Think of transitions as entry transitions for the background, Master Slide elements, and any element without animation.

NOTE

Every slide starts with No Transition applied. This might seem boring, but many presentations work well without transitions when slides have content that flows smoothly from one slide to another.

To find the transitions and apply one, do the following:

1. Select the Animations tab.
2. Go to the large Transition to This Slide group.
3. From the gallery, hover your mouse over a transition to see a live preview, and click on one to apply it (see Figure 15.19).

NOTE

Although this is just an example of a particular transition, many professionals think this dissolve transition is ugly, outdated, and should be avoided. For the purposes of this book, it translates best into print so that you can "see" the transition.

Drop down the gallery to expand it. This will show more transitions organized into the following types:

- No Transition
- Fades and Dissolves
- Wipes
- Push and Cover
- Stripes and Bars
- Random

Figure 15.19

Hover your mouse over a slide transition on the Animations tab and watch it preview on the main slide.

How you use these depends on your content; definitely try them out and see what fits best with your presentation.

Transition Sounds

If you look to the right of the Transitions gallery on the Animations tab, you will find more options to customize your transition, such as the ability to add a sound that will play once or loop until the next sound if you check the box at the bottom of its drop-down, as shown in Figure 15.20.

By default, the sound is set to No Sound, which we recommend as well because most sounds end up sounding pretty tacky. However, feel free to prove us wrong by using your own sound, which you can do by selecting Other Sound from the drop-down.

NOTE

Live Preview works here as well, in that hovering over a sound will preview it. However, these get annoying pretty fast.

Transition Speed

The Transition Speed drop-down is right underneath the Transition Sound button. The transition speed is handy if you need to use up more time. By default, the speed is set to Fast, and the drop-down allows you to set it to Medium and Slow. These are the only options for the speed of the transition, and they vary from one transition to another.

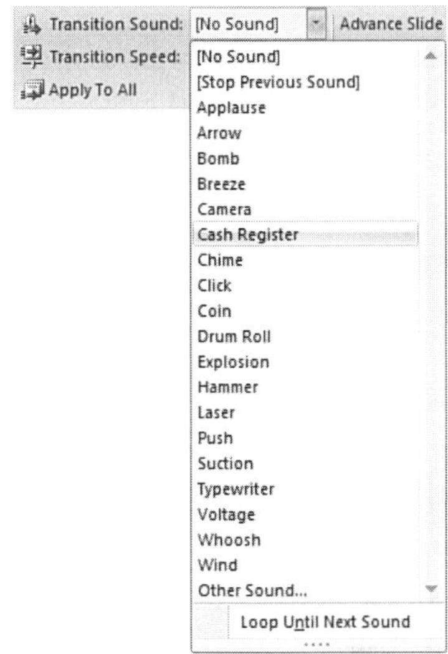

Figure 15.20

The Transition Sound drop-down. A sound plays once unless you select the last option in the dialog to have the sound loop until the next sound.

Advancing to the Next Slide

For those who fear accidental clicks or want to really make sure that your Custom Animation trigger works perfectly, make sure to use the On Mouse Click feature and make sure that it is unchecked (see Figure 15.21). Because triggers start a custom animation when an object is clicked, this check box prevents any missed clicks from advancing the slide.

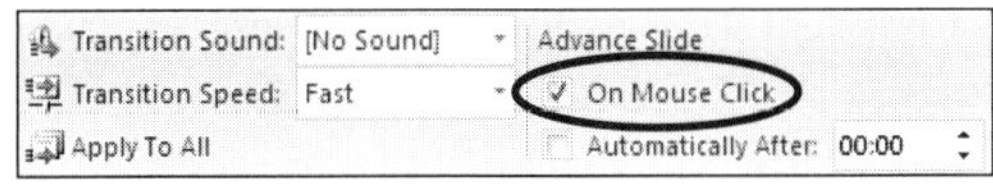

Figure 15.21

Uncheck the On Mouse Click box to prevent the mouse from advancing to the next slide.

To automatically advance to the next slide after a period of time, check the Automatically After box and set an amount of time into the timer on the right. If this is set to 00:00, the slide will advance automatically after all animations in the timeline finish.

Creating Custom Shows

This is one of our favorite features that is not widely known. Custom Show allows you to take slides from your presentation and build a new show with them. This is really powerful when you want to rearrange the slides for the presentation only but leave the slides in the same order in the physical presentation file. In addition, this allows you to repeat a slide as many times as you want, rather than duplicating the slides in the document.

To access Custom Show, first create many slides in a presentation and then do the following:

1. Click on the Slide Show tab.
2. Under the Start Slide Show group, click Custom Shows to reveal a drop-down.
3. Here you can either click on an existing Custom Show you have created in order to launch it or create a new one.

To create a new Custom Show:

1. Select Custom Shows from the Custom Shows drop-down (Slide Show tab, Start Slide Show group).
2. From this dialog, click on the New button.
3. Now give this Custom Show a Name.
4. Select Slides from the presentation on the left pane and click Add to put them into your custom show. If a slide does not have a title, only the slide number is shown.
5. Repeat until you have created a custom show to your liking. Also, repeat all the steps to create multiple custom shows.

At this point, you can reorder slides and add multiple slides at the same time. Also, custom shows only exist within one presentation and cannot be linked to from outside.

Now under the Custom Shows drop-down, you will find your new show, which you can launch by clicking on it. This list is ordered by the order in which you created the shows.

This is a great way to display different slides to diverse audiences if you plan on showing your presentation to a varied set of people.

Use this feature in combination with Action Settings or Hyperlinks, which we explain in the next section, to create a really cool hidden feature using hidden links to custom shows.

Hyperlinks

By now, everyone's familiar with links on Internet web pages. PowerPoint supports links as well. You can put one on just about any shape or text:

1. To insert a shape, go to the Home tab, and in the Drawing group on the Shapes drop-down, select a shape and click on the slide to insert it. (We could just as easily type some text and select it, but for this example, we will use a shape.)
2. On the Insert tab in the Links group, choose Hyperlink (or just press Ctrl+K). In the dialog that comes up (see Figure 15.22), type in a web address such as http://www.ironjeff.com, and click OK.

TIP

Alternatively, you can select text, right-click the selection, and choose Hyperlink. If the text you selected is spelled incorrectly though, you will see a spelling correction menu instead, and you will need to fix the spelling of the selected words before you can use this method to apply a hyperlink.

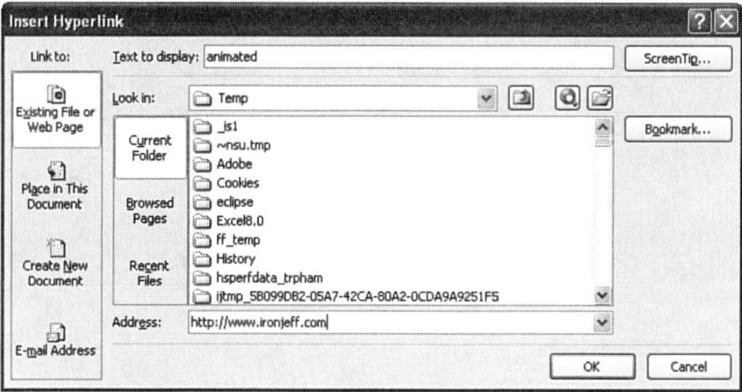

Figure 15.22

Hyperlink dialog.

3. Click the shape. Uh, nothing happened. In Excel, that would launch the web site. In PowerPoint, hyperlinks are only active in Slide Show.
4. Go to the Start Slide Show group on the Slide Show tab and choose From Beginning. Or, just press F5.
5. Now that you're in Slide Show mode, click the shape to activate the hyperlink. Note that when you hover your mouse over the shape, the cursor changes to a hand to show that it's clickable.

NOTE

Hyperlinks cannot be placed on placeholders. If you apply a hyperlink on a placeholder, the hyperlink applies to all the text inside the placeholder. Microsoft probably figured that there was no need for hyperlinks on placeholders because most placeholders contain just text and don't have anything you can really click on.

Set Off Actions During Your Presentation

Advanced

Now that we've explored basic hyperlinks, let's say that we want PowerPoint to link to something more interesting, such as to the next slide in the presentation. That's where Actions come into play.

Inserting Action Buttons

The easiest way to create an Action link is to insert an Action button:

1. Go to the Home tab's Drawing group and choose Shapes. Choose one of the Action buttons in the bottom category of the Shapes gallery (see Figure 15.23).

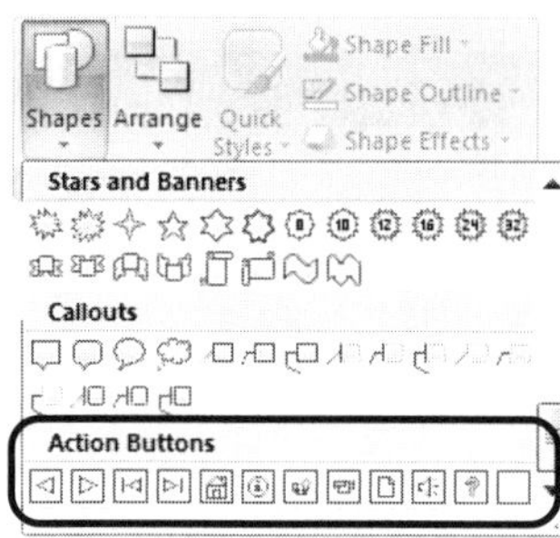

Figure 15.23

The choices at the bottom of the shapes gallery are Action buttons.

2. After you insert the Action button, the Action Settings dialog comes up (see Figure 15.24). You can click OK to just accept the default choice. We discuss each of the choices in greater depth in the "Different Types of Actions" section later in this chapter. If you ever change your mind about what Action to use, select the Action button, go to the Insert tab in the Links group, and choose Action.

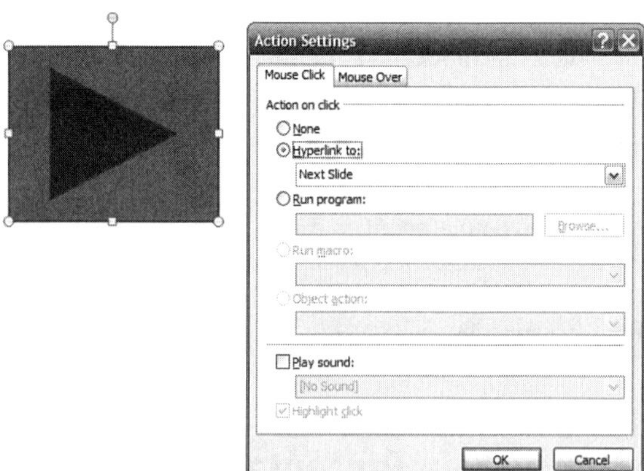

Figure 15.24

Action Settings dialog.

3. Enter Slide Show mode by going to the Slide Show tab's Start Slide Show group and choosing From Current Slide.
4. Click on the button you inserted to see what happens.

NOTE

Depending on which Action button is chosen, nothing might happen when you click on it in Slide Show. For example, if you click the Home Action button (the one that looks like a house), this takes you to the first slide. Clicking it on the first slide will make it look as if nothing happened. Try a few different buttons to experiment.

Repeat for all the different Action Button types to see what they all do. Also, by default the Action buttons aren't all that beautiful. Use the shape formatting skills you learned in Chapter 12, "Formatting Shapes, Text, and More" to spruce them up.

Before accepting the Action Settings dialog, take a quick look at the bottom of the dialog. Here you can choose to

- Play a sound when the link click occurs. This only works with `.wav` files.
- Highlight the button when the link click occurs. Note that this has no effect on Action buttons, which will always be highlighted when clicked.

These two actions will happen on the side in addition to anything else you've specified. Don't overdo either, or you risk annoying your audience.

Mouse Over

If you look carefully at the Action Settings dialog, you will note that there are tabs at the top—one for Mouse Click and one for Mouse Over (see Figure 15.25). The options on both tabs are virtually identical, except that the choices on the second tab occur when you mouse over the button rather than click on it.

WHAT IS A MOUSE OVER?

A mouse over occurs when the mouse is hovered over a shape or text during the slideshow. You can jump to the next slide when someone moves the mouse over your button, for instance.

For a mouse over to work when the cursor is already on a shape, the cursor must leave the shape and then return back over the shape. This is a good reason not to set mouse over effects over large shapes that cover the entire slide.

Different Types of Actions

Let's describe all the different types of actions to which you can link using the Action Settings dialog (seen previously in Figure 15.24):

- **None**—What's the point of an Action button that does no action? You might want something to happen on Mouse Over but not on Mouse Click, or vice versa, so you'd choose None for the one you want to do nothing. You might also set an action to None if all you want to do is trigger one of the Side Actions described in the previous section, but you don't want the link to actually go anywhere.

Figure 15.25

The action can appear when you click or when you mouse over.

- Hyperlink to
    - **Next Slide**—Fairly self-explanatory. For custom shows, mentioned earlier in this chapter, this does not jump to the next slide in the sequence but to the next slide in the original slide order. Also, this does not skip hidden slides, which we talk about at the end of this chapter. These two caveats apply to the next three items as well.
    - **Previous Slide**
    - **First Slide**
    - **Last Slide**
    - **Last Slide Viewed**—This is usually equivalent to Previous Slide, but if you used another action to link to the current slide, the Last Slide Viewed could be a totally different slide. For example, let's say that someone going through your slideshow follows a hyperlink from slide 3 to slide 20. Clicking a Previous Slide link on slide 20 would go back to slide 19. Clicking a Last Slide Viewed link on slide 20 would go back to slide 3.
    - **End Show**—In a regular slideshow, this ends the current slideshow. For a custom show, it just ends the custom show and returns to the slide that started the custom show. For external slideshows, it closes the external show and returns back to the slide that started the external show.
    - **Custom Show**—We discussed custom shows previously in this chapter. Here you can link to one of them. You also get the option to select a check box labeled Show and Return. If you check this, when the linked custom show finishes playing, PowerPoint continues the slideshow on the slide containing the link. If it's unchecked, after the custom show finishes, the entire slideshow finishes.
    - **Slide**—Links to any slide in the presentation.

- **URL**—Similar to a normal hyperlink, such as one that links to http://www.waynekao.com.
- **Other PowerPoint Presentation**—You choose another presentation, and it shows that presentation before returning to the current slide.

CAUTION

Be careful if when linking to files on your disk with the Other PowerPoint Presentation or Other File choices. If you send your presentation to someone else using another computer, those links won't work anymore unless the recipient has the same files sitting on the same places on his hard disk. To avoid headaches like this, we recommend only linking to files in the same folder as your presentation. It makes it less likely that you will forget to send the files when you email the presentation, plus PowerPoint is less likely to be confused where to find the files. And **always** test your links before making your big presentation.

- **Other File**—You can link to an Excel spreadsheet, a text file, or just about any document.

- **Run Program**—Choose a program to run. You can run Solitaire, Microsoft Word, World of Warcraft, or just about any other program you have. For those technical folk out there, note that you can have PowerPoint pass command-line switches when launching a program. Because this links to the actual program path on the current computer, make sure to test these links if you move the presentation from one computer to another. Also, note that during the slideshow, PowerPoint shows a scary warning message about external content before it actually runs the linked program.
- **Run Macro**—Here you can run your favorite macro. Read more about macros at the end of Chapter 10, "Formatting Your Presentation."
- **Object Action**—Only applicable if you're putting an action on an OLE object, which you can read about in Chapter 7. So, if you've embedded an Office document—such as an Excel spreadsheet—or you've embedded a sound or video, you can select the object, launch the Actions dialog, and the Object Action option will have some useful commands such as Edit and Open for the spreadsheet and Play for the sound or video.

TIP

Always test your hyperlinks and Action buttons. It's very easy to get unexpected behavior, and you don't want to be surprised halfway through an important presentation.

Nothing Special About These Buttons

It's not just Action buttons that can use Actions and Action Settings. You can select any shape, text, or even a chart or SmartArt, and then go to the Insert tab, Links group and choose Action to apply the same actions.

NOTE

In PowerPoint 2003, you could right-click a shape or text and select Action Settings directly from the context menu. This functionality no longer exists in PowerPoint 2007.

ACTION SETTINGS OR HYPERLINKS?

There is some functionality overlap between the Hyperlink dialog (found by going to the Insert tab, Links group and clicking Hyperlink) described in the previous section and the Actions dialog (also in the Links group, under Action). For instance, both let you link to a particular slide. There are two dialogs because the hyperlink dialog is the generic Microsoft Office dialog, very similar to the one used in Word and Excel, whereas the Actions dialog is specific to PowerPoint and showcases functionality only found in PowerPoint. In general, unless we're creating a quick link to a website, we prefer to use the Actions dialog because it contains all the functionality of the hyperlink dialog, plus more.

There's actually one special behavior you get with Action buttons that isn't equivalent to adding an Action to other objects. When in Slide Show, if you click on an Action button, the button changes slightly to show its being pressed. You can duplicate this behavior by adding an animation to your object, but it won't come automatically as it does with Action buttons.

Cool Things You Can Do with Actions

That's enough nitty-gritty. Let's talk about some neat uses of PowerPoint Actions.

LINK TO FIRST SLIDE

It's always nice having a link to the title slide of the presentation, no matter what slide you're currently on. Let's add one to the master:

1. On the View tab, go to the Presentation Views group and choose Slide Master to enter Slide Master view.
2. On the Home tab, go to the Drawing group and choose Shapes, and then select the Home Action button. That's the one with the house on it (see Figure 15.26). Click on the slide to insert it.

CAUTION

Make sure that a master is selected in the left pane, not a layout. Masters are the top-level slides with a number to the left of them; layouts are the ones that appear underneath them slightly indented. If you add to a layout on accident, the link will only appear on some slides. If you are really diligent, instead of adding the link to the master, you can just add it on several slide layouts where it makes sense and omit the link on layouts on which it doesn't make sense, such as the Title Slide Layout.

3. By default, the Action Settings dialog indicates that the Action button will link to the First Slide. That's what we want, so just click OK.

NOTE

Even if you click Cancel in the dialog, the Action button and the link are still inserted. The dialog just comes up, so you can change the link if you prefer.

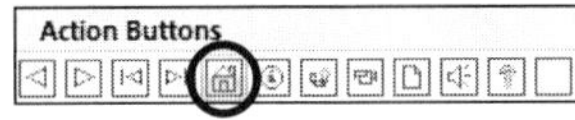

Figure 15.26

Insert the Home Action button.

That's it. If you enter Slide Show mode, every slide now has a link to the first slide in the presentation.

CREATE INTERACTIVE PROTOTYPES

Before companies spend a lot of time and energy building a software program such as Microsoft Office, they usually build a prototype and test it on people to see if they like it. PowerPoint makes it very easy to build a quick prototype of your idea.

Let's say that we're building a special check box library for a client and we want to test it to see how it will behave. That's easy enough to do:

1. Create a new presentation.
2. On the first slide, add a picture of an unchecked check box. Or, be lame like us, and insert a donut shape from the Home tab's Drawing group under Shapes.
3. Insert a new slide (on the Home tab in the Slides group, choose New Slide).
4. Now go to slide 2 and insert a picture of a checked check box. Or, we're going to be lazy and insert a No symbol. Put it on the slide in exactly the same place you put the unchecked check box in step 2 (see Figure 15.27).

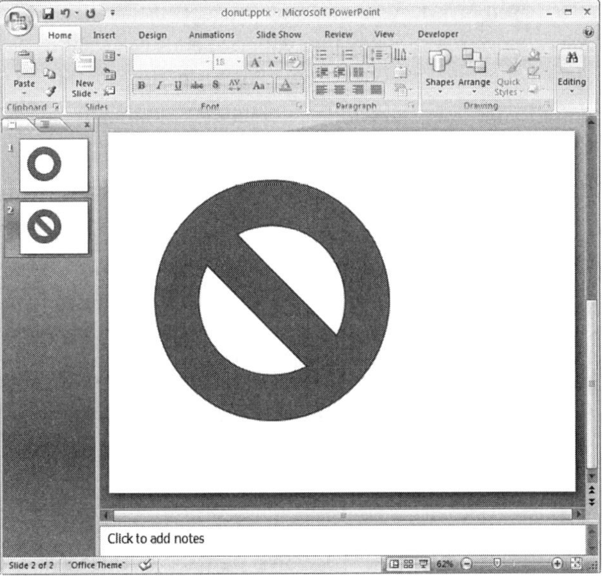

Figure 15.27

Insert two symbols in the same place on two different slides.

NOTE

In this simple example, it's probably easier to use triggered animations in which clicking one shape triggers the appearance of the other shape. Triggers are explained earlier in this chapter. Using triggers gives you the flexibility to have multiple controls without having to create a large number of slides. For more complicated prototypes with more than a simple shape, however, using the technique described here is often useful.

5. Now let's make this interactive. On slide 1, select the unchecked check box and choose the Insert tab and then Action in the Links group. Click Hyperlink To and choose Next Slide from the drop-down.
6. On slide 2, we're going to do something very similar. Select the checked check box and choose the Insert tab and then Action from the Links group. Click Hyperlink To and choose Previous Slide from the drop-down.
7. Now, enter Slide Show mode (press F5). When you click the button, watch how it checks itself. If you click it again, it will uncheck itself.

NOTE

If clicking a shape triggers both an animation and a hyperlink (or action), the hyperlink will happen first.

HIDDEN LINK DEPENDING ON AUDIENCE REACTION

Adjust your presentation based on how your audience reacts. Let's say that after you present the first slide of your presentation, you're not sure whether your audience will want to dive into details or whether they will want a higher level overview. PowerPoint is perfect for this:

1. Create a new presentation with three slides. Number them 1–3 in their title placeholders so that you can tell them apart later.
2. Let's pretend that slide 2 contains details and slide 3 has the high-level overview. On slide 1, let's create some hidden links to slides 2 and 3.
3. Insert a shape on slide 1.
4. Get rid of the outline by going to the Shapes Styles group on the Format tab, clicking Shape Outline, and then clicking No Outline.
5. Set the fill to be barely visible. Back on the Format ribbon, click Shape Fill, choose More Fill Colors, and set the transparency at the bottom of the dialog to 99% (see Figure 15.28).

NOTE

In PowerPoint 2007, hyperlinks on shapes do nothing in Slide Show unless the shape has a fill or a line. This is also the behavior in the PowerPoint Viewer. This differs from PowerPoint 2003 behavior. To work around this problem, set a nearly invisible fill or line on the shape, as we did in this section's example.

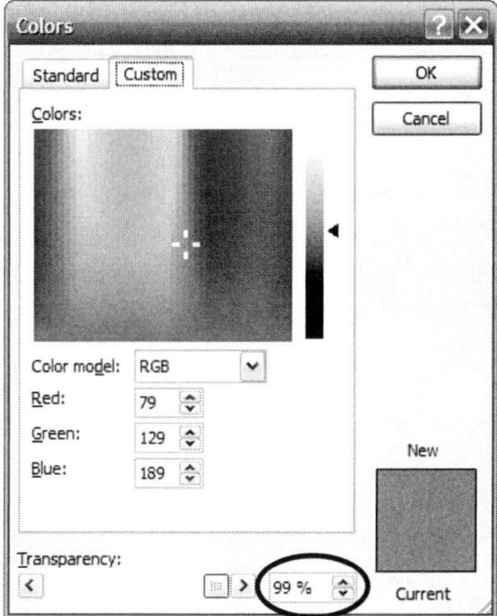

Figure 15.28

Set a high transparency fill.

6. Now insert an Action Setting. Go to the Insert tab in the Links group and click Action. Choose Hyperlink To so that this one links to the details slide, which is slide 2. Click OK.
7. Now duplicate your invisible shape by pressing Ctrl+D. Move the new shape so that it's not so close to your original shape.
8. Let's change this one's link to the high-level overview on slide 3. Add an action by going to the Insert tab's Links group and choosing Action yet again. Choose Hyperlink To. Then, choose Slide from the drop-down. Select slide 3 in the list of choices (see Figure 15.29).

Figure 15.29

Choose Hyperlink To and then choose Slide from the Action Settings dialog.

9. Now, if you go into Slide Show (press F5), you can present a spiel for the first slide, ask for questions, and then based on the answers, click on the link to the details page or the overview page.

TIP

A similar technique can be accomplished using Slide Show shortcut keys, detailed in Chapter 16. For example, you could press 3, and then press Enter to jump to slide 3. There's less setup work, but the downside is that you will have to remember the slide number. Another way to accomplish this is to create custom shows of several topics that the audience might be interested in and then create menu slides that use Actions to link to each of them.

Presenting Tools

Although we claim that we cannot help you become great speakers, we can help you become great presenters. Or, we can at least show you some tools to help with your presentations.

Rehearse Timings

The old saying "practice makes perfect" might or might not work for you when giving presentations. Some people like to have every word memorized; some like to have just the general idea of what they will say and use talking points. Whatever style you use, it's important to practice.

Rehearse Timings guides you through a dry run of your presentation by walking through it and recording how long you should spend on each slide. When you're done recording, you can keep the timings of when to switch slides. Later, you can even use them during an actual presentation if you so desire.

To access Rehearse Timings, go to the Slide Show tab in the Set Up group and choose Rehearse Timings button. This will launch Slide Show for you with an added little widget to show you how much time has elapsed (see Figure 15.30). This widget is nice because it gives you a Next button to switch to the next slide, a Pause button to take a break from the timing, the current time that has been spent on the current slide, a Repeat button to restart timing on this slide, and the total time that has been recorded in the presentation as a whole.

NOTE

Pausing the time for the slide pauses the time for the whole presentation timer as well.

Figure 15.30

The Slide Show Widget gives you information about your rehearsal.

At the end of your presentation, you will notice a nice pop-up that says "The total time for the slide show was H:MM:SS. Do you want to keep the new slide timings to use when you view the slide show?" (Figure 15.31 shows this.)

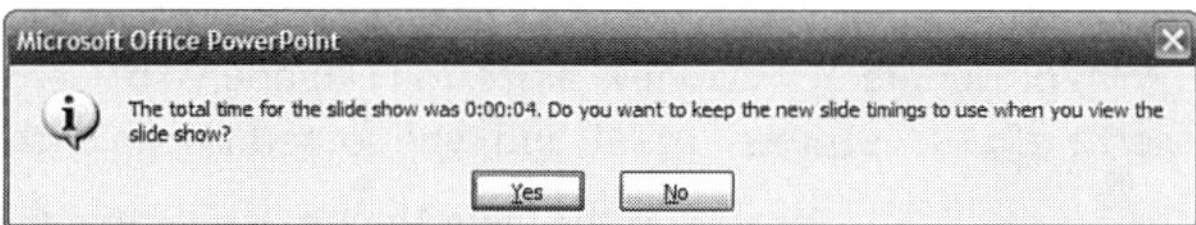

Figure 15.31

When finished with Rehearse Timings, a pop-up asks if you want to keep the timings for use during Slide Show.

If you choose Yes, the timings for each slide are saved. The next time you enter Slide Show (press F5), you won't have to manually transition between slides. They will automatically change based on the timings you recorded. If you want to keep the timings, but then want to enter the slideshow without using the timings temporarily, go to the Slide Show tab in the Set Up group and uncheck the Use Rehearsed Timings box.

NOTE

If you save the timings, your view will automatically be changed to Slide Sorter View so that the timing for each slide can be verified and adjusted.

If you choose No, nothing will happen, and you can continue as normal or try to rehearse again. Perhaps you only wanted to get a rough estimate of how much time the presentation will take and still transition between slides yourself during the real thing.

Additionally, if you choose No and remove the timings from the slides, it might take a second for PowerPoint to remove all the timings. Also, if you save timings on one pass and don't save them on the next pass, the first timings are restored. In other words, the timings are not removed.

TIP

When estimating how much time a presentation takes, don't assume that your actual presentation will take exactly the same amount of time as your rehearsal. Always leave a little buffer time for audience questions. If the presentation involves feedback from the audience, factor in even more time for discussion.

Also be sure to remember the pause/black/white buttons that are available at presentation time. More on this can be found in Chapter 16.

Creating Self-Playing Presentations

Ever see those self-playing PowerPoint presentations that jump by themselves between slides? We used to regularly see these while waiting in line at the local Taco Bell, looping though the 3 to 4 monthly specials, and we don't think they had a guy in the back advancing the slides by hand.

Let's make deeper use of the Rehearse Timings feature to construct a self-playing presentation.

RECORD HOW LONG TO STAY ON EACH SLIDE

Similar to the previous section, we need to record how long we want to stay on each slide.

1. Create a PowerPoint presentation with a few slides. You can open a presentation you already have. Or, just insert a few slides (press Ctrl+M) and type something on each inserted slide.
2. Now start the Rehearse Timings Feature on the Slide Show tab by going to the Set Up group and choosing Rehearse Timings.
3. You're now in Slide Show mode with a timer. This records how long to stay on each slide. So, if you want your final show to stay on slide 1 for 10 seconds, wait 10 seconds before you advance to the next slide. You can use the leftmost Play arrow to advance slides, the Pause arrow to pause, or the third button to reset the clock for the current slide.

> **NOTE**
>
> It's a good idea to have someone else read the content aloud to ensure that those viewing the presentation will be able to keep up.

4. When you arrive at the last slide, press Esc to exit the slideshow. PowerPoint will ask you whether to keep the timings; choose Yes.

REVIEW TIMINGS

You're now plopped into Slide Sorter view (see Figure 15.32). Notice how each slide has a time underneath it, telling you the timing value for each slide.

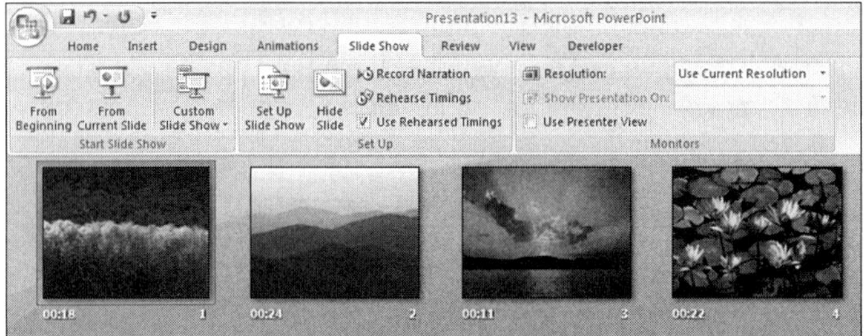

Figure 15.32

Slide Sorter view shows you the timings for each slide.

If it's massively off, just reread the "Record How Long to Stay on Each Slide" section earlier in this chapter to start over.

If just one or two slides need to be fixed up, select the slide and go to the Animations tab in the Transition to This Slide group. You will see the current time value in the rightmost text box labeled Automatically After (see Figure 15.33). Change the number to change the timing information for the selected slide.

NOTE

The time you enter is very precise, not just to the nearest second; it goes to the nearest millisecond.

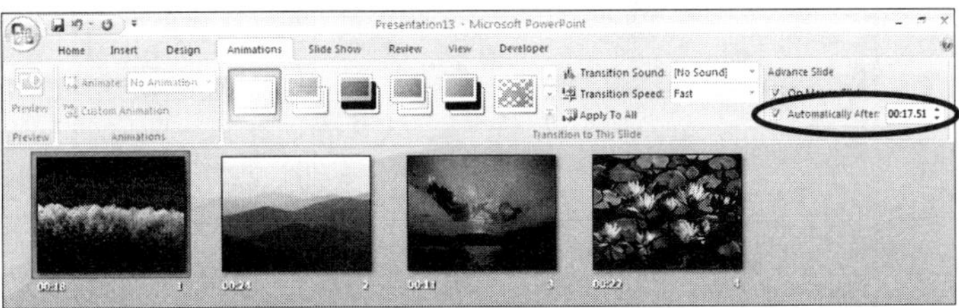

Figure 15.33

Update timing information for a particular slide under the Animations tab.

SET UP THE LOOP

Okay, now we have timing information for each slide. To make this self-running, we need to make sure that the presentation loops, repeating itself when it reaches the end of the presentation. To do that,

1. Go to the Slide Show tab in the Set Up group and choose Set Up Slide Show to launch the Set Up Slide Show dialog, which is covered more in Chapter 16.
2. In the Show Options section, check Loop Continuously Until 'Esc' and click OK.

RUN THE SHOW

And that's it. Just enter the slideshow (press F5), and your presentation will play and loop by itself until you press the Esc key.

NOTE

Another way to set up a self-running presentation is via Kiosk mode, which is described more in Chapter 16.

Pre-Record Your Presentation (Record Narration)

Along the same lines as Rehearse Timings is a feature that lets you record yourself giving a presentation. This is extremely useful for giving lectures and sharing presentations with those who cannot attend. It gives you a way to attach your voice to the slides that is helpful for those who want to review your presentation without bringing a recorder to your presentation and pausing and rewinding while looking at your slides.

NOTE

You need a microphone to use this feature.

Start the Record Narration feature by going to the Slide Show tab in the Set Up group and choosing Record Narration. This brings up the Record Narration dialog (see Figure 15.34).

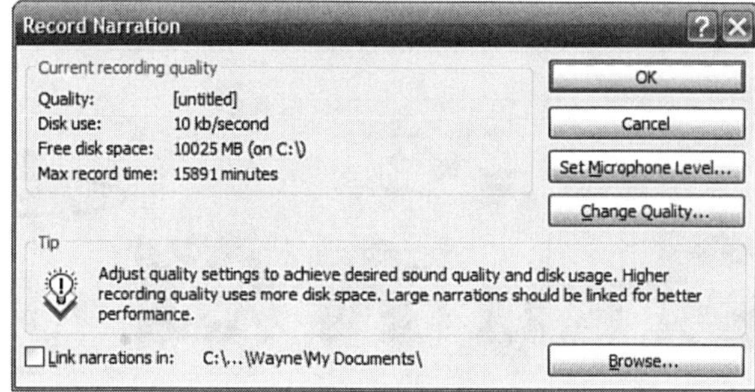

Figure 15.34

The Record Narration dialog.

SOUND QUALITY

Notice the Current recording quality section describing the current quality of the sound used. You can change the quality used, which is dependent on the format of audio used and the attributes of the audio. Based on the Quality setting, a Disk Use summary is shown, indicating how much disk space is taken up per second. This gives you a nice little summary of how much free space you have at the current save location and how many minutes you can record without running out of space.

You can change the Quality setting to decrease the amount of disk space you are using, for example. Click on the Change Quality button.

TESTING THE MICROPHONE

Next, a good thing to do is test the microphone level. This will tell you whether you need to adjust the sensitivity of your microphone to avoid too much noise and also whether it is loud enough to capture your voice. It's important that you give a few test words into the microphone with this Microphone Check dialog open. It will help you ensure that a quality recording is made.

It's recommended to read the sentence shown in the dialog because it is set up to help ensure that things work correctly. The test is self adjusting; it will set the level correctly based on the input.

LINKED NARRATIONS

If you select the Link Narrations In check box at the bottom of the dialog and select a location, the audio for each slide will be recorded into a `.wav` file and saved into that directory. PowerPoint creates links to those sounds inside your presentation. This is good practice if you want to edit the narration later with a separate sound editor.

CAUTION

If you decide to Record Narration and Link narrations into a separate folder, remember to transfer the sound files whenever you transfer your presentation somewhere. If you do not, the presentation will have no way of knowing where to get the sound from. We recommend saving the sounds to the same folder as your presentation.

If you start narration in the middle of a presentation, a dialog asks you whether to start recording on the current slide or the first slide.

NARRATIONS AND SLIDES

Now notice that the slide has a sound icon in the lower right corner, indicating that audio will play when this slide is encountered in Slide Show mode (see Figure 15.35).

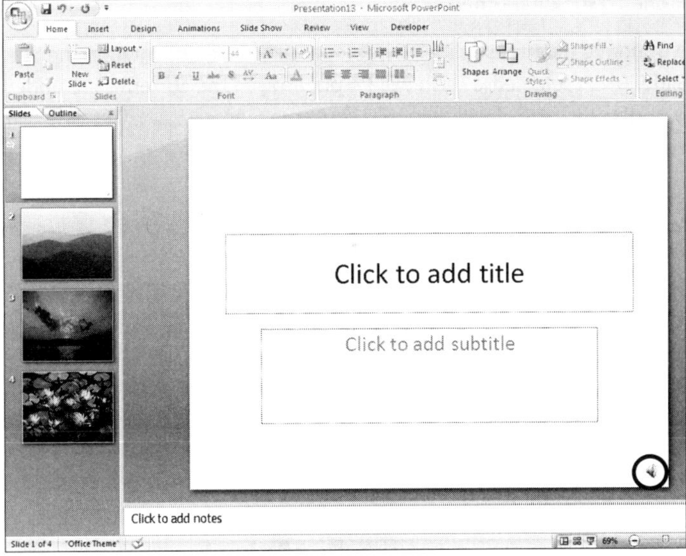

Figure 15.35

The narrations come as sounds attached to slides, which play automatically when in Slide Show mode.

What if I want to start halfway through my presentation? You can! Select a slide that isn't the first one and click on Record Narration, and you will be greeted with a nice prompt, as shown in Figure 15.36, asking whether you want to start recording from the current slide or the first slide. This is a great way to rerecord only select slides without having to redo the entire presentation.

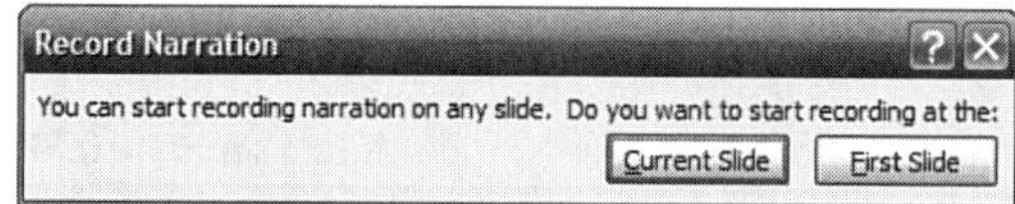

Figure 15.36

It's possible to start recording the narration from any slide.

When finished with the recording, another prompt asks if you want to save the slide timings. This is exactly the same as Rehearse Timings. If you save it, the next time you start Slide Show, it will know when to transition to the next slide.

Hide Slide

Sometimes you do not want certain slides to appear in your slideshow, but you don't want to delete the slides yet for one reason or another.

You can find the option to hide these slides by going to the Slide Show tab in the Set Up group and choosing Hide Slide. When selected, a slash will be put around the current slide under the Slide Thumbnail pane, and its thumbnail will be grayed out (see Figure 15.37). The slide will not automatically appear during the presentation in Slide Show mode.

Figure 15.37

With Hide Slide selected, a slash is added to the slide number in the Thumbnail pane to denote that this slide is hidden and will not appear during Slide Show Mode.

TIP

Hidden slides do not appear when going through the presentation slide by slide, but they can be navigated to using the slide number or a hyperlink.

16

Running Slide Show Like a Pro

IN THIS CHAPTER

- Four Ways to Start Slide Show
- Working with the View Mode Buttons
- Inking
- Editing During a Presentation
- Set Up Slide Show
- View Notes on Your Laptop While the Audience Sees Normal Slides (Presenter View)
- Slide Show Keyboard Shortcuts
- Widescreen (Custom Slide Sizes)
- Fixing Flickering Problems

At this point in the book, we've hopefully convinced you that there's a great deal more to PowerPoint than just jotting down some thoughts and starting up Slide Show. Now that you have created your slides and perfected every element, PowerPoint Slide Show is how you present them. Slide Show is a core part of PowerPoint because it is the vehicle you use to communicate your ideas to the audience.

Four Ways to Start Slide Show

Can you believe that there are four ways to start a slideshow? Check out the list that follows to find your favorite method.

- Press F5 on the keyboard to start at the beginning of the show.
- Choose the View indicator at the bottom of the window on the status bar to start at the current slide.
- Click Slide Show on the View tab (see Figure 16.1) to start at the beginning of the show.
- Choose options on the Slide Show tab to start at the beginning of the show or at the current slide, depending on the button clicked.

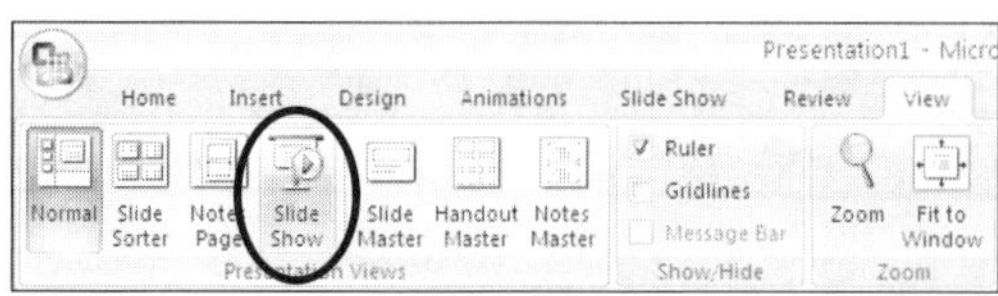

Figure 16.1a

Access Slide Show via the View tab.

Figure 16.1b

Access Slide Show via the status bar.

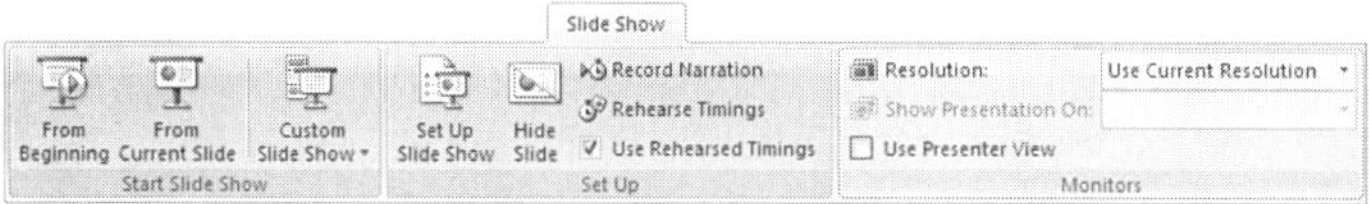

Figure 16.1c

Access Slide Show via the Slide Show tab.

Working with the View Mode Buttons

You're undoubtedly familiar with the three little buttons near the right side of the status bar (see Figure 16.2) that let you switch views:

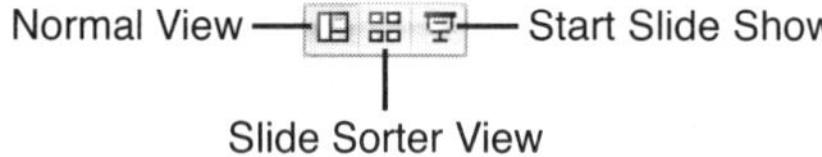

Figure 16.2

You can find these view buttons on the lower right part of your window on the status bar. From left to right, we have Normal View, Slide Sorter View, and Slide Show.

Did you know that you could press Ctrl or Shift while clicking the View mode buttons to invoke all sorts of crazy commands?

Table 16.1 summarizes what you can do using modifier keys.

Table 16.1 Use Modifier Keys to Trigger Special Behavior

Modifier Key	Normal View (left button)	Slide Sorter View (middle button)	Slide Show (right button)
Normal	Normal View	Slide Sorter View	Slide Show from current slide
With Shift	Slide Master View	Handout Master View	Setup Show
With Ctrl	Normal View	Slide Sorter View	Mini Slide Show
With Ctrl+Shift	Normal View without thumbnail and notes panes	Outline	Setup Show

Here are a few more shortcuts:

- Clicking (or Ctrl+clicking) Slide Sorter View toggles between Slide Sorter and Normal View.
- Shift+clicking Slide Sorter View switches to Handout mode, no matter where you start.
- Ctrl+Shift Slide Sorter View, followed by Slide Sorter View toggles between Outline and Slide Sorter View.

NOTE

In PowerPoint 2003 when you hovered over the different views with a shortcut key pressed, the ToolTip would tell you what it does. With PowerPoint 2007 it does not do that, but that's why we made this nice table for you.

Two notable shortcuts exist out of those shown in Table 16.1 that we want to emphasize. They're notable primarily because we don't think that there's a way to invoke them except through these shortcuts.

The coolest one is Ctrl+Slide Show. We often find ourselves playing the full screen Slide Show just to preview an animation. With this, we can display a little Slide Show window and simultaneously edit slides in the main window. The little window is a fully working instance of the Slide Show. Here we've inked in it, just as we can in the real Slide Show (see Figure 16.3).

NOTE

The mini-slideshow shows up on the same monitor as the main slideshow.

The second trick is the ability to edit text in PowerPoint without having to worry about how it looks. Ctrl+Shift+Slide Sorter View displays a full page outline to let you focus on your text. The text here must be in a text placeholder for it to show up here; otherwise, if the text is within a SmartArt or Shape, it won't show up.

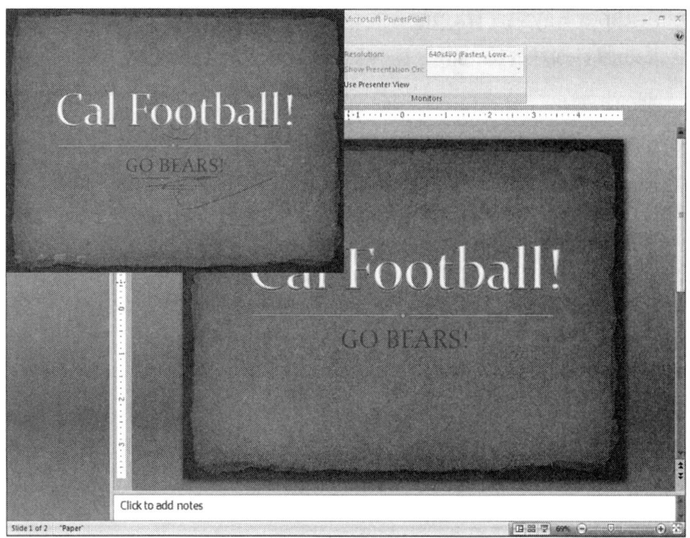

Figure 16.3
Inking inside the mini-slideshow.

SHIFT+F5

While we're on the subject of the three dinky little buttons, it pains us whenever we see someone trying to click on that little slideshow button during their presentation to resume their slideshow.

Pressing F5 starts the slideshow over again from the first slide, but what if the presenter wants the presentation to start on the current slide? Going to the Slide Show tab on the Start Slide Show group and choosing From Current Slide does the right thing but takes a little longer. So, most people start aiming for that tiny Slide Show button.

As you guessed from the title of this section, the answer is by pressing Shift+F5. This functionality has been around since PowerPoint 2003. Next time you're at a presentation and you see someone painfully trying to get the mouse to click that little slideshow button, be a hero. Yell out, "Shift+F5!"

Inking

Few people know that while you're in Slide Show mode, you can use the Ink feature to draw and label while you're presenting. Be sure to read more about Ink in Chapter 9, "Inserting Content into PowerPoint."

Why Ink?

PowerPoint makes it very easy to create freehand ink notes while in Slide Show. You might use this to

- Circle something on the slide you want to draw attention to
- Draw a quick diagram, perhaps to answer an audience member's question

How to Ink

To draw

1. Make sure that you're in Slide Show. Press F5 or go to the Start Slide Show group on the Slide Show tab and click the From Beginning button.
2. Switch to the Pen tool by clicking on the Pen icon in the bottom-left corner of the screen and then clicking one of the pens (see Figure 16.4). Alternatively, you can get to the pen from the contextual menu during Slide Show (see Figure 16.5).

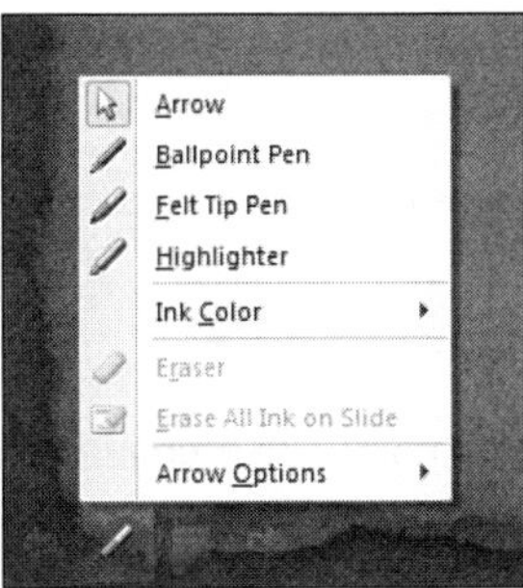

Figure 16.4

The Pen tool found in the lower left corner of Slide Show mode.

3. Then, use your mouse to draw. Click to put the pen against the paper and just drag the mouse around to draw. (If you have a Tablet PC or a Wacom tablet, you can use your pen to draw.)

TIP

Since the release of PowerPoint 2003, PowerPoint has saved slideshow ink using the Tablet PC hooks (APIs) that Windows provides. If you use the pen on a Tablet PC with an active digitizer—which is the case with most Tablet PCs—PowerPoint records pressure sensitivity information about each stroke, which it can't record if you use the mouse or a Wacom tablet. In short, if you want prettier ink, use a Tablet PC.

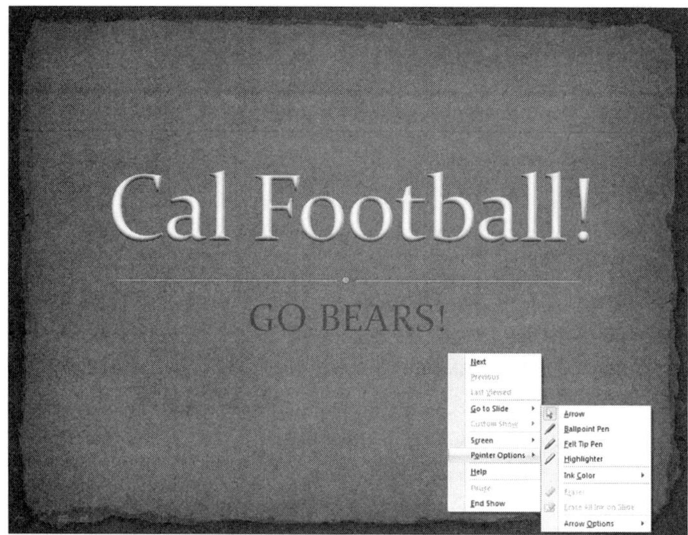

Figure 16.5

The Pen tool can also be accessed from the contextual menu during Slide Show mode.

Saving Your Ink

Sometimes you ink to make a temporary point. Other times, you ink to record some important information that you'd like to save for later. For example, maybe you're giving a dry run of your talk and you ink some comments people in your audience gave so that you can refer to them later.

When you are ready to exit Slide Show, press Esc and PowerPoint asks you whether you want to save the ink (see Figure 16.6). Click Keep if you want to save the ink with the presentation.

NOTE

Keep in mind that the ink added to a presentation cannot be selected via Ctrl+A; you must click the ink object to select it.

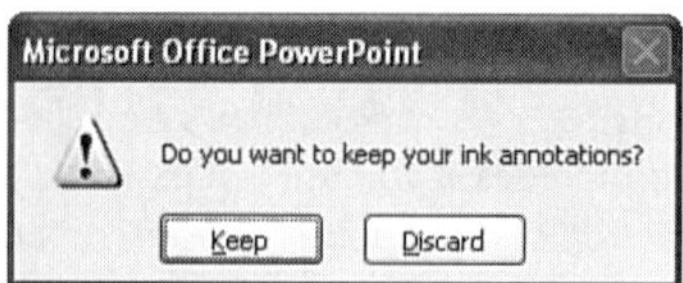

Figure 16.6

When you exit Slide Show, PowerPoint asks whether you want to save your ink.

CAUTION

PowerPoint Document Recovery can save your neck when you forget to save your presentation. If you haven't saved in a long time and PowerPoint or Windows crashes, the next time you open PowerPoint, it usually still has your data and any changes (see the "Customizing AutoSave" section in Chapter 18, "Publishing Your Presentation to Any Format"). Unfortunately, this is never true for slideshow ink until you exit Slide Show and choose to "keep" your ink. If you're inking information you can't afford to lose, periodically exit Slide Show and save your presentation.

Editing During a Presentation

Ever see a mistake while you're presenting your slideshow and have the immediate need to fix it? Your first reaction might be to exit the slideshow, fix the mistake, and then restart the slideshow. But that's overkill.

CAUTION

Be very careful when you decide to edit a presentation during the presentation. This can be seen as unprofessional and will definitely distract you. The audience might lose interest or become bored.

When you're presenting your slideshow, PowerPoint simply opens a big Slide Show window and plops it on top of everything.

This Slide Show window is automatically synced with the content in the main PowerPoint window, so any changes you make to the presentation while you're presenting it updates instantly in Slide Show. So, there's no need to exit Slide Show at all. All you need to do is get back to the main PowerPoint window to make the changes and then switch back to Slide Show:

- While in Slide Show, press Ctrl+T to display the Windows taskbar. Click Microsoft PowerPoint—[*Presentation Name*]. Make sure that you don't click on PowerPoint Slide Show because that will just bring you back into the slideshow. You can also press the Windows button on your keyboard, which brings up the Windows taskbar and activates the Start menu.
- Another method for switching back to the main PowerPoint window is to hold down Alt and while it's held down, keep pressing Tab to navigate through all the open windows. Release the Alt key when you've selected the Microsoft PowerPoint—[*Presentation Name*] window (see Figure 16.7).

NOTE

This image is taken from a computer running Microsoft Windows Vista without Aero enabled; if you have a different operating system or configuration, you might see something different.

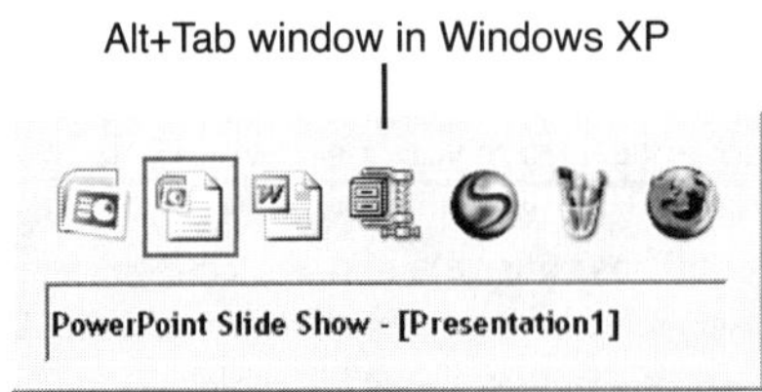

Figure 16.7

Alt+Tab is a common way to switch between programs in Windows and is useful even outside of your PowerPoint adventures.

Now that you're back in the main PowerPoint window, go ahead and make your changes. When you're done, switch back to the Slide Show window by clicking the PowerPoint Slide Show option in the Windows taskbar or by using Alt+Tab again, and your changes should be updated instantly.

CAUTION

Sorry Office XP and 2003 users: Apparently the changes don't show up in your slideshow after making changes like this.

Set Up Slide Show

This is an important dialog to explain because it has a lot of options that help you customize how you can use Slide Show for different purposes.

You can access the Set Up Slide Show dialog from the Slide Show tab, Set Up Slide Show group, as shown in Figure 16.8.

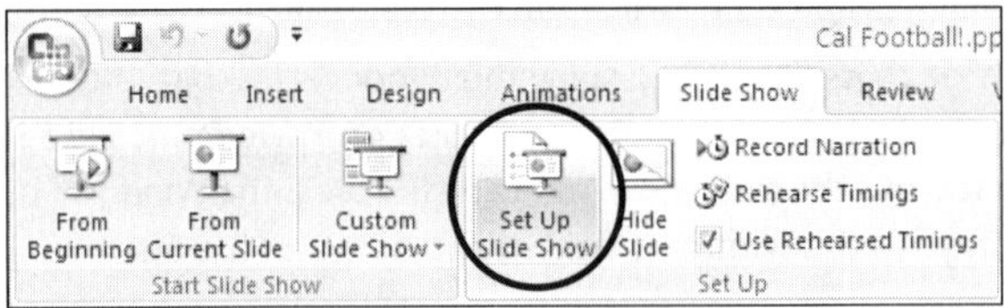

Figure 16.8

Opening the Set Up Show dialog.

Show Type

The three types of Slide Shows you can use PowerPoint for are Speaker, Individual, and Kiosk. See the top left area of Figure 16.9 for the show types.

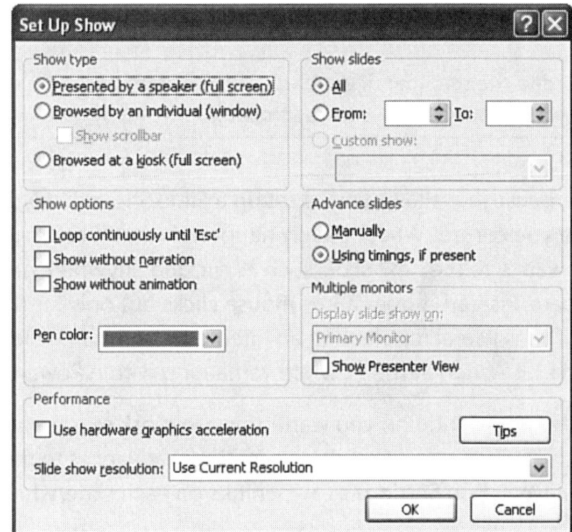

Figure 16.9

The Set Up Show dialog.

Speaker, used when the Presented by a Speaker (Full Screen) option is selected from the dialog, launches the Slide Show in a mode that consumes the entire screen and is useful for presenting to an audience.

Individual is meant for viewing a slide deck or presentation or reading through it. This view arranges all slides into one window and allows you to scroll down to view the next slide. Figure 16.10 shows an example of this.

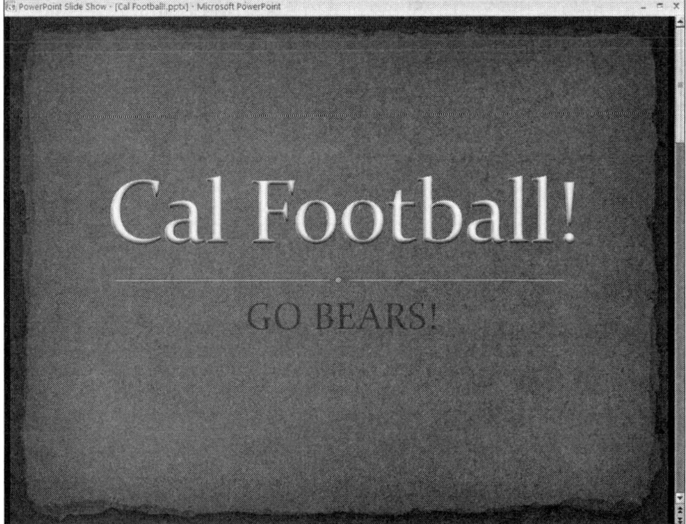

Figure 16.10

Individual browsing mode lets you read through a presentation and scroll through slides in a separate window.

TIP

After you start dragging the scrollbar (if enabled), a description of the slide and the slide number appear so that you know how far you are scrolling.

Kiosk mode is interesting because it allows you to set up a Slide Show that is interactive, yet contained in an environment you control. What actually happens is that Kiosk mode does not allow any of the normal input to advance to the next slide, such as clicking anywhere on the slide or using the right arrow on the keyboard. Instead, it does allow mouse clicks but only for things such as Action Settings and Hyperlinks. This is useful for creating an interactive setup in which users can advance to slides based on their clicks on Action Settings, while remaining within PowerPoint.

This means that if you have a presentation you want to use in Kiosk mode, you must either use Automatic Slide Transition Timings setup (which automatically advances to the next slide after a certain amount of time), or have Action Settings or Hyperlinks on each slide, which a user can click to advance the slide.

This is useful for setting up displays and demos that users can play with, but remember not to include a keyboard; otherwise, the user can press the Esc key to exit Kiosk mode.

Present a Range of Slides

Custom shows are described in Chapter 15, "Going Beyond Slide-by-Slide," and you can choose to start a specific Custom Show from this dialog. In addition, you can select a range of slides to show by choosing a From and To slide, and only those will show up in Slide Show mode.

Presenting in Different Resolutions

Under the Performance area of the Set Up Show dialog is a drop-down that lets you choose the resolution used for displaying the Slide Show (see Figure 16.11). Because this is performance related, you really want to use this when you feel that your presentations are sluggish or you know that the computer you are presenting on will not handle your presentation well.

As you probably already know, lower resolutions result in faster performance (more responsive, less of a lagged feeling) but also look worse.

NOTE

If the resolution used in Slide Show in the Set Up Show dialog is different from the default resolution used for the computer, the display might flicker when it enters Slide Show and switches resolutions. Similarly, this could happen when exiting Slide Show mode.

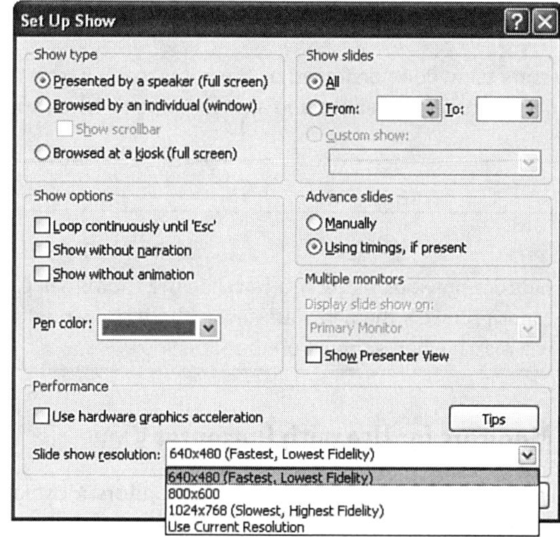

Figure 16.11

You can change the Slide Show resolution from the Set Up Show dialog to improve performance.

View Notes on Your Laptop While the Audience Sees Normal Slides (Presenter View)

"You know what you guys should add to PowerPoint? The ability for me to see my slides and notes on my laptop screen while I'm projecting just the slides with the projector."

This is one of the most requested PowerPoint features, and...wait for it...it's one that's already in the product.

NOTE

Presenter View is not new to PowerPoint 2007—it's been around since PowerPoint 2002—but it did get a big makeover for the 2007 release.

Presenter View Features

While all the audience sees your normal slides, you, the presenter, can

- View thumbnails of upcoming slides.
- Click a thumbnail to jump to a particular slide quickly.
- See your notes.
- See the elapsed time.
- Black out the screen (there are other ways to do this; see the keyboard shortcuts later in this chapter).

NOTE

While you're in Presenter View, don't be fooled by the notes that you see. You cannot actually edit them while you're in this view even though a cursor appears when you click on text in that pane.

TIP

To view upcoming slides or previous slides, you can slide the Thumbnail pane scrollbar. Unfortunately, you cannot preview them in your view without showing the audience yet because your view will match what is shown on the Slide Show.

Setting Up Multiple Monitors for Use with Presenter View

To set this up, your machine must have support for multiple monitors. Most laptops made in the last couple of years have this built-in, so you can project on a screen while still viewing stuff on your laptop screen. To do this on a desktop computer, though, you likely need two video cards or one really spiffy video card.

Before you can set this feature up, you need to make sure that you're not using monitor mirroring:

1. Right-click a blank area of your desktop and click Properties.
2. Click the Settings tab.
3. Click the picture of the other monitor. It might be grayed out.
4. Check the Extend My Windows Desktop onto this Monitor box.
5. Click OK. Your screen will flicker for a bit. Answer Yes when asked whether you want to keep the new settings. If it doesn't flicker, your machine might not support this.

After you've finished with the settings, do the following:

1. Launch PowerPoint.
2. Go to the Slide Show tab, Monitors group.
3. Check the Use Presenter View check box at the bottom (see Figure 16.12).
4. Click the Show Presentation On select box to choose which monitor you want to display the slideshow on. If this is grayed out, you don't have multiple displays set up correctly (or your video card won't support the feature).

Figure 16.12

Presenter View.

TIP

You can also choose which monitor to use and whether to enter Presenter View by going to the Slide Show tab, Set Up group and clicking Set Up Show.

USING MULTIPLE MONITORS WITHOUT USING PRESENTER VIEW

Alternatively, if you don't check the Show Presenter View check box but you still select a different monitor, you can have the PowerPoint editing screen open on one monitor and the Slide Show running for the audience on another.

How is this helpful?

- Presenter View's optimized for showing you the most important information that you will typically need during a presentation, but this gives you access to all of PowerPoint, not just the Presenter View subset.
- All the tips from the "Editing During a Presentation" section earlier in this chapter still apply. So, you can make edits to the presentation that update in the slideshow immediately. Plus, because all your edits are happening on a different monitor, the audience doesn't have to see the process going on. (They might just think their eyes were tricking them that there was a mistake, as you can quickly fix it without anyone being the wiser.)

Slide Show Keyboard Shortcuts

In addition to using the modifier keys with the View Mode buttons listed back in Table 16.1, PowerPoint has a bunch of shortcut keys you can use while presenting in Slide Show mode. A few of our favorites are

- Pressing B blacks out the screen, and pressing W turns the screen white. Press any key to go back to your slides. We find this useful for hiding slides during breaks in the middle of a presentation.
- Type a number and then press Enter to jump to a particular slide. For example, pressing 5+Enter jumps to slide number 5. Or, if you're not so secretive, press Ctrl+S to display a dialog that lets you jump to any slide. Or, if you don't remember either of those, just right-click while in the slideshow and use the Go to Slide menu command, as shown in Figure 16.13.

TIP

Here's a cool trick: Type 9999 and Enter, and this will take you to the last slide in the show. Thanks, Kathy Jacobs!

- Pressing Ctrl+A makes the cursor visible so that you can use the mouse to point to something.
- Hold both mouse buttons down for two seconds, and you will jump back to the first slide.
- Press F1 while you're in a slideshow to see a more complete list (see Figure 16.14).

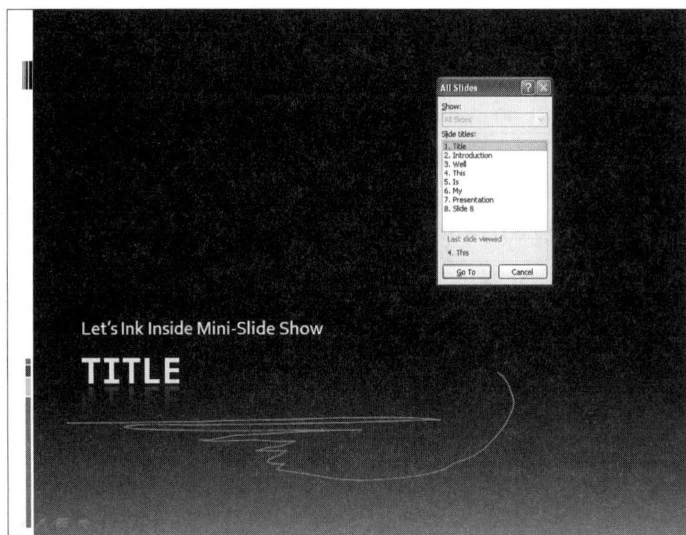

Figure 16.13

Ctrl+S shows a list of slides; choosing Go to Slide on the context menu shows a list of slides as well.

TIP

If you are using Presenter View, this same list can be accessed via the Help button on the Presenter View screen.

- Use the arrow keys to advance to the next slide or return to the previous slide. This trick does not work in Kiosk mode.
- Press Esc to exit from Slide Show mode.

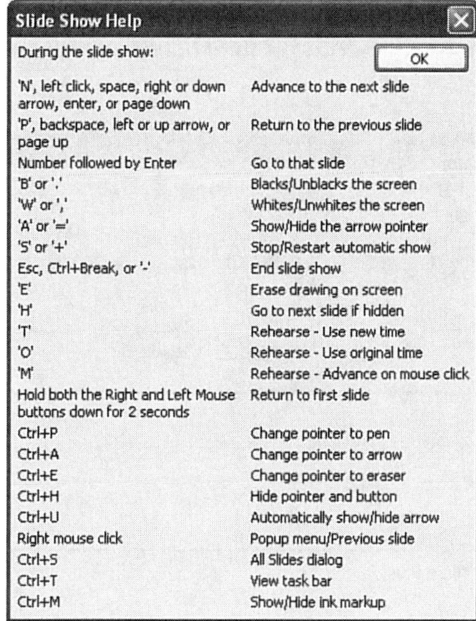

Figure 16.14

Bring up a list of slideshow shortcuts by pressing F1 during a slideshow.

Widescreen (Custom Slide Sizes)

By default, PowerPoint assumes that you're going to be presenting on a screen with 4×3 dimensions. With the proliferation of widescreen monitors these days, this means that you waste some screen space in a slideshow. Or, perhaps you plan to print your presentation on wide paper, which doesn't have 4×3 dimensions.

PowerPoint addresses this by letting you change the slide size. To do this, go to the Design tab in the Page Setup group and click Page Setup (see Figure 16.15).

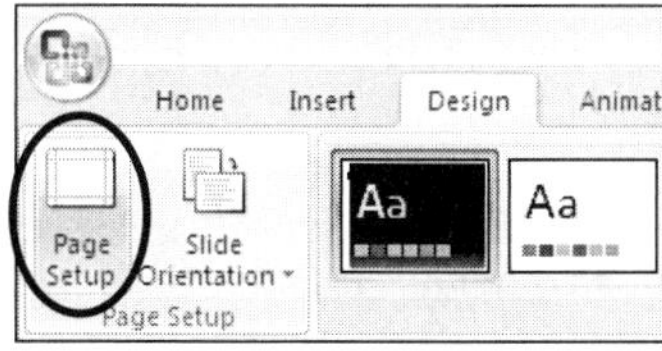

Figure 16.15

Click the Page Setup on the Ribbon to launch the Page Setup dialog.

This brings up the Page Setup dialog box shown in Figure 16.16. If you have a widescreen you're going to be presenting on, choose the second or third options, which are On-Screen Show (16:9) or On-Screen Show (16:10).

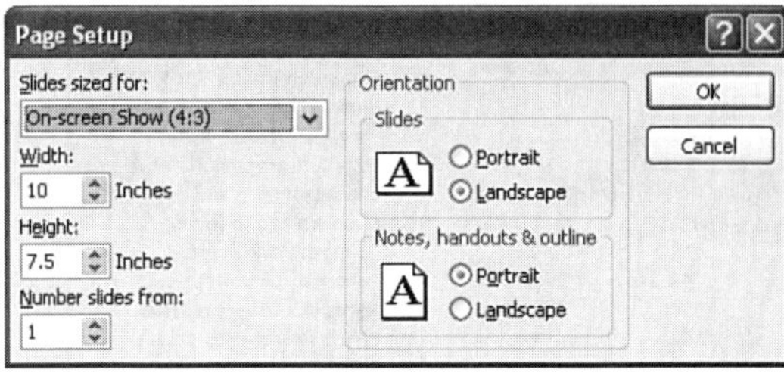

Figure 16.16

Page Setup dialog.

CAUTION

The safest way to change slide sizes is to do this before you add any content to your slides. When you change slide size, all existing content is scaled to fit the new size. For example, if you add a circle to a slide but then resize the slide to be tall and thin, the circle will be squished to fit the new size. Unless your slides are very simple, you will get the best results by resizing the slide first and then adding your content. Even though your laptop might have a widescreen, you could ultimately be showing your presentation using a projector that isn't widescreen. If all your content was prepared using a widescreen page setup, it will be squished when you present it on a normal 4:3 screen. So, it's always a good idea to see where you're presenting rather than get hosed at the last minute.

Another thing to pay attention to is that when switching to widescreen, the textual content changes locations and anything set to word wrap can change.

Fixing Flickering Problems

Occasionally, people have had issues in which PowerPoint continually redraws, flashes, or blinks continuously.

Usually, this is because of bad hardware drivers. Unreliable drivers are one reason why PowerPoint doesn't enable hardware acceleration by default. It's also why PowerPoint has a hard time creating pretty animations and effects; it can't depend on all the necessary hardware being reliable.

Getting New Graphics Drivers

Graphics drivers are often out-of-date and need to be updated even after buying a brand new machine.

The best way to resolve this issue is to get the newest graphics drivers from your graphics card or computer manufacturer. For example, Dell customers can get up-to-date drivers from: http://support.dell.com/support/downloads.

Microsoft might also have the updated drivers up on Microsoft Update. Microsoft Update scans your machine for updates and might list a newer drive as one of the optional hardware updates: http://update.microsoft.com.

CAUTION

Don't install new graphics drivers the day before a big presentation. Updating your drivers usually helps, but sometimes they can cause unexpected system instability too. Give yourself a few days to work out the kinks.

Disabling Hardware Acceleration

If you find no success with updating drivers, many have had success disabling hardware acceleration. Go to the Slide Show tab, Set Up group and click Set Up Slide Show. Make sure that the Use Hardware Graphics Acceleration box is unchecked.

If that doesn't work, try disabling graphics acceleration throughout Windows by right-clicking the Desktop and clicking Properties. On the Settings tab, click Advanced, and then click the Troubleshoot tab. Use the slider to reduce hardware acceleration.

Making Graphics Faster

On the other hand, if everything's working great for you but feels a bit slow, try enabling hardware acceleration by doing the opposite of what is described in the previous section. When acceleration is on, PowerPoint tries pushing off a bunch of work to the hardware, which should speed things up.

It probably doesn't need to be said, but if your slideshow is still slow after doing that, you might need to get a new computer, purchase a better graphics card, or install more memory.

You would think learning about files would be as easy as telling you to click Save and then open files up again. Surprisingly, there's much more to say about Open and Save than just that.

V

PowerPoint Files Unleashed

17 Migrating Files to PowerPoint 2007 337

18 Publishing Your Presentation to Any Format 351

17

Migrating Files to PowerPoint 2007

IN THIS CHAPTER

- Open Options
- Converting Objects
- Opening PowerPoint 2007 Files Using PowerPoint 97–2003 (Compatibility Pack)
- How Presentations Are Windowed
- PowerPoint Command-Line Parameters
- What's a Command-Line Parameter?
- Starting in PowerPoint Safe Mode
- Inside the New PPTX File Format

Opening a presentation is probably one of the most basic operations in PowerPoint. Although it is easy to do, a few interesting topics related to this can improve your productivity, as you will see in this chapter.

Open Options

A subtle feature surrounding the Open command is the ability to open the file in a specific manner. In addition to opening files in the traditional manner, the other options are

- **Open as Read Only**—PowerPoint won't let you save the file. This is useful if you want to present something, for instance, and ensure that you don't accidentally make an edit.
- **Open as Copy**—Edit a copy of the presentation so that you still have the original.
- **Open in Browser**—A rare option only used for PowerPoint presentations saved in HTML format. It gives you the option to open it in the browser instead of in PowerPoint.
- **Open and Repair**—If opening a presentation in the traditional manner didn't work, this tells PowerPoint to open the presentation however it can, even if it means throwing away corrupted portions of the presentation.

To access these open options, you can either use the shortcut key Ctrl+O to get to the Open File dialog or click the Office button and select the Open option. At this point, the default operation would be a simple Open, but to access these specific types of Open options, click the arrow next to the Open button (see Figure 17.1).

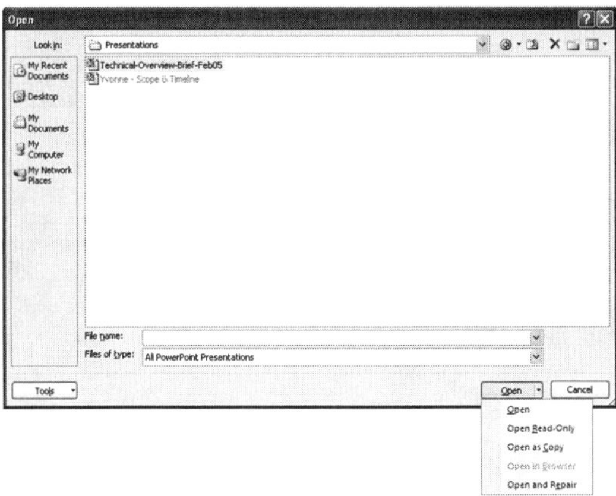

Figure 17.1

The Open command's alternative options.

Converting Objects

As you know, there are many new content types in PowerPoint 2007, such as the renovated charts (see Chapter 6, "Rediscover Charts") and the new SmartArt (see Chapter 5, "Diagrams and SmartArt"). These have replaced the charts and diagrams from PowerPoint 97–2003, which exist in millions of PowerPoint presentations that are "out in the wild."

When opening a `.ppt` file that was created in PowerPoint 97–2003, any charts or diagrams that exist in the presentation are replaced with what we call *compatible objects*.

At first glance, it seems as though these objects are exactly the same as they were when created in previous versions of PowerPoint, but if you try to double-click one to edit it, you are prompted with whether you want to convert the object to its newer equivalent (see Figure 17.2).

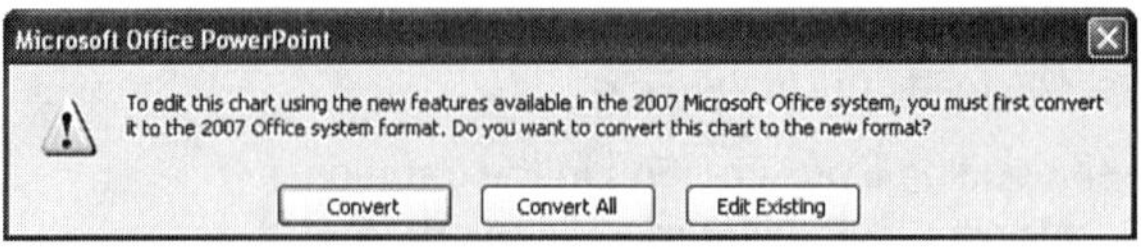

Figure 17.2

When trying to edit a legacy diagram or chart, you are prompted to convert to the 2007 format first.

The prompts are different for diagrams and charts. For diagrams, to edit the diagram, you must convert it to a 2007 format, but you are given two options: Convert to SmartArt and Convert to Shapes. In most cases, you will want to convert it to the SmartArt to maintain its semantics as a diagram so that PowerPoint still treats it as a diagram.

For charts, you have two options: Converting or Edit Existing.

NOTE

There is a third option of Convert All, but it does the same thing as Convert; it just allows you to convert more than one object at a time.

If you choose Edit Existing, the OLE Chart Object User Interface is launched, and you can continue editing it in OLE mode (see Figure 17.3). Unlike editing a diagram, you aren't forced to upgrade the chart to continue editing it.

NOTE

This section discusses the complications involved when opening PowerPoint 97–2003 diagrams and charts with PowerPoint 2007. Nearly all other old PowerPoint content—including shapes, text, and pictures—simply converts automatically to the 2007 format, so there's nothing noteworthy to mention.

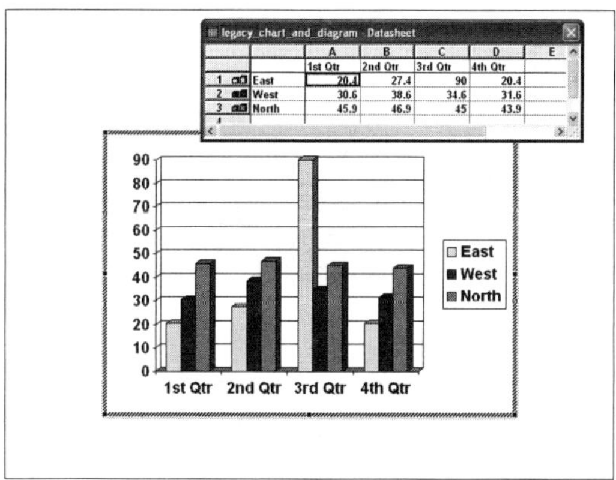

Figure 17.3

Edit Existing on a legacy chart leaves it as an OLE object.

Opening PowerPoint 2007 Files Using PowerPoint 97–2003 (Compatibility Pack)

This section is more helpful for those who have not upgraded to Office 2007. However, it's also useful to understand this stuff so that you can help colleagues or friends who are still using older versions of Office. That way, they can open your shiny new `.pptx` files.

By default, if you try to open a `.pptx` in Office 2003, it will not know what that file is or even recognize that it is a PowerPoint file. However, if the latest service pack for Office 2003 is installed, the new `.pptx` file extensions will show up (see Figure 17.4). To install the latest updates, simply head to http://windowsupdate.microsoft.com, and it should find the updates for Office 2003.

We talk in more detail about the `.pptx` file extension and saving your PowerPoint 2007 presentation in the `.pptx` and old `.ppt` format in Chapter 18, "Publishing Your Presentation to Any Format."

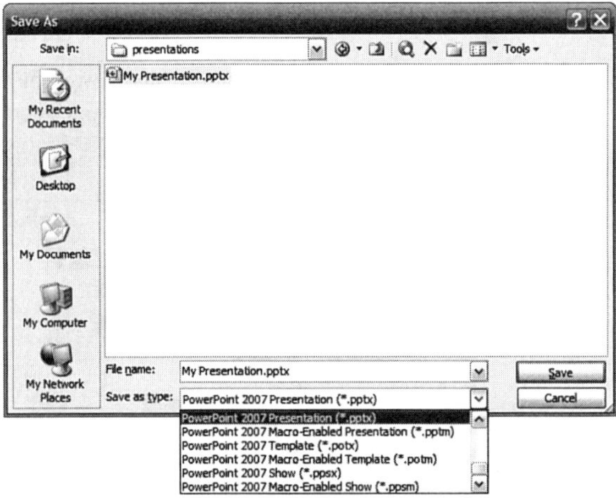

Figure 17.4

Whoa! PowerPoint 2007 files can be opened in PowerPoint 2003? After the compatibility pack for Office 2007 has been installed, new options for the 2007 formats appear in the PowerPoint 2003 Open or Save As dialog boxes.

NOTE

After you download the latest Office 2003 service pack, you can try to open a `.pptx` file. You will be greeted with a friendly message about downloading a compatibility pack in order to open the file. This opens your default browser and sends you to a site where you can download the pack. After this is downloaded and installed, any new files created using Office 2007 can be opened in Office 2003 applications.

How Presentations Are Windowed

PowerPoint windows are confusing to many PowerPoint users, and users often request that Microsoft change this behavior. Let's take a look at what actually happens when multiple files are open in PowerPoint. If you have multiple PowerPoint presentations open at the same time, the taskbar displays a different button for each presentation. It's as if each one is a separate open instance of PowerPoint (see Figure 17.5).

Figure 17.5

Each open presentation creates a taskbar button.

When you click a taskbar button for one of the open presentations, it appears in the main PowerPoint window. If you click a different presentation's taskbar button, it opens into the same window, replacing the one you opened previously.

This behavior is due to how PowerPoint is structured. It is currently a Multiple Document Interface (MDI) application in which one main window exists and many sub-windows can be created. MDI applications were very popular in the earlier days of Microsoft Windows, when PowerPoint was first created.

To see an example where sub-windows are created, do the following:

1. Select the View tab.
2. Under the Window group, select New Window, Arrange All, or Cascade.
3. Notice sub-windows within the main window, which can be manipulated and resized.

In this example, you can have multiple views of the same presentation if the New Window option is selected. Compare this behavior to Word, which is a Single Document Interface (SDI) application in which each document open is in its own Window.

NOTE

A shortcut to Cascade view is Ctrl+F5.

The main reason we point this out is to help you understand why you cannot display and edit two separate presentations side by side in separate windows or on separate monitors.

TIP

Technically, you can edit two presentations on two different monitors by manually stretching the main PowerPoint window across your two monitors and then resizing the presentation windows so that there's one on each monitor; but it's a little painful to set up, and it's incredibly ugly.

If you have multiple sub-windows, you can cycle through them by pressing Ctrl+F6. Neat, huh?

PowerPoint Command-Line Parameters

In this section, we discuss launching PowerPoint from the command line, which is useful if you're comfortable using the Windows command line.

What's a Command-Line Parameter?

When a Windows computer program is run from the Start menu or by double-clicking an icon, it runs a program sitting on your hard disk. For example, click the Start button and choose All Programs; then choose Accessories. Right-click the Calculator icon and choose Properties. You will see that the shortcut in the All Programs menu runs PowerPoint by invoking the application's executable file from `%SystemRoot%\system32\calc.exe`. Although Calculator doesn't support them, some programs let you add additional text after the program name to run the program in a special mode.

Command-Line Parameters in PowerPoint

Now let's talk specifically about PowerPoint. PowerPoint supports a handful of command-line parameters. Use these to create special Windows shortcuts (right-click the desktop and choose New, Shortcut) or to perform PowerPoint tasks quickly from the command prompt or a batch file.

> **TIP**
>
> Learn more about writing batch files at this website: www.computerhope.com/batch.htm.

You will need to modify the commands based on where you installed PowerPoint. Following are three basic examples of adding parameters to the PowerPoint startup file to cause it to perform a specific operation:

- Open a Presentation

  ```
  "x:\Program Files\Microsoft Office\Office12\powerpnt.exe" "x:\ folder\filename.pptx"
  ```

- Print a Presentation

  ```
  "x:\Program Files\Microsoft Office\Office12\powerpnt.exe" /p "x:\
  folder\filename.pptx"
  ```

- Start a Presentation in Slideshow

  ```
  "x:\Program Files\Microsoft Office\Office12\powerpnt.exe" /s
  "x:\folder\filename.pptx"
  ```

Note that you need to include the full path for the filename, as well as for the PowerPoint executable file. Also, these only work if PowerPoint is not already running.

PowerPoint Parameter Example

Do the following to test this alternative method for printing a PowerPoint presentation.

1. Create a presentation and save it as **`c:\spiffy.pptx`**.
2. Right-click the Desktop and choose New Shortcut. In the location box, type, as shown in Figure 17.6:

```
"c:\Program Files\Microsoft Office\Office12\powerpnt.exe" /p "x:\spiffy.pptx"
```

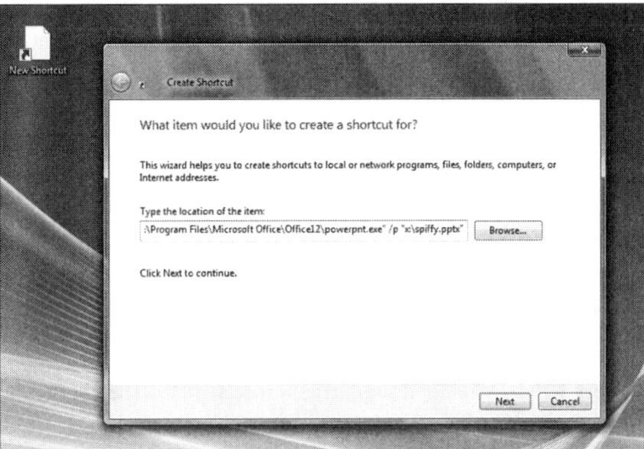

Figure 17.6

Create a shortcut to directly perform a PowerPoint operation, like printing a file in this example.

3. Click Next.
4. Give the shortcut a name, such as `Print Spiffy`.
5. Notice that there's now a new shortcut on your desktop. If you double-click it, it will print spiffy.pptx.

TIP

You can also print a presentation from Windows by right-clicking the presentation and choosing Print from the context menu, which is much less work. But, this illustrates the command-line concept that you can use at the command line and in batch files to save time. Creating shortcuts is also handy if this is a task you do so often that it's worth saving that extra click.

Starting in PowerPoint Safe Mode

Just as in Windows, PowerPoint has a safe mode that disables functionality and add-ins to make sure that PowerPoint can start without crashing.

If PowerPoint crashed the last time you tried to start it up, it will launch into safe mode the next time you start it up. It's doing its best to make sure that your second attempt to launch PowerPoint doesn't crash.

If you want to enter safe mode yourself, simply hold down the Ctrl key while launching PowerPoint, and the dialog shown in Figure 17.7 appears. The dialog will say that it noticed you have the Ctrl key held down and will ask if you really want to start PowerPoint in safe mode.

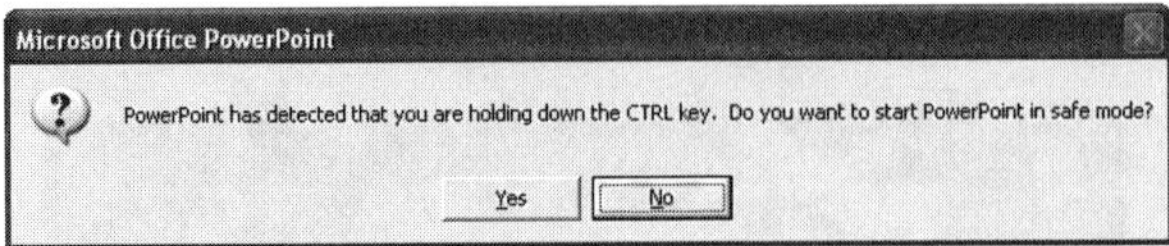

Figure 17.7

Hold down Ctrl while launching PowerPoint until this dialog appears.

Inside the New PPTX File Format

Office 2007 introduces a new file format dubbed the Microsoft Office Open XML. For the nerds out there, it's essentially a zip file containing XML files, and the binary resources, such as images, videos, and VBA macros.

XML

Never heard of XML? XML is designed to be human readable and is essentially just a text file, along with tags around pieces of the text that tell you what the text is talking about. Here's a short XML document example that we made up:

```
<instructions>
 <step number=1 >Put on pants.</step>
 <step number=2 >Put on shoes.</step>
</instructions>
```

Here's some sample XML from inside a PowerPoint file. It takes some expertise to know what each item means, but it's perfectly readable (and editable) text.

```
<Properties …>
  <TotalTime>0</TotalTime>
  <Words>0</Words>
  <Application>Microsoft Office PowerPoint</Application>
  <PresentationFormat>On-screen Show (4:3)</PresentationFormat>
  <Paragraphs>0</Paragraphs>
  <Slides>1</Slides>
```

Why a New File Format?

So why a new file format? Microsoft touts these advantages of the new format compared to the binary formats from Office 2003 and before:

- **Smaller size**—Zip files use industry standard compression techniques to compress files down to the smallest possible size, which is better than something custom Microsoft might come up with on its own.

- **Safer**—Macros are stored in a separate part of the file, so system administrators can strip out the dangerous parts more easily. Plus files are macro free by default, as described in the previous section. Storing components as different parts of the same zip file also means that if one part of the file is damaged, most of the rest of the presentation is still recoverable. So, the entire presentation is less likely to get corrupted.
- **Transparency**—Microsoft has had public relations nightmares in the past when people discovered that Word documents often hid the names of authors inside Word files. People would send these files to others, not realizing what data was inside. Zip files and XML are open standards, so anyone can peer inside a file to make sure that nothing is hidden inside.
- **Easier to manipulate**—Using Zip and XML standards means that developers can create handy tools for manipulating Office files. They're no longer hindered by needing Office macros to change stuff inside a file. Even if you're not a developer, this means that more tools will eventually be available for you to do neat stuff to your files.

Peering Inside a PPTX File

Advanced Let's look within the raw insides of a file. You will need to save a `.pptx` file:

1. Create a new presentation in PowerPoint.
2. Click the Office button and choose Save (or just press Ctrl+S). In the Save As dialog, check that the Save As Type drop-down is set to PowerPoint Presentation. Click Save.

NOTE

This section is slightly more advanced than most of the rest of this book. We assume that you're familiar with changing filename extensions in Windows and with opening Zip files. It's hard for us to walk you through these step-by-step because the steps can be very different, depending on how your computer is set up. If these concepts sound foreign to you, skip to the next section or find your favorite geek to help you out.

OPEN IT UP

We need to have Windows stop hiding file extensions so that we can change the extension later. In Windows XP, go to My Computer or Windows Explorer, find the Tools menu, and choose Folder Options. In Windows Vista, click Start, Control Panel, Appearance and Personalization, and then Folder Options. For both Windows XP and Windows Vista, after you have the Folder Options dialog open, go to the View tab and make sure that Hide Extensions for Known File Types is *not* checked. Then click OK.

Now let's break open that file.

1. Using My Computer or Windows Explorer, locate the file you saved.
2. Right-click the file and choose Rename. Change the file's extension from `.pptx` to `.zip`. Confirm that you want to change the extension when Windows asks you. You should notice the icon change from your friendly PowerPoint presentation icon to a Zip folder icon.

3. Now right-click the presentation's icon and choose Explore to open the presentation as a Zip file. This should show you the contents of the file.

NOTE

We're using the Windows built-in Zip file viewer here, but feel free to use any Zip program you're comfortable with, such as WinZip.

You will see some folders such as _rels, docProps, and ppt. (see Figure 17.8).

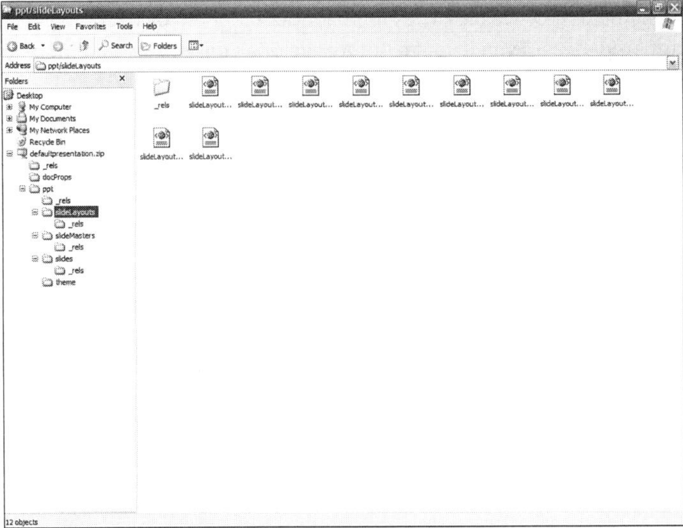

Figure 17.8

View the contents of a PowerPoint presentation, as a Zip file, in Windows XP.

TERMINOLOGY (PARTS AND CONTAINERS)

Inside the folder are a bunch of files, such as slideLayout1.xml. Because these are parts of the presentation, Microsoft calls these files inside the file "parts." Most of these are standard XML files that you can edit using your favorite text editor, such as Notepad.

TIP

Even though XML is editable by any text editor, the files are designed to be mostly read by computers and not humans, so everything is crammed onto one line. You're best off using a text editor that can "pretty print" text, such as Microsoft Visual Studio. You can download Visual Studio Express free at http://msdn2.microsoft.com/en-us/express/default.aspx. Internet Explorer will also format XML nicely as well if you only want to read XML.

The entire Zip file is called a *container* because it contains the parts. A container is just a fancy way of saying Zip file.

CONTAINER INVENTORY

Here's a quick rundown of what's inside a typical presentation container. We will describe roughly the parts inside each folder:

- **docProps**—These properties apply to the document—stuff you want to know without opening the presentation, such as the number of slides in there and who authored the presentation. You will find PowerPoint-specific information inside app.xml and application-agnostic information inside core.xml. You will also find an image thumbnail.jpeg that Windows uses to show the little preview of your presentation in Save dialogs and into the Windows Explorer.
- **ppt**—Here PowerPoint stores very PowerPoint-specific information. Presentation.xml stores the core stuff, and some auxiliary data is split out into presProps.xml and viewProps.xml. For example,
    - presentation.xml stores the following:
        - Ordered lists of Custom Shows (see Chapter 15, "Going Beyond Slide-by-Slide")
        - Slides
        - Masters
        - Slide sizes
        - Presentation-wide text properties, such as the embedded font list (see Chapter 18)
        - Save properties, such as how to compress pictures (see Chapter 4, "Working with Pictures")
        - Editor properties
        - Content properties
    - presProps.xml stores information such as what pen color to use when you annotate in Slide Show (see Chapter 16, "Running a Slide Show Like a Pro")
    - tableStyles.xml describes how your tables will look (see Chapter 8, "Tables Like You've Never Seen Before").
- ppt\slideLayouts stores all the slide layouts. Slide layouts are described in Chapter 10, "Formatting Your Presentation." One slideLayout1.xml file exists for each layout.
- ppt\slideMasters stores slide masters, also described in Chapter 10. One slideMaster1.xml file exists for each master, though the default presentation only starts with one master.
- ppt\slides are the actual slides in your presentation; one slide1.xml file exists for each slide. Everything that lives on a slide is stored inside these files from shapes, placeholders, and text positioning and formatting to animation information.
- ppt\theme stores a copy of the theme used by this presentation. Themes are described more in Chapter 11, "Dissecting Themes."

RELATIONSHIPS OF THE PARTS

You might have also noticed a bunch of directories named _rels scattered throughout the file. Inside, you will find files that describe the relationships that files have with other files inside the presentation.

As a simple example, let's say that slide 1 uses layout 2. You will find slide 1 at `ppt\slides\slide1.xml`. Its list of relationships lives at `ppt\slides\_rels\slide1.xml.rels`. The relationship file always has the same name as the file you're looking at—only it's inside the _rels subfolder and with an extra `.rels` appended at the end of its name. Inside `slide1.xml.rels`, you will see something like this:

```
<?xml version="1.0" encoding="UTF-8" standalone="yes" ?>
<Relationships
➥xmlns="http://schemas.openxmlformats.org/package/2006/relationships">
<Relationship Id="rId1"
Type=
➥"http://schemas.openxmlformats.org/officeDocument/2006/relationships/slideLayout"
Target="../slideLayouts/slideLayout1.xml" />
</Relationships>
```

The core piece here is the reference to `"../slideLayouts/slideLayout1.xml"`. The `".."` describes a relative path, which means that you go up a directory into the ppt directory. So, this means that you will find the layout at `ppt\slideLayouts\slideLayout1.xml`. The file also notes that this relationship is called `"rId1"`.

Neat huh? All this means is that the part `ppt\slides\slide1.xml` has a relationship called `"rId1"` to another part `ppt\slideLayouts\slideLayout1.xml`. If you look inside slide1.xml, it probably references rId1 and has more details about the relationship.

EDIT AWAY

Feel free to experiment by editing any of the files inside the Zip file, saving your edits back into the Zip file, renaming the file back to a `.pptx` extension, and reopening the file with PowerPoint. The language is fairly esoteric; however, PowerPoint is very picky about what you write, so it might warn you that the file is corrupt if you mistype anything in your edits.

CAUTION

Always work on a copy of presentation. It's very easy to corrupt a presentation when editing it in this way, and a corruption is often not obvious immediately after it has occurred. For example, after accessing a specific element on a certain slide days later, you might notice that something is corrupted.

Also, be careful not to change the names of files inside the Zip file unless you know what you're doing. Filenames can be referenced from multiple `.rel` files throughout the container.

Also, while the specifics differ for each application, you can use a similar technique to crack open Word 2007 and Excel 2007 files, such as `.docx` document and `.xlsx` spreadsheet files. The core concepts of containers, parts, and relationships apply to those files as well.

FURTHER RESOURCES

If you found the file format fascinating, you're in luck. Microsoft published the Office 2007 file format as an open standard, so you can read the full Office 2007 file format specifications that were accepted by the ECMA standards body here: www.ecma-international.org/news/TC45_current_work/. They're very technically detailed, describing what all the jargon is inside each XML part inside a presentation container.

Brian Jones, a Microsoft Office program manager who worked on the file format, also has a blog that talks about the Office 2007 file formats here. Though he has yet to cover PowerPoint in great depth, he talks about the file format in great detail and includes tutorials on how to create a Word document or an Excel document from scratch: http://blogs.msdn.com/brian_jones/. In this post, Brian describes how to make a minor edit to the presentation part to reorder slides in your presentation: http://blogs.msdn.com/brian_jones/archive/2006/04/11/573529.aspx.

18

Publishing Your Presentation to Any Format

IN THIS CHAPTER

- PowerPoint File Format Types
- Embedding Fonts in a Presentation
- Making a Presentation That Just Plays (`.ppsx`)
- Advanced Publishing Tricks
- Collaboration Using Comments
- Encrypting Presentations with a Password
- Exporting a Presentation as a Picture Slideshow
- Saving to a Network Share
- Save as Web Page
- Removing Sensitive Information from Presentations (Document Inspector)
- Using PowerPoint Shapes in Other Office Applications
- Saving to the 97–2003 File Format
- Compressing Pictures to Create Smaller Files
- Publishing Your Presentation to a CD

Outputting a PowerPoint presentation isn't always as easy as clicking Save. This chapter discusses various ways to publish a presentation and how to overcome all the inevitable complications.

PowerPoint File Format Types

New PowerPoint has always had a variety of different file types. There are regular presentation files and design template files that most everyone is familiar with, but then there are exotic file types such as Add-In and Show files. PowerPoint 2007 introduces a brand new file format, `.pptx`—explored in great detail in Chapter 17, "Migrating Files to PowerPoint 2007"—which complicates the matter even more.

Understanding PowerPoint File Formats

PowerPoint 2007 saves to quite a number of different file format types. Table 18.1 gives a brief summary of each file type. The new formats are marked in the table as New, whereas the old binary formats from past versions of PowerPoint are marked as Old.

Table 18.1 File Format Types in PowerPoint 2007

Extension	Description	Macros	File Format
.pptx	Regular presentation	No	New
.pptm	Regular presentation	Yes	New
.ppt	Regular presentation	Yes	Old
.potx	Design template	No	New
.potm	Design template	Yes	New
.pot	Design template	Yes	Old
.ppsx	Show	No	New
.ppsm	Show	Yes	New
.pps	Show	Yes	Old
.ppam	Add-In[1]	Yes	New
.ppa	Add-In	Yes	Old
.thmx	Theme	No	New
.eftx	Effect Scheme	No	New
.xml	Font Scheme, Color Scheme, or other[2]	No	New

[1]*PowerPoint Add-Ins extend what PowerPoint can do. Creating and using add-ins is not described in this book, but read this unofficial add-in FAQ online to learn more: http://skp.mvps.org/ppafaq.htm.*

[2]*PowerPoint only uses* `.xml` *for font schemes and color schemes, but the* `.xml` *format is not specific to PowerPoint or to Office, and other applications can use it for other purposes.*

Macros

Because previous versions of Office (mostly Word and Excel) suffered a black eye from allowing macro viruses to plague users' computers, Office 2007 has the concept of macro-free file formats and macro-enabled file formats. Any file with a macro has to be saved to one of the macro-enabled formats that ends with the letter "m," such as `.pptm`. If you receive a file in a format that's macro free, such as `.pptx`, PowerPoint guarantees that it won't contain macros that could damage your computer.

More information about macros can be found in Chapter 10, "Formatting Your Presentation."

Embedding Fonts in a Presentation

Advanced Not all computers have the same fonts. Office comes with a few—such as your friends Arial, Times New Roman, and Verdana—but fonts beyond the standard Office set vary computer by computer.

If you're like most people, there are some occasions when you need to send your presentations to others. Obviously, you want everyone to see the same font that you used to create the presentation, so it's important to verify that your recipient owns all the fonts that you use in your presentations.

Otherwise, PowerPoint will just select a replacement font, and it might be positioned incorrectly or displayed at the wrong size.

Stick to the Office Fonts

If you do need to distribute your presentation without a lot of control over what fonts the end user might have, your best bet is to stick with the standard Windows and Office fonts. Everyone with Office has these fonts, so they're a safe bet. Take a look at the Microsoft Typography website at www.microsoft.com/typography/fonts/ to see which fonts came with Office 2003 and Windows XP. Office 2007 and Windows Vista come with a superset of those fonts. You can choose a product from the list to see which fonts come with it.

If you are sure that the recipient of your presentation has PowerPoint 2007, you can also use the new fonts mentioned in Chapter 2, "Everything You Need to Know About Text."

To ensure that your presentation looks exactly as it did when you created it, your other option is to embed the fonts.

Embedded Fonts

If you do not know what fonts exist on the machines of the people who will be looking at your presentation, you can embed the font in the presentation.

1. Click the Office button and choose PowerPoint Options.
2. Choose Save in the left pane of the dialog. In the bottom section, check the box next to Embed fonts in the file (see Figure 18.1). You can also choose whether you embed the entire font—which makes editing the presentation easier—or just embed the characters used in the presentation, which saves a little disk space but makes editing more painful.

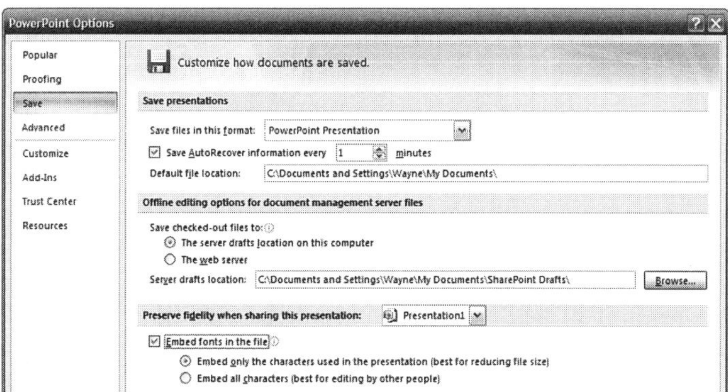

Figure 18.1

Choose to embed the font in the presentation.

CAUTION

PowerPoint respects a licensing level that is set inside of each font. Some fonts are set as Print or Preview-Only, which means that your recipients will be able to view the presentation with the embedded fonts, but they won't be able to edit the presentation at all. Other fonts are licensed as Installable, which means that editing is allowed, but the font can be used only inside the presentation in which it is embedded. Finally, the most liberally licensed fonts are installable, which means that you can install the font to Windows and use it in any program later. This Microsoft KB article explains more: http://support.microsoft.com/kb/826832.

Making a Presentation That Just Plays (`.ppsx`)

Advanced There are several different scenarios in which the `.ppsx` format comes in handy. This format saves the presentation as a slideshow only—the file will no longer be editable and will open automatically into Slide Show view.

For example, if you're planning to show a presentation and don't want the editing interface in front of the audience, save the file as `.ppsx`.

Save the file in the PowerPoint Show format by clicking the Office button and choosing Save As. Choose PowerPoint Show as the Save As type (see Figure 18.2).

CAUTION

`.ppt` files created in older versions of PowerPoint can be renamed with a `.pps` extension to change them to PowerPoint Show files. Unfortunately, the new `.pptx/.ppsx` file format used in PowerPoint 2007 writes whether the file is a PowerPoint Show file directly into the contents of the file. So, a simple rename is no longer sufficient, and you must go through the Save As process now.

TIP

Not sure if your recipient has the latest version of PowerPoint? Save as type PowerPoint 97–2003 Show, which has a `.pps` extension. It's the equivalent of `.ppsx` but for older PowerPoint versions. Opening `.ppsx` files is not a problem if the recipient has the latest PowerPoint Viewer or the Office 2003 compatibility pack. But if you're not sure or you think that the recipient has Office XP or older, saving in the older format is the way to go. The downside to doing this is that the `.pps` file will always be larger than just sending the `.ppsx` file.

This saves your file with a `.ppsx` extension instead of a `.pptx` file extension. When you open the `.ppsx` file—by double-clicking it from Windows Explorer, for instance—PowerPoint sees the `.ppsx` extension and launches directly into the slideshow. This can be a useful way to distribute presentations you intend for most of your viewers to watch using Slide Show.

TIP

Likewise, if you want to view a `.pptx` or `.ppt` file directly in Slide Show, you can do this by right-clicking the file and choosing Play.

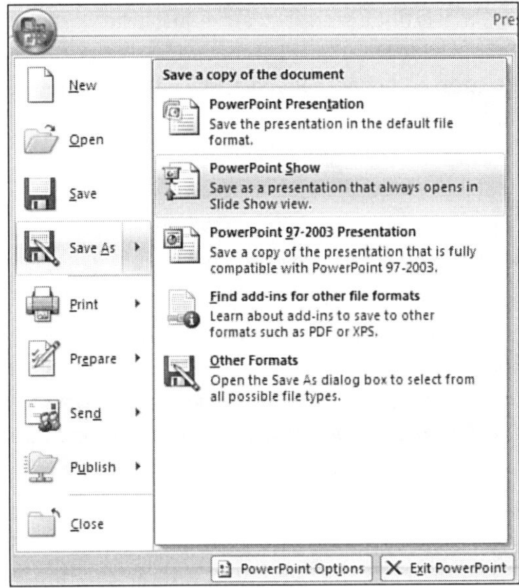

Figure 18.2

Choose PowerPoint Show as the Save As type, which by default starts the presentation in Slide Show mode.

Advanced Publishing Tricks

Suppose that you are done editing your presentation, you want to send the presentation to others, but you don't want them to edit the presentation. The next sections discuss two ways to send a presentation in a finalized form.

Mark as Final

Mark as Final lets you declare a presentation as finished. Later, if the presentation is opened, it's opened in a read-only format so that people don't accidentally edit it.

When a presentation is marked as final, it means

- Typing, editing commands, and proofing marks disappear.
- When opened, the presentation is set to read-only so that it cannot be accidentally edited.

To mark a presentation as final, do the following:

1. Click the Office button and choose Prepare, Mark as Final.
2. Click OK. Notice the finalize icon that appears in the status bar.

Change your mind? Mark as Final is not a security feature, just a suggestion noted in the file. So if you or anyone you send the file to decides that the file is not so final after all, it's easy to "unfinalize" the file: Simply click the Office button and choose Prepare, Mark as Final. These are basically the same steps you took to finalize it.

Save as PDF/XPS

Another way to publish a presentation is to save it as a PDF or XPS file. PDF files can be viewed by anyone with Adobe Reader; XPS files can be viewed with a built-in viewer that comes with Windows Vista.

1. Install the 2007 Microsoft Office Add-in named Microsoft Save as PDF or XPS from this location online: www.microsoft.com/downloads/details.aspx?familyid=4D951911-3E7E-4AE6-B059-A2E79ED87041. Unfortunately, that address is a little hairy. You can also get to it by searching Google for "PDF XPS Office add-in." Download and install the add-in. If you don't have installation privileges on your computer, contact your friendly IT person.
2. After the add-in is installed, click the Office button, click the arrow to the right of Save As, and then choose PDF or XPS (see Figure 18.3). There are some options at the bottom to tweak, such as whether the PDF is intended to ever be printed. You can click the Options button if you want to get really detailed about what to save in the PDF, such as hidden slides, document properties, or accessibility information.

NOTE

To get more information about each of the advanced PDF saving options, click Options to launch the Options dialog. Then click the question mark button at the top right of the dialog.

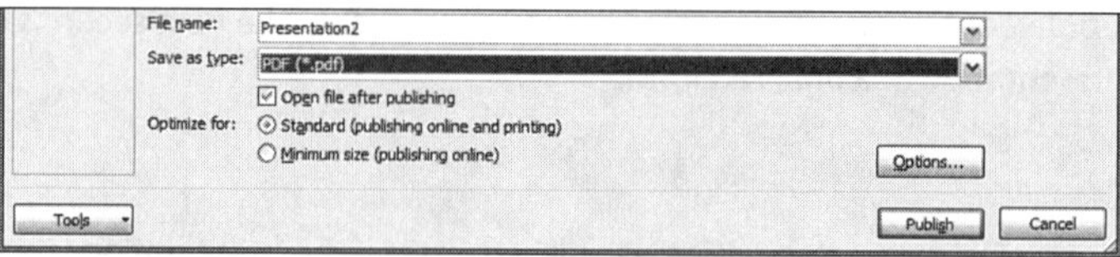

Figure 18.3

Save as PDF or XPS from the Office menu.

3. You can then view the saved document without using PowerPoint. If you save to PDF, you can use the Adobe Reader to view it; download it free here: www.adobe.com/reader.

Collaboration Using Comments

Advanced PowerPoint is being used more in nontraditional ways because presentations are being utilized as documents to convey information instead of simply a presentation aid. As you might have noticed, PowerPoint is the Office application best tailored to view and manage graphics, and if a document is rich with media and graphics, people typically use PowerPoint instead of Word to present their content.

The Comments feature can help you and your peers manage working on the same document. It allows you to add annotations without modifying the actual presentation.

Adding Comments

You might be familiar with the Reviewing ribbon in Word 2007 (it was the Reviewing toolbar in previous versions), which allows changes to be tracked and allows one person's modifications to be viewed by another.

Although this highly popular feature is not found in PowerPoint, it is possible to obtain similar functionality using the Comments feature. The basic idea is that you can annotate slides by adding Comments that contain who created the comment, and when it was created, as well as some text. All Comments on a slide can be cycled through, edited, and deleted.

To insert a Comment, go to the Review tab in the Comments group and click New Comment.

A balloon is inserted in the upper left corner of your current slide by default; or if you have an object selected, the comment will be placed next to it (see Figure 18.4). Multiple comments are cascaded and offset from each other.

Using Comments

Here are some things to keep in mind about comments:

- Comments can only contain text, not graphics.
- Comments cannot be formatted.
- The title of the comment is made up of the initials used to register PowerPoint followed by the comment number.
- Comments expand to accommodate the text placed in them.
- Navigation from one comment to another using Next and Previous will open the comment text.
- Comments can be made invisible by clicking the Show Markup button, but note that this does not delete them from the presentation.

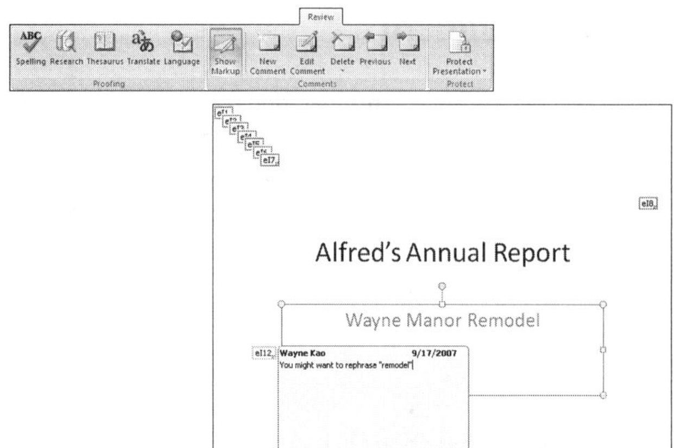

Figure 18.4

Add a new comment to annotate your presentation.

This is a great way to add notes to a presentation without actually modifying the content. The comments do not show up in Slide Show mode, so only editors of the presentation will notice them.

NOTE

Previous versions of PowerPoint had the capability to Send for Review and also a Revisions Pane, which were quite helpful for collaborating on presentations. These features were removed in PowerPoint 2007.

Encrypting Presentations with a Password

Advanced You, as a reader of this book, might very well be a spy and need to email a super secret PowerPoint presentation back to headquarters. The presentation might get intercepted by baddies, and you want to be absolutely certain that no one will be able to read its contents unless they have the secret password.

Password to Open

You're in luck. PowerPoint makes it very easy to encrypt presentations so that they are completely unreadable without the correct password:

1. Open your presentation in PowerPoint (click the Office button and choose Open).
2. Click the Office button again and click the arrow next to Prepare. Choose the Encrypt Document option.
3. Type your secret password into the box and click OK (see Figure 18.5). PowerPoint asks you to enter it again to make sure that you entered it correctly.

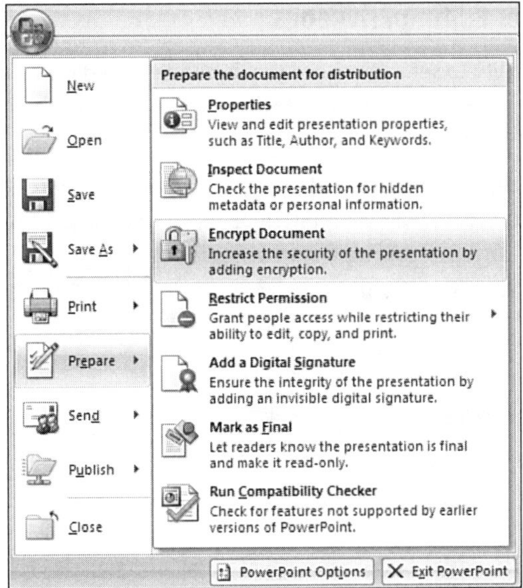

Figure 18.5

Encrypt Document lets you add a password so that nobody can open it without first entering the password.

4. Save your presentation and close PowerPoint.
5. Restart PowerPoint and open the presentation. PowerPoint now prompts you for a password.

CAUTION

This uses real encryption, so you won't be able to get into your file if you forgot your password. Really! Even if you paid someone at Microsoft a million dollars, they wouldn't be able to recover your presentation if you forget the password. So don't forget it. Also, passwords are case sensitive, so a capital A is not the same as a lowercase a.

On the other hand, don't put complete faith in Office's password protection either. No program is perfect, and tools exist to attack encrypted PowerPoint presentations. Your best safeguard to prevent this it to choose good passwords that are long, combine uppercase and lowercase letters, numbers, and symbols (such as @%!$).

If you edit an encrypted presentation and save your changes, the encryption stays in place. You don't need to manually encrypt every time.

To remove encryption for a presentation, go back to the Office button. Again, go to Prepare and select Encrypt Document again, which will deselect the option and unprotect your presentation.

Setting a Password for Editing Privileges

PowerPoint also has an ability to set a password that is needed to edit the presentation. If an editing password is set and the recipient doesn't know the password, the presentation will be opened in read-only mode and won't be editable.

To use this feature, click the Office button, and then click the arrow next to Save As. Choose Tools, General Options (see Figure 18.6). Yeah, we know; it's a really weird place to hide password options.

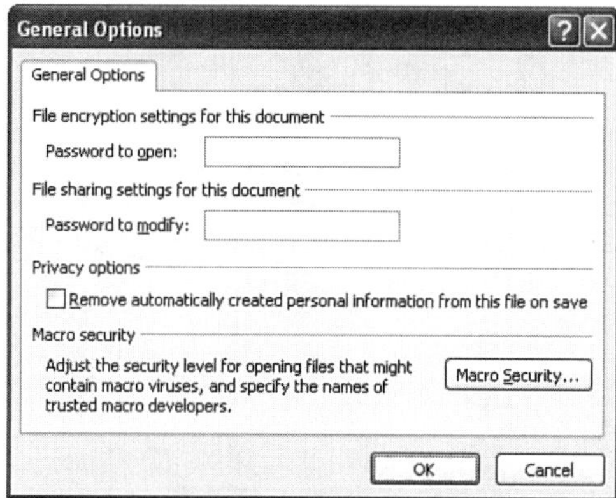

Figure 18.6

Choose General Options from the Tools menu on the Save As dialog.

In this dialog, you can set a password to allow a user to modify the presentation. The password you enter in the Password to Modify field is required for someone to edit the presentation. Note that there's also a text box in the dialog that lets you set a password to open the presentation, which is described in the previous section.

Unlike the password to open, which encrypts the entire presentation, this password is much less secure. Someone with a little technical knowledge can remove or change this password. So please don't rely on this one for top secret content.

CAUTION

Once again, passwords for edit are not nearly as secure as passwords to open. If you send your favorite computer nerd (like us) a presentation that requires a password to edit, rest assured that we will be able to edit it if we really want to. Programs are also available that let people easily break these passwords. The password to edit just keeps honest people honest.

To clear out the edit password, return to the dialog by clicking the Office button and choosing Save As. Again, go to Tools and then General Options. Clear out the password you don't like, and click OK.

Exporting a Presentation as a Picture Slide Show

Advanced Save Presentation as Pictures

PowerPoint lets you save presentations in many formats. One useful format is as a picture:

1. Open your favorite presentation.
2. Now save the presentation as an image by clicking the Office button, and then clicking the arrow next to Save As. For the Save As type, choose PNG Portable Network Graphics Format or another picture format.
3. Choose a location to save to, such as your Desktop, and then give the presentation a name. Click OK.
4. When PowerPoint asks whether to export every slide in the presentation or just the current slide, choose Every Slide (the first choice).

Now you have a folder full of PNG images on your desktop, which you can view with any image viewing program as a collection of picture slides.

CAUTION

Because these are pictures, you will lose any effects, animations, or media in the original presentation. What you're getting is a static shot of each slide in its initial state.

Slides on an iPod

Do you have an iPod that supports pictures? You can transfer the images of your presentation that you saved to the iPod to make your presentation more mobile. This can be very helpful for students or if you are traveling to a remote location where you might not be able to take a laptop.

Do the following to copy the images of your presentation that you just created to your iPod, and enjoy your slides on the road:

1. Connect your iPod to your computer.
2. If iTunes doesn't start automatically, launch iTunes from the Start menu.
3. In iTunes, select the iPod's icon. You will see it in the Devices section at the bottom of the left pane.
4. Click the Photos tab. (If you don't see a Photos tab, your iPod probably doesn't support photographs, unfortunately.)
5. Check the Sync Photos From box and navigate to the folder of slide PNGs you saved.

6. Choose whether to copy all your folders or just the selected folders and albums. You probably just want to copy the selected ones.
7. When you're happy with your choices, click the OK button, and your iPod will sync the slides.

NOTE

These steps were based on Apple iTunes 7.4 for Windows. They might vary if you're using an older or newer version of iTunes.

Save Anything as a Picture

In addition to saving entire slides from your presentation as a picture, just about any element you create in PowerPoint can be saved as a picture. Let's walk through an example:

1. Create a new presentation and add a text placeholder to the slide.
2. Type some text into the placeholder.
3. On the Insert tab, go to the Drawing group and click Rectangle. Click anywhere on the slide to insert the rectangle.
4. Select the rectangle and the placeholder by dragging a marquee to select both objects. Or, use Ctrl+A to select everything on the slide.
5. Right-click one of the selected objects and choose Save as Picture and save it.

Neat, huh? This works with just about any type of PowerPoint object. It makes it very easy to whip up a quick diagram, save it out to a picture, and email it to a friend.

NOTE

Notice how the default file format for saved pictures in PowerPoint 2007 is PNG. This is so that saved objects can have a transparent background without much fuss. In PowerPoint 2003, the default was Enhanced Windows Metafile (`.emf`), which also did the job, but did not work as well on non-Windows platforms.

Save a Picture as a Picture

Yes, this means that you can save a picture as a picture also. Go ahead:

1. Insert a picture on your slide.
2. Right-click it and choose Save as Picture. By default, this saves the image at its current dimensions. PowerPoint probably shrunk the image when it was inserted, so you won't be saving the picture at its full size. To save it at its full original size, click the little arrow to the right of the Save button and choose Save Original Picture.

NOTE

Save Original Picture saves the original picture stored in the presentation. If someone were to use the PowerPoint 2007 picture compression tools or removes cropped regions from all saved pictures, the original picture would no longer be in the presentation, so you wouldn't be able to save it.

So what's the point? You might want to save a picture as a picture to take advantage of PowerPoint's picture effects. For example, with a picture selected, you can go to the Picture Tools Format tab and go to the Picture Styles group, where there's a gallery of pretty picture effects. Then, when the picture's formatted the way you like, use Save as Picture to save the picture as a picture again.

Saving to a Network Share

Advanced When saving a presentation using the Save As dialog, you might think that the text box only allows you to type in the filename to save under. But, you can actually type in remote locations to save your presentation directly to a remote server (see Figure 18.7).

Figure 18.7

The Save As dialog box that lets you enter a server location as well as a filename to which PowerPoint saves your file.

You can save to a network share by typing in a UNC path such as \\waynes-computer\documents\.

To save to a website that supports WebDAV or a Microsoft SharePoint Document Workspace, type a URL such as www.example.com/Documents.

Many companies use SharePoint internally, and Microsoft will host SharePoint for you free through its Office Live service (http://officelive.com). You can get WebDAV by signing up for a premium Microsoft Office Live service such as Live Essentials or from Apple by signing up for its .Mac service. Inside a corporation, you're best off using Slide Library, which you can read more about in Chapter 9, "Inserting Content into PowerPoint."

CAUTION

Saving over a network is typically less reliable than saving to your local hard drive. For a super important presentation, your best bet is to steer clear of network saving, or save a copy locally just in case the other one fails to save or becomes corrupt.

CUSTOMIZING AUTOSAVE

Advanced One cool thing about PowerPoint is that it periodically saves what you've done so far. That way, if PowerPoint crashes, your computer crashes, or aliens attack, you won't lose any changes you have made to your presentation.

By default, PowerPoint saves your work every 10 minutes. We're paranoid, so we prefer to save more often. To do this

1. Click the Office button and choose PowerPoint Options.
2. Choose the Save tab on the left.
3. Make sure that Save AutoRecover Information Every ___ Minutes is checked, enter **1** for the number, and click OK to save.

If you often edit a large presentation, saving every minute slows down your whole system. Just use a higher number for the time increment to create an AutoRecover file to keep from eating up all your processor's performance.

Save as Web Page

PowerPoint lets you save a presentation in HTML, the native web format. Because most people can view PowerPoint presentations these days either with PowerPoint itself, the free PowerPoint Viewer, or another program such as Open Office, we don't find ourselves using this feature for publishing that often. However, this feature does have its uses.

In this section, we discuss using the Save as Web Page feature to extract your media from a presentation and explain why Office HTML is as ugly as it is.

Easily Extract Pictures, Movies, and Sounds from Your Presentation by Saving the Presentation as a Web Page

Ever add a picture, movie, or sound to a presentation, lose the original content, and want to pull the original object back out of PowerPoint? Or maybe someone sent you a presentation containing a pretty picture that you'd like to save out to use on your own. There are various ways to accomplish this, but the easiest is to save the presentation as a web page:

1. Open the presentation you need to get something from.
2. Click the Office button, and then click the arrow next to Save As.
3. Choose Web Page for the Save As type, choose a location to save to such as the Desktop, and click Save.
4. Navigate to the place you saved the presentation as a web page. You will find a folder there with a similar name as your presentation. Inside, you will find the original pictures, movies, and sounds from the presentation.

Ugly Office HTML

As web developers, one of our biggest gripes with Office used to be the bloated HTML it would save out. Really, we type two words in a PowerPoint presentation. We expect something like this:

```
<html>
 <head>
  <title>Wayne Kao</title>
 </head>
 <body>
  <div class="slide">Wayne Kao</div>
 </body>
</html>
```

Instead, PowerPoint produces this *huge* file that *barely* resembles HTML, with all this extra gunk:

```
<html xmlns:v="urn:schemas-microsoft-com:vml"
xmlns:o="urn:schemas-microsoft-com:office:office"
xmlns:p="urn:schemas-microsoft-com:office:powerpoint"
xmlns:oa="urn:schemas-microsoft-com:office:activation"
xmlns="http://www.w3.org/TR/REC-html40">

<head>
<meta http-equiv=Content-Type content="text/html; charset=windows-1252">
<meta name=ProgId content=PowerPoint.Slide>
<meta name=Generator content="Microsoft PowerPoint 12">
<link rel=File-List href="Wayne%20Kao_files/filelist.xml">
<link rel=Preview href="Wayne%20Kao_files/preview.wmf">
<link rel=Edit-Time-Data href="Wayne%20Kao_files/editdata.mso">
<title>Wayne Kao</title>
<!--[if gte mso 9]><xml>
 <o:DocumentProperties>
  <o:Author>Wayne Kao</o:Author>
  <o:LastAuthor>Wayne Kao</o:LastAuthor>
  <o:Revision>2</o:Revision>
  <o:TotalTime>0</o:TotalTime>
  <o:Created>2007-09-25T14:28:29Z</o:Created>
  <o:LastSaved>2007-09-25T14:28:50Z</o:LastSaved>
  <o:PresentationFormat>On-screen Show (4:3)</o:PresentationFormat>
  <o:Slides>1</o:Slides>
  <o:Version>12.00</o:Version>
 </o:DocumentProperties>
 <o:OfficeDocumentSettings>
  <o:PixelsPerInch>80</o:PixelsPerInch>
 </o:OfficeDocumentSettings>
</xml><![endif]-->
<link rel=Presentation-XML href="Wayne%20Kao_files/pres.xml">
<meta name=Description content="9/25/2007: Wayne Kao">
<meta http-equiv=expires content=0>
```

```
<![if !ppt]><script>
<!--
    var ver = 0, appVer = navigator.appVersion,
➥msie = appVer.indexOf( "MSIE " )
    var msieWin31 = (appVer.indexOf( "Windows 3.1" ) >= 0),
➥isMac = (appVer.indexOf("Macintosh") >= 0)
    if( msie >= 0 )
        ver = parseFloat(
➥appVer.substring( msie+5, appVer.indexOf ( ";", msie ) ) )
    else
        ver = parseInt( appVer )
    browserSupported=0
    if( !isMac && ver >= 4 && msie >= 0 ) {
        browserSupported=1
        window.location.replace(
➥'Wayne%20Kao_files/slide0001.htm'+document.location.hash )
    }
//-->
</script>
<![endif]>
</head>

<body>
<script><!--

if( browserSupported )
    document.writeln('<div style="visibility:hidden">');

//--></script><font face=Arial size=2><b>

<p>This presentation contains content that your browser
➥may not be able to show properly.</p>

<p>If you would like to proceed anyway, click <a
href="Wayne%20Kao_files/slide0001.htm">here</a>.</p>

</b></font><script><!--

if( browserSupported )
    document.writeln('</div>');

//--></script>
</body>

</html>
```

Actually, there's a very good reason that PowerPoint saves out all this stuff. Although it's *definitely* not optimized for the Web, the designers of this feature figured that customers would expect to be able to open the PowerPoint HTML back up without *any* data loss. After all, they said if PowerPoint can save it, it should be able to open it.

Therefore, the HTML needs to be as expressive as the normal `.pptx` format. Because PowerPoint has added a good number of features over the years, this obviously requires saving a lot of information, which does explain the size of the HTML source.

NOTE

Word contains a Filtered HTML option that produces cleaner code that cannot be reopened in high-fidelity. Unfortunately, PowerPoint doesn't have a similar filtered HTML option.

Removing Sensitive Information from Presentations (Document Inspector)

Advanced Have you heard about those scandals in which a government official posted a Word document on the Internet and accidentally revealed confidential information that had been embedded in the doc?

Yeah, that's not good. Office 2007 includes some new tools for sanitizing documents to make sure that you don't accidentally send out private stuff when sending your file to others:

1. Open a presentation, click the Office button, and then click the arrow next to Prepare. Choose Inspect Document.
2. You will be prompted to save the presentation if you have changes that you have not already saved.

TIP

The Document Inspector's changes cannot be undone, so consider making a copy of your presentation before using it.

---

3. Check all the boxes and click OK. PowerPoint shows you some information saved in the presentation that you might not know about and gives you an opportunity to strip it out (see Figure 18.8).

This tool can help strip out comments, ink notations, document properties, custom XML data, invisible content that was hidden with the content pane, off-slide content, and notes.

CAUTION

Not all off-slide content is bad. For example, you might have some notes not on the slide that you like to pull in for quick edits. Sometimes this is worth getting rid of; sometimes it's good to keep around. The Document Inspector will point out potential problems, but don't follow it blindly.

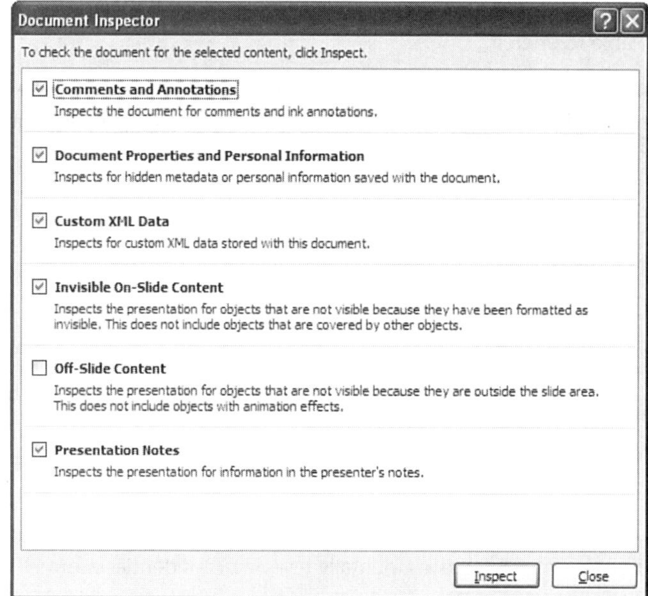

Figure 18.8

There are many types of hidden data that PowerPoint can help remove from your presentation.

TIP

If you have a presentation with a lot of notes that are taking up too much space, use the Document Inspector to remove all the notes from your presentation to make the file smaller.

Using PowerPoint Shapes in Other Office Applications

Advanced It's easy to export PowerPoint content to Word and Excel. Because slides are structured as one large canvas, it's often easier to create quick diagrams in PowerPoint and move it over to Word or Excel rather than create it in Word or Excel.

Copying Shapes to Microsoft Excel

Copying content from PowerPoint to Excel is easy:

1. Launch PowerPoint.
2. Insert a few shapes using tools on the Home tab, Drawing group under the Shapes button. Choose a shape and click on the slide to insert it.
3. Select all the shapes you inserted (press Ctrl+A to select everything or Shift+click to select individual shapes), and then choose Copy (press Ctrl+C or go to the Home tab under the Clipboard and choose Copy).

4. Launch Excel.
5. Paste the shapes (press Ctrl+V).
6. Excel 2007 uses the same underlying drawing code as PowerPoint 2007, so you can continue tweaking your diagram in Excel. For example, you can select a shape, go to the Format tab in the Shape Styles group, and choose Shape Fill to change the fill on a shape right in Excel.

Most of what's created in PowerPoint—including shapes, charts, pictures, and diagrams—can be copied over and edited in Excel with full fidelity.

NOTE

If you're using PowerPoint 2007 with Excel 2003 or older, the objects will be pasted into Excel as pictures. So, they will look great, but they won't be editable since older versions of Excel don't have the new Office 2007 user interface.

The opposite technique, moving Excel content into PowerPoint, is discussed in Chapter 9, "Inserting Content into PowerPoint."

Copying Shapes to Microsoft Word

Word's drawing engine was not upgraded in Office 2007 as Excel and PowerPoint's were. Diagrams and charts can be brought from PowerPoint over to Word and edited in full fidelity, but moving over a shape keeps it in locked form.

Give it a try:

1. Follow steps 1–3 from the steps in the Excel section given previously.
2. Launch Word.
3. Paste the copied shape(s) (press Ctrl+V).

Notice how individual shapes can't be formatted or selected. If you want to make edits, make them in PowerPoint and then recopy and repaste into Word. You know that you like PowerPoint better anyway.

You can insert Office 2003 era shapes in Word using Insert, Illustrations, Shapes, choosing a shape, and clicking in the document to insert it. No pretty effects exist like glows, soft shadows, reflections, or real 3D on native Word shapes though. Word 2007 does have galleries though (with a Word shape selected, go to Drawing Tools Format and look at the Shape Styles group), so you can use the PowerPoint 2003 era effects in Word with greater effectiveness.

Saving to the 97–2003 File Format

New PowerPoint 2007 introduces a new `.pptx` file format. For at least the next few years, you will likely be sharing files with folks who still have older versions of PowerPoint. Some might have PowerPoint 2002 or older, which doesn't include the file format Compatibility Pack (read more about the Compatibility Pack in Chapter 17, "Migrating Files to PowerPoint 2007"). Others might be using Open Office or Google docs, which don't support the new file formats. In any case, people will often request that you send them a `.ppt` file.

That's easy enough. Just click the Office button, click the arrow next to Save As, and choose PowerPoint 97–2003 Presentation. Now you can save the file in the `.ppt` format that all versions of PowerPoint from 97 to 2007 are capable of opening without a hitch.

DON'T CHOOSE A WEIRD FILE FORMAT

To keep your presentation size small, stick to the new 2007 file formats (`.pptx`, `.ppsx`, `.pptm`, and so on) if you can.

Saving to the older binary formats (`.ppt`, `.pps`) is best when you're collaborating with others who may have PowerPoint versions that are older than PowerPoint 2003. (PowerPoint 2003 users can use the Compatibility Pack to view the new file formats.) But, when you save to the older format, PowerPoint essentially saves two copies of the file. For example, if you save as presentation.ppt, it shoves a full presentation.pptx copy of your presentation inside the `.ppt` file. That way, if a PowerPoint 2007 user opens the file, he will get all the data from the embedded `.pptx` file; if a PowerPoint 2003 user opens the file, he will get all the data from the binary `.ppt` file.

The new file formats produced by PowerPoint 2007, which are zipped XML, are typically smaller than the old binary `.ppt` format produced by PowerPoint 2003, especially if fast saves are turned on in PowerPoint 2003. There are rare cases in which PowerPoint 2003 will produce smaller files. But one thing is clear: For compatibility reasons, the `.ppt` binaries produced by PowerPoint 2007 will *always* be bigger than the native `.pptx` files it produces. So, stick to `.pptx` when possible.

A similar tip applies when you're using older PowerPoint versions such as PowerPoint 2003. Save as the default `.ppt` format. If you save as PowerPoint 97–2003 & 95 Presentation, PowerPoint essentially saves two copies of the presentation, which can massively increase file size.

Also, don't worry about having to always save to `.ppt` or the 2003 formats if your friends, peers, or co-workers have yet to upgrade to Office 2007. Read about the Compatibility Pack in Chapter 17, which allows them to open files created in 2007 with their previous versions of PowerPoint!

Change Your Default File Format

If you anticipate saving mainly in the old file format, you can set PowerPoint 97–2003 file as your PowerPoint default:

1. Click the Office button, and then click the PowerPoint Options button.
2. In the PowerPoint Options dialog, choose Save in the left panel.
3. For the Save Files in This Format section, select a file format that you want to be your default. Then click OK to save your choice.

CAUTION

Unless there's a good reason to do this—for example, everyone you know is using ancient versions of PowerPoint—you should steer clear of changing your default format to PowerPoint 97–2003. When saving to the PowerPoint 97–2003 format, you won't be able to use many of the new drawing features introduced in PowerPoint 2007.

Using the Compatibility Checker

PowerPoint 2007 supports many new features that aren't supported when you save in the older file format. PowerPoint 2007 contains a Compatibility Checker that warns you when it needs to "dumb down" your file to save in the old format.

For example,

1. Create a new presentation.
2. Type some text into the title placeholder and select it.
3. On the Format tab, go to the WordArt Styles group and select one of the fancier effects.
4. Click the Office button, and under the Save As options, choose PowerPoint 97–2003 Presentation, select a filename, and click Save.
5. This automatically pops up the Compatibility Checker (see Figure 18.9). Carefully read what saving will do and press Continue when you're satisfied. Be careful though because you cannot undo this.

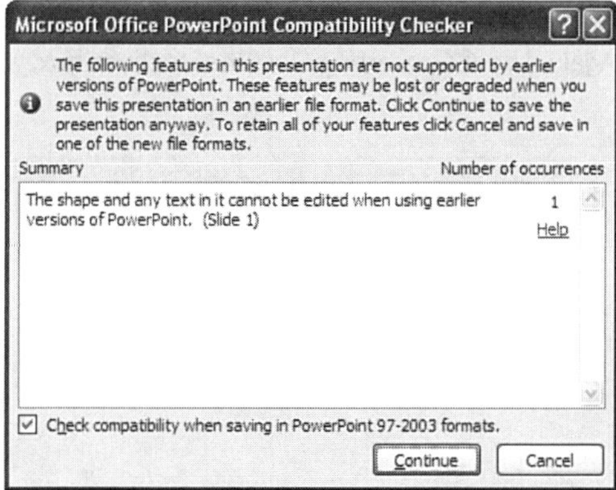

Figure 18.9

The PowerPoint Compatibility Checker.

Compatibility Mode

When you save a file in the older `.ppt` file format or when you open a file that's in the old format, note that the title changes to say Compatibility Mode, as shown in Figure 18.10.

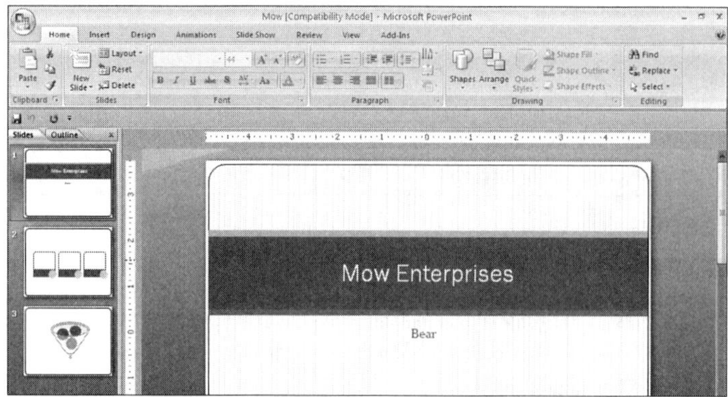

Figure 18.10

Compatibility Mode.

When in this mode, PowerPoint makes sure that you don't do anything to the file that is incompatible with PowerPoint 97–2003. For example, click into the title placeholder and then go to the Home tab in the Drawing group and open the Quick Styles gallery. Note how all the styles are disabled.

If you change your mind and want the full power of PowerPoint 2007, you need to upgrade to the new file format that supports all the latest features. To do that, click the Office button and then choose Convert.

A dialog appears, asking whether you want to upgrade (see Figure 18.11). If you accept, the file format changes and the words "Compatibility Mode" disappear from the title bar. Click OK to accept. If you check the Do Not Ask Me Again About Converting Documents check box, you won't be prompted anymore in the future.

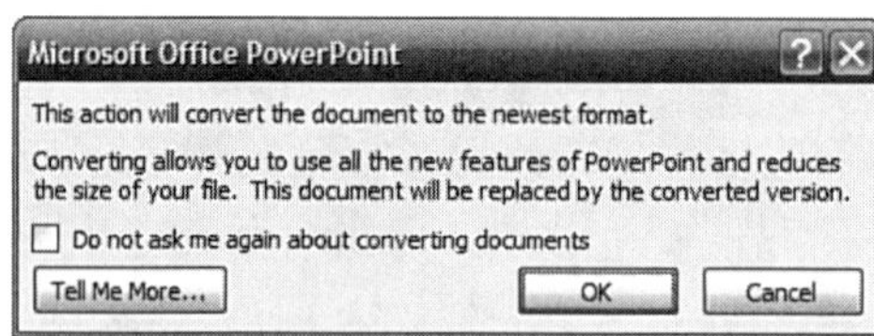

Figure 18.11

A dialog asks whether to upgrade your file to the new PowerPoint 2007 file format.

Now if you click into the title placeholder, go to the Home tab, Drawing group, and open the Quick Styles gallery, you can see that all the options are available.

Compressing Pictures to Create Smaller Files

Advanced Having many large photos is one way to bloat the size of your saved presentations. Unlike previous versions of PowerPoint, PowerPoint 2007 does a lot by default to compress pictures so that they take up very little space.

This process is very customizable, however:

1. With a presentation that contains pictures open, click the Office button and then click the arrow next to Save As.
2. Click the Tools button and choose Compress Pictures.
3. Click Options to bring up the dialog shown in Figure 18.12.

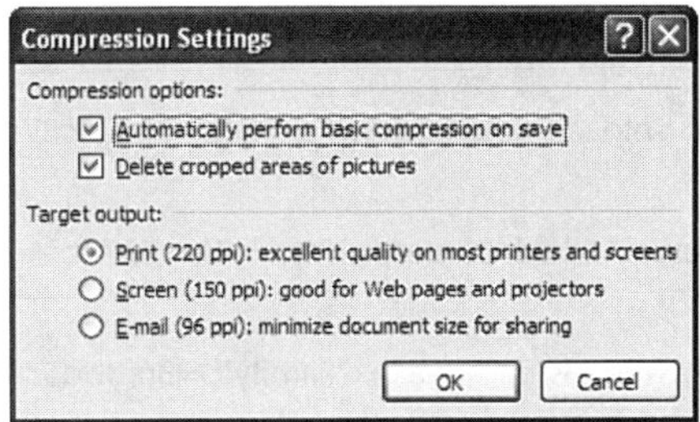

Figure 18.12

PowerPoint lets you customize how pictures are compressed.

Uncheck the first check box if you want to pick and choose which pictures are compressed and uncheck the second check box if you often re-crop pictures within PowerPoint and don't want the cropped portions deleted. Most of the time, you should just keep both checked to keep your presentations smaller.

If you don't intend to print your presentation and just want view it onscreen, you can change the Target Output option to Screen to further compress your images to make the presentation even leaner in size.

Publishing Your Presentation to a CD

With PowerPoint 2007 comes a brand new PowerPoint Viewer (www.microsoft.com/downloads/details.aspx?FamilyID=048dc840-14e1-467d-8dca-19d2a8fd7485).

OLDER VIEWERS

The 2007 Viewer now requires Windows 2000. The 2003 Viewer distributed with PowerPoint 2003 ran on Windows 98 SE as well, but the system requirements were bumped to Windows 2000 during the Office 2007 to make the code more secure. If you need to view PowerPoint presentations when using older versions of Windows, you can grab the older PowerPoint 2003 Viewer here—www.microsoft.com/downloads/details.aspx?FamilyId=428D5727-43AB-4F24-90B7-A94784AF71A4—and the even older PowerPoint 97 Viewer here—http://office.microsoft.com/downloads/2000/Ppview97.aspx. The PowerPoint 2003 Viewer added newer animations and slide transitions, support for password protected presentations, and animated GIFs.

The nice thing about Microsoft Office viewers is that they're free, so you can use them even if you don't own the associated program. This also applies to the Word viewer, the Excel viewer, and the Visio viewer (and we're sure that there are others):

- www.microsoft.com/downloads/details.aspx?FamilyID=95e24c87-8732-48d5-8689-ab826e7b8fdf
- www.microsoft.com/downloads/details.aspx?FamilyID=c8378bf4-996c-4569-b547-75edbd03aaf0
- www.microsoft.com/downloads/details.aspx?FamilyID=3fb3bd5c-fed1-46cf-bd53-da23635ab2df)

Why Care About a Viewer If I Own PowerPoint?

"But I own PowerPoint! Why do I care that there's a new viewer? I can just view my presentation in PowerPoint."

One point of anxiety you face as a PowerPoint user is being unsure whether the presentation that took you *hours* to create and looks *marvelous* on your home machine will turn to ugly mush after you are forced to present on some old machine running a decade old version of PowerPoint that's already connected to a projector but that doesn't support half the animations you're using.

Fear no more.

The coolest feature of this viewer is that it can be run without any installation or setup, which means that it can be run directly off your USB keychain or even off write-protected media such as a CD or DVD.

Replacing the old Pack and Go Wizard, a new Package for CD feature (found under the Office button in the Publish options) was added in PowerPoint 2003 to make it easy to burn your presentation to a CD along with the new PowerPoint Viewer (see Figure 18.13). Then, you can just stick the CD into any machine running Windows 2000 or later, even if the computer doesn't have PowerPoint, and your presentation will play automatically using the new viewer.

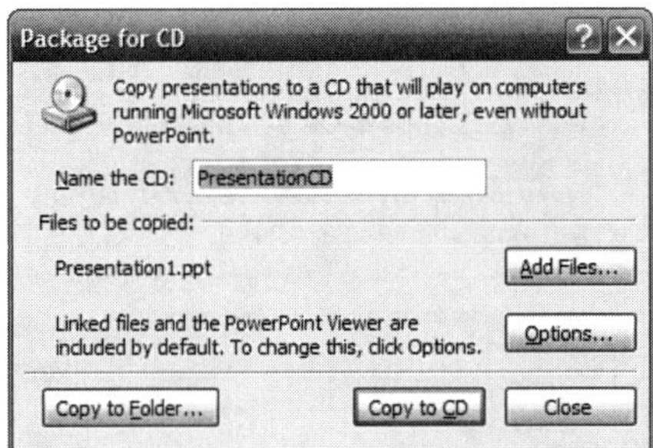

Figure 18.13

The Package for CD dialog.

TIP

Need to view PowerPoint files on your little Windows Mobile device? If you have a device running Windows Mobile 5.0, you have PowerPoint Mobile. This application only allows you to view PowerPoint files, but it does so very accurately since it runs the same underlying code as the PowerPoint 2003 Viewer.

Package for CD Customizations

You can choose multiple presentations when selecting which files to copy. PowerPoint lets you create a playlist of presentations so that you can order the presentations (see Figure 18.14). The Select How Presentations Will Play in the Viewer choice in the Options dialog (see Figure 18.15) lets you choose whether to play the presentation in your playlist in order or whether to let the user choose which presentation to play.

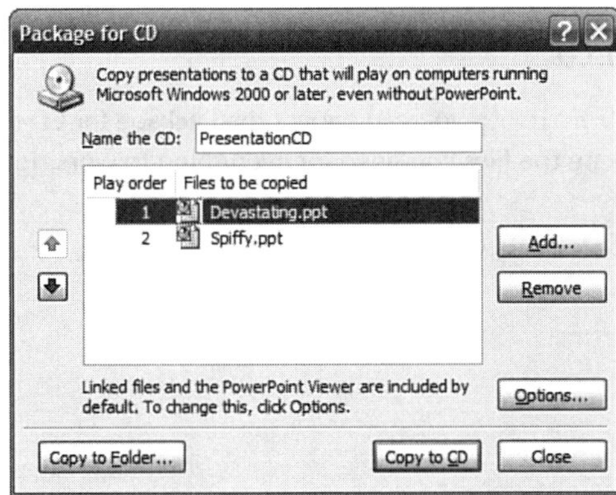

Figure 18.14

The Package for CD playlist dialog.

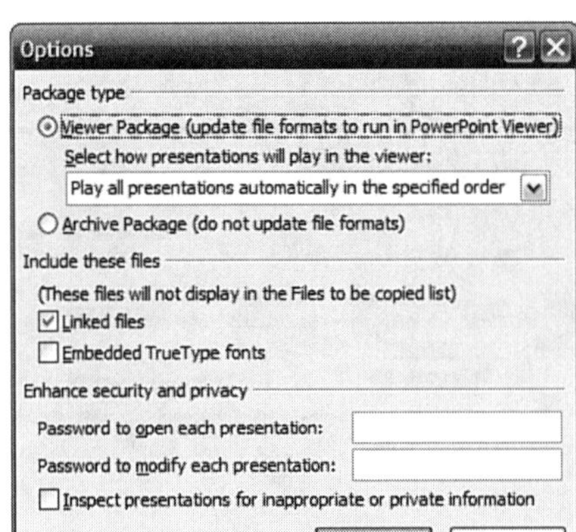

Figure 18.15

Select options for how the presentation will be played.

The PowerPoint 2007 viewer still only plays older binary `.ppt` files natively, so this dialog also lets you choose whether you want to downgrade your new `.pptx` files to play natively in the viewer. Unless you choose Archive Package, all your files will be down converted to the old `.ppt` binary format. If your files contain presentations that are not in the old `.ppt` format (this includes files for which you've used Convert to change to the new format), you will get a warning asking whether to convert to "compatible file formats," which means that PowerPoint wants to convert them to the old format.

The middle options in the dialog let you choose whether to include linked files and embedded fonts in your package. As always, beware of including linked files unless you trust the source.

Other options let you set a password for the entire package and choose whether to inspect the presentations for inappropriate content. (Read about Document Inspector earlier in this chapter.)

Bypassing Package for CD

If you really know what you are doing, you can bypass the Package for CD feature and copy the Viewer files yourself. These are the files you need for everything to work right. They all need to be in the same directory:

- pptview.exe
- gdiplus.dll
- intldate.dll
- ppvwintl.dll
- saext.dll
- unicows.dll

So create your presentation and burn it to a CD, knowing that you can stick it in practically any old Windows machine, and it will play exactly the way you expect it to.

Other Notes About the Viewer

Here are some other caveats about the Viewer that might not be obvious:

- There are a few limitations to the Viewer: no VBA Macros, no programs, no IRM, no OLE.
- There are a few special command switches for launching the Viewer. For example, you can open a list of presentations instead of just one, you can use the Viewer to print a presentation, or you can open a presentation starting at a particular slide. This article has more details: http://support.microsoft.com/default.aspx?scid=kb;EN-US;830040.

Now that we are nearing the end of the book, we look at some resources you can use to learn more about PowerPoint and to answer any questions you might still have.

VI

Finding Help

19 Using Help and Other Resources 381

19

Using Help and Other Resources

IN THIS CHAPTER

- Integrated Help
- microsoft.public.powerpoint Newsgroup
- Knowledge Base
- Microsoft Employee Blogs
- Community Sites

Some people see using help as a sign of weakness. We suppose that it's like having to ask for directions after you get lost. This chapter provides you with some resources to get help from within PowerPoint itself, in addition to the online PowerPoint community.

Integrated Help

The Help feature in PowerPoint is useful; we use it all the time. You can think of it as a search engine for PowerPoint related material. To access the Help feature:

1. Click the question mark Help icon near the top right of PowerPoint (see Figure 19.1).
2. The Help window that pops up contains a large text box that you can type questions into (see Figure 19.2).

This searches all the help databases that came on your Office CD, but if you are connected to the Internet, it also searches the large database on a website that the Microsoft Office team maintains. You can use it to find answers just as you would search Google.

NOTE

In case you don't have PowerPoint installed but are itching to get your question answered, the same content is available on the Microsoft Office Online website: http://office.microsoft.com/en-us/powerpoint/

Figure 19.1

Click the question mark Help button near the top right of the application window.

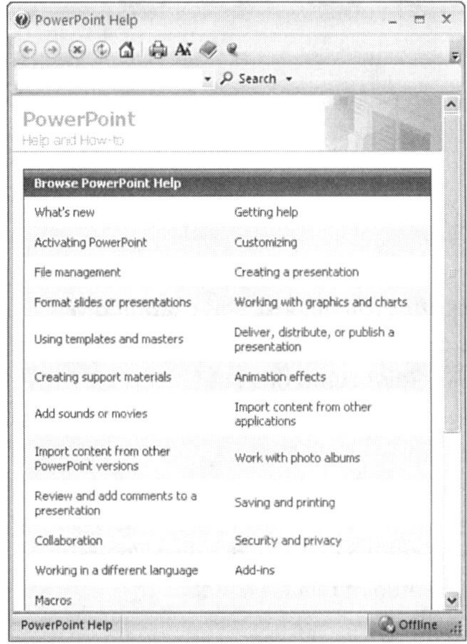

Figure 19.2

Help can search for answers to your PowerPoint questions.

microsoft.public.powerpoint Newsgroup

If you couldn't find the answer for an obscure question using the built-in PowerPoint Help feature, the next place to turn is to the PowerPoint newsgroup. This group is full of passionate PowerPoint users and partners who have answers to even your most obscure PowerPoint question.

- You can access the newsgroup via Google Groups: http://groups.google.com/group/microsoft.public.powerpoint

- Microsoft also has a web interface to it. You can hunt for it by starting here: www.microsoft.com/office/community/en-us/default.mspx

Knowledge Base

Though not as accessible as the Help feature or as comprehensive as the newsgroup, the Microsoft Knowledge Base is where the Microsoft support teams write articles about how to solve common PowerPoint issues that people run into. It also has a search box that you can type questions into: http://support.microsoft.com/search/

Microsoft Employee Blogs

These blogs give you fascinating insight behind the development of PowerPoint. Though they might not solve your immediate problem, they will definitely contribute to your knowledge of the product:

- The PowerPoint team has a blog discussing new features in PowerPoint 2007: http://blogs.msdn.com/powerpoint/
- Jensen Harris has a blog about the motivation behind the new Office 2007 user interface: http://blogs.msdn.com/jensenh
- Brian Jones writes about the new Office 2007 Open XML file format: http://blogs.msdn.com/brian_jones/

Community Sites

Here are a handful of our favorite independent PowerPoint websites. These are all pretty awesome.

- **The PowerPoint FAQ**—Our favorite independent PowerPoint site. It contains great tips and tricks about most areas of PowerPoint:
  www.pptfaq.com
- **A PowerPoint Blog**—A frequently updated blog devoted to PowerPoint. Often links to beautiful templates you can download, in addition to links to other interesting PowerPoint websites:
  www.indezine.com/blog/
- **PowerPoint Heaven**—A collection of advanced PowerPoint presentations you can download from which you can draw inspiration. These presentations push PowerPoint animations to the limit, and the site offers recipes you can follow to create similar effect:
  www.pptheaven.mvps.org/

- **PowerPoint Tips Blog**—This blog offers a grab bag of advanced PowerPoint tips, walking through fun step-by-step recipes:
  www.ellenfinkelstein.com/PowerPoint_tips_blog.html
- **Beyond Bullets**—Whereas the book you are holding focuses entirely on the technical aspects of using PowerPoint software, the Beyond Bullets blog teaches the softer skills on delivering a great presentation:
  www.beyondbullets.com/
- **Office Tips**—For aspiring PowerPoint VBA programmers, this is the place to view sample code and go through code tutorials:
  http://skp.mvps.org/

Index

Numbers

3-D Format dialog, 255-256

3D graphics, 245
- 3-D Format dialog, 255-256
- 3D rotation
  - custom rotations, 251-254
  - object position, 255
  - preset rotations, 250
  - resetting, 255
  - text, 254
- angle, 261
- bezel, 256
- capabilities and limitations, 249
- consistency, 263
- contour, 258
- depth, 257
- design tips, 262-263
- lighting, 259-260
- materials, 259
- resetting, 262
- sphere example, 245-248
- surfaces, 259-261

4x4 Transformation Matrix, 254

A

Action buttons, 302

Action Settings dialog, 303-305

actions
- Action buttons, 302
- Action Settings dialog, 303-305
- applications
  - creating interactive prototypes, 307-308
  - hiding links depending on audience reaction, 308-310
  - linking to first slide, 306-307
- compared to hyperlinks, 306
- types of, 303-305

Add Bullet command (SmartArt), 96

Add Shape command (SmartArt), 95

add-ins, Microsoft Office Sounds, 23

Align options, 278-279

Alt key
- keyboard shortcuts
  - F6 key, 17
  - finding, 16
  - Office 2003 shortcuts, 16-17
- resizing objects with, 275
- rotating objects with, 277

angle (3D objects), 261

animation
- custom animations
  - adding, 288-289
  - Custom Animation pane, 286-287
  - options, 289-291
  - previewing, 291
  - Selection pane, 287-288
- motion paths
  - creating, 292
  - editing, 294
- preset animations, 284-285
- SmartArt, 96-97
- table cells, 142-143
- text, 294-296
- triggers, 296-299

Arc tool, 123

audio. *See* sounds

Auto Correction feature (Picture Manager), 80

AutoContent Wizard, 200

AutoCorrect, 44
- clickable hyperlinks, creating, 45-46
- custom phrases, 46
- default text corrections, 44-45
- pranks, 46
- Smart Tag, 152-153

AutoCorrect dialog, 44-46

Autofit, 34

AutoSave, 364

auxiliaryThemeThumbnail.jpeg file, 213

B

backgrounds
- adding, 175-176
- background fills, 229-231
- hiding, 178

batch editing (Picture Manager), 83-84

bevel, 256

bevel effect, 238

Beyond Bullets, 384

black-and-white color mode, 69

block arrows, stretching, 122

blogs
- Microsoft employee blogs, 383
- PowerPoint Blog, 383
- PowerPoint Tips Blog, 384

brightness (pictures), 67

bulleted lists
- Bullets and Numbering dialog, 43
- custom bullets, 42-44
- default bullets, 41

Bullets and Numbering dialog, 43

C

Calibri font, 32

Cambria font, 32

Candara font, 32

caps, formatting text as, 38

CDs
- packaging presentations for, 165-166
- publishing presentations to, 373-377

cells (tables)
- animating, 142-143
- margins, 149
- sizing, 148
- splitting and merging, 149

center tab stops, 48

changing
- charts, 111-112
- color schemes, 24
- default file format, 370
- effect schemes, 212
- font schemes, 207
- pictures, 70
- shapes, 242-243
- slide layouts, 179-180

character spacing, 39

charts, 101
- compatible objects, converting to PowerPoint 2007, 338-339
- copying/pasting into PowerPoint, 102-103
- formatting, 105-107
- inserting from scratch, 103-105
- inserting objects into, 107
- layouts, 107
- legacy charts
  - converting to Office 2007 format, 114-115
  - corruption, 115
  - undo operations, 115
- modifying, 111-112
- pie charts, 113-114
- styles, 108-109
- templates
  - applying, 110-111
  - creating, 110
  - managing, 111

Choose a SmartArt Graphic dialog, 87

clearing text formatting, 55

ClearType, 32

clickable hyperlinks, creating, 45-46

clipboard formats, 154-156

Coleman, Paul, 12

color. *See also* fills
- color modes, 69
  - overview, 195
  - per-object color mode, 195-196
  - viewing, 195
- color schemes, 24, 203-204, 208-210
- lines, 232
- recolor feature (duotone effect), 68-69
- transparency, 70

columns (tables), inserting, 147-148

command-line parameters, 342-343

commands
- File menu, 14-15
- finding, 11-12
- Interactive PowerPoint 2003 to PowerPoint 2007 Command Reference Guide, 11-12
- QAT (Quick Access Toolbar), 19
- SmartArt Create Graphic commands
  - Add Bullet, 96
  - Add Shape, 95
  - Layout, 96
  - Right to Left, 96

comments
- adding, 357
- overview, 357
- tips and guidelines, 357-358

community sites, 383

Compatibility Checker, 371

Compatibility mode, 371-372

compatible objects, converting to PowerPoint 2007, 338-339

compressing pictures, 69-70, 81, 373

confidential information, removing with Document Inspector, 367

configuring Slide Show
- keyboard shortcuts, 329-330
- overview, 324
- Presenter View, 327-329
- ranges of slides, 326
- resolution, 326
- show types, 324-326
- widescreen slide sizes, 331-332

connectors, 126-127
- customizing, 129-130
- inserting, 128
- rerouting, 129
- SmartArt, 91

Consolas font, 32

Constantia font, 32

containers (PPTX files), 347

Content pane (SmartArt), 89-90

contour of 3D objects, 258

contrast of pictures, 67

converting
- existing content to SmartArt, 88-89
- legacy charts to Office 2007 format, 114-115
- objects, 338-339
- placeholders to SmartArt, 97-98

copying
- charts, 102-103
- copying and pasting, 154-156
- Excel tables, 141
- formatting with Format Painter, 239-241
- slides from Slide Library, 161-162
- text, 28

Corbel font, 32

corruption of OLE objects, 115

Create Graphic commands (SmartArt)
- Add Bullet, 96
- Add Shape, 95
- Layout, 96
- Right to Left, 96

cropping pictures, 71-72, 80

.crtx file extension, 110

Ctrl key
- Ctrl+Enter keyboard shortcut, 187
- moving objects with, 277
- resizing objects with, 273-274
- rotating objects with, 276

Custom Animation pane, 286-287

Custom Shows, 299-300

Custom Tab Picker, 47

customizing
- 3D rotations, 251-254
- animations
  - adding, 288-289
  - Custom Animation pane, 286-287
  - motion paths, 292-294
  - options, 289-291
  - previewing, 291
  - Selection pane, 287-288
  - text, 294-296
  - triggers, 296-299
- AutoSave, 364
- bullets, 42-44
- default shapes, 239
- headers/footers, 190
- lines, 129-130
- placeholders, 187-188
- QAT (Quick Access Toolbar), 17-19
- slide layouts, 181-182
- status bar, 22
- tab stops, 47-48

D

decimal tab stops, 48

default bullets, 41

default file formats, changing, 370

default shapes, customizing, 239

default tab stops, 47

depth of 3D objects, 257

design templates, 200, 204

designing presentations
- 3D effects, 262-263
- design templates, 200, 204
- themes
  - advantages, 199-200, 205
  - applying entire themes, 200-202
  - applying parts of themes, 202-203
  - color schemes, 203-204, 208-210
  - compared to design templates, 200, 204
  - compared to presentations, 204
  - creating, 214-215
  - effect schemes, 203, 210-212
  - font schemes, 203-207
  - overview, 199
  - saving, 214
  - slide layouts, 213
  - slide masters, 213
  - thumbnails, 212-213

diagrams. *See also* charts
- compatible objects, converting to PowerPoint 2007, 338-339
- SmartArt, 85-87
  - accentuating photos with, 98
  - advantages, 91-92
  - animations, 96-97
  - connectors, 91
  - Content pane, 89-90
  - converting existing content to, 88-89
  - converting placeholders to, 97-98
  - Create Graphic commands, 95-96
  - inserting, 87-88
  - layouts, 92-93
  - nodes, 90, 96
  - styles, 94
  - Text pane, 90
  - themes, 94
  - types, 86

dialog box launcher (Ribbon), 10

dialogs
- 3-D Format, 255-256
- Action Settings, 303-305
- AutoCorrect, 44-46
- Bullets and Numbering, 43
- Choose a SmartArt Graphic, 87
- Font, 39-40
- Format Chart Area, 105
- Format Selection, 105-107
- Format Shape, 36, 219-220, 248-251
- Grid and Guides, 270-271
- Hyperlink, 301
- Insert Object, 65, 133
- Insert Table, 138-139
- Open File, 337-338
- Picture Fill, 227-228
- Select Data Source, 111
- Select Multiple Objects, 132
- Size and Position, 265-267
- Text Box, 34

dictionary, 57

direction of text, 30

disabling
- hardware acceleration, 333
- ScreenTips, 23
- sounds, 23

Distribute options, 278

distributed text, 52

distributing presentations with sound, 165-166

docProps (PPTX files), 347

Document Inspector, 367-368

dragging text, 28-29

Draw Table option, 139, 149

drawing
- during presentations, 321
- ellipses, 234

Drawing Tools Format tab
- shape fill, 121
- shape styles, 120-121

drivers (graphics), 332-333

dummy text, generating, 60

duotone effect (pictures)
- color modes, 69
- dark variations, 68
- light variations, 68-69

duplicating shapes, 118

E

Edit Points mode, 124

editing
- charts, 111-112
- motion paths, 294
- Photo Albums, 78
- pictures, 66
  - associating text with, 73-75
  - brightness/contrast, 67
  - changing shape of, 72-73
  - compression, 69-70
  - cropping, 71-72
  - Picture Manager, 79-84
  - preset picture effects, 66

recolor feature (duotone effect), 68-69
restoring to original state, 71
transparency, 70
PPTX files, 348
shapes, 124-125
SmartArt nodes, 96
text
dictionary, 57
direction/orientation, 30
during presentations, 323-324
inline editing, 56-57
spelling checker, 57-58
thesaurus, 57-58
translation, 57-58

effect schemes, 203, 210-212
adding, 212
applying, 211-212
changing, 212

effects
3D rotation, 238
applying to tables, 146
bevel, 238
effect schemes, 203, 210-212
adding, 212
applying, 211-212
changing, 212
glow, 237
reflection, 237
shadows
inner shadows, 236
perspective shadows, 236
setting, 236
soft versus hard, 235
soft edges, 237

ellipses, drawing, 234

embedding
fonts, 352-354
objects from other applications, 133-134
pictures, 63-64
sounds/video, 164-165

employee blogs (Microsoft), 383

enabling
hardware acceleration, 333
ruler, 268

encrypting presentations, 358-359

equalizing character heights, 38

Equation Shapes group, 122

Equation Tools Design ribbon, 169-170

equations, 169-170

Esc key, 134

Excel charts, 101
copying/pasting into PowerPoint, 102-103, 141
copying shapes to, 368-369
formatting, 105-107
inserting from scratch, 103-105
inserting objects into, 107
layouts, 107
legacy charts
converting to Office 2007 format, 114-115
corruption, 115
undo operations, 115
modifying, 111-112
pie charts, 113-114
styles, 108-109
templates
applying, 110-111
creating, 110
managing, 111

Excel Spreadsheet option, 139

exporting
pictures from Picture Manager, 82-83
presentations as slideshows, 361

Extensible Markup Language (XML), 344

F

F6 key, 17

Fade Up Transform Effect, 55

File menu, 14-15

files
auxiliaryThemeThumbnail.jpeg, 213
default file format, changing, 370
migrating to PowerPoint 2007
converting objects, 338-339
Open options, 337-338
PDF format, 356
.potm files. *See* templates
.potx files. *See* templates
PowerPoint 2007 files, opening with PowerPoint 97–2003 compatibility pack, 340
PPTX format
advantages, 344-345
containers, 347
docProps, 347
editing, 348
online resources, 349
opening, 345-346
overview, 344
parts, 346
ppt, 347

relationships of parts, 348
saving, 345
.pps format, 354
.ppsx format, 354
presProps.xml, 347
table of file formats, 351-352
tableStyles.xml, 347
.thmx files. *See* themes
thumbnail.jpeg, 213
XPS format, 356

fills, 121
background fills, 229-231
gradient fills, 220-223
applying, 221
custom gradients, 221-223
gradient overlays, 223-226
picture fills, 226-228
solid fills, 220

Filtered HTML option, 367

finding
commands, 11-12
keyboard shortcuts, 16

First-Line Indent Marker, 47

first slide, linking to, 306-307

Fitts Law, 15

flickering problems, troubleshooting
disabling hardware acceleration, 333
enabling hardware acceleration, 333
replacing graphics drivers, 332-333

floatie (mini toolbar), 20-21

Follow Path Transforms, 56

Font dialog, 39-40

fonts
Calibri, 32
Cambria, 32
Candara, 32
Consolas, 32
Constantia, 32
Corbel, 32
embedded fonts, 352-354
Font dialog, 39-40
font schemes, 203-207
adding, 207
applying, 206
changing, 207
Live Preview, 30-31
Office 2007 new fonts, 32
previewing, 30-31
replacing, 33
Segoe UI, 32
theme fonts, 31

footers, customizing, 190

Format Chart Area dialog, 105

Format Painter, 189
capabilities, 240
example, 240
overview, 239
tips, 240-241

Format Selection dialog, 105-107

Format Shape dialog, 36, 219-220, 248-251

formatting presentations
3D rotation, 238
bevel, 238
charts, 105-107
color modes
overview, 195
per-object color mode, 195-196
viewing, 195
copying formatting with Format Painter, 239-241
glow, 237
headers/footers, 190
line color, 232
line styles, 232-233
object fills
background fills, 229-231
gradient fills, 220-223
gradient overlays, 223-226
picture fills, 226-228
solid fills, 220
objects
with Format Shape dialog, 219-220
overview, 218
with Ribbon, 219
with style gallery, 218
outlines
creating, 182-183
creating slides from, 183-184
placeholders
custom placeholders, 187-188
definition, 185
moving between, 187
standard placeholders, 185-187
reflection, 237
shadows
inner shadows, 236
perspective shadows, 236
setting, 236
soft versus hard, 235
slide backgrounds
adding, 175-176
hiding, 178
slide layouts
applying, 179
changing, 179-180

customizing, 181-182
overview, 179
reordering slides
with Thumbnail pane, 173-175
Slide Masters
creating, 177
hiding background graphics on, 178
modifying, 176-177
multiple Masters, 177-178
SmartArt nodes, 96
soft edges, 237
text, 29-30, 36
AutoCorrect, 44-46
character spacing, 39
clearing all formatting, 55
distributed text, 52
equalized character heights, 38
Follow Path Transforms, 56
inline editing, 56-57
justified text, 52
kerning, 40
keyboard shortcuts, 61-62
mouse shortcuts, 62
paragraph markers, 50-52
placeholders, 54-55
shape-editing mode, 53
small caps/all caps, 38
strikethrough, 38-39
subscript, 38
superscript, 38
tab stops, 46-50
text-editing mode, 53
underline, 36
warped text, 55
transparent overlay, 238
widescreen slide sizes, 331-332

Freeform tool, 123

functions, rand(), 60

G

galleries
overview, 11
Shapes, 117-118

glow, 237

gradient fills, 220-223
applying, 221
custom gradients, 221-223

gradient overlays, 223-226

gradient stop, 223

grammar checking, 57

graphics
3D graphics, 245
3-D Format dialog, 255-256
3D rotation, 250-255
angle, 261
bevel, 256
capabilities and limitations, 249
consistency, 263
contour, 258
depth, 257
design tips, 262-263
lighting, 259-260
materials, 259
resetting, 262
sphere example, 245-248
surfaces, 259-261
animation
custom animations, 286-291
motion paths, 292-294
preset animations, 284-285
text, 294-296
triggers, 296-299
charts, 101
copying/pasting into PowerPoint, 102-103
formatting, 105-107
inserting from scratch, 103-105
inserting objects into, 107
layouts, 107
legacy charts, 114-115
modifying, 111-112
pie charts, 113-114
styles, 108-109
templates, 110-111
connectors, 126-127
customizing, 129-130
inserting, 128
rerouting, 129
custom bullets, 42-44
pictures, 63
associating text with, 73-75
auto correcting, 80
batch editing, 83-84
brightness/contrast, 67
changing format of, 82
changing shape of, 72-73
compressing, 69-70, 81
cropping, 71-72, 80
embedded pictures, 63-64
linked embedded pictures, 65-66
linked pictures, 64-65
Photo Album, 75-78
Picture Manager, 78-84
preset picture effects, 66
recolor feature (duotone effect), 68-69
resizing, 81-82

restoring to original state, 71
transparency, 70
shapes. *See* shapes
SmartArt, 85-87
accentuating photos with, 98
advantages of, 91-92
animations, 96-97
connectors, 91
Content pane, 89-90
converting existing content to, 88-89
converting placeholders to, 97-98
Create Graphic commands, 95-96
inserting, 87-88
layouts, 92-93
nodes, 90, 96
styles, 94
Text pane, 90
themes, 94
types, 86
transitions
adding, 297-298
sounds, 298
speed, 298

graphics drivers, 332-333

graphs. *See* charts

grayscale color mode, 69

Grid and Guides dialog, 270-271

grids, snapping objects to, 269-271

grouping
pictures/text, 73
Ribbon groups, 9
shapes, 135-136

guides, snapping objects to, 269-271

H

Handout Master, 193-194

handouts
Handout Master, 193-194
printing, 192-193

hard shadows, 235

hardware acceleration, 333

Harris, Jenson, 10, 15, 383

headers, customizing, 190

help
community sites, 383
Help feature, 381
Interactive PowerPoint 2003 to PowerPoint 2007 Command Reference Guide, 11-12
Microsoft employee blogs, 383
Microsoft Knowledge Base, 383
microsoft.public.powerpoint newsgroup, 382
ScreenTips, 23

hiding
background graphics, 178
links depending on audience reaction, 308-310
portions of pictures, 125-126
slides, 316

horizontal text boxes, 34

HTML, 365

Hyperlink dialog, 301

hyperlinks, 300-301
clickable hyperlinks, creating, 45-46
compared to actions, 306
to first slide, 306-307
hiding depending on audience reaction, 308-310
Hyperlink dialog, 301
linked embedded pictures, 65-66
linked narrations, 314-315
linked pictures, 64-65
sounds/video, 164

I

Insert Table dialog, 138-139

images. *See* graphics

Ink, 168-169, 320-322

inline text editing, 56-57

inner shadows, 236

Insert Object dialog, 65, 133

Interactive PowerPoint 2003 to PowerPoint 2007 Command Reference Guide, 11-12

interactive prototypes, 307-308

iPods, publishing presentations to, 361-362

J-K

Jones, Brian, 349, 383

justified text, 52

kerning text, 40

keyboard shortcuts, 16
Alt key
resizing objects, 275
rotating objects, 277
Ctrl key
Ctrl+Enter, 187
moving objects, 277

resizing objects, 273-274
rotating objects, 276
Esc key, 134
F6 key, 17
finding, 16
Office 2003 shortcuts, 16-17
positioning objects with, 272-273, 277-278
Shift key
moving objects, 277
resizing objects, 275
rotating objects, 276
Slide Show, 329-330
Tab key, 132
text formatting shortcuts, 61-62

Knowledge Base (Microsoft), 383

L

Layout command (SmartArt), 96

layouts
applying, 179
changing, 179-180
charts, 107
customizing, 181-182
overview, 179
SmartArt, 92-93

Left Indent Marker, 47

left tab stops, 48

legacy charts
converting to Office 2007 format, 114-115
corruption, 115
undo operations, 115

libraries, Slide Library
adding slides from PowerPoint, 159-160
adding slides from SharePoint, 160-161
checking slides for changes, 162-163
copying slides from, 161-162
overview, 157
setting up, 157-158

lighting (3D objects), 259-260

lines, 126-127
color, 232
customizing, 129-130
editing, 124-125
inserting, 128
rerouting, 129
styles, 232-233

links, 300-301
clickable hyperlinks, creating, 45-46
compared to actions, 306
to first slide, 306-307
hiding depending on audience reaction, 308-310
Hyperlink dialog, 301
linked embedded pictures, 65-66
linked narrations, 314-315
linked pictures, 64-65
sounds/video, 164

lists
bulleted lists
custom bullets, 42-44
default bullets, 41
ordered lists, 42
shopping list, 48-49

Live Preview, 13-14, 30-31

Lock Drawing Mode, 119-120

looping
presentations, 313
sounds, 166

M

.m3u playlists
applying to presentations, 168
creating, 167-168
overview, 166

macros
adding to QAT, 197
creating, 196-197
online resources, 198
overview, 196
publishing, 352

margins
table cells, 149
text boxes, 34

Mark as Final option, 355-356

materials (3D objects), 259

mathematical equations, 169-170

measurement units (ruler), 269

merging table cells, 149

microphones, testing, 314

Microsoft
employee blogs, 383
Knowledge Base, 383
SQM (Service Quality Monitoring), 10
Visual Studio Express, 346

Microsoft Graph, 101

Microsoft Office Sounds add-in, 23

microsoft.public.powerpoint newsgroup, 382

migrating files to PowerPoint 2007
converting objects, 338-339
Open options, 337-338

mini toolbar (floatie), 20-21

minimizing Ribbon, 10

modeless dialogs, 107

modifying. *See* changing

monitors, configuring for Presenter View, 328-329

motion paths
- creating, 292
- editing, 294

mouse
- positioning objects with, 271
- text formatting shortcuts, 62

moving
- lines, 129
- text
  - copying and pasting, 28
  - dragging, 28-29

multimedia. *See also* sounds
- distributing presentations with multimedia, 165-166
- embedding, 164-165
- linking, 164
- looping, 166
- overview, 163-164
- playlists
  - applying to presentations, 168
  - creating, 167-168
  - overview, 166
- sounds spanning multiple slides, 166

multiple monitors, configuring for Presenter View, 328-329

multiple Slide Masters, creating, 177-178

multiple undo operations, 242

N

narration
- linked narrations, 314-315
- recording, 313-316

network shares, publishing presentations to, 363

New Slide button, 179

newsgroups, microsoft.public.powerpoint, 382

nodes (SmartArt), 90, 96

notes
- Notes Page, 191
- Notes pane, 190-191
- overview, 190
- Presenter View, 327-329
- when to use, 192

Notes Page, 191

Notes pane, 190-191

O

object linking and embedding. *See* OLE objects

objects. *See also* graphics; pictures; text
- compatible objects, converting to PowerPoint 2007, 338-339
- fills
  - background fills, 229-231
  - gradient fills, 220-223
  - gradient overlays, 223-226
  - picture fills, 226-228
  - solid fills, 220
- formatting
  - with Format Shape dialog, 219-220
  - overview, 218
  - with Ribbon, 219
  - with style gallery, 218
- inserting into charts, 107
- OLE (object linking and embedding) objects, 101, 133
  - converting to Office 2007 format, 114-115
  - corruption, 115
  - undo operations, 115
- pasting, 154-156
- positioning
  - Align options, 278-279
  - Distribute options, 278
  - with keyboard, 272-273, 277-278
  - with mouse, 271
  - ruler, 268-269
  - Size and Position dialog, 265-266
  - snapping to grids and guides, 269-271
  - zoom slider, 271-272
- resizing
  - with Alt key, 275
  - with Ctrl key, 273-274
  - with Shift key, 275
  - Size and Position dialog, 266-267
- rotating
  - with Alt key, 277
  - custom rotations, 251-254
  - object position, 255
  - options, 277
  - preset rotations, 250
  - resetting, 255
  - with Shift key, 276
  - SmartArt nodes, 96
  - text, 254

Office 2003, 12, 16-17

Office button, 14-15

Office Tips, 384

Office User Interface Blog website, 15

OLE (object linking and embedding) objects, 101, 133
- converting to Office 2007 format, 114-115
- corruption, 115
- undo operations, 115

On-Screen Show, 332

Open and Repair option, 337

Open as Copy option, 337

Open as Read Only option, 337

Open command, 337-338

Open File dialog, 337-338

Open in Browser option, 337

opening
- PPTX files, 345-346
- presentations, 337-338

ordered lists, 42

orientation of text, 30

outlines
- creating, 182-183
- creating slides from, 183-184

Overflowing Text Smart Tag, 153-154

overlays
- gradient overlays, 223-226
- transparent overlay, 238

P

Package for CD feature, 374-376

packaging presentations for CD, 165-166, 375-376

paragraph markers, 50-52

parts (PPTX files), 346

password protection, 358-360

Paste Smart Tag, 151-152

pasting objects, 154-156
- charts, 102-103
- Excel tables into PowerPoint, 141
- text, 28

PDF format, 356

per-object color modes, 195-196

perspective shadows, 236

Photo Album, 75-78
- adding pictures to, 75-76
- editing, 78

photos. *See* pictures

Picture Fill dialog, 227-228

Picture Manager, 78
- advantages of, 82
- batch editing, 83-84
- changing picture formats, 82-83
- compressing pictures, 81
- editing pictures, 79-80
- exporting pictures, 82-83
- resizing pictures, 81-82

pictures, 63
- accentuating with SmartArt, 98
- associating text with
  - grouping pictures/text, 73
  - shapes with picture fill, 73-75
- auto correcting, 80
- batch editing, 83-84
- brightness/contrast, 67
- changing format of, 82-83
- changing shape of, 72-73
- compressing, 69-70, 81, 373
- cropping, 71-72, 80
- embedded pictures, 63-64
- fills, 226-228
- hiding part of, 125-126
- linked embedded pictures, 65-66
- linked pictures, 64-65
- Photo Album, 75-78
  - adding pictures to, 75-76
  - editing, 78
- Picture Manager, 78
  - advantages of, 82
  - batch editing, 83-84
  - changing picture formats, 82-83
  - compressing pictures, 81
  - editing pictures, 79-80
  - exporting pictures, 82-83
  - resizing pictures, 81-82
- positioning
  - Align options, 278-279
  - Distribute options, 278
  - with keyboard, 272-273, 277-278
  - with mouse, 271
  - ruler, 268-269
  - Size and Position dialog, 265-266
  - snapping to grids and guides, 269-271
  - zoom slider, 271-272
- preset picture effects, 66
- publishing presentations to, 362-363
- recolor feature (duotone effect), 68-69
  - color modes, 69
  - dark variations, 68
  - light variations, 68-69
- resizing, 81-82
  - with Alt key, 275
  - with Ctrl key, 273-274

with Shift key, 275
Size and Position dialog, 266-267
restoring to original state, 71
saving as pictures, 362-363
transparency, 70

pie charts, 113-114

placeholders
converting to SmartArt, 88-89, 97-98
custom placeholders, 187-188
definition, 185
moving between, 187
standard placeholders, 185-187
text placeholders, 54-55

playlists
applying to presentations, 168
creating, 167-168
overview, 166

positioning objects, 265
Align options, 278-279
Distribute options, 278
with keyboard, 272-273, 277-278
with mouse, 271
ruler
aligning objects, 268
enabling, 268
units of measurement, 269
Size and Position dialog, 265-266
snapping to grids and guides, 269-271
zoom slider, 271-272

.potm files. *See* templates

.potx files. *See* templates

PowerPoint 97, opening PowerPoint 2007 files in, 340

PowerPoint 97–2003 format, saving presentations as, 369-370
Compatibility Checker, 371
Compatibility mode, 371-372

PowerPoint 2007 files, opening with PowerPoint 97–2003 compatibility pack, 340

PowerPoint Blog, 383

PowerPoint FAQ, 383

PowerPoint Heaven, 383

PowerPoint Tips Blog, 384

PowerPoint Viewer, 373-374, 377

.pps format, 354

.ppsx format, 354

PPTX file format
advantages, 344-345
containers, 347
docProps, 347
editing, 348
online resources, 349
opening, 345-346
overview, 344
parts, 346
ppt, 347
relationships of parts, 348
saving, 345

presentations. *See also* Slide Show; slides
comments
adding, 357
overview, 357
tips and guidelines, 357-358
compared to themes, 204
confidential information, removing with Document Inspector, 367
editing during slideshows, 323-324
encryption, 358-359
formatting
color modes, 195-196
copying with Format Painter, 239-241
reordering slides with Thumbnail pane, 173-175
slide backgrounds, 175-178
slide layouts, 179-182
Slide Masters, 176-178
widescreen slide sizes, 331-332
headers/footers, 190
narration
linked narrations, 314-315
recording, 313-316
opening, 337-338
outlines
creating, 182-183
creating slides from, 183-184
packaging for CD, 165-166, 375-376
password protection, 358-360
pictures, 63
associating text with, 73-75
auto correcting, 80
batch editing, 83-84
brightness/contrast, 67
changing format of, 82
changing shape of, 72-73

compressing, 69-70, 81
cropping, 71-72, 80
embedded pictures, 63-64
linked embedded pictures, 65-66
linked pictures, 64-65
Photo Album, 75-78
Picture Manager, 78-84
preset picture effects, 66
recolor feature (duotone effect), 68-69
resizing, 81-82
restoring to original state, 71
transparency, 70

placeholders
converting to SmartArt, 88-89, 97-98
custom placeholders, 187-188
definition, 185
moving between, 187
standard placeholders, 185-187
text placeholders, 54-55

publishing
to 97–2003 file format, 369-372
to CD, 373-377
compressing pictures, 373
Document Inspector, 367-368
embedded fonts, 352-354
to Excel, 368-369
file format issues, 370
to iPods, 361-362
macros, 352
Mark as Final option, 355-356
to network shares, 363
PDF format, 356
as pictures, 362-363
.pps format, 354
.ppsx format, 354
as slideshows, 361
table of file formats, 351-352
as web pages, 364-367
to Word, 369
XPS format, 356
rehearsing timings, 310-311
restarting on current slide, 320
self-playing presentations, 311-313
looping presentation, 313
recording how long to stay on each slide, 312
reviewing timings, 312
running, 313
windows, 341

presenter notes
Notes Page, 191
Notes pane, 190-191
overview, 190
Presenter View, 327-329
when to use, 192

Presenter View, 327-329

preset 3D rotations, 250

preset animations, 284-285

preset picture effects, 66

presProps.xml file, 347

previewing
animations, 291
fonts, 30-31
styles, 13-14

printing handouts, 192-193

proofing text
dictionary, 57
example, 58-59
spelling checker, 57-58
thesaurus, 57-58
translation, 57-58

prototypes, 307-308

publishing presentations
to 97–2003 file format, 369-370
Compatibility Checker, 371
Compatibility mode, 371-372
to CD, 373-377
comments, 357-358
compressing pictures, 373
Document Inspector, 367-368
embedded fonts, 352-354
encryption, 358-359
to Excel, 368-369
file format issues, 370
to iPods, 361-362
macros, 352
Mark as Final option, 355-356
to network shares, 363
password protection, 358-360
PDF format, 356
as pictures, 362-363
.pps format, 354
.ppsx format, 354
as slideshows, 361
table of file formats, 351-352
as web pages, 364-367
to Word, 369
XPS format, 356

Q-R

QAT (Quick Access Toolbar), 17
- adding macros to, 197
- commands, 19
- customization limitations, 19
- customization tips and tricks, 19
- customizing, 18-19

rand() function, 60

random text, generating, 60

ranges of slides, presenting, 326

recolor feature (duotone effect)
- color modes, 69
- dark variations, 68
- light variations, 68-69

recording narration, 313-316
- linked narrations, 314-315
- microphones, 314
- sound quality, 314

reflection, 237

regrouping shapes, 135-136

rehearsing timings, 310-311

relationships of parts (PPTX files), 348

_rels directories, 348

reordering slides, 173-175

Repeat feature, 241-242

replacing fonts, 33

rerouting lines, 129

Reset Picture tool, 71

resetting
- 3D effects, 262
- 3D rotation, 255

resizing objects
- with Alt key, 275
- with Ctrl key, 273-274
- pictures, 81-82
- with Shift key, 275
- tables, 147

resolution in Slide Show, 326

resources
- community sites, 383
- Help feature, 381
- Microsoft employee blogs, 383
- Microsoft Knowledge Base, 383
- microsoft.public.powerpoint newsgroup, 382
- PPTX files, 349

restoring pictures to original state, 71

reusing slides
- from another presentation, 156
- overview, 156
- with Slide Library
  - adding slides from PowerPoint, 159-160
  - adding slides from SharePoint, 160-161
  - checking slides for changes, 162-163
  - copying slides from, 161-162
  - overview, 157
  - setting up library, 157-158

Ribbon, 7-8
- design, 8, 12
- dialog box launcher, 10
- Drawing Tools Format tab
  - shape fill, 121
  - shape styles, 120-121
- Equation Tools Design ribbon, 169-170
- formatting objects from, 219
- galleries, 11
- groups, 9
- minimizing, 10
- tabs, 8-9

right tab stops, 48

Right to Left command (SmartArt), 96

rotation
- with Alt key, 277
- custom rotations, 251-254
- object position, 255
- options, 277
- preset rotations, 250
- resetting, 255
- with Shift key, 276
- SmartArt nodes, 96
- text, 254

rows (tables), inserting, 147-148

ruler
- aligning objects, 268
- enabling, 268
- units of measurement, 269

S

Safe mode, 343-344

saving
- ink, 322
- PPTX files, 345
- presentations. *See* publishing presentations
- themes, 214

schemes
color schemes, 203-204, 208-210
effect schemes, 203, 210-212
adding, 212
applying, 211-212
changing, 212
font schemes, 203-207
adding, 207
applying, 206
changing, 207

ScreenTips, 23

Scribble tool, 123

SDKs (Software Development Kits), 154

security, password protection, 358-360

Segoe UI font, 32

Select Data Source dialog, 111

Select Multiple Objects dialog, 132

selecting
shapes, 132
text, 27-28

Selection pane, 131-132, 287-288

self-playing presentations, 311-313
looping presentation, 313
recording how long to stay on each slide, 312
reviewing timings, 312
running, 313

sensitive information, removing with Document Inspector, 367

sepia color mode, 69

Service Quality Monitoring (SQM), 10

Set Transparent Color wand, 70

shadows
inner shadows, 236
perspective shadows, 236
setting, 236
soft versus hard, 235

shape-editing mode, 53

shapes, 117
Arc tool, 123
changing, 242-243
connectors, 126-127
customizing, 129-130
inserting, 128
rerouting, 129
converting to SmartArt, 88-89
copying
to Excel, 368-369
to Word, 369
creating, 122-123
default shapes, customizing, 239
duplicating, 118
editing, 124-125
ellipses, 234
embedding from other applications, 133-134
fills, 121
background fills, 229-231
gradient fills, 220-223
gradient overlays, 223-226
picture fills, 226-228
solid fills, 220
Format Painter, 240
formatting
with Format Shape dialog, 219-220
with Ribbon, 219
with style gallery, 218
Freeform tool, 123
grouping, 135-136
hiding portions of pictures with, 125-126
inserting, 117-119
lines
color, 232
styles, 232-233
Lock Drawing Mode, 119-120
new shapes, 122
of pictures, 72-75
regrouping, 135-136
Scribble tool, 123
selecting with Tab key, 132
Selection pane, 131-132
Shapes gallery, 117-118
styles, 120-121
turning text boxes into, 35-36
ungrouping, 135
yellow diamond adjust handles, 130-131
z-order, 132

Shapes gallery, 117-118

SharePoint
adding slides to Slide Library, 160-161
definition, 157

Shift key
moving objects with, 277
resizing objects with, 275
rotating objects with, 276

shopping list, 48-49

Single File Web Page save option, 166

Size and Position dialog, 265-267

sizing objects
with Alt key, 275
with Ctrl key, 273-274

pictures, 266-267
with Shift key, 275
table cells, 148

skins, 24

Slide Library
adding slides from PowerPoint, 159-160
adding slides from SharePoint, 160-161
checking slides for changes, 162-163
copying slides from, 161-162
overview, 157
setting up, 157-158

Slide Masters
creating, 177
hiding background graphics on, 178
modifying, 176-177
multiple Masters, 177-178
schemes, 213

Slide Miniature pane, 173-175

Slide Show
Custom Shows, 299-300
editing during presentations, 323-324
Ink feature, 320
advantages, 321
drawing during presentations, 321
saving ink, 322
keyboard shortcuts, 329-330
Presenter View, 327-329
ranges of slides, 326
resolution, 326
show types, 324-326
starting, 317-318
View mode buttons, 318-319
widescreen slide sizes, 331-332

slides. *See also* presentations
creating from outlines, 183-184
hiding, 316
layouts, 213
applying, 179
changing, 179-180
customizing, 181-182
overview, 179
linking to first slide, 306-307
reordering, 173-175
reusing
from another presentation, 156
overview, 156
with Slide Library, 157-163
Slide Library
adding slides from PowerPoint, 159-160
adding slides from SharePoint, 160-161
checking slides for changes, 162-163
copying slides from, 161-162
overview, 157
setting up, 157-158
Slide Masters
creating, 177
hiding background graphics on, 178
modifying, 176-177
multiple Masters, 177-178
schemes, 213
Slide Show
Custom Shows, 299-300
editing during presentations, 323-324
Ink feature, 320-322
keyboard shortcuts, 329-330
Presenter View, 327-329
ranges of slides, 326
resolution, 326
saving presentations as, 361
show types, 324-326
starting, 317-318
View mode buttons, 318-319
widescreen slide sizes, 331-332
transitions
adding, 297-298
sounds, 298
speed, 298

small caps, formatting text as, 38

Smart Tags
AutoCorrect Smart Tag, 152-153
contextual nature of, 154
Overflowing Text Smart Tag, 153-154
Paste Smart Tag, 151-152
Software Development Kit (SDK), 154

SmartArt, 85-87
accentuating photos with, 98
advantages, 91-92
animations, 96-97
connectors, 91
Content pane, 89-90
converting existing content to, 88-89

converting placeholders to, 97-98
Create Graphic commands
Add Bullet, 96
Add Shape, 95
Layout, 96
Right to Left, 96
inserting, 87-88
layouts, 92-93
nodes, 90, 96
styles, 94
Text pane, 90
themes, 94
types, 86

snapping to grids and guides, 269-271

soft edges, 237

soft shadows, 235

Software Development Kits (SDKs), 154

solid fills, 220

sounds
distributing presentations with sound, 165-166
embedding, 164-165
linking, 164
looping, 166
Microsoft Office Sounds add-in, 23
narration
linked narrations, 314-315
recording, 313-316
overview, 163-164
playlists
applying to presentations, 168
creating, 167-168
overview, 166
sounds spanning multiple slides, 166
transitions, 298

spacing, character, 39

speed of transitions, 298

spelling checker, 57-58

spheres, creating, 245-248

splitting table cells, 149

SQM (Service Quality Monitoring), 10

standard placeholders, 185-187

starting Slide Show, 317-318

status bar
components, 22
customizing, 22
definition, 21

stretching block arrows, 122

strikethrough text, 38-39

styles
charts, 108-109
line styles, 232-233
previewing, 13-14
shape styles, 120-121
style gallery, 218
table styles, 144-145

subscript text, 38

Super ScreenTips, 23

superscript text, 38

surfaces (3D objects)
angle, 261
lighting, 259-260
materials, 259

T

Tab key, selecting shapes with, 132

tab stops, 46-47
center tab stops, 48
Custom Tab Picker, 47
custom tab stops, 47-48
decimal tab stops, 48
default tab stops, 47
First-Line Indent Marker, 47
Left Indent Marker, 47
left tab stops, 48
right tab stops, 48
shopping list example, 48-49
tips, 50

Table button, 137-138

tables
cells
animating, 142-143
margins, 149
sizing, 148
splitting and merging, 149
columns, inserting, 147-148
Draw Table option, 149
effects, 146
Excel tables, copying and pasting into PowerPoint, 141
inserting
with Draw Table option, 139
with Excel Spreadsheet option, 139
with Insert Table dialog, 138-139
with Table button, 137-138
overview, 137
resizing, 147
rows, inserting, 147-148
styles, 144-145

tableStyles.xml file, 347

Tablet PCs, 168-169, 321

Tags, Smart. *See* Smart Tags

templates
chart templates
applying, 110-111
creating, 110
managing, 111
compared to themes, 200, 204

testing microphones, 314

text, 27
3D rotation, 254
animating, 294-296
associating with pictures
grouping pictures/text, 73
shapes with picture fill, 73-75
AutoCorrect
clickable hyperlinks, creating, 45-46
custom phrases, 46
default text corrections, 44-45
pranks, 46
bulleted lists
custom bullets, 42-44
default bullets, 41
copying/pasting, 28
direction/orientation, 30
dragging, 28-29
dummy text, generating, 60
fonts, 30
Calibri, 32
Cambria, 32
Candara, 32
Consolas, 32
Constantia, 32
Corbel, 32
embedded fonts, 352-354
Live Preview, 30-31
Office 2007 new fonts, 32
previewing, 30-31
replacing, 33
Segoe UI, 32
theme fonts, 31
formatting, 29-30, 36
character spacing, 39
clearing all formatting, 55
distributed text, 52
equalized character heights, 38
Follow Path Transforms, 56
inline editing, 56-57
justified text, 52
kerning, 40
keyboard shortcuts, 61-62
mouse shortcuts, 62
paragraph markers, 50-52
placeholders, 54-55
small caps/all caps, 38
strikethrough, 38-39
subscript, 38
superscript, 38
underline, 36
warped text, 55
ordered lists, 42
proofing
dictionary, 57
example, 58-59
spelling checker, 57-58
thesaurus, 57-58
translation, 57-58
selecting, 27-28
shape-editing mode, 53
tab stops, 46-47
center tab stops, 48
Custom Tab Picker, 47
custom tab stops, 47-48
decimal tab stops, 48
default tab stops, 47
First-Line Indent Marker, 47
Left Indent Marker, 47
left tab stops, 48
right tab stops, 48
shopping list example, 48-49
tips, 50
text boxes
Autofit, 34
converting to SmartArt, 88-89
horizontal text boxes, 34
margins, 34
options, 34-35
text wrap, 34
turning into shapes, 35-36
vertical text boxes, 34
text-editing mode, 53
text wrap, 34

Text Box dialog, 34

text boxes, 34
Autofit, 34
converting to SmartArt, 88-89
horizontal text boxes, 34
margins, 34
options, 34-35
text wrap, 34
turning into shapes, 35-36
vertical text boxes, 34

text-editing mode, 53

Text pane (SmartArt), 90

themes
advantages, 199-200, 205
applying entire themes, 200-202
applying parts of themes, 202-203

color schemes, 203-204, 208-210
compared to design templates, 200, 204
compared to presentations, 204
creating, 214-215
effect schemes, 203, 210-212
adding, 212
applying, 211-212
changing, 212
font schemes, 31, 203-207
adding, 207
applying, 206
changing, 207
overview, 199
saving, 214
slide layouts, 213
slide masters, 213
SmartArt, 94
thumbnails, 212-213

thesaurus, 57-58

.thmx files. *See* themes

Thumbnail pane, 173-175

thumbnail.jpeg file, 213

thumbnails, 212-213

timings, rehearsing, 310-311

toolbars, QAT (Quick Access Toolbar), 17
commands, 19
customization limitations, 19
customization tips and tricks, 19
customizing, 18-19
floatie (mini toolbar), 20-21

transformed text
Follow Path Transforms, 56
warped text, 55

transitions
adding, 297-298
sounds, 298
speed, 298

translation, 57-58

transparency, 70

transparent overlay, 238

triggers (animations), 296-299

troubleshooting flickering, 332
disabling hardware acceleration, 333
enabling hardware acceleration, 333
replacing graphics drivers, 332-333

turning off
floatie (mini toolbar), 21
ScreenTips, 23
sounds, 23

U

underlining text, 36

undo operations
multiple undo, 242
OLE objects, 115
picture cropping, 72

ungrouping shapes, 135

units of measurement (ruler), 269

University of Chicago School of Business, 2

URLs, clickable hyperlinks, 45-46

user interface, 7
color schemes, 24
floatie (mini toolbar), 20-21
Interactive PowerPoint 2003 to PowerPoint 2007 Command Reference Guide, 11-12
keyboard shortcuts
F6 key, 17
finding, 16
Office 2003 shortcuts, 16-17
Live Preview, 13-14
Microsoft Office Sounds add-in, 23
Office button, 14-15
QAT (Quick Access Toolbar), 17
commands, 19
customization limitations, 19
customization tips and tricks, 19
customizing, 18-19
Ribbon, 7-8
design, 8, 12
dialog box launcher, 10
galleries, 11
groups, 9
minimizing, 10
tabs, 8-9
ScreenTips, 23
status bar
components, 22
customizing, 22
definition, 21

V

vertical text boxes, 34

video. *See also* sounds
distributing presentations with video, 165-166
embedding, 164-165
linking, 164

overview, 163-164
playlists
applying to presentations, 168
creating, 167-168
overview, 166

View mode buttons (Slide Show), 318-319

Viewer, 373-374, 377

Visual Studio Express, 346

W

warped text, 55

washout color mode, 69

web pages, publishing presentations to, 364-367

widescreen slide sizes, 331-332

windows, 341

wizards, AutoContent Wizard, 200

Word
copying shapes to, 369
creating equations in, 169-170
paragraph markers, 51

WordArt, 29-30

X-Y-Z

XML (Extensible Markup Language), 344

XPS format, 356

z-order, 132

zoom slider, 271-272

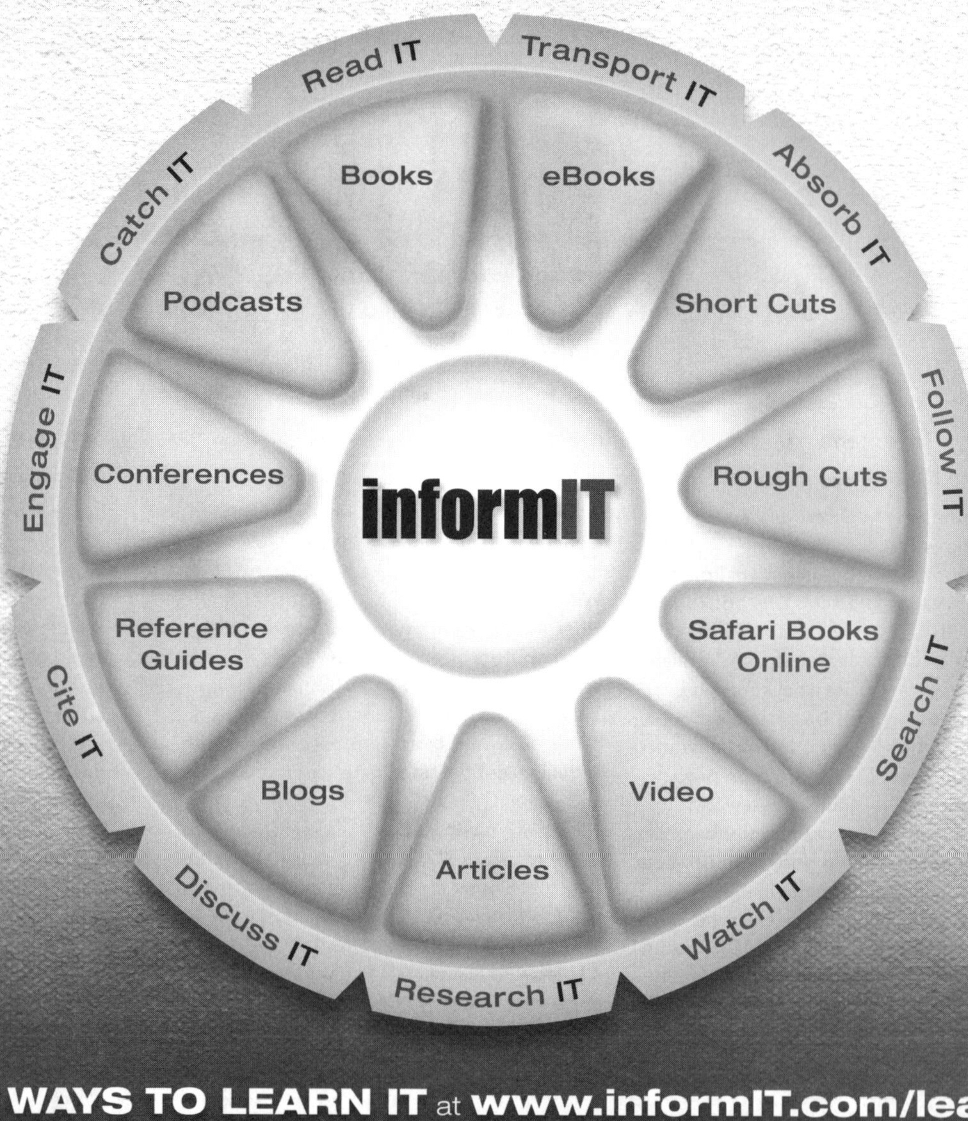